A Sociolinguistic Approach to Bilingual Education

Experiments in the American Southwest

Andrew D. Cohen
Department of English
University of California, Los Angeles

NEWBURY HOUSE PUBLISHERS, INC.

Language Science
Language Teaching
Language Learning

68 Middle Road, Rowley, Massachusetts 01969

ISBN: cloth   912066-35-0
        paper   912066-34-2

Printed in the U.S.A.   First Printing: October, 1975

FOREWORD

Bilingual education is a critical issue in American education today, but its goals are unclear, its methods not agreed on, and the term itself means very different things to different people. In all the welter of federal and state laws, experimental projects, and educational controversies, there are almost no informative descriptions of the language situation in communities where bilingual education is being tried and almost no careful evaluative studies of bilingual programs in progress. Andrew Cohen has written a pioneering book which provides both these things. It belongs on the same shelf with *Bilingualism in the Barrio* of Fishman and his colleagues as an innovative, multi-method study of a bilingual community. Equally it belongs with Lambert and Tucker's *Bilingual Education of Children* as the evaluation of a sustained educational experiment in a bilingual setting. For American educators, however, the Cohen book is more valuable than these shelf mates, because it focuses directly on the Mexican-American bilingualism which is the biggest linguistic challenge in American education, and because it tries to reply directly to the very questions the conscientious educator wants answered. It is a book to be studied by everyone concerned with Mexican-American educational problems and by all advocates and opponents of bilingual education on the American scene.

Cohen's book starts where all reports, proposals, and analyses of bilingual education projects *should* start, but rarely do: with a description of the particular bilingual community, its people, and the respective roles of the two languages in it.

He then proceeds to a description of the particular school system and its bilingual education project. With this full background he is then able to present an explanation of his own evaluative research on the effects of the project and their possible implications for other communities and school systems.

The findings are clear enough. Over a three-year period the bilingually educated children in the Redwood City project did about as well in *two* languages as the monolingual Anglo children in the control group did in English alone, and, further, the Mexican-American children of the project improved in attitude toward school and school attendance while their parents' views of their minority language became more favorable.

It is my hope that Cohen's study will be a model for evaluative studies of bilingual education programs in other communities and in different educational settings, as well as a stimulus for other researchers to refine and develop the methods of investigation. I hope also that the author's careful limitations on the generalizability of his results will be noted by his readers, who must see the study as he sees it—an important contribution to the discussion rather than a general recommendation for policy.

The interested reader will find many suggestive ideas in this volume, sometimes explicit and highlighted and other times mentioned in passing or left in the background. Some of the most striking aspects of the book and the research it reports depend on Cohen's personal background, present interest and personality. Two features of his research style may serve as examples: his own active bilingual participation in the project, which made some of the research methods possible, and the substantial involvement in the conduct of the investigation of a cadre of Chicano students from Stanford University. These features reflect the author's Peace Corp experience in Bolivia, his two years of guiding Stanford's undergraduates in a community tutored program, and his equal commitment to educational research and to work in community and classroom.

Although this book may still have some marks of the dissertation format from which it grew, its import goes far beyond the evaluation of the single bilingual education project which it reports. It offers food for thought on a wide range of topics, from broad national issues such as cultural pluralism and the education of ethnic minorities to specialized theoretical issues such as the nature of linguistic change and the standarization of language tests. May it lead to more sociolinguistically oriented educational research and to more informed discussion of language problems in our society.

Committee on Linguistics
Stanford University

Charles A. Ferguson

ACKNOWLEDGMENTS

My deepest gratitude goes to Charles Ferguson and to Robert Politzer for their encouragement and guidance during the years of the study. My special thanks go to Robert Cooper, G. Richard Tucker, Wallace Lambert, Joshua Fishman, and Joan Rubin for their help at various stages in the research. I am also grateful to Martin Carnoy for his comments.

I wish to acknowledge the assistance of Janet Elashoff and Richard Snow in planning the data analysis, and that of Eleanor Chiang in familiarizing me with the appropriate computer programs.

I appreciate all the cooperation that I received from the Redwood City School District while I was employed as Internal Evaluator for the Title VII Project. I particularly wish to thank Jim Abbott, Richard Cochran, César Muñoz-Plaza, Mike Fernández, Ken Woody, Edith Cunningham, and all the staff, teachers, teacher aides, and children for their participation and support of the research effort.

A special debt of gratitude goes to all those Stanford students who took part in the data collection, especially to Jose Martínez, George Ybarra, Dee Briones, Jose Cerda, Anna Lange, and Armando Rivera.

And finally, a world of thanks goes to my wife, Sabina, who intermittently put aside her own work to help me with mine.

NEWBURY HOUSE SERIES

STUDIES IN BILINGUAL EDUCATION

Sponsored
by
The International Center
for Research on Bilingualism
Laval University
Quebec City, Canada

Published:

BILINGUAL EDUCATION IN A BINATIONAL SCHOOL
by William F. Mackey

THE LANGUAGE EDUCATION OF MINORITY CHILDREN
Selected Readings
Edited by Bernard Spolsky

BILINGUAL EDUCATION OF CHILDREN: The St. Lambert Experiment
by Wallace E. Lambert and G. R. Tucker

A SOCIOLINGUISTIC APPROACH TO BILINGUAL EDUCATION
by Andrew D. Cohen

Forthcoming:

BILINGUAL SCHOOLING AND THE SURVIVAL
OF SPANISH IN THE UNITED STATES
by A. Bruce Gaarder

THE AMERICAN BILINGUAL TRADITION
IN EDUCATION AND PUBLIC ADMINISTRATION
by Heinz Kloss

CONTENTS

PREFACE

This book is intended as a research report on one bilingual education program in the United States. But the book is designed to offer more than just a report of research data. The first several chapters provide background in two areas, bilingualism and the Mexican American people. Particularly for the newcomer to the field, a report on a bilingual education program only takes on significance against the backdrop of an understanding of bilingualism and various approaches to bilingual schooling. Furthermore, it is necessary to consider the special characteristics of the Mexican American people to fully understand the ramifications of bilingual education for their children.

Before discussing the findings of the study, there is a discussion of some of the pedagogical aspects of the program. Thus, the reader doesn't just read about the results of pre- and posttesting, but also learns something about the instructional process. There is also a description of some of the Spanish and English language forms used by the children in the study, to provide teachers with insights into the interpretation of the child language of Mexican American bilinguals.

The research techniques utilized in the study span a broad range, from survey research to psychological testing to observational techniques. Thus, the various methodological chapters not only serve the purpose of reporting findings for this one study, but are also intended to provide a format for research elsewhere.

In short, this book is designed both for people in universities and in the public schools. I hope teachers, administrators, bilingual program evaluators and a variety of other people will find parts or all of this book useful to them in planning and thinking about bilingual education programs.

A.D.C.

INTRODUCTION

This book is about bilingual schooling. It describes the research findings of several years' efforts to provide instruction through both Spanish and English to a group of Mexican American school children. Since the program involved innovations in language instruction in the classroom, a primary emphasis of the study was to better understand the sociolinguistic characteristics of the children and their families—both at the outset of the program and on a continuing basis. The introduction that follows concerns itself primarily with the notion of sociolinguistics and its relationship to bilingual schooling.

As Andersson and Boyer so aptly put it:

> . . . bilingual schooling is not exclusively either the learning of a
> "foreign" language or the learning of English—though both of these
> are involved; it is rather a new way of conceiving of the whole
> range of education, especially for the non-English-speaking child
> who is just entering school. It necessitates rethinking the entire
> curriculum in terms of the child's best instruments for learning,
> of his readiness and motivation for learning the various subjects,
> and of his own identity and potential for growth and develop-
> ment. (Andersson and Boyer, 1971, pp. 43-43)

With 163 bilingual education programs funded under the Bilingual Education Act[1] during the 1971-72 school year and numerous other projects receiving funding from some other source, an attempt is being made to meet the linguistic and cultural needs of minority school children. However, the proliferation of bilingual education programs has prompted sociolinguists to call attention to the lack of investigations of existing language situations as part of program planning. Whereas these does exist a small legacy of sociolinguistic studies of bilingual communities (see Barker, 1947; Weinreich, 1951; Haugen, 1953; Diebold, 1961; Rubin, 1968; Fishman, Cooper, Ma et al., 1971), there have been only a few truly sociolinguistic studies of bilingual schooling programs.

Fishman and Lovas (1970) state that most existing bilingual programs have not utilized recent insights into societal bilingualism in their program designs. Staff personnel offer educational, psychological, or linguistic reasons for project characteristics, but ignore the language situation existing in the community involved. The only quoted statistics refer to the number of people with Spanish surnames, and it is assumed that such statistics provide reliable and meaningful data about the language situation. Valdez (1969) warns against the mistake of trying to assess bilingual proficiency from surnames. Fishman and Lovas (1970) point out that more than census data and school records are necessary. They emphasize that a survey should be undertaken to identify the languages and varieties used by parents and children by social domain, to estimate relative proficiency in each language by domain, to indicate the community's attitudes toward the language varieties in the community, and to indicate community attitudes toward changing the language situation.

Sociolinguists have shown how language can be studied in relation to its social environment. As Fishman defines it, *sociolinguistics* is "the study of the characteristics of language varieties, the characteristics of their functions, and the characteristics of their speakers as these three constantly interact, change, and change one another within a speech community" (Fishman, 1971c, p. 4). As both Hymes (1967) and Ervin-Tripp (1964) have pointed out, language always exists and functions within some social context. Therefore, the description of language should reflect its function in the local society.

Studies which trace the progress of children schooled bilingually have appeared abroad and are beginning to appear in the U.S. (see Chapter 2). Mention is made of tests that the students took and of their charted progress. Occasionally, mention is also made of the language used in the home, but rarely is there any systematic study of how the child's language behavior in school relates to his language behavior out of school and to the language patterns of parents and siblings. Nor is there mention of the effect of bilingual schooling on his language behavior over time.

The language use and proficiency of Mexican American children schooled bilingually in California is a virtually untapped field, but one of great importance in determining the effectiveness of bilingual education in the State. Several language use studies were conducted in Texas and New Mexico, but, for the most part, didn't involve children in bilingual programs. Patella and Kuvlesky (1970) related language use of Texas high school children to occupational aspirations.

---

[1] The Bilingual Education Act is Title VII within the Elementary and Secondary Education Amendment (ESEA) of 1967.

Mahoney (1967) did a secondary analysis of data collected by the Texas Agricultural Experiment Station in 1962. Language use items were one part of a 14-page questionnaire designed to find out more about the Spanish-American labor force in Texas. Mahoney studied the language choices of rural and urban household heads and their children in a variety of language use situations. She then related language use information to demographic variables such as age, birthplace, education, income, and occupation.

Thompson (1971) did a study to determine whether Spanish is being dropped in favor of English among the Spanish-speaking population of Austin, Texas. He conducted two surveys in a neighborhood containing over half of the city's Mexican population. 136 heads of households rated the frequency that Spanish was used in the home by themselves and the other adults with various family members, friends and neighbors. The language use data were analyzed with respect to the variables of age, generation, place of birth, locality of childhood, education, and occupation. Because "location of childhood" was the only highly significant variable, a second survey was conducted just with household heads who were raised in Austin, thus controlling for that variable while examining the relation of the use of Spanish at work, occupational mobility, and the degree of Northern or Southern accent to the use of Spanish in the home and with friends.

Timmins (1971) studied the relative bilingualism of 60 Spanish-surnamed school children grades 1-4 in the Armijo Elementary School in Albuquerque, New Mexico. An attempt was made to determine if language use and proficiency varied in relation to the number of years in public school and in relation to social domain. A Spanish usage rating schedule was used to assess language use with various "bilingual" interlocutors in the domains of education, religion, neighborhood, and family. A word naming task and a picture response task were used to assess aspects of language proficiency in the same domains.

One of the few available studies which considers a bilingual education program from a sociolinguistic perspective was conducted in a small community in Albuquerque, New Mexico, by Mallory (1971). She looked at whether a bilingual program effected "a sociolinguistic performance change" in six selected first graders in the program as compared with older children in their families. Additionally, the sociolinguistic performance of the children was compared with that of their parents. Language attitude measures were also given to the children and to their parents.

Ornstein (1971) introduces a "sociolinguistic research kit" aimed at specifying categories of information that should be given priority in sociolinguistic research projects in the Southwest. His "kit" includes the following:

1) *Linguistic Data*
   a) regional and non-standard variants of Spanish in the fields of phonology, grammar, and lexicon, according to use by different social strata;

b) non-standard features of the English employed by various socio-economic groups;

c) interference phenomena.

2) *Socio-Attitudinal Data*

a) attitudes toward the different varieties of Southwestern Spanish and English and the degree of "language loyalty";

b) attitudes toward comparative life-styles and value systems of the *anglo* and *hispano.*

3) *Bilingual Communication Data*

a) patterns of linguistic dominance;

b) distributive roles of Spanish vs. English in Southwest communication networks;

c) ranges of codes employed;

d) code switching. (Ornstein, 1971, p. 56)

Gaarder (1971) also provides a framework for research in sociolinguistics, as he lists twenty-two socio-cultural factors affecting the maintenance or shift of Spanish in the United States. Some of these factors were originally identified by Weinreich (1953). Among the factors are the following:

1. Size and homogeneity of the bilingual group.
2. Access to renewal from the hinterland.
3. Reinforcement by in-migration and immigration.
4. Relative proficiency in both languages.
5. Modes of use (reading, writing, listening, speaking).
6. Specialized use by domain and interlocutor.
7. Status of the bilingual groups.
8. Attitudes toward each language.
9. Function of each language in social-advance.

Kjolseth (1972) points out that there is a lack of hard evidence on the effects of bilingual education programs upon community language use patterns. He registers a plea for research on shifts in the bilingual dominance configurations of specific groups. He calls for the consideration of changes in subgroup language use patterns in domains outside of the school. He views the real innovation to be the investigation of language use patterns, as opposed to measuring only changes in individual language skills and language attitudes.

Since one of the aims of the Redwood City Bilingual Education Project was to maintain the minority group's language and culture, a longitudinal study was implemented to assess whether the program was achieving that aim. The Redwood City School District began its bilingual schooling in the fall of 1969, under the auspices of the ESEA Bilingual Education Program, Title VII. The Redwood City project was initiated with one Pilot first-grade class of twenty lower-class Mexican Americans and ten middle-class Anglos at the Garfield Elementary School in the Fair Oaks neighborhood. The following school year, 1970-71, a new first grade and kindergarten were added, to be referred to as the Follow Up I and Follow Up II groups respectively.

In the fall of 1970, a longitudinal study of the Pilot, Follow Up I, and Follow Up II groups was begun. At that time, comparison groups of Mexican American students were selected from a school in the nearby Middlefield neighborhood. Pretest or baseline data on language use and proficiency were collected from the children in the Bilingual and Comparison groups, using a pupil's language use inventory, a test of oral comprehension, a word naming by domain task, storytelling tasks, reading tests, math tests, and a measure of academic aptitude. Parents of the Bilingual and Comparison children were administered a home interview schedule which asked about the language use and proficiency patterns of all family members, and which included a series of socioeconomic, educational, and demographic questions. These parents were also given a language orientation questionnaire to determine their "language loyalty."

At the end of the 1971-1972 school year, the Bilingual and Comparison students were given the same instruments as a posttest, plus a language use observation instrument and a writing sample (at the Pilot level only). At that time, the students' parents were asked to describe the current language use and proficiency patterns of their children in the Bilingual or Comparison group, and the language loyalty of the parents were again assessed. The cultural attitudes of the Bilingual and Comparison students were also assessed.

This study incorporates many of the suggestions for research enumerated by Ornstein, Gaarder, and Kjolseth (see above). The research concerns itself with patterns of language proficiency in four skills in both languages and with the distributive roles of Spanish and English by societal domain, and with attitudes toward language maintenance and attitudes toward culture (Ornstein, see above points 3a, 3b, 2a, 2b; Gaarder, see above points 4-9). Baseline data also include information on the size and homogeneity of the bilingual group, access to renewal from the hinterland, and reinforcement by in-migration and immigration (Gaarder, see above, points 1-3). Hopefully other studies will replicate this research in these same areas and concern themselves with research areas that are not covered by this sociolinguistic study of bilingual education in Redwood City, California.

Chapters 1 through 4 treat background topics related to the research study described in this book. Chapter 1 describes the phenomenon of bilingualism itself, Chapter 2 deals with the concept of bilingual education, and Chapter 3 discusses the relationship between bilingualism and intelligence. Chapter 4 provides a broad-ranging discussion of the Mexican American people, focusing on both supposed and actual characteristics of this emergent ethnic group.

Chapters 5 through 12 deal with the Redwood City study. Chapter 5 describes the research design and the methodological procedures, and includes a description of the Redwood City community. Chapter 6 details the school instructional programs or "treatments" during the time of the study, complemented by a list of instructional materials by grade level in Appendix 2.

Chapter 7 discusses the measurement of the Spanish and English language proficiency of children in the bilingual program and in the comparison group, and Chapter 8 gives a linguistic account of many of the deviant forms found in the children's spoken language. Chapter 9 provides a sociolinguistic account of the language use patterns, over time, of the children in the study.

Chapter 10 looks at the effects of bilingual schooling upon acqusition of mathematical skills and upon the development of certain intellectual abilities. Chapter 11 deals with the children's attitudes toward Mexican and Anglo culture and toward school, and with the parental attitudes toward the Spanish and English languages. Chapter 12 states the conclusions of the study and offers a series of recommendations.

1. BILINGUALISM

This chapter provides an overview of bilingualism. Definitions are given, followed by a discussion of several instruments designed to measure degree of bilingualism, and then a series of studies on bilingualism are briefly described.

1.1 *Definitions*

Although the terms "bilingualism" and "bilingual" are frequently used, the users rarely define what they mean when they use the terms (see John and Horner, 1971). Individuals are referred to as "bilinguals" as if there were some fixed notion of what that meant. Bartlett observes the following about bilingualism:

> Despite the widespread appearance of the phenomenon, we do not
> yet have a satisfactory general theory of bilingualism. Indeed, it was
> not until this century that attempts were made to analyze the phe-
> nomenon scientifically, and to assess its effects on human behavior
> and its influence on social structures. From what evidence we have
> of earlier periods, bilingualism appears as a rare and unusual quality,
> suspect except in those societies which valued another language as a
> key to culture. Indeed, in former times the word had overtones of
> deceitfulness, and a little of this aura still hangs about it. (Bartlett,
> 1969, pp. v-vi)

Jakobovits (1970) points out that both nonprofessional and professional judges have their own versions of "folk bilingualism." To the nonprofessional judge, accent, pronunciation, and fluency may be given a disproportionate degree of importance. Thus, a speaker with a poor accent and less fluency but with greater knowledge of the language might not impress them as being bilingual. Some professionals require equal facility in two languages before they are willing to talk of bilingualism, while others are willing to speak of "incipient bilinguals" (Diebold, 1961). Jakobovits (1970) asserts that there is no particular advantage in setting arbitrary limits for a definition of bilingualism. Instead, emphasis should be placed on specifying the extent of an individual's knowledge of his two languages.

Figure 1 provides a chart, based on Bordie (1970), Macnamara (1967a), and Cooper (1968, 1970), showing five elements of each of the four major skills in each language. This particular chart is set up, for illustrative purposes, just to measure a speaker's ability in one variety of Spanish and one variety of English. Let us suppose that the variety of Spanish is central-Mexican standard Spanish. A language "variety" here refers to either a dialect, a register, a style, or a level of formality. Thus, we could do a separate subchart for a child's language proficiency in his school register of Spanish and in his non-school register. Notice that four of the five elements of each of the four skills are the same. Speaking, writing, listening, and reading all involve semantics (the meaning of words and phrases), syntax (the arrangement of words in sentences), morphology (the grouping of parts of words into words) and lexicon (a listing of all words and word particles in a language). Phonemes (the meaningful sound units in a language) comprise the fifth element in the *oral* skills—i.e., speaking and listening, and graphemes (the units that represent the phonemes in the orthography) comprise the fifth element in the *written* skills—i.e., writing and reading.

Macnamara terms bilinguals "persons who possess at least one of the language skills even to a minimal degree in their second language" (Macnamara, 1967a, pp. 59-60). This writer prefers to define a bilingual as a person who possesses at least some ability in one language skill or any variety from each of two languages. This definition takes into account both very young children with some listening comprehension in each of two languages but minimal speaking ability, as well as English speakers who read a little French or understand a little German. The one remaining problem with the above definition is that of determining what constitutes a language. As Gumperz (1967, 1969) has documented, peoples' perceptions of language may cross-cut long-existing notions of what languages are, especially in places where languages are in contact (see Weinreich, 1953). It is possible, for instance, that one variety of a Chicano's speech viewed by an outsider as mixing of English and Spanish, is viewed by the speaker as a language in its own right. For the purpose of this study, if a variety cross-cuts two languages, it will be designated as such. Otherwise, varieties will refer to one language exclusively.

FIGURE 1

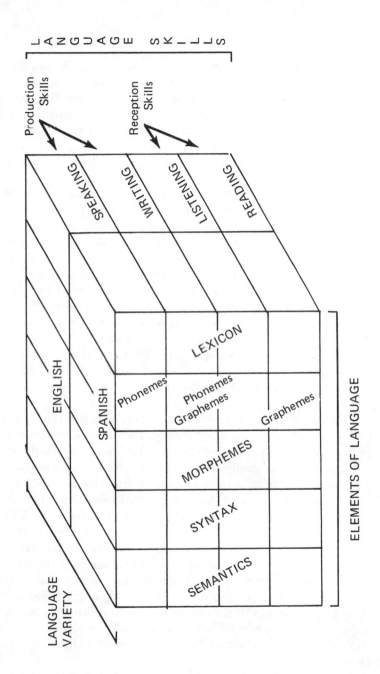

1.2 *Measurement of Bilingualism*

Social scientists have devised a series of measures of bilingualism, including report of language use and language proficiency, as well as both direct and indirect measures of performance. Direct measures include language activities that a person would perform regularly, such as listening comprehension tasks, storytelling, and reading. Indirect measures are farther away from everyday experience —activities like naming words for a particular domain (e.g., neighborhood) (see Macnamara, 1967a; Kelly, 1969; and Fishman, 1971b, on measurement of bilingualism).

Hoffman (1934) devised an instrument for measuring the extent of bilingual background or environment to which an individual is exposed by asking the subject to estimate the extent to which each of his languages is used in his home. More recent research is still using the Hoffman Bilingual Scale (see Jones, 1960; Lewis and Lewis, 1965; Riley, 1968) to assess degree of bilingualism. However, as Haugen points out (Haugen, 1956, pp. 94-95), this is a rather imperfect instrument when trying to measure the subtleties of bilingualism. Hoffman made no attempt to assess where and when one language would be chosen instead of the other. Bilingualism was viewed as present or not present, with no attempt to differentiate the conditions under which a person spoke one language, the other language, or both. Macnamara (1969) used a Hoffman-type scale in his own research with sixth-grade pupils in Montreal and also found it to be a weak measure of bilingualism when related to performance measures of bilingual proficiency.

Fishman (1964, 1965, 1966a), drawing on Weinreich (1953) and Gumperz (1964), provides a theoretical framework for a more complete study of bilingualism than that suggested by Hoffman. Fishman advanced the notion of the bilingual dominance configuration, which describes the bilinguality of an individual in terms of language use and proficiency for each of the four language skills, across language varieties and across societal domains. Fishman (1971c) defines a domain as a cluster of social situations which are typically constrained by a common set of behavioral rules. The domains which are relevant for a given bilingual community may vary, but they often include family, neighborhood, religion, education, and the occupational sphere. Note that a domain is more than a context or a place. A domain also comprises the roles of interlocutors within the particular setting and the topics that these interlocutors are likely to discuss. For instance, within the occupational domain, the boss and an employee (two interlocutors in a socially prescribed role relationship) may be talking in the boss's office (setting) about a salary boost for the employee (topic).

A major innovation in the Fishman model was the addition of the domain dimension to the measurement of bilingualism. Domains of language use had been discussed by Weinreich (1953) but not operationalized in sociological research. Fishman observed that the traditional measures of degree of bilingualism which subtracted a score obtained in one language from a score obtained in another may be insufficiently revealing of relative proficiency, since bilingual speakers may use each language under socially-differentiated circumstances (Fishman, 1965). The traditional difference-score approach labeled a person a "balanced" bilingual if his score was the same in each language for the particular linguistic task required (Macnamara, 1969). Yet, Fishman points out that the notion of balance is unrealistic for the following reason:

> . . . Socially patterned bilingualism can exist as a stabilized phenomenon *only* if there is functional *differentiation* between two languages rather than merely global dominance or balance. From the point of view of sociolinguistics, any society that produces functionally balanced bilinguals (i.e., bilinguals who use both their languages equally and equally well in all contexts) must soon cease to be bilingual because no society needs two languages for one and the same set of functions. (Fishman, 1971b, p. 560)

While the degree of bilingualism is an attribute of a person, the term "diglossia" has emerged (Ferguson, 1959; Gumperz, 1964; Fishman, 1967, 1971c) for describing this "functional differentiation between two languages" at the societal level (mentioned in the above quote by Fishman). For a bilingual Mexican American community to be diglossic, for example, one language must be used more in certain domains, while the other is used more in other domains. For instance, English may be the predominant language in the occupational sphere (particularly at the higher levels of employment), while Spanish is the language of the home. As soon as the uses of the two languages begin to overlap, Spanish will give way to English—the societally-dominant, more prestigious language, unless conscious efforts are made to create functional specialization of Spanish and English. Efforts such as bilingual education in the schools and special practices in the homes (see Christian, 1971) may not be enough.

Fishman (1971b) criticizes the measures of bilingualism that do not take into account the bilingual respondent's use and proficiency as related to domains of social interaction. Unfortunately, the bulk of research on bilinguals makes no allowances for differences by domain. Riley (1968), for instance, made an effort to relate word recognition abilities in bilinguals to their degree of bilingualism. However, he used the Hoffman scale (Hoffman, 1934) which falls short of a domain analysis.

The insights of Fishman into the field of bilingualism are of importance because they suggest a new research direction to help shed new light on a controversy that has been raging for decades, primarily among educators and psychologists, over the supposed detrimental effects of being bilingual. John and Horner (1971) point out that between the ages of five and seven, children use language at an accelerating rate for purposes of problem solving. In early learning, the child is ordering the world around him and language is critical in this ordering process. Does the introduction of a second, weaker language at this point simply confuse the ordering process? The authors point out that if bilinguals have the opportunity to develop two languages fully, they may demonstrate cognitive skills superior to those of their monolingual peers. Jones (1969) cites psychological, neurological, pedagogical and socio-political research supporting the favorable effect of learning a second language early.

1.3   Studies on Bilingualism

The literature on bilingualism is quite extensive, and some of it, particularly that relating to Mexican Americans, will be cited in Chapter 3. At this point, attention will be given to five particularly relevant studies. Note that all of these studies look at bilinguality as a global phenomenon, rather than as being domain-specific, as Fishman would suggest is important.

Lynn (1945) found that when English was introduced to young Spanish-speaking children in Arizona before their Spanish was well-established, the children made a variety of oral language mistakes in Spanish. The conclusion was that forced early learning of a second language before the first language was mastered causes impairment of first language development.

In his studies in Ireland, Macnamara found that children had greater difficulties in reading and in doing math problems in their weaker language. Macnamara and Kellaghan (1967) found that sixth-standard boys whose first language was English had more difficulty reading Irish than English versions of math problems aloud, regardless of whether they had been taught in Irish or in English. Macnamara (1967b) reports on results with twenty-four English-speaking girls who had had French in high school and in college. They had greater difficulty in semantic decoding of French words and sentences than of English words and sentences.

Macnamara (1966) studied the effects of teaching arithmetic in Irish to children from English-speaking homes. He selected five groups of English-speaking children in their fifth year from 100 schools selected at random. The groups ranged from those receiving all math in English to those receiving all math in Irish. The findings were that, while children from English-speaking homes showed no loss in mechanical arithmetic when learning in Irish, they were retarded 11 months in arithmetic age in problem solving. Perhaps a careful study of the bilingual dominance configuration of those students would have given greater insights into the problem-solving lag these students demonstrated. For instance, how were these students in other subjects in Irish? With whom did they use Irish, under what circumstances, where?

Peal and Lambert (1962) selected two groups of 10-year-old French-Canadian children, one group monolingual in French and the other bilingual, equating them with respect to socioeconomic level, age, and sex. Both groups received a word association test, a word detection test, the Peabody Picture Vocabulary Test, and an I.Q. test. Bilinguals came out higher on all measures, including verbal and nonverbal I.Q. The authors suggested that because of their training in two languages, the bilinguals had become more adept at concept formation and abstract thinking than the monolinguals. Macnamara (1966) argues that selecting balanced bilinguals as subjects, as Peal and Lambert did, is likely to yield bilinguals who are more able than the monolingual controls. Lambert and Anisfeld (1969) reply that the implication of Macnamara's criticism is that only the more intelligent children become balanced bilinguals. "It is difficult to understand," comment Lambert and Anisfeld, "how studies purportedly showing that bilinguals are inferior can be used to support the interpretation that the more intelligent become bilingual, rather than vice versa" (p. 127).

Worrall (1970, 1971) studied 30 Afrikaans-English bilinguals ages 4-6 and 7-9 from Pretoria, South Africa. Each bilingual was matched with two monolingual children—one Afrikaans and the other English-speaking—on intelligence, age, sex, school grade, and social class. Worrall was interested in the nature of the bilingual experience and the ways that it might influence the cognitive development of bilingual children. After Leopold (1949), Worrall viewed bilingualism as enriching the early childhood experience, and she felt that her results tended to support this view. On a semantic and phonetic preference test, for example, the preschool bilinguals showed a greater ability to separate the sound of a word from its meaning than did either group of monolinguals. She concluded that bilinguals are aware that different words can mean the same thing earlier than monolinguals (because they are used to giving the same object two names —one from each of their languages). This research employed a home-language-use interview, similar to that of Hoffman, but only as a screening device for selecting monolinguals and bilinguals for the experiments.

Riley (1968) attempted to test out the "balance effect" notion in language learning—that if a child develops skills in one of his two languages, he generally pays for it by a deficit in the other. He took 120 first-grade Mexican Americans from Fort Worth and Laredo, Texas, and gave one-third of them the Peabody Picture Vocabulary Test in English, another third the same test in Spanish, and the final third the same test in both languages simultaneously. Riley also obtained a rough measure of language use in the home using the Hoffman Schedule (Hoffman, 1934). He found that the students did better on the Spanish-English version than on the English version alone. He concluded from this that bilingualism doesn't impair word recognition in both languages. A flaw in his procedures, however, was that he gave the Spanish and English stimuli for a word simultaneously and thus didn't know whether the child was responding to the Spanish or the English word, or whether the double stimuli somehow worked together to help him point to the right picture.

Riley then correlated degree of bilingualism with word recognition ability and found that the more bilingual the subject, i.e., the more his Spanish use at home was equal to his English use, the better he did on the test in both languages simultaneously. The finding that interested Riley was that the bilinguals in Laredo were a different kind of group from those in Fort Worth, since the Laredo children were reported to use Spanish in the home, whereas the Fort Worth group were reportedly encouraged not to do so. Consistent with their reported language use patterns, the Laredo children performed much better than did the Fort Worth children on word recognition in Spanish. Although lacking description by domain, the Hoffman instrument did give Riley some insights into the different nature of the bilingual communities these two groups of school children came from. Furthermore, the data analysis indicated how much these environments influenced the measured bilingualism of the children, dispelling the myth that all Spanish-surnamed children are bilingual in Spanish and English in the same way.

Lewis and Lewis (1965) did a study of the degree to which bilingualism affected the written language performance of sixth-grade children. They looked at lower socioeconomic-level monolingual Americans, Chinese bilinguals, and Spanish bilinguals. As did Riley, the authors used the Hoffman Bilingual Schedule as a measure of bilingualism. Controlling for socioeconomic level and intelligence (something that many studies on the performance of bilinguals do not do), they found that the bilinguals did as well in written language performance (verbal output, range of vocabulary, accuracy of spelling, grammatical correctness, quality of sentence structure, and effectiveness of expression) as did monolinguals.

Only with the work of Fishman, Cooper, Ma et al. (1971), employing Fishman's bilingual dominance configuration theory, did there begin to appear research on the bilingual that truly considered factors such as domains of bilingual proficiency and use. These authors studied 431 Puerto Ricans ranging in age from below six to sixty-four, from a four-block neighborhood of Jersey City, New Jersey. The major intent of the research was to pioneer a series of techniques for better describing bilinguals, and to determine the interrelationships and relative effectiveness of these techniques.

Two pieces of research from the massive study, Cooper (1971) and Edelman, Cooper, and Fishman (1971) are perhaps illustrative of some of the approaches used. Cooper (1971) took 38 subjects, thirteen years old and above, and administered tasks of word naming by domain and word association to them. The word naming task asked subjects to name, in one minute, as many different words referring to a specified domain as they could. This task was administered first in one language and later in the other. For "family," they were asked to name things seen or found in a kitchen; for "neighborhood," things seen or found in the street; for "religion," things seen or found in a church; for "education," subjects studied in school; and for "work," the names of jobs, occupations, or professions. On the word association task, respondents were asked to give, within one-minute periods, as many continuous associations as possible for each of the following stimulus words in English and Spanish: *factory, school, church, street,* and *home.*

Cooper related word naming and word association to six criterion measures —years in the U.S., occupation, accentedness of speech in English, English repertoire range (number of English speech styles), and listening comprehension in Spanish and English. Relative proficiency in word naming varied significantly as a function of context, age, and recency of arrival in the United States. The bilinguals were more proficient in Spanish than in English word naming in the tradition-oriented domains of home and religion. In the domains of neighborhood, education, and work, some age groups performed better in English. In interpreting the results, the authors pointed out that if word naming had not been broken down by domain, the performance of the six demographic subgroups (ages 13-18, 19-34, or 35 and above, with more than 11 years or less than 11 years on the mainland) would have been described as "balanced" in terms of the difference between their English and Spanish average *total* scores. Yet, all but one of these groups exhibited significant differences between English and Spanish average scores in one or more domains.

Edelman, Cooper, and Fishman (1971) tested 34 six-to-twelve year-old Puerto Rican boys and girls attending a parochial school in Jersey City. All were born in the United States. The students were asked how much they used Spanish and English with various bilingual interlocutors in school, at church, in the neighborhood, and at home (representing the domains of education, religion, neighborhood, and family, respectively). Students also received a word naming instrument similar to the one used in the Cooper research mentioned above. However, the occupational domain was eliminated because it did not apply.

Results showed that the children reported using more Spanish in the domains of family and neighborhood and more English in the domains of education and religion. There were no differences for the domain of family. In comparing the results from self-report of language use with those on word naming, we see that children reported using more Spanish than English in the neighborhood and yet performed better on word naming for the domain of neighborhood in English than in Spanish.[1] Ervin-Tripp (1971) points out that perhaps the problem here is one of using self-report rather than recordings of natural conversation. She suggests that perhaps the children's conversations *were* in Spanish, but that vocabulary for nameable shapes and objects was primarily in English and that the children could actually be using considerable English when believing their conversations were normally in Spanish.

Ervin-Tripp is perhaps pointing out one major weakness in the Jersey City research. Fishman plays down the importance of the languages-in-contact aspect of bilingual use and proficiency (see Fishman, 1971b, for instance), and except for passing mention in an article by Ma and Herasimchuk (1971), *Bilingualism in the Barrio* all but ignores the phenomena of loan words and language mixing.[2] Not only has considerable language mixing been observed in bilingual communities in the U.S. (see Espinosa, 1917; Lance, 1969; Gumperz & Hernández, 1970), but it is increasingly evident that some bilinguals do not model their speech on any variety used by unilingual speakers of their language, but rather on local bilingual usage, which shows considerable linguistic fusion of two languages (Gumperz, 1967, 1969).

1.4 *Summary of Points and Relevance to the Redwood City Study*

1.4.1   The terms "bilingualism" and "bilingual" are frequently used without being adequately defined. Language skills include various aspects of the production skills, speaking and writing, and of the comprehension skills, listening and reading. Bilinguals are persons who possess at least one language skill in two languages. A bilingual may speak one or more different varieties of a language, which may be either different dialects, registers, styles, or levels of formality.

1.4.2   Measures of bilingualism include both report of language use and proficiency and performance measures like storytelling or word naming. Joshua Fishman devised the bilingual dominance configuration to provide a truly comprehensive picture of a person's bilingualism. The individual's bilingual ability is examined in the various skill areas across a series of societal domains, which are social situations constrained by a common set of behavioral rules, and often include family, neighborhood, religion, education, and occupation.

---

[1] An earlier version of this article (Edelman, 1968) reports this discrepancy.

[2] See Weinreich (1953) for a detailed description of the phenomenon of languages in contact.

1.4.3 A long-raging dispute has centered around the effects of being bilingual. Research suggests both that bilingualism impairs intellectual functioning and that it enhances it. In much of this research, the degree of bilingualism of subjects is not assessed to any extent, such as through determining the bilingual dominance configuration for the subjects involved.

1.4.4 Research by Fishman, Cooper, and others in Jersey City investigates the effectiveness of various instruments aimed at obtaining a more comprehensive picture of a bilingual's language use and proficiency than has previously been available in the literature. The results clearly show that bilingual language use and proficiency vary with respect to societal domain.

In the evaluation of the Redwood City Bilingual Education Project, Fishman's bilingual dominance model was used to try to obtain a comprehensive picture of the patterns of bilingualism among the Mexican American children and their parents in Redwood City. The intent was to gain insights into how the bilingual proficiency and language used by the students varied according to societal domain, and particularly, *with* and *without* the influence of bilingual schooling.

The next chapter will deal with the notion of bilingual education, starting with definitions and descriptions, and then proceeding to the description of various experiences in bilingual education both at home and abroad.

2. BILINGUAL EDUCATION

Before describing one bilingual education program in particular, it is necessary to discuss bilingual education in general. "Bilingual education" may well fall into that category of terms that are much talked about but little understood. This chapter will include definitions of bilingual education and will also provide research findings from bilingual education programs in other countries and at home.

2.1 *Definitions and Descriptions*

"Bilingual education" is the use of two languages as media of instruction for a child or group of children in part or all of the school curriculum. Bilingual education may be one-way or two-way. In two-way bilingual education, the children in each ethnic and linguistic group learn curricula through their own language and through a second language. All curricula may be taught in both languages to both groups, or perhaps just certain subject matter (such as social studies). However, bilingual education usually implies that more than just language is being taught in the second language. In two-way bilingual education, the different native language groups may be kept segregated (sometimes just for the first two or three years of primary school). In one-way bilingual schooling, only one group learns bilingually.

One model calls for repeated teaching of the same subject matter in both languages—e.g., math in English in the morning, math in Spanish in the afternoon. Another model, alternate days bilingual education, involves teaching a subject matter in one language on one day and then continuing on to new content in that subject matter in the other language on the following day. A third model, simultaneous translation, provides that a bilingual teacher give, say, a math lesson in both languages simultaneously, by translating word by word, sentence by sentence, or paragraph by paragraph. Another model calls for functional specialization—some subjects in one language and other subjects in the other. Still other models expect learning of subject matter to go on primarily in one language, with the intent being to shift all or most students to instruction in the dominant or official language in certain content areas (such as math and science) or in the entire curriculum.

Mackey (1971) points out that an aim of bilingual education for over fifty years has been to keep the two languages of instruction separate out of fear that the children will otherwise come to mix them indiscriminately, both by mixing words and phrases and by confusing word associations across languages. The thought was that if the two languages were used for teaching in *separate* contexts, the children would be less likely to mix them. Andersson and Boyer (1970, Vol. 1, p. 102) argue against mixing two languages freely throughout the day. In referring to bilingual instruction at the Nye Elementary School in Texas, Treviño (1968) comments, "The two languages were never mixed in the classroom, but were used alternately in instruction, questioning, and discussions. The aim was to have all children learn to use each language correctly. Every effort was made to prevent and discourage the children from expressing themselves in a mixture of both languages. For example, the teachers would tell a story in English and the entire class would discuss it and answer questions in English; immediately after the same story would be told in Spanish, and the entire class would discuss it and answer questions in Spanish" (p. 65).

The Dade County Bilingual Education Program was also designed to keep Spanish and English language use in two separate contexts—instruction through the vernacular being from 10:30 A.M. to 11:30 A.M. and through the second language from 2:00 P.M. to 3:00 P.M. (Inclán, 1971). According to John and Horner (1971), the Las Cruces, New Mexico, Bilingual Education Program started with Spanish in the morning and English in the afternoon, but eventually, either the two languages became mixed in the same lesson, or English and Spanish lessons were used in alternation. Andersson and Boyer assert that if P.M. instruction is a carbon copy of A.M. instruction, the students will get bored (Andersson and Boyer, 1970, Vol. 1, p. 102). Also, the students will wait for the content to be taught in the language that they know better. Furthermore, elaborate and expensive precautions to keep the two languages separate call for double staffing and other measures.

Mackey (1971) describes the John F. Kennedy School in Berlin, where children have become bilingual through free language alternation in school over a ten-year period.[1] At this school, 50% of the children are from German families,

---

[1] See Mackey (1972) for a more detailed description.

40% from American families, and the other 10% from the international community. Most classes outside of language are bilingual in their grouping. Teachers alternate considerably between languages within the same lesson. Mackey notes that the teachers at the Berlin School use at least five approaches: (1) part of a lesson in one language, another part in the other language, (2) all material in one language, repetition of the same material in the other language, (3) all material in one language, a summary in the other language, (4) continual alternation of one language and the other, (5) speaking to some persons in one language, to others in the other language. At the Berlin School continual alternating is prevalent. Apparently, teachers try to sense each child's dominant language and his comprehension at a given moment in order to better communicate with him. Mackey is not at all worried that this free alternation will produce children who indiscriminately mix their two languages. He feels that evidence over the last ten years at the Berlin School speaks in favor of this method. Regardless of whether this method is "the best" or one of the best, the Mackey findings suggest that it should not be discarded as a possible alternative without being given a fair trial.

Bilingual education may be used as a stopgap measure until the second language is learned (the assimilationist approach) or it may be continued as something valued in itself (the pluralistic approach).[2] In those programs where bilingual education is not phased in and then phased out, the goal is to reach grade-level achievement in all subjects by the end of sixth grade, with native or almost-native abilities in the second language. (For a more complete discussion of definitions and models for bilingual education, see Andersson, 1965, 1968, 1969a, 1969c; Andersson & Boyer, 1970; Gaarder, 1966, 1967; Ulibarrí, 1970; Zintz, 1969; Saville and Troike, 1970; John and Hörner, 1971; Mackey, 1970, 1971; Valencia, 1969; Fishman and Lovas, 1970; Krear, 1971a).

Neither "Foreign Language in the Elementary School" (FLES) nor "English as a Second Language" (ESL) are rightly speaking bilingual education programs. FLES is simply a foreign language program, designed to teach languages like Spanish and French to Anglo children in the later elementary grades and in junior high (see McKim, 1970). It has been pointed out that FLES programs do not start early enough in the grades, nor are they intensive enough to produce satisfactory results (Andersson, 1969b). ESL is usually a crash program throughout the grades (1-12) to teach productive and receptive skills in English, using foreign language teaching techniques. Whereas the ESL component is an essential part of a bilingual program, ESL pays no attention to first-language development. To have a bilingual program, ESL instruction must be accompanied by instruction in and through the first language of the students.

---

[2] See Kjolseth (1972) for an excellent discussion of characteristics of a bilingual education program which uses a cultural pluralistic model as compared to an assimilationist one.

The pluralistic approach to bilingual education considers the various languages and cultures found in a country to be a national resource that must be conserved. Educators have advanced the "salad bowl theory" as the pluralistic model in opposition to the assimilationist "melting pot theory" (for more on assimilation vs. pluralism, see Warner and Srole, 1945; Glazer and Moynihan, 1963; Gordon, 1964). The salad bowl theory simply states that tomatoes, cucumber, radishes, and carrots can all be in the bowl together without losing their individual identities. If a country does not train native speakers of minority languages to read, write, and speak their languages, these individuals will lose these language skills for technical or professional purposes, and thus, lose unique career potential. Currently, the U.S. spends a billion dollars a year teaching primarily Spanish and French to Anglos at Foreign Service Institutes, the Department of Defense, the Agency for International Development, etc. Yet, little effort is made to develop the *native* language competence of some four million native Spanish and French speakers (Gaarder, 1969).

A bilingual education program usually commences as a unilingual program of instruction in the vernacular of the students. Gudschinsky (1971) presents the pedagogical, social, and psychological reasons for teaching a student in his vernacular first, reiterating statements made by UNESCO (1953). The pedagogical reasons include exploiting the student's fluency in his own language in learning how to read and write, with the expectation that he will transfer the reading skill gained in the first language to reading in the second language—and thus, increase his degree of exposure to the second language. The social and psychological reasons for learning in the vernacular (whether first, or concurrently with learning in the second language) are that it minimizes culture shock for the child (the traumatic experience of facing a strange school environment with a foreign language and foreign cultural values), it augments his sense of personal worth (since language is an exteriorization of self), and it helps him establish a habit of academic success (Gudschinsky, 1971).

2.2 *Bilingual Education: The Foreign Experience*

In foreign nations, children have often received their schooling in several languages, sometimes not including their own mother tongue (see Andersson and Boyer, 1970). Frequently, the children emerge from these programs bilingual. For the most part, however, the programs are not examples of "bilingual education," in the way that the term was defined above, since the students receive the content subjects in only one language. They are not actually being taught bilingually. In some cases, students are taught in their mother tongue. In other cases, the students are taught in a second or third language, while their mother tongue may be taught as a subject. In the few instances where researchers have described and evaluated such programs, it is usually because the language selected for instructional purposes runs counter to what would be expected. For instance, the mother tongue is used as the language of instruction in an area where another, dominant language, is generally used in school. Or students are taught in a second language in an area where their own mother tongue is used for teaching most or all such students.

The research results from abroad for both kinds of programs that produce bilingual students are generally mixed. A study in Mexico (Modiano, 1966, 1968) shows the advantages of instruction through the *mother tongue*. On the other hand, a series of studies from the Philippines suggests that this approach is disadvantageous (see The Department of Education, Manila, 1953; Davis, 1967; Revil *et al.,* 1968). Results of studies in Canada (Lambert and Macnamara, 1969; Lambert, Just, and Segalowitz, 1970; Lambert, Tucker, d'Anglejan, and Segalowitz, 1970; Tucker, Lambert, d'Anglejan, and Silny, 1971; Lambert and Tucker, 1971; Lambert and Tucker, 1972) and in the Philippines (The Department of Education, Manila, 1953; Davis, 1967; Revil *et al.,* 1968) show the advantages of schooling in a *second* language. One study in Ireland (Macnamara, 1966) points up disadvantages of schooling in the second language. One study in South Africa (Malherbe, 1946, 1969) reports the advantages of being schooled simultaneously in two languages.

Perhaps the mixed research results reflect the general foreign trend towards using only one language at a time as the medium of instruction. The single study that reports using both languages (Malherbe, 1946, 1969) cited the decidedly superior achievement of those who had received the bilingual schooling as compared with those in monolingual schools.

In comparing results of bilingual education programs in different foreign countries, it is important to remember that no two language communities and school situations are the same. There are differences in the relative numbers of people who speak the vernaculars and the dominant or official language (see, for instance, Fishman, Ferguson, and Das Gupta, 1968), and there are differences in attitudes on the part of all concerned—parents, teachers, and children—toward the languages of the community (see Le Page, 1964; Gardner and Lambert, 1972). The societal prestige afforded each language, the socioeconomic level of the students, and the quality of the instruction are all important factors. For these reasons, research results for one community must only be viewed as suggestive of how effective a similar program may be in another community. It is also important to keep in mind that assimilationist models of bilingual education (i.e., rapid transfer to the dominant language), while frequently opposed by minority groups in the United States, are accepted and encouraged by speakers of the vernaculars—the subordinate languages—in many countries (see Gudschinsky, 1971).

The following are detailed discussions of some of the foreign programs that have received substantial mention in the literature. The purpose of including the information here is that some of the actual studies are difficult to obtain.

2.2.1 *South Africa*

By the Act of Union in 1910, both English and Afrikaans (a variety of Dutch) were considered official languages to be taught as subjects in all public schools in South Africa. Malherbe (1946) surveyed 18,773 pupils from standards IV-X in over 200 representative schools. In 1938, at the time the survey was conducted, Afrikaans-English bilingual schools were still very common. Malherbe (1969) reports that since the Nationalist regime had come into power in 1948, bilingualism in South Africa had deteriorated because children had been segregated into two distinct linguistic groups, ignoring the language group which used both languages at home.

With respect to the question of how bilingually-schooled children fare in English and Afrikaans language proficiency, Malherbe looked at three groups of South African school children: 4,736 from unilingual Afrikaans homes, 6,044 from unilingual English homes, and 7,993 from bilingual homes. He had identified these three groups by means of a sociolinguistic survey of language use in the home. In comparing bilingually-schooled children from unilingual Afrikaans homes with a unilingually-schooled group matched on intelligence, the bilingually-schooled children were considerably superior in measured language attainment (vocabulary, same-opposites, story completion, speed and comprehension of reading). This was particularly true for the lower intelligence group. Not only did these students do as well as the control group in Afrikaans, but they performed nearly twice as well as the higher-intelligence control group in English language attainment. As Malherbe states, "Contrary to general expectation, children with low intelligence have a relatively much better chance of becoming bilingual citizens (without loss in their mother tongue or in their content subjects. . .) by attending the bilingual school than by attending the unilingual school" (Malherbe, 1946, p. 64).

Bilingually-schooled children from unilingual English homes performed as well as the control group in English and made one year's progress in Afrikaans over the English unilingually-schooled group. Finally, bilingually-schooled children from *bilingual* homes achieved the greatest degree of bilingualism in English and Afrikaans.

With respect to the question of how bilingually-schooled children fare in content areas, children in bilingual schools surpassed those in unilingual schools by 4/5 of a year in geography and by half a year in mathematics. Malherbe comments that "it has often been maintained that, while the partial use of the second language as a medium may help the second language, the child loses in 'content.' This contention has been definitely disproved in the case of the bilingual school where the results in the ordinary subjects are consistently better than those attained by pupils in unilingual schools—intelligence and home language being kept constant in the two types compared" (Malherbe, 1946, p. 117).

The South African experience, therefore, supports the contention that education by means of the vernacular followed by second language learning can lead to success in acquiring bilingual skills and to academic success.

2.2.2 The Philippines

The Philippines experience, until recently, has been somewhat different from that of South Africa. Although two or more languages have been taught as subjects in the Philippine schools, these languages have not been simultaneously used as media of instruction in the classroom. Recently, however, an alternate days approach to bilingual education was implemented (Tucker, Otanes, and Sibayan, 1970). For many years, English was the sole medium of instruction in Philippine schools, although Pilipino (popularly called Tagalog) was studied as a subject since 1940. In 1957, a decision was made to use the prevailing local vernacular as the medium of instruction in grades 1 and 2, with English being introduced as the primary medium of instruction in Grade 3.

Research in the Philippines has been concerned with the results of switching at various grade levels from instruction through a vernacular to instruction through English, as opposed to starting directly with English. Although these language-switch studies are not actually experiences in bilingual education in the way that the term is currently being defined, they do reflect attempts at making children bilingual in all four language skills in each language—listening, speaking, reading, and writing. For this reason, they are given a place in our discussion.

The Department of Education, Manila (1953) reports that when native Hiligaynon speakers were schooled in their vernacular instead of in English for grades 1 and 2, they scored higher in reading and in language than a control group schooled only in English. However, the equality of the two groups' scores was in doubt because the experimental group took the tests in Hiligaynon and the control group in English. At the end of the third year, when both groups were tested in English, there was no difference between the two groups in reading or in language, and at the end of the fifth year, the control group excelled in language. The researchers concluded that the groups schooled in the vernacular were able to make a satisfactory transfer to English.

Orata (1953) found the same results with children who spoke Tagalog as their vernacular. A group schooled in Tagalog for two years that switched to English in the third year was compared with a control group that used English throughout. The experimental group showed noticeable superiority in achievement during the first two years when they were tested in their native language and the control group was tested in English. In the third year when both groups were tested in English, the experimental group was still higher but not significantly.

Davis (1967) reports on two language-teaching experiments. In one, 900 Hiligaynon-speaking students participated in an experiment in which the number and order of second languages introduced as subjects were varied. One group received both Pilipino (Tagalog) and English as second languages in first grade, one group received just English, and a third group was introduced to Pilipino as a subject in second grade, and then English was added in third grade. The finding was that it was better for English achievement to teach English all three years, not just beginning in second grade. However, the time of introduction of Pilipino didn't affect achievement in that language. Furthermore, the extra introduction of Pilipino as a second language at the same time as English as a second language didn't seem to interfere with the learning of English.

Davis (1967) also reports on the Rizal Experiments, part of which looked at the importance of varying the grade at which English was introduced as the medium of instruction to native Pilipino speakers. One group received English instruction from grades 1-6 with Pilipino as a subject, another group used Pilipino as the medium of instruction for grades 1 and 2 and then switched to English, and a third group was instructed through Pilipino for grades 1-4 before switching to English. The effects of these different approaches on language and subject-matter achievement were measured at the end of grades 4 and 6. Davis found that later introduction of English meant poorer performance in English language achievement at the end of grade 4. Those using English as the medium of instruction in grades 1-4 did best on the English version of the subject-matter tests. Those schooled in Pilipino did best on the Pilipino version of the tests. By grade 6, those schooled in English from the start were better on all tests—even Pilipino reading—than those schooled in Pilipino for a period of time. Also, the group that switched to English in the third grade performed better in English than did the group that didn't switch to English until the fifth grade.

Revil *et al.* (1968) did a follow up to the Rizal Experiments, using 64% of the original sample, in their second year of high school (8th grade). Their findings confirmed those of the earlier experiments with respect to English proficiency, namely that English proficiency was directly related to the number of years it was used as the medium of instruction. However, at the high-school level, the group that had switched to English instruction in the fifth grade performed as well in English as did the group that had switched to English in the third grade. Thus, the group with an English language handicap were essentially "catching up" in this area over time.

Revil *et al.* also looked at performance by the three groups in the content areas, specifically Philipino; Philippine history, government, and current events;

general science; and general math computation and problem solving. The group
schooled exclusively in English performed best in all areas, as they had done at
the end of sixth grade. This meant that the group schooled in English exceeded
the other two groups in a test of Philipino grammar and literature by a wide margin, whereas at the end of grade 4 there had been no differences across groups and
at the end of grade 6 the English group were only slightly ahead. These authors
conjectured that the tests of Pilipino grammar in grades 4 and 6 did not have a
high enough ceiling, thus depressing the scores of the students schooled exclusively in English. Their conclusion was that language shift in and of itself somehow
affected those students involved in it, not only in English performance and in
content-area performance, but also in performance in their native language.

The Philippine experience does *not* tend to support the argument that it is best
to begin education in the vernacular alone as a means for achieving bilingual ability and academic success. Those students who started in the second language alone
appear to have emerged more proficient bilinguals and academically more successful. Apparently, when students began their studies in the vernacular and in English
simultaneously, as with the more recent alternate days approach (see Tucker,
Otanes, and Sibayan, 1970; Philippine Normal College, n.d.), these students
emerged as proficiently bilingual as students beginning their studies in English
alone. However, students who began their studies only in the vernacular were
experiencing a lag, consistent with the earlier research findings.

2.2.3 *Perú and Mexico*

Whereas the Summer Institute of Linguistics established bilingual education
programs in Perú for jungle Indians in 1953, now reaching 20 different indigen-
ous language groups, and for highland Quechuan Indians in 1965 (see Gudschinsky, 1971), reports of systematic evaluations of these programs are not available
in the literature. See Burns (1968) for an impressionistic account of a program for
Quechuan Indians in Perú.

One program for Tzeltal- and Tzotzil-speaking Mexican Indians in the highlands
of Chiapas, Mexico, however, was evaluated and has received widespread publicity.
Students in 13 schools run by the National Indian Institute were instructed for
one year in the vernacular, while students in another 13 federal and state schools
were taught directly through Spanish, their second language. The students who
started schooling in the vernacular prior to reading in Spanish scored significantly
higher on a Spanish language instrument and were more frequently rated by their
teachers as able to read Spanish with comprehension than were those students who
started school directly in Spanish (Modiano, 1966, 1968). Note that in remote
areas like that studied by Modiano, the students were not likely to speak much
Spanish outside of school.

The results from the Chiapas study seem to support the contention that education begun in the vernacular enhances the acquisition of the second language.

2.2.4 *Canada*

English Canadian parents in Montreal, in collaboration with the staff at McGill University, initiated a French immersion program for their children in the fall of 1965. They were concerned that non-French speakers in the Province of Quebec might in time encounter increasingly stronger social and economic pressures to learn French (Lambert and Macnamara, 1969). One group of kindergarteners in an English elementary school who were from middle-class English-speaking homes, became participants in a French kindergarten. A French teacher conducted the whole year's program exclusively in French. As of the 1971-72 school year, that group was in sixth grade and a follow-up group was in fifth grade. During the 1966-67 school year, Wallace E. Lambert and his associates at McGill University started an intensive evaluation of this program, and through their efforts a number of subsequent reports on the project have appeared (see Lambert and Macnamara, 1969; Lambert, Just, and Segalowitz, 1970; Lambert, Tucker, d'Anglejan, and Segalowitz, 1970; Tucker, Lambert, d'Anglejan, and Silny, 1971; Lambert and Tucker, 1971; Lambert and Tucker, 1972).

Lambert was interested in finding out whether home-school language switch resulted in native-language or subject-matter deficit, and whether it would be detrimental to the cognitive development of the children in the program. The program began as one of French immersion with English not being introduced as a subject until grade 2. However, in grade 5, the program became bilingual with one subject per year taught through the medium of English—arithmetic in fifth grade, science in sixth grade, geography in seventh grade, and so forth.

The Lambert study involved the administration of a comprehensive battery of language proficiency tests to the experimental groups, French controls, and English controls. Tests included language arts (word knowledge, word discrimination, reading, spelling, etc.), listening comprehension, vocabulary, storytelling and retelling, and word association. Students were also tested in mathematics, in intelligence, and in creativity. Furthermore, data were collected on parental and student attitudes toward French Canadians, European French, and English Canadians.

After six years, the findings were that the program had not resulted in any native-language or subject matter (i.e., arithmetic) deficit. Nor did there appear to be any cognitive retardation attributed to participation in the program. The experimental pupils were able to read, write, speak, and understand English as well as youngsters instructed via English in the conventional manner. In addition, they could read, write, speak and understand French in a way that English pupils who follow a traditional FLES program never do. Their French listening comprehension score was comparable to that of the controls from grade 2 on, and by grade 4, their performance on a French picture vocabulary test and their free association in French was equal to that of the French controls. Although they still made more errors in their French oral production, especially in gender and contractions, and scored noticeably lower than the French controls in rhythm and intonation and in overall expression, their verbal content in French was as long and complex as that of the controls and showed a similar degree of comprehensiveness and vocabulary diversity (Lambert and Tucker, 1971). Swain (1972) provides a teacher's testimonial on the high quality of French spoken by the English Canadian students.

The program also measured attitudes of the students and found that home-school language switch improved the students' attitudes toward French people, both French Canadians and European French, in comparison with the English Control classes. Although their attitudes were not stable over time (in the spring of 1970, attitudes toward French Canadians turned negative and those toward European French neutral), by the spring of 1971 the attitudes of the immersion program children toward both French groups were solidly positive. The interpretation offered was that the Experimental children were able to use the French language so effectively that they were able to communicate with and establish satisfying friendships with French-speaking people (Lambert and Tucker, 1971).

Since the McGill staff were fully aware that part of the success of this program could possibly be attributed to the middle-class status of the children in the Experimental group, they started another program of French immersion for working-class children in two separate schools (see Tucker, Lambert, and d'Anglejan, 1972). Each group was compared separately with an English and French control group. The Pilot group (first graders) and the control groups were given a battery of tests similar to those used with the middle-class children. In one school, the Experimental group performed as well as the English control group in English language arts. This was somewhat surprising since the *middle-class* Experimental group had scored *lower* than the control in English language arts until the third grade, a result attributed to their not starting formal schooling in English until second grade. In the other working-class school, the control group performed better than the Pilot in first-grade English language arts, as Lambert *et al.* expected. Although clearly behind the French controls in many French language skills, the Experimental groups at both schools performed as well in French listening comprehension as did the controls and showed that they were acquiring command of other skills. In mathematics, the Experimental groups did significantly better than the controls although the test was in English, indicating that they were not experiencing a deficit in math when learning it through French.

Although some people draw a parallel between the French immersion situation Lambert *et al.* have designed and the English immersion situation that Mexican

Americans, for example, find themselves in, Lambert warns against making such a comparison: "The contrast . . . between Spanish American children who are coming into a school system in the United States and learning English is not a valid parallel (to the St. Lambert project in Montreal). For the minority group in the United States, giving up the home language and entering an American school is like kissing his home language goodbye. In the case we are dealing with, however, English is clearly the most powerful language, so much so that these parents can be sure to have English-skilled children who can afford to learn some French" (Lambert, Just, and Segalowitz, 1970, p. 276).

The Montreal experience tends to suggest that it isn't important to start schooling in the vernacular—that in fact it is possible to start in another language and learn the vernacular formally later on, without suffering set-backs in language proficiency or in the content subjects. Yet the above admonition expressed by the authors suggests that these findings apply to comparable socio-political situations where the languages in question share the same relative degree of prestige.

2.3 The History of Bilingual Education in the United States

The U.S. experience with bilingual schools falls into two different periods, pre-World War I and post-1963.[3] The first bilingual schools were founded before 1800 and were non-public (chiefly parochial) elementary schools. German schools existed throughout the country, French schools in New England, and Scandinavian and Dutch schools in the Midwest. Many of these schools were not actually bilingual in their curricula. Rather, they were non-English schools where English was taught as a subject (Andersson and Boyer, 1970). The first public bilingual school was founded in 1840 in Cincinnati, where there were a large majority of German-speaking immigrants (Andersson, 1971). To attract German students to public schools, the state of Ohio passed a law in 1840 making it the duty of the board of trustees of common schools to provide German schools—schools where German was introduced as an optional subject. But this and other programs failed to provide an authoritative curriculum model for bilingual education. Often they only had a language program, not a bilingual program.

German was taught extensively in the elementary schools between 1840 and 1919—from Indianapolis to Baltimore to New Ulm, Minnesota (Andersson and Boyer, 1970). In fact, the Missouri Superintendent of Public Instruction in 1887 was complaining that not enough English was being taught in several of his districts (Fishman, 1969; also see Fishman, 1966b). During the same period that German was used so extensively, French was used as a medium of instruction in Louisiana, and from 1848, Spanish was used in New Mexico.

---

[3] See Kloss (1971) for a thorough history of federal and state laws regarding the languages of instruction in the schools.

Espinosa (1911) cites a then long-standing Colorado State law requiring that in the school districts where the majority of the children were of Spanish parents, the teachers had to know both Spanish and English, and could teach them to read in Spanish and use Spanish as a medium of instruction for other subjects as well. Espinosa points out that at the same time there was a greater need for Spanish instruction in New Mexico, but no legislation to support it, and "great animosity on the part of the school authorities, lest the Spanish-speaking children learn to read Spanish" (Espinosa, 1911, p. 18). Espinosa (1917) notes that in 1896 the New Mexican public schools began a systematic attempt to have English taught in all the schools. In some cases "the American authorities . . . in their enthusiasm for the English language have gone so far as to forbid the use of Spanish by the Spanish children during their play" (Espinosa, 1917, p. 411).

Leibowitz (1971) notes that "the original California State Constitution was drafted in a context of linguistic equality. Although only eight of the forty-eight delegates to the 1849 Monterey Constitutional Convention were native speakers of Spanish (deducing this from their Spanish surnames), the Convention elected an official translator, and all resolutions and articles were translated before being voted upon. The final document was similarly published in Spanish and English; it recognized the importance of Spanish by providing that all laws should be published in English and Spanish" (pp. 46-47). At the end of 1848, there were 15,000 residents in California, half of them of Mexican descent. With the Gold Rush, there were 95,000, almost all Anglo-Americans. In 1855 the State Bureau of Public Instruction stipulated that all schools had to teach exclusively in English. In the early 1850's the State passed statutes suspending the publishing of State laws in Spanish and requiring that all court proceedings be in English.

Southern California remained Spanish-speaking for some time (see Leibowitz, 1971). Spanish newspapers and bilingual schools flourished in the 1870's. There were Spanish-speaking judges, elected officials, and community leaders. In 1870 a statute was issued stipulating that all schools had to teach only in English. An amendment to the California Constitution in 1894 restricted voting to those who could read and write English. As Leibowitz remarks, "The decisions to impose English as the exclusive language of instruction in the schools have reflected the popular attitudes towards the particular ethnic group and the degree of hostility evidenced toward that group's natural development" (Leibowitz, 1971, p. 4).

As a result of the Americanization movement in the decade from 1913 to 1923, states passed statutes requiring English to be the language of instruction in the public and private schools. By 1923, 34 states had such laws. The purpose of these statutes was to ensure that the schools would serve as a melting pot to transmit the means to participate in and contribute fully to American life. The desire to assist the adjustment of aliens was inextricably bound up with a desire to seek uniformity of language (Leibowitz, 1969). This same rejection of alien cultures and languages in favor of everything American carried through the World War II period.

The 1940's were marked by considerable expansion of programs in English as a second language. Intensive English drills were designed to facilitate later instruction through English in school subjects, with no effort to develop the children's knowledge of their own language and culture (Cannon, 1971). Primarily out of concern for national defense, the U.S. government started stimulating foreign language programs in the late 1950's, especially for college-age students and for adults. Programs for young children began in the 1960's. The first modern bilingual education program was established at the Coral Way Elementary School, Dade County, Miami, Florida, in 1963 for grades 1-3, supported by a grant from the Ford Foundation. The program was designed for Spanish-speaking Cubans and for Anglos, but at first only part of the school participated, mostly children with English-speaking parents. By the second year all Spanish- and English-speaking children were involved (Andersson, 1971).

The National Education Association meeting in 1966 focused on the improvement of elementary schooling for Spanish-speaking children in the Southwest. The discussants emphasized the difficulties Mexican American students were having in adjusting to Anglo culture at school. An NEA survey noted that one-sixth of the school-age population in the Southwest were Spanish-speaking (NEA, 1966). The study suggested that pre-school and lower elementary instruction should be conducted in both Spanish and English, and that Mexican cultural traditions should be fostered so that the pupils would take pride in their ethnic identity. The NEA report recommended the repeal of state laws specifying English as the sole language of instruction.

Both as a result of this NEA study and other similar studies, and as a result of politicking by concerned statesmen and educators (see Gaarder, 1969; Tobier, 1969; Andersson, 1971; Kloss, 1971; Badillo, 1972), the Bilingual Education Act became a federal statute under Title VII of the Elementary and Secondary Education Amendment (ESEA) of 1967. The statute authorized appropriation of funds to (1) develop special instructional materials for use in bilingual education programs, (2) provide in-service training for teachers, teacher aides, and counselors participating in bilingual programs, and (3) establish, maintain, and operate special programs for children of limited English-speaking ability (Andersson and Boyer, 1970, Appendix A).

In enacting legislation for the Bilingual Education Act of 1967, Congress provided official endorsement of the concept of cultural pluralism and of the importance of developing children's skills and concepts in their first language. At the same time, these children would be learning English as a second language. Some states have recently passed laws enabling schools to legally conduct bilingual education programs (Leibowitz, 1969; Kloss, 1971; Cannon, 1971).

As of the 1971-72 school year, there were 163 bilingual education programs supported by the Bilingual Education Act, serving 86,154 children (Andersson, 1971). Nonetheless, interpretations of what the ingredients of bilingual education in the U.S. actually are and how these ingredients are to be effectively integrated into a bilingual program has been a subject of controversy (see, for instance, Gaarder, 1970; Ortego, 1970; Tucker and d'Anglejan, 1971; Cannon, 1971; Kjolseth, 1972).

In April of 1971, the Bureau of Elementary and Secondary Education issued a manual defining bilingual education and specifying the objectives of the Title VII Bilingual Education Program (U.S. Office of Education, 1971). Bilingual education is defined as "the use of two languages, one of which is English, as mediums of instruction for the same pupil population in a well-organized program which encompasses part or all of the curriculum and includes the study of the history and culture associated with the mother tongue. A complete program develops and maintains the children's self-esteem and a legitimate pride in both cultures" (U.S. Office of Education, 1971, p. 1). Note that both languages are to be used as "mediums of instruction." Thus, a program which teaches math, science, social studies, and physical education in English and teaches language arts in both English and Spanish is not a bilingual program, regardless of whether the students are native English-speaking or native Spanish-speaking. The students may emerge from such a program as bilinguals, but they are not being schooled in the subject matter in both languages, and therefore are not receiving bilingual education (*The Linguistic Reporter,* 1971).

Under a section in the manual on objectives of bilingual education, the target group is specified as children with limited English-speaking ability who come from low-income families where the dominant language is other than English. The educational goals for these children include developing greater competance in English, becoming more proficient in their dominant language, and profiting from increased educational opportunity. The Office of Education's position with respect to mother-tongue instruction is that although the "primary importance of English" is emphasized, use of the children's mother tongue in school "can have a beneficial effect upon their education" (U.S. Office of Education, 1971, p. 1). Instructional use of the mother tongue can help to prevent retardation in school performance until sufficient command of English is attained. But beyond "transitional" value, the development of literacy in the mother tongue should result in more broadly educated adults (U.S. Office of Education, 1971, p. 1).

Under characteristics of bilingual education programs, the manual points out that children are taught one or more academic subjects in their dominant language. This is a requisite for a bilingual program. It is also stipulated that provision be made (1) for children whose dominant language is English to be taught the dominant language of the other children and (2) for increasing the instructional use of both languages for both groups in the same classroom. The rationale given for this last stipulation is as follows: "Though the legislation was written with the intention of benefiting children who come from homes where English is not spoken, it is essential that they not be segregated from the rest of the school population, even if this kind of grouping might seem to make instruction more effective" (U.S. Office of Education, 1971, p. 21).

An irony of bilingual education is that program staffs are now encouraging children to behave in a way that had been shunned for fifty years or more in most U.S. schools: to use their native language at school. In a sense, it is reverse socialization. Whereas school children have been subjected to the English-only rule whereby they have been punished, even suspended or expelled, for using a language other than English in the U.S. schools of the past, now they are encouraged to use that language at school (see Espinosa, 1917; Bernal, 1969; Carter, 1970; Ortego, 1970; Cannon, 1971, on this issue).

One key purpose of bilingual education programs in the U.S. is to eliminate the stigma that has been attached to the "handicap" of being bilingual (see, for instance, Rowan, 1950). The majority of bilingual programs strive to make each bilingual *functionally* bilingual—namely, able to understand, speak, read, and write in both his first and second languages. Such programs are attempting to demonstrate that bilingualism need not be a detriment, but rather an advantage in a world with ever-increasing multilingual demands. And in the short run, the creation of functional bilinguals is also intended to produce individuals with a strong self-concept and pride in their cultural heritage, who experience academic success in school from the first day they enter the classroom

2.4 *Evaluations of 1963-1971 U.S. Bilingual Education Programs Primarily Aimed at Spanish-Dominant Students*

There are two major ways that bilingual education programs for the Spanish speaking have been evaluated. The first approach asks whether bilingually-schooled children meet curriculum objectives or tasks that are specified by the project staff. This approach provides feedback as to whether instructional objectives within a program have been met. However, the reader of this type of an evaluation may be left wondering whether the objectives were appropriate in the first place. The second approach asks whether students participating in such programs have a better school experience than comparable students schooled traditionally. This approach provides feedback as to the effectiveness of bilingual education programs as compared with monolingual schooling. There are few thorough evaluations of U.S. Spanish-English bilingual education programs as compared to English-only monolingual programs in the literature. To do a comparative study calls for a comparison group and hence involves all the problems associated with finding comparable students, arranging and executing a testing program, and analyzing the results. The following are descriptions of some of the bilingual programs for Spanish speakers that have been evaluated.

The descriptions below are of programs in Dade County, Florida (see Inclán, 1971); Webb County, Texas (see Treviño, 1968); the San Antonio Independent School District, Texas (see Horn, 1966a, 1966b; Ott, n.d.; Stemmler, 1966; Arnold, 1968; Taylor 1969, 1970); the Harlandale Independent School District, Texas (see Pryor, 1967; John and Horner, 1971); San José, California (see Owens, 1972); Sacramento, California (see Hartwig, 1971); and Compton, California (see Goodman and Stern, 1971). These reports yield generally favorable results. Spanish-speaking students instructed bilingually tend to perform as well in English language skills and in the content areas as comparable students schooled only in English. At the same time, the Spanish-speaking students are developing language skills in Spanish. Anglo students in such programs do not appear adversely affected in their English language development and in the content subjects, and are learning a second language, Spanish (see particularly Inclán, 1971).

2.4.1 Dade County, Florida

The Coral Way Elementary School in Dade County, Florida, was the site of the first bilingual education program in the second period of bilingual schooling in the U.S., beginning in 1963. The program involved two-way bilingual education for Cuban and Anglo students, with subject matter presented in one language in the morning and repeated in the other language in the afternoon. As of 1970, Cubans in grades 3-8 who were schooled bilingually were as good in English reading (using the Inter-American Tests of Reading) as Cuban control students schooled conventionally. At the junior high school level (7th and 8th grade), however, the Cuban control students were better in Spanish reading (Inclán, 1971). Inclán (1971) points out that the Cuban control group was taking a class in Spanish as a first language. Still, since the experimental group was exposed to reading in Spanish for all its subjects, they would have been expected to do better in Spanish reading than the control group. The Anglo bilingual sixth graders were tested in Spanish reading, and although far below the Cuban students, they were considered to be doing well (Inclán, 1971).

In assessing bilingual education in Dade County as a whole (as bilingual schooling was extended to other schools besides Coral Way), it was found that the Experimental students, both Spanish-speaking and English-speaking, performed as well as did Control students in language arts and in math achievement. At the same time, the Spanish-speaking pupils were learning to read and write their native language, and the English-speaking pupils were learning a second language (Inclán, 1971).

2.4.2 *Webb County, Texas*

The second bilingual program in the U.S., according to Andersson (1971), was begun at the Nye Elementary School, in the United Consolidated Independent School District, Webb County, Texas. Treviño (1968) studied 87 Mexican American and 96 Anglo children schooled bilingually in math over three years, in the Nye Elementary School. In the first and second grades, the students were instructed in both languages by bilingual teachers. The content was first given in one language and then translated into the other. In the third grade, the children were team taught with math content presented by one teacher in one language in the morning and then repeated by the other teacher in the afternoon. The classrooms were fully integrated so that native Spanish speakers and native English speakers were both exposed to math instruction in both languages.

At the end of the first grade, the students were given the Arithmetic Subtest of the California Achievement Tests. At the end of the third grade, the group was given a more advanced form of the test. Both forms have sections on math reasoning (meanings, number symbols, problems) and math fundamentals. The word problems were read to the first graders. Third graders read them themselves. The performance of the students at the first-grade and at the third-grade levels was compared with that of comparable students at each grade level. (There was no continuing comparison group.) Analysis of Bilingual group performance was carried out both for the total group and with the elimination of students retained in grade an extra year.

Results showed that Mexican American children taught bilingually performed higher than those taught in English alone. When in first grade, Bilingual-group Spanish speakers scored better in math fundamentals than the Control group, and were at least as proficient when students repeating the grade were eliminated from the analysis. There was no difference between the groups in math reasoning. At the third-grade level, the Bilingual group came out ahead in math reasoning, and equal in math fundamentals, both when data from the retainees were included in the analysis and when they were left out.

At the first-grade level, the Anglos outperformed the Anglo Control group in math fundamentals, both with and without retainees in the analysis. Similarly, there was no difference in math reasoning. At the third-grade level there was no difference in math fundamentals between the Anglo Bilingual and Control groups, but the Bilingual group excelled in math reasoning.

Furthermore, Mexican Americans in the Bilingual group performed as well as Anglos in math fundamentals and reasoning at both the first- and third-grade levels. This is particularly surprising since the Mexican Americans were from rural backgrounds and the Anglos from suburban areas. Treviño concluded that bilingual instruction didn't retard progress in mathematics. Rather, she contended that bilingual instruction enhanced it.

2.4.3 *San Antonio, Texas*

The third bilingual program in the U.S. was started with 735 children from 28 first-grade classes in nine schools of the San Antonio Independent School District (Andersson, 1971). Almost all of the students in each class were native speakers of Spanish. The project utilized an oral-aural approach to initial reading instruction, employing science content because of its culture-free nature (Stemmler, 1966). The oral-aural materials were based on English-as-a-second language techniques, using pattern drills and dialogs to deliver the material (Horn, 1966a, 1966b; Ott, n.d.). The major research question was the effect of instruction in the students' native language (Spanish) upon the development of oral and then written English. One group was given the oral-aural approach to science just in English, another group just in Spanish, and a third group was given the science content in English without the oral-aural structures. A fourth group was set up as a control. This group represented a cross section of socioeconomic levels in contrast to the three low-income groups receiving the treatments.

The results of research on the projects are mixed. Arnold (1968), in reporting the findings after two years, noted that second-grade Spanish speakers receiving Spanish oral-aural science with the other subjects in English performed on a par in English reading with Spanish speakers receiving oral-aural science and all other instruction in English. Those first graders given the oral-aural English treatment were most successful. This finding coincides with findings in the Philippines to the effect that earlier introduction of English reading meant better performance in English reading (see above).

Taylor (1969, 1970) looked at the San Antonio project when the treatment groups were at the end of grades 4 and 5. The year that the groups were in grades 2 and 3 the treatment group receiving science without the oral-aural structures was eliminated "because of operational conditions" (Taylor, 1969) and those students were merged with the other two treatment groups. At the end of five years, Taylor reports that there had been considerable attrition from the treatment groups, partly because students moved away and partly because students were removed from the treatment classes by administrative decisions. Furthermore, the original mixed-income control group had been discontinued.

In her study, Taylor gave randomly-selected students from the two treatment groups (those receiving the oral-aural science materials in English and those receiving them in Spanish), and students from newly-devised control groups, an English language proficiency test. She found that the fifth-grade experimental group receiving the Spanish language treatment obtained higher scores than either the English treatment group or the control group in English fluency and in total oral production (pronunciation, intonation; and fluency), while those instructed only in the oral-aural English treatment were better in pronunciation.

There were no differences among the fourth-grade groups, either on the subtests or on the total test.

The author explains the higher performance in English oral production of the fifth graders schooled partially in Spanish as follows: Hearing their own language reinforced the phonemic and syntactic contrasts between English and Spanish, thus making it easier for these Spanish speakers to learn English (Taylor, 1969). She concluded from her research that partial instruction in Spanish has a beneficial effect on the English-speaking proficiency of Mexican American children (Taylor, 1970).

Another bilingual program in San Antonio, Texas, was initiated in the Harlandale Independent School District with Spanish-speaking students in one first-grade classroom in each of four schools—Columbia Heights, Collier, Flanders, and Stonewall. The bilingual section at each school was taught Spanish language arts for one hour and twenty minutes each day.[4]

Looking at gains in English reading over the course of grade 1 in each of the four schools, Pryor (1967) reports that the Spanish-speaking students in the Bilingual section at each school either maintained a position they established relative to the other three-to-five comparison sections in the pretesting at the beginning of the year, or pulled ahead. At the same time, the Bilingual sections demonstrated skills in Spanish reading, as measured by the *Pruebas de Lectura, Serie Interamericana.* Three Bilingual sections scored significantly lower in Spanish reading than in English reading, but the Bilingual group at Stonewall did *better* in Spanish reading than in English reading. Pryor explains that the bilingual teacher at that school had taught Spanish language arts the year before and had all the materials ready, suggesting the importance of the teacher's experience in bilingual education and the existence of appropriate curriculum materials.

John and Horner (1971) indicate that results at the end of the second year of the Harlandale project showed that the Bilingual sections once again were doing as well in reading English as classes instructed only in English. John and Horner also report that a bilingual project for four first-grade classrooms at the Garfield Elementary School in Del Rio, Texas, during the 1966-67 year showed the experimental group as good as the control group in English language skills and superior in measures of socialization and adjustment.

2.4.4 San José, California

Owens (1972) reports on a bilingual preschool program in San José, California, called the Spanish Dame Project. It was given that name because paraprofessional teachers conducted school sessions in the children's homes, utilizing the mother of

---

[4]The students apparently also received some instruction in the content subjects in Spanish (see John and Horner, 1971, p. 89), although this fact is not evident from the first-year evaluation report (Pryor, 1967).

the household as the teacher aide. A pretest-posttest control group design involving three experimental and three control groups indicated that the Bilingual preschool students had experienced significantly greater oral language growth than the control groups.

2.4.5 Sacramento, California

In the Sacramento City Unified School District, 402 kindergarten through third graders, 60% Spanish-dominant and 40% English-dominant, received bilingual instruction in language arts, social students, and math. At the end of the 1970-71 year, Hartwig (1971) found that the Experimental group was better than the comparison group in third-grade reading and in first- and third-grade math, using the California Achievement Tests. The Experimental first- and second-grade groups were just as proficient as the control groups in English reading. Unfortunately, the analysis didn't distinguish between Spanish-dominant and English-dominant children, nor between Mexican Americans and Anglos, in analyzing and reporting the results.

2.4.6 Compton, California

In the Compton City Schools, 299 students, 80% Spanish-dominant, in grades K-2 received at least 80 minutes of Spanish-medium instruction per day. Goodman and Stern (1971) report that the Spanish-dominant Bilingual kindergarten and first graders were better in Spanish and English on the Stern Expressive Vocabulary Inventory than comparison groups. Spanish-dominant Bilingual-group first graders were better in English oral comprehension and as good in Spanish oral comprehension as the comparison group, as measured by the Inter-American Tests of Oral Comprehension. Although no test of English reading was given,[5] the Spanish-dominant first- and second-grade Bilingual groups did better than the comparison groups in Spanish reading on the *Pruebas de Lectura, Serie Interamericana*. The English-dominant students were not included in the formal evaluation.

The above evaluations of bilingual programs in the U.S. speak highly for bilingual education. It could be argued that some of their success was attributable to experimental or Hawthorne effect, i.e., the children knew that they were involved in something special and consequently they performed better. It is also possible that results were a direct reflection of the number of adults in the classroom, i.e., not just the teacher, but a teacher aide and possibly the coordinator and curriculum writer from time to time. Ideally, every bilingual child from a low-income

---

[5] The project staff assumed that all students would take the English reading test given to all children in the District in the past. But the District decided on a random sampling test program and none of the children from the project were included.

family should be part of an educational experiment if it improves his skills in both languages, as well as his performance in non-language subjects. With the continuing increase in federal and state programs, however, it is difficult to find a "control" group of low-income minority children who are receiving a *completely* traditional or conventional educational program. In discussing the "treatment" for the Redwood City Project, the programs that have benefited the "comparison" groups in that school district will also be mentioned.

Cannon (1971) points out a reason why past evaluations of bilingual education programs have not been impartial: "Since a generally positive assessment was necessary in order to secure funding for the following year, some of their conclusions may have been less than dispassionate." Cannon goes on to say, "The new concept of 'outside' auditors is providing more detachment" (Cannon, 1971, p. 456). Yet even the outside audit may not be impartial, particularly if he wants his contract with the bilingual program renewed for the following year.

As of December of 1971, the Bilingual Education Branch of the Office of Education had only received perhaps half of the 1970-71 Title VII evaluations for California projects. Many of those that were received were not very informative about the successes and failures of the project. There appears to be a real reluctance to commit the findings to paper. It is for this reason that the Redwood City evaluation has been written up so extensively. Clearly too little information about the results of bilingual education for Mexican Americans in California has been made available in the literature.

2.5 Summary of Points and Relevance to the Redwood City Study

2.5.1 Bilingual education is defined as the use of two languages as media of instruction for a child or group of children in part or all of the school curriculum.

2.5.2 Bilingual education is one-way (for one dominant language group) or two-way (for two dominant language groups). There are a variety of models for bilingual schooling, such as morning-afternoon, alternate days, and simultanteous translation.

2.5.3 A bilingual education program is also usually bicultural. The program may aim at either assimilation of the minority group into the majority culture or at dual language and cultural maintenance.

2.5.4 Experiments with bilingual schooling in South Africa, Mexico, and Canada have been highly successful. Results in the Philippines have been mixed, but generally supportive of immersion education in the second and highly prestigious language, English.

2.5.5 Bilingual schooling in the U.S. falls into two distinct periods, pre-World War I and post-1963. World War I brought a sharp trend away from "foreign language" schooling toward English-only schooling as a part of an Americanization process. The year 1963 saw a renewed trend toward instruction through minority-group languages in the schools.

2.5.6 Available evaluations of bilingual education programs for Spanish-speakers and Anglos in Florida, Texas, and California yield generally favorable results. Spanish-speaking students instructed bilingually tend to perform as well in English language skills and in the content areas as comparable students schooled only in English. At the same time the Spanish-speaking students are developing language skills in Spanish. Anglo students in such programs do not appear adversely affected in their English language development and in the content subjects, and are learning a second language, Spanish.

The Redwood City Project staff recognized that bilingual education did not mean simply the teaching of two languages, but the use of both languages as media of instruction. The rationale for using both languages was to give greater legitimacy to the less prestigious language, namely Spanish, and to enhance language learning, since a good way to learn a language is to have to use it as a vehicle for learning something else. As will be discussed in Chapter 6 the Redwood City Project involved two-way bilingual education, with both Mexican Americans and Anglos instructed in the content subjects (math, social studies, science, etc.) through both Spanish and English. The Project also utilized several models of bilingual schooling, including simultaneous translation and the alternate days approach.

Research results on bilingual education, particularly those from other projects in the United States, were considered encouraging enough to warrant the implementation of the Redwood City Bilingual Education Project. Such research had demonstrated that valuable bilingual and bicultural skills could be acquired without impairing progress in the content subjects.

Unquestionably one of the goals of bilingual schooling is that the students achieve or maintain bilingualism. Since it has been suggested that being or becoming bilingual may have detrimental effects on intelligence, the following chapter will be devoted to a discussion of the relationship between bilingualism and intelligence. The emphasis will be placed on adequate assessment of that which is referred to as intelligence.

3. TESTING THE INTELLIGENCE OF BILINGUALS

This chapter deals with the literature on the relationship between bilingualism and intelligence. Chapter 1 referred to several studies relating intelligence to bilingualism, most notably Macnamara's study in Ireland (Macnamara, 1966). This chapter will pursue the topic more fully, and will include mention of current themes regarding the testing of I.Q. among Mexican American students, namely, the proper language for testing, the proper test, and the proper norms.

Because so much of the educational literature of the past decades has linked bilingualism to lower intelligence and to poor grades in school, bilingualism has been referred to as a "disadvantage," a "handicap," and a "problem" (see Rowan, 1950, for example). These references have attributed negative connotations to the quality of being bilingual. Bilingualism has been viewed by some as an educational ill that must be eradicated before the U.S. educational system can function efficiently. As recently as June 11, 1970, the San Francisco Chronicle editorialized, "Unless it (bringing language deficient children up to higher levels of competence in English) is done, parts of California will tend to degenerate into a bilingual society."

Diebold (1968) summarizes the literature on bilingualism and intelligence from the early 1920's to the present.[1] He points out that many studies have shown the superiority of monolinguals over bilinguals, but often only on sub-

---

[1] Also see Darcy (1953, 1963) and Macnamara (1966).

41

tests of verbal intelligence. In nonverbal intelligence, there have been few differences. Thus, what appears to be a bilingual's lack of intelligence, may simply be a lack of verbal ability in English. Whereas intelligence should be a measure of how a child can deal with what he knows (De Avila, 1972), a child won't be able to deal with what he knows in a language he doesn't know.

Furthermore, Diebold points out that studies finding monolinguals more intelligent than bilinguals were conducted in communities where the monolingual groups were speakers of the socially-dominant language, the language of greater prestige. Also, bilinguals were generally from a lower socioeconomic level, as well as being subject to racist attitudes in the community. Diebold cites the research of Peal and Lambert (1962) for demonstrating that when the above factors are truly controlled, not only are bilinguals on a par with monolinguals, but they surpass them on both verbal and nonverbal intelligence tests. Lambert and Anisfeld (1969) point out that they began their research with the intent of finding out *how* bilingualism adversely affected cognitive development. They were interested in determining appropriate means for overcoming the handicap. But the results of their research showed that bilinguals were *not* inferior.

Taylor (1970) provides another summary of research on bilingualism and intelligence. She mentions many of the same points as Diebold, and also notes that the sex, age, educational background, and dominant language of the student should be controlled in careful research on the relation between bilingualism and intelligence. Furthermore, she emphasizes that the tests should be given in the language in which the bilinguals are most proficient.

With regard to the intelligence of the Mexican American bilingual, there have been numerous studies over the years. Paschal and Sullivan (1925) found that Mexican children did worse on performance tests of mental ability than American children in Tucson, Arizona. The authors asserted that these tests were free from language handicaps and felt that poor performance was a result of mental inferiority. Garretson (1928) administered both a verbal test and a nonverbal test of intelligence (Meyer's Pantomime Group Intelligence Test) to first through eighth graders. He found that the language difficulty was a disadvantage for Mexican Americans in first and second grade, but that this was less important in grades 3-8. Mexican Americans tested at least 10.53 months more "retarded" than Anglos, and 30% more individuals of the Mexican American group were retarded than of the Anglo group. The author concluded that the prime factor governing the retardation of the Mexican child was his mental inferiority as measured by the group test. There was no control for socioeconomic level.

Carlson and Henderson (1950) tested 115 Mexican and 105 Anglo fifth and sixth graders from Los Angeles longitudinally on a battery of intelligence tests. The American children of Mexican parentage were found to have consistently lower mean scores on all tests, including the verbal and nonverbal subtests of the California Test of Mental Maturity. The difference between the two groups increased from the first to the last testing period over a span of 5½ years, primarily because of a drop in the mean I.Q. of the children of Mexican parentage. The authors suggested that differences may be due to heredity, but that some environmental factors were not controlled. For instance, the authors controlled for " neighborhood," but not for socioeconomic level. The authors mentioned two other factors that were not controlled: "the bilingual factor" (the language proficiency of the Mexican American children in both languages) and the background of the parents (either rural or urban).

Pasamanick (1951) criticized the Carlson and Henderson study for its lack of attention to the problems of bilingual and environmental variables. Pasamanick stressed that a Mexican American ghetto area is not necessarily comparable to that of Anglos, using census data to support his case, and that whereas parent's education was mentioned, it was not discussed as a control variable. He also pointed out that Mexican Americans were significantly older at the outset and that the age differential increased at later testing, suggesting retentions of Mexican Americans during those years. He concluded that the mental inferiority of Mexican Americans was not proven by the study.

Studies by Johnson (1953) and Altus (1953) both had mixed results. Johnson found that on a performance test, the Goodenough Draw-a-Man, 30 nine-year-old and twelve-year-old Spanish-English bilingual boys came out average in comparison with other students, but on a verbal (Otis) test they were way below average. He measured the linguistic balance of the bilingual speakers by dividing the number of words produced in English in five minutes by the number produced in Spanish. Johnson found that the more bilingual the subjects were, the better they did on the performance tests and the poorer on the verbal test. Altus tested a group of slower students, matched for age and I.Q. using the Wechsler scale. Results showed that monolinguals were higher achievers on the verbal scale, but that there was a nonsignificant difference on the performance scale.

A study by Jensen (1961) found that Mexican Americans were not of inferior intelligence. Jensen carefully selected bilingual Mexican Americans and monolingual Anglos in grades 4 and 6 in Contra Costa County, California, on the basis of age, father's occupation, and location of residence. He divided them into low and high I.Q. groups on the basis of the California Test of Mental Maturity. Then he gave them a battery of nonverbal and manual tests. Jensen remarked that current I.Q. tests were actually "static measures of achievement which sample the knowledge and skills the child has acquired in the past" (Jensen, 1961, p. 148). Jensen wished to measure present learning ability. Thus, he developed nonverbal tests using materials familiar and comprehensible to different subcultures, and which involved three types of tasks: immediate recall, serial learning, and paired-associates learning; and two types of materials: familiar and abstract. Mexican Americans who were classified low on I.Q. performed better on all the tests than did low I.Q. Anglo children. Low I.Q. Mexican Americans also performed as well as high I.Q. Anglos on two of the tests. The author concluded that the standard I.Q. tests were not measuring the ability of Mexican Americans accurately and should not be a basis for putting Mexican Americans in slow-learners' classes.

The themes that seem to run through the literature on testing Mexican Americans' I.Q. are those of (1) the proper language for testing, (2) the proper test, and (3) the proper norms.

3.1   *The Proper Language for Testing*

Over forty years ago, Wright and Manuel (1929) found that simply translating the Stanford Reading Achievement Test into Spanish didn't insure that Mexican Americans would do better. The authors had five translations of the test made, three of them by Mexican Americans. They found that more than 50% of a group of Mexican American high-school and college students in Texas did better on the English than on the Spanish test. The authors were puzzled by these results. They suggested that the results may have been a product of differences in the English and Spanish versions of the test.

Sánchez (1932b) found that if Mexican American children were given a test of verbal I.Q. in English and then given the same test after enough time had elapsed to minimize the practice effect, the children performed better on the second testing. The author submitted that this was due to an increased facility in the use of the English language. The same author also spoke of "mental confusion" resulting from a dual language handicap. He pointed out that so-called "nonverbal" tests also resulted in mental confusion because the students had to follow verbal directions (Sánchez, 1932a). Sánchez felt that the language handicap got worse through the grades because a greater amount of language was required at each grade level.

Keston and Jiménez (1954) used English and Spanish editions of the Stanford-Binet Intelligence Test on 50 Spanish-surnamed fourth graders in Albuquerque, New Mexico. The results showed that the students performed better in English. The authors concluded that the children had trouble with the Spanish version because it used standard Peninsula Spanish, while the Spanish of the group sampled contained "archaisms, contaminations, and Anglicisms" (Keston and Jiménez, 1954, p. 268). Furthermore, Spanish was not taught in the school, and it was felt that the children were not truly balanced bilinguals—that they were actually dominant in English. Further differences in the scores on the Spanish and English versions were attributed to the fact that the test depended on educational achievement in school where the language of instruction was English.

Carrow (1957) did a "language handicap" study, controlling for intelligence and socioeconomic status. She looked at the performance of Spanish-English bilinguals and monolingual English-speaking third graders in San Antonio, Texas. She didn't specify whether the monolinguals were Mexican Americans. On tests of reading, she found that monolinguals did better altogether. However, Mexican Americans testing over 121 on the Otis Alpha test of mental ability performed as well as, or better than, monolinguals on every test. Perhaps only at this I.Q. level were intelligence and socioeconomic factors truly controlled.

Linn (1967), in a follow-up study to that of Carrow, confirmed her results when he looked at bilingual Mexican American and monolingual Anglo seventh and eighth graders. The conclusion he derived from his research was that Mexican Americans who start school as bilinguals still have the same handicap in junior high that Carrow found in primary school. However, he also looked at monolingual English-speaking Mexican Americans and found that their performance on English reading tests was just as high as that of the Anglos, attesting to the fact that performance differences were a result of language differences and not a result of ethnic group membership.

Galvan (1967) used Spanish and English versions of the Wechsler Intelligence Scale for Children on third-through-fifth-grade Spanish Americans in Dallas, Texas, and found that the children produced lower scores on the English version. Chandler and Plakos (1969) retested 47 pupils, grades 3-8, who had been put in classes for the educable mentally retarded in California after testing in English. The results of retesting on a Spanish version of the Wechsler test produced an average gain of over 12 points. They concluded that the population tested lacked an understanding of the English language. Mycue (1968) found that if Mexican American children were given an English storytelling task in *Spanish,* as a warm up, they subsequently performed better than peers who were just given the task in English.

De Avila (1972) points out that it is wrong to assume the Mexican American child speaks one language or another. Of course, he may *speak* Spanish but not be taught how to read in Spanish. If so, he may have trouble with a written test in Spanish. Furthermore, if the child is not functional in English reading, then he has trouble on the English version as well (see Moreno, 1970). Problems of translating tests go beyond the question of the frequency of the translation equivalents. De Avila observes that a direct translation implies that the test still has the same cultural and cognitive biases, even though the test is presented in Spanish.

3.2 *The Proper Test*

The problem of constructing the proper test for the Mexican American is becoming an ever-growing concern. In reference to I.Q. tests, Herschel Manuel (1930) pointed out, "One does not know how well or how poorly adapted to Mexican children this test is, even when the directions are translated" (p. 29). Sánchez (1934) also questioned the validity of standardized tests for the Mexican American students. More recently, Manuel (1963) has devoted time and energy to the task of constructing tests especially for the Spanish speaker of the Southwest.

It is of note that intelligence tests are no longer being used by school systems in New York City, Washington, D.C., and Los Angeles because such tests have been found to extract only a single group of abilities—perhaps of lesser importance—from a range of mental abilities necessary for successful functioning in our society (Bordie, 1970). Research has also shown that existing I.Q. tests do not adequately assess the learning abilities of children with a lower socioeconomic background. As it turns out, many of the Spanish-English bilinguals of the Southwest are from such backgrounds. Whereas such I.Q. tests may be good predictors of achievement in the schools, they have been unenlightening with respect to assessing the abilities of minority students. De Avila (1972) speaks of some more appropriate instruments that he and his staff developed.

Galvan (1967) emphasized the inadequacy of using verbal tests of intelligence on Spanish American children. He suggested that nonverbal tests would be a better indication of ability. Palomares and Cummins (1968) used a variety of I.Q. tests, both verbal and nonverbal, on rural Mexican American pupils, preschool through twelfth grade, in Wasco, California. They found that the students had trouble with most of the tests. In grades 4-6 and 8-12 where forms of the Wechsler intelligence tests were given, students did better on the nonverbal than on the verbal subtests, particularly in grades 8-12. These findings corroborate those of Galvin, and those of Johnson (1953) and Altus (1953) mentioned above.

3.3 *The Proper Norms*

Proper norming of tests for Mexican Americans is another real problem. Chandler and Plakos (1969) assert that many children in the classes for the educable mentally retarded (EMR) have linguistic and cultural differences that invalidate the I.Q. tests—based on white middle-class norms—which place them in EMR classes. They point out that in 1967, over 26% of the children in the EMR classes in California had Spanish surnames whereas only 13% of the children attending public schools had such names. More recently, the rate of placement of Spanish-surnamed children in EMR classes in California has been reported as three times higher than for Anglo children (Light, 1971).

De Avila (1972) points out that educators have generated regional norms or "bonus points" to be given to Chicanos, instead of changing the test. He feels that tests cover materials that the Mexican American children haven't been exposed to. He asserts that many so-called intelligence items are actually testing socialization and exposure (i.e., where you've been). De Avila is currently working on more appropriate instruments for assessing what the Chicano child knows and how well he can deal with what he knows.

In the Santa Ana Unified School District in 1969, Mexican-American students made up almost 53% of the enrollment in EMR classes, although they were only 26% of the total school enrollment. The Mexican American parents took legal action to ensure that their children be tested by means of an I.Q. test normed to the California Spanish-speaking child population, and that they be tested in both Spanish and English and be allowed to respond in either language (Light, 1971).

Aside from considerations as to the proper language to use, the proper test, and proper norms, there is the question of the proper tester. Mycue (1968) found that the use of Mexican American testers increased the Oral English proficiency scores of Mexican-American children. Savage and Bowers (1972) similarly found Black students performed significantly higher on an intellectual task when the testers were also Black. In both studies, a tester with the same ethnic background reduced the students' anxiety level. It could be argued that *any* sympathetic tester could do this, but similar cultural and linguistic background appear to be helpful.

3.4 *Summary of Points and Relevance to the Redwood City Study*

3.4.1 The literature on bilingualism and intelligence that finds various ethnic groups of bilinguals less intelligent than monolinguals often leaves important factors uncontrolled, such as the ability of the student in the language of the test and the student's age, educational background, and socioeconomic level.

3.4.2 The negative literature on the intelligence of the Mexican American bilinguals falls prey to the same criticisms leveled at all such literature. Too many factors are left uncontrolled to call Mexican American children inferior with respect to intelligence.

3.4.3 When the importance of language is minimized in I.Q. testing, as in nonverbal tests, the bilingual Mexican American students perform as well as, or better than, monolinguals.

3.4.4 Some literature says that Mexican Americans should be tested in Spanish. Other literature cautions against assuming the child has test-taking skills in Spanish. Still other literature says to test in both Spanish and English. Ideally, the child's language dominance should be determined before testing.

3.4.5 Not only should I.Q. tests be normed separately for Mexican Americans in California, but if possible the tests themselves should be free of cultural and cognitive biases against the Chicano.

In the evaluation of the Redwood City Bilingual Education Project, there was clearly a need to assess intellectural growth, but there was also an awareness of the problems associated with testing the Mexican American, such as finding the "right" test with respect to language, content, and so forth. The Non-Verbal Ability Subtests of the Inter-American General Ability Test were ultimately chosen (see Chapter 10). Instructions were given in both Spanish and English. Since national or even State norms for the test were not available, the intellectual growth of the Mexican American students in the Bilingual Project was assessed by comparing their results on the test to those of comparison Mexican American students who were receiving conventional English-only schooling.

Now that issues concerning bilingualism have been discussed, and before moving on to the description of the Redwood City study, it is important to take a closer look at the group of people from which the subjects for the study were drawn, namely the Mexican Americans. The following chapter discusses the attributes of Mexican Americans, and their situation and expectations with respect to the educational system.

4. MEXICAN AMERICANS OF THE SOUTHWEST

The Mexican Americans are clearly one of the most significant of the newly emergent ethnic minorities, and yet there remain many misconceptions about them. This chapter will address itself to the issue of portraying the Mexican American more accurately. The chapter will also look at the educational situation of Mexican Americans in the Southwest, with particular emphasis on "the language problem," case studies of Mexican Americans in school, studies of Mexican American student achievement and parental and student attitudes toward education, and suggestions for educational reform.

4.1 *In Search of the Mexican American People*

There are a number of more or less accepted facts about Mexican Americans. They are the second largest minority in the United States, numbering more than 5.5 million, 90% of whom live in the Southwestern states of California, Arizona, Colorado, New Mexico and Texas (Rodríguez, 1969). As of 1960, Mexican Americans comprised about 12% of the Southwest's population and 9% of California's population (U.S. Commission on Civil Rights, 1968). Furthermore, immigrants from Mexico have been coming at the rate of 40,000 per year and 78% are unskilled or of low skills. The Mexican American birthrate is 50% higher than that of the population as a whole (U.S. Commission on Civil Rights, 1968). In California, 20% of the poor (income of $3,000 or less) are Mexican American (Galarza, Gallegos, Samora, 1969). Because of large families, the per capita Mexican American income in the Southwest is 47% below that of the Anglos (Greb-

ler, Moore, Guzman, *et al.,* 1970). The unemployment rate in 1966 was 7.7%
for Mexican Americans in the urban areas, and the median level of education
was 8.6 years, as compared to 12.1 for Whites and 10.5 for Blacks (Rodríguez,
1969).

Unfortunately, however, there are many more fictions about Mexican Americans than there are facts. For instance, one Anglo misconception about Mexican
Americans is that they are primarily in farm labor, whereas actually more than
80% are urban dwellers (Rodríguez, 1969; Peñalosa, 1967). It is well known that
TV advertising has done a lot to reinforce these misconceptions (see Wagner &
Haug, 1971b). Much of the literature on Mexican Americans, often written by
well-meaning Anglos, is fraught with misconceived notions. Hernández (1970)
asserts that a person needs more than casual familiarity with, and sensitivity to,
Mexican Americans to study them. Galarza *et al.* (1969) point out that too few
publications on the Mexican Americans are written by members of their own
group. These authors report that out of the 790 articles, pamphlets, brochures,
and books on Mexican Americans that they studied, only 10% were written by
Mexican Americans.

4.1.1 *Stereotypic Portrayals of the Mexican American*

Peñalosa (1967) perhaps started a recent wave of criticism aimed at studies
of Mexican Americans by social scientists. He denies the validity of studies
which describe them with reference to a traditional Mexican folk culture. He
further maintains that all popular images of the Chicano population are anach-
ronistic, particularly in Southern California, the area with which he is most
familiar.

Romano (1968) criticizes two works written by Anglos on Mexican Americans. Romano finds that Madsen's *The Mexican-American of South Texas* (Madsen, 1964) ignores the history of Mexican Americans and draws a social por-
trait of them based on a stereotyped "traditional culture." The study was meant
to depict Mexican American communities ranging from rural folk society to a
bicultural urban center. The "traditional culture" analysis depicts the Chicano
as fatalistic, passive and lazy, and frequently implies that only through acculturation to Anglo, "American" values of activism and deferred reward will the
Mexican Americans be able to advance socially and economically. Romano shows
that Mexican Americans have displayed activism and recognition of self-interest
in their various movements in the United States, in criticism of Madsen's ahis-
toric approach to Mexican Americans. A Chicano newspaper review also had un-
favorable things to say about the Madsen book:

> What (Madsen) writes will surely not result in better understanding
> of the Chicano, as he intends, but in increased misunderstanding be-

tween policy makers, teachers, social workers, administrators, public officials, etc., and the Mexican American community. (Martínez, 1970, p. 5)

Romano (1968) also attacks the often-cited Heller book, *Mexican-American Youth, Forgotten Youth at the Crossroads* (Heller, 1966). As Romano describes it, Heller's Mexican Americans are not quite Americans and unusually homogeneous ethnically. Romano further states:

> In less than 40 pages, then, this sociologist has said that Mexican Americans are not Americans, that they are all virtually alike, that they tend to speak with a foreign accent, that they are held down by their own families, that their sons are helpless victims of parental indulgence which retards them, and that they are fatalistically resigned to this cultural miasma. (Romano, 1968, p. 21)

Romano insists that Chicano society is pluralistic and that Mexican Americans cannot be described by a simplistic formula.

Hernández (1970) criticizes studies by A.J. Schwartz (1969) and W. Gordan, A.J. Schwartz, *et al.* (1968) for causally relating the cultural values of Mexican American high-school pupils with their low academic achievement in the public schools. The cultural variable is "affectivity orientation" (values, attitudes, beliefs). Hernández contends that intervening variables, namely poverty, low status family occupation, prejudice, segregation, hostile personal contacts, poor quality school facilities, and biased teachers are responsible for academic achievement. According to Hernández, the Mexican American family is criticized by Schwartz *et al.* as the "Typhoid Mary" of the child's difficulties. Hernández feels that these stereotyped images are "Anglo fabrications about Mexican Americans, and they become the school rationale for the treatment and manipulation of this ethnic group" (Hernández, 1970, p. 42). She stresses that "... the adult society for the Mexican American is not the Anglo adult society but a hybrid Mexican-Anglo adult society, which can be a highly individualized mixture ... (the Mexican American) is not isolated in an encapsulated Mexicanism, nor is he, nor can he ever be, in an absolutely Anglo sphere" (Hernández, 1970, p. 21).

Jiménez (1971) reiterates Romano's criticisms mentioned above. Jiménez feels that one of the biggest problems facing the Chicano is that of patronizing racism *(patronismo)*. The Anglo says he wants the Chicano to develop his best potential, but views the Chicano against the backdrop of a mythical folk culture. Jiménez notes that even Carter in his largely sympathetic book, *Mexican Americans in School: A History of Educational Neglect* (Carter, 1970), provides information that reinforces stereotypic notions. Although Carter attempts to point out that the characteristics he describes are true only for some Chicanos in some localities, some of the time, Jiménez feels that most educators will regard the traits that Carter mentions as being widespread.

Both Guerra and Cabrera (1966) and Galarza, Gallegos, and Samora (1969) criticize the massive volume, *The Mexican-American People: The Nation's Second Largest Minority* (Grebler, Moore, Guzman, *et al.,* 1970), as the archetype example of ill-guided research conducted on the Mexican American people. Guerra and Cabrera feel that the work is assimilationist—that it is not supportive of cultural pluralism and the goodness of being Mexican American. The data are seen as outmoded and obsolete. Although the Spanish language is depicted in the work as "the real villain," there is little mention of language and of the literature on bilingual education programs. Both Guerra and Cabrera and Galarza *et al.* feel that the resource people were misused. Galarza *et al.* assert that this study may be "both a capstone for what has preceded in research, and a turning point toward new uses and perhaps even new methods in this field" (Galarza *et al.,* 1969, pp. 55-56).

Galarza *et al.* join other Mexican Americans in protesting the stereotypic portrayal of the Mexican American in the literature:

> . . . the Mexican-American southwesterners may not be regarded as
> a bloc, but rather as a demographic aggregate differentiated within
> by citizenship status and the distance in time from the ancestral
> Mexican culture. (Galarza *et al.,* 1969, p. 77)

As if foreseeing criticism, one of the authors of *The Mexican American People,* Joan Moore, wrote an article on how difficult it was to research the Mexican American people. She pointed out that the Mexican American community was suspicious and defensive upon learning that Anglo authorities wanted to do a study on them. The people feared that researchers were immigrant officers or FBI agents (Moore, 1967). Moore felt that the Mexican Americans were not like other ethnic groups in terms of acculturation and enculturation because of their nearness to their mother country. She stated that the reference group must support the research—that there must be a bargain struck between pure research and social action. It appears that the research she was engaged in failed to strike this bargain with the community although an advisory board from the community was apparently set up. An ultimate irony of the project was that the book was published only in hard cover at $15 a copy, putting it out of the range of many of the community members who may have wanted to read the findings.[1]

Rodríguez (1969) discusses the prevalent stereotypic notion of the Mexican American as disadvantaged. He says that Chicanos reject the "disadvantaged" notion. They say that they are advantaged in having differences in culture and language—differences that are part of the American Dream: freedom, democracy,

---

[1] In a personal conversation, Ralph Guzman, co-author, indicated that there were no current plans to bring out the book in a more accessible form.

plurality. He stresses that a different language and culture are *not* shackles that must be stripped off before a full partnership in the American society can be attained.

McWilliams (1949), in one of the only Anglo works on Mexican Americans that has not undergone criticism (see, for instance, a review by López, 1970), refutes the stereotype of the docile Latin. McWilliams discusses many incidents that occurred in the mining camps and in the community. Not only has Mc-Williams refrained from ignoring the history of the Mexican Americans, he has portrayed it most honestly.

4.1.2 Research into Stereotypes

Some research studies have examined the recurring stereotypes which Anglos have about Mexican Americans and vice versa. There are also studies which inquire into stereotypes that Mexican Americans have of themselves. Such studies often suggest several things. First, Anglos and Mexican Americans don't interact very much (see Grebler, Moore, Guzman, *et al.,* 1970, Ch. 16). Second, Mexican Americans don't stereotype the Anglo as much as Anglos stereotype Mexican Americans (see Parsons, 1965). And third, Mexican Americans tend to internalize certain negative stereotypes about themselves which are perpetrated by Anglos (see Ulibarrí, 1968).

A study by Simmons (1961) found Anglos describing Chicanos as homogeneous, inferior, unclean, criminal, and immoral, and Mexican Americans describing Anglos as defensive of themselves, industrious, ambitious, cold, mercenary, and exploitive. Parsons (1965) categorized ratings on Mexican Americans and Anglos by the other group according to four levels of frequency: characteristics most of the group attributed to the other group, those that three-quarters of the group attributed to the other group, one-third of the group, and a few. Parsons reported that it was harder to get Mexicans to rate Anglos as a group because there is "no Mexican parallel of the Anglo belief in group homogeneity" (Parsons, 1965, p. 192).

4.1.3 Equating Value Orientations with Economic Status

Some of the literature on the Mexican American equates value orientations with economic status. Ulibarrí (1968) states that values of Mexican Americans which conflict with occupational success, such as low competitiveness, timidity, present time orientation, and aspirational level are a function of being in the lower class, and are not ethnic traits. A study by Peñalosa and McDonagh (1966) on the Chicano community of Pomona, California, found that the Mexican Americans themselves equated value orientations with economic status. That is, the Chicanos identified the "strivers" as middle class and those who "don't care" as members of the lower class.

Casavantes (1969, 1971) deals with the relationship between Chicano values and ethnicity and the values of the disadvantaged, the culture of poverty. He cites research by Cohen and Hodges (1963) which found that attributes in Chicanos close to the poverty line were common to Blacks and Anglos with a similar economic status, and therefore not derived from traditional Mexican folk culture. These attributes included preference for tradition, fear of innovation, anti-intellectualism, male authoritarianism, and fatalism. Casavantes estimated that 33% of all Chicanos share values of Anglos and Blacks in the lower class, such as extended family, conservatism, inability to postpone gratification, dependence on physical force, and fatalism. He feels that these attributes are *not* ethnically based.

Lewis (1966), in his research on the "culture of poverty," was attempting to identify a life style and a set of values determined not by ethnic characteristics but rather motivated by adaptation to the situation and to necessity. Lewis believed that the middle-class researchers did not recognize the presence of a culture common to the lower class in a class-stratified, capitalistic society (such as that of the U.S.), and spoke only of deprivation, lack of order, and instability. Lewis saw behavior in this culture as clearly patterned and predictable.

Valentine (1968) challenges the culture-of-poverty concept. He feels that values cross-cut situational or class differences. Valentine distinguishes between cultural patterns and external conditions, such that the cultural values of the poor may be much the same as middle-class values, merely modified in practice because of situational stresses. Essentially, Valentine doesn't feel that Lewis substantiates his theory. Furthermore, the characteristics that Lewis ascribes to the culture of poverty are predominantly negative—group disintegration, personal disorganization, resignation, fatalism, and lack of purposeful action. Hernández (1970) reinforces Valentine's position when she refers to the error many authors have made of equating economic determinism with cultural determinism. She feels that a group's social manifestation does not necessarily reflect its cultural values. Thus, although class status plays a part in determining Mexican-American culture, it is only one factor of many.

4.1.4 Towards a More Accurate Portrayal of the Mexican American

Perhaps the place to start in more accurately portraying the Mexican American is with the Spanish surname. Valdez (1969) feels that school administrators act as if all Spanish-surname children had identical language and educational "problems." Valdez emphasizes the error in classifying a totally divergent group on the basis of one criterion: Spanish surname. A survey of the Spanish-surnamed population of a given area provides *only* a tally of the Spanish-surnamed, Valdez points out. Thus, the name alone is not very informative about the characteristics of the Mexican American.

Peñalosa (1967) asserts that the Mexican American subculture in its most common form can best be explained as a variant of a U.S. subculture. Chicanos are partially Mexicanized Americans rather than partially Americanized Mexicans. He substantiates his belief by showing the wide divergence between the Mexican lower class and the Mexican American lower class. He defines a Mexican American as a person permanently residing in the United States who is descended from Spanish-speaking persons permanently residing in Mexico and who in childhood and youth became enculturated into Mexican American subculture. He sees these Mexican Americans as moving away from lower-class Mexican traditional culture and toward Anglo American middle-class culture.

Peñalosa (1970) later broadens his description of Mexican Americans. He points out that Mexican Americans are not a separate race in the 19th century physical-anthropological sense, but a mixture of races. Mexican Americans consider themselves as being of three ethnic groups: Americans of Mexican ancestry (detached from their Mexican descent); Mexican Americans (always conscious of Mexican ancestry and important in their self-concept); and Chicanos (acutely aware of Mexican identity and descent and committed to defending Mexican American subculture values). Furthermore, Mexican-American culture is seen as a combination of five factors:

(1) "traditional" Mexican culture—way of life brought from Mexico
(2) influence of the surrounding majority Anglo culture
(3) class influence
(4) minority status—in the sense of politically, economically, and socially prejudicial treatment
(5) historical, regional, and ecological variants.

Casavantes (1969) submits a set of attributes that he feels do apply to the majority of Mexican Americans. He calls these "structural-demographic" attributes. The majority of Mexican Americans are either immigrants from Mexico, or have parents or grandparents who were. They speak Spanish and may have an accent in their English. They are Roman Catholics and some of their practices reflect this. Many have dark skin, dark hair, and brown eyes, thus setting them apart physiognomically from other Americans. Casavantes feels that attributes relating to the state they live in, their educational level, and their income (all mentioned above), although not irrelevant to being Mexican American, are certainly not givens simply because they are Mexican Americans. Casavantes refers to *Chicano* as the Spanish language contraction and nickname for "Mexican American," and says that to be truly Chicano is "to speak Spanish well, to enjoy Mexican music and Mexican food, to periodically recall the customs and ways of life of Spain and of Mexico" (Casavantes, 1969, p. 6).

Several research articles have pointed up the differences in cultural values and other attitudes of U.S.-born and Mexican-born Mexican Americans, and how important it is to view these two groups somewhat separately. Dworkin (1965) found that Mexican-born adults were less negative toward Anglos and less pessimistic about themselves than were Mexican Americans born in the United States. Dworkin (1971) adds an important qualification to his earlier work. He found that the length of time that the Mexican-born Mexican American is in the United States has a bearing on his attitudes toward Anglos and towards himself. Mexican Americans in the U.S. for six months or less were found to be more positive toward Anglos and more optimistic about themselves than those living in the U.S. for a longer time.[2]

Derbyshire (1969) studied the attitudes and behaviors of East Los Angeles Mexican American teenagers born in Mexico (or whose parents were born in Mexico) with those of second- and third-generation Americans. He found that immigrant teenagers dissociated themselves from "Mexicans" whereas second- and third-generation Mexican American teenagers highly identified themselves as "Mexican." The author speculates that the strong identification with Mexican values is functional to identity maintenance for established Mexican American adolescents, but not necessary for new immigrants. As Derbyshire puts it:

> . . . after one or two generations in the United States it may be adaptively necessary for Mexican adolescents to overly view themselves as highly Mexican in order to defend against "the cultural stripping" process of American society. (Derbyshire, 1969, p. 102)

Most recently, the term "Chicano" is gaining wider usage in reference to the emergent Mexican American culture (see Wagner, and Haug, 1971a, for example). Nava (1970) refers to how the Mexican American youth use "Chicano" positively and prefer it to "Mexican American." Nava asserts that "Chicanos demand recognition of, and respect for, the importance and meaningfulness of their own language and customs" (Nava, 1970, p. 47).

Rivera (1970) goes as far as to posit two norms for the emergent Chicano culture:

(a) the norm of non-materialistic achievement
(b) cooperation of effort and the sharing of resources toward mutual achievement.

Rivera states that Mexican Americans were assigned a deviant or non-person status through the denial of Chicano community and culture:

---

[2] In Dworkin's sample, the median length of time for those living in the U.S. for over six months was 9.6 years.

. . . the forced death of one culture, that of Mexico in the United States, has meant the forced birth of a new culture, that which in its emergent stages we have called "Mexican American" and that which we are now calling *Chicano*. (Rivera, 1970, p. 44)

4.2 *The Educational Situation of Mexican Americans in the Southwest*

Frequently Mexican American students have been referred to as "handicapped" as a result of their bilinguality (see, for example, Rowan, 1950) and home environment. The truth is that Mexican American students have not had a record of success in the schools in the Southwest. Whereas the reasons have been attributed to a failing in the child or in his culture for not preparing or motivating him for school, emphasis is more recently being placed on the failing of the schools (see Grebler, Moore, Guzman, *et al.,* 1970, Ch. 7). This section will discuss some educational statistics about the Mexican American, touch on the language problem, discuss several case studies of the Mexican American in school, report on studies of Mexican American student and parent attitudes toward education, and end with some literature pointing to problems in schooling the Mexican American and giving suggestions for reform. The literature in all these areas is quite extensive and the articles referred to here are just suggestive of what has been written.

4.2.1 *Educational Statistics about the Mexican American*

According to an article in the *San Francisco Chronicle* (December 8, 1971), the United States Commission on Civil Rights had finished the second in a series of seven reports on the Mexican American, entitled "The Unfinished Education." This report covered 532 school districts in the five states of Arizona, California, Colorado, New Mexico, and Texas. The report estimated that out of 100 Mexican Americans who enter first grade in the survey area, only 60 graduate from high school. Sixty-seven out of 100 Black students graduate from high school, and 86 out of 100 Anglos do so. (See Grebler, Moore, Guzman, *et al.,* 1970, Ch. 7, for a more extensive breakdown of educational attainment for the different ethnic groups, based on the 1960 U.S. Census.)

The report stated that if the present school dropout rates in California fail to improve, more than one of three Mexican-American pupils in grades one through six (120,000 pupils out of 330,000) will fail to graduate from high school. The report noted that this represents "a staggering loss of potentially well-educated and productive manpower." Although California tends to fare slightly better than the five Southwestern states taken altogether, the figures are still alarming. Among Mexican Americans the English reading skills are low, dropout rates are high, and grade repetition and subsequent "overagedness" (students older than other students in their grades) are frequent. In an informal study of 225 California schools with 50 to 90% Spanish-speaking students, one Mexican American educator (Del Buono, 1971) found that only 5% of these students were reading at the national average.

The U.S. Commission on Civil Rights (1968) pointed out that in California, more than 25% of all those in classes for the educable mentally retarded (EMR) were Mexican Americans. On May 25, 1972, the *San Francisco Chronicle* reported that although the 705,894 children of Mexican American descent in California were only about 15% of the school population, they represented 40% of the students in EMR classes. Williams (1968) reports that data available from three states in the Southwest with large Mexican American populations indicated that the proportion of Mexican Americans enrolled in special education classes was twice that of their representation in the general population. The reasons she gives for such placement are: medical and environmental conditions in these students' homes, economic disadvantage, cultural disadvantage, and unfamiliarity with the language of the schools, English, and with the culture of the schools. Chapter 3 above suggested improper test procedures as a further, perhaps principal, reason for such placement.

4.2.2   *The Language Problem and the Schools*

The real question with respect to language problems is, "Whose language problem is it?" Until recently, a so-called "linguistic handicap" or "bilingual handicap" was often associated with Mexican American students. Burma (1954), for example, singles out the language handicap as instrumental in the child's school failures and eventual school drop out. But what about Mexican Americans who do not have a problem with the English language? Mexican Americans comprise at least four distinct language groups: those who speak no English, those who speak more Spanish than English, those who speak more English than Spanish, and those who speak no Spanish. Thus, there are Mexican Americans who are either dominant in English or even monolingual English speakers. Many of these students also have difficulties at school. Part of their problem may be socioeconomic. Another factor is that they are speakers of nonstandard English and not adequately familiar with "school" English to perform well in school.

Recently more emphasis is being placed on the handicap certain *teachers* have in not being able to speak the language or dialect of their students. In an often-cited book, *The Spanish-Speaking Children of the Southwest,* Manuel (1965) puts in a plea for the use of Spanish in the classroom for the child whose English language skills are limited at the outset and who lives among Spanish speakers. At the time the book was written, Manuel lamented the language policies of the schools:

> At present in the Southwest, it is the policy of the public schools to use English as the language of instruction throughout the school grades . . . It is the general practice to minimize its (Spanish) use and to use English exclusively. In fact, many teachers have little or no knowledge of Spanish. (Manuel, 1965, p. 119)

Yet the no-Spanish rule perseveres. As Carter (1970) reports, teachers of the Southwest give four reasons for this rule:

(1) English is the national language and must be learned. The best way is to prohibit Spanish.
(2) Bilingualism is mentally confusing.
(3) The Spanish of the Southwest is a substandard dialect.
(4) Teachers don't know Spanish

Even at the college level, Guerra (1969) points out that English language problems, as well as insecurity with college-level Spanish, jeoparidze the chances of Mexican Americans in higher education. Language problems often mean poor reading skills and therefore poor academic performance.

Since the language that the Mexican American student feels most comfortable with is not necessarily Spanish, the teacher must determine what language is best for the student for the particular subject and the particular task within that subject. Perhaps a combination of Spanish and English instruction is best, with an emphasis on oral work in Spanish and written work in English. Perhaps instruction should only be in English. Possibly "school" English as a second dialect may be most appropriate, particularly if the student speaks a Chicano variety of English (see Krear, 1971a, 1971b). As Ferguson (1971) points out, if more than one variety of a language is used in a speech community, curriculum planners must decide on the relative emphasis to be accorded each variety in the curriculum, the order in which they are to be studied, and whether skill in one variety can be maintained when the learning is concentrated on the other variety.

4.2.3 Case Studies of Mexican Americans in School

Perhaps the most extensive case study of a Mexican American school in the Southwest was conducted by Parsons (1965) in a Southern California combined elementary-junior high school. Essentially, the study is an exposé of injustices toward Mexican Americans in the classroom. For instance, tracking of students was apparently based on teacher records rather than on the basis of I.Q. or standard achievement tests, and teachers' treatment of pupils was seen to relate to the student's ethnicity. Furthermore, there appeared to be more Anglo student exclusion of Mexican Americans than Mexican American withdrawal from contacts with Anglos. Also, fourth-through-eighth-grade Anglos were shown to possess the characteristic negative stereotypes about Mexican Americans—and Mexican Americans supported many of these stereotypes as indicated by their own sociometric choices.

Carter (1970) reports on visits to many schools throughout the Southwest. Some of his findings were as follows:

(a) The academic success of a Mexican American child depends on the degree to which his home has been oriented to Anglo middle-class culture. Teachers drill minority-group children to accept middle-class norms of achievement, individual responsibility, and good manners to gain a good grade or teacher acceptance. The child might forget these norms right away if they are different from those of his home or peer group. Some Mexican American children reject the school culture, others reject the home culture, and some are caught in between which may lead to personal disorganization.

(b) Children entering school directly from Mexico achieve better than the local Mexican Americans. Also, the older the immigrant, the better he does in school. Carter speculates that the immigrant's status is looked at with more favor than that of a U.S.-born Mexican American.

(c) Mexican Americans remain close to Anglos in achievement through third or fourth grade and then Anglos move up while Mexican Americans lose ground. On standard math tests, Mexican Americans are good in fundamentals but not in problem solving (perhaps a result of difficulties with the English language used in the problems).

(d) Carter accredits the general optimism of teachers toward Mexican American students in the primary grades to the minority group children's tendency to perform well, appear adjusted, and seem happy. However, in the upper elementary grades, rejection of the school begins, adjustment problems become evident, and the intermediate and secondary teachers give up.

(e) Whereas Mexican American teachers are sought for Mexican American students, schools often get upper middle-class teachers who have nothing in common with lower-class Chicanos. Carter feels that a Spanish speaker is needed, but not necessarily a person of Mexican descent. The Mexican American role model doesn't work because the Mexican American and Anglo teachers think alike. Carter also found that Mexican American teachers sometimes expect more from their Mexican American students than from their Anglo students, and they are harsher on the Chicanos if they don't achieve.

4.2.4 Studies on Mexican American Student Achievement and on Student and Parent Attitudes toward Education

There have been numerous studies of the correlates of academic achievement among Mexican Americans. Social scientists have been intrigued by the persistent low-achievement levels of Mexican American students in the schools. Research interest has also focused on the educational and occupational aspirations and expectations of Mexican American students and parents.

4.2.4.1 Achievement

Coleman (1966), in a study of 5% of the nation's schools, grades 1, 3, 6, 9, and 12, found that only about 20% of the variance in Mexican Americans' achievement was attributable to kinds of schools attended. The big factor was whether the student thought he could control the environment through his own efforts. Variations in school characteristics had little effect on this. What little effect teacher attitudes and ability had on pupils' achievement was primarily evidenced in the later grades (also see Mayeske, 1969).

Córdova (1969), in a study of 477 sixth-grade Mexican Americans from 16 schools, found that a low level of assimilation resulted in low achievement. He found that the low assimilation level helped create poor teacher-pupil relations which alienated the Spanish American students, further limiting their achievement potential. Córdova found that as Mexican American students were increasingly accepting of the dominant society's values and beliefs concerning education and politics, there was a decrease in the feeling of alienation. But accepting the dominant society's values made Mexican Americans feel like traitors to their culture, family, and friends.

Anderson and Johnson (1968) found that low achievement among Chicanos in grades 7-12 was due to low SES (socioeconomic status), use of Spanish, and low self-confidence. Low achievement was not a result of low motivation but of poor educational programs in the schools. Anderson and Johnson (1971) found that the best predictors of achievement in English classes were self-concept, sex, father's education, degree of use of English in the family, and parental emphasis on education. Girls with high self-concept coming from English-speaking homes had the highest achievement in English classes.

Taylor (1970a) looked at the relation between the sociocultural attitudes and values of Mexican American and Anglo working-class and Anglo middle-class parents in the San Joaquín Valley, and the achievement of their third- and fourth-grade children. According to Taylor, parents' attitudes toward education affected the achievement of their children, particularly in reading comprehension. For Mexican Americans and the Anglo middle-class, the greater the value on education, the higher the achievement of the children. This was not the case for the Anglo lower class, where the reverse pattern prevailed. Perhaps lower-class Anglo children were in open rebellion to their parents. The author also concluded that Mexican American children were achieving at a higher level than Anglo lower-class children when I.Q. was held constant.

Gill and Silka (1962) studied 60 Mexican American high school juniors and seniors, 15 high- and 15 low-achieving males and females (as determined by grade point average). They found that high-achieving girls and low-achieving boys came from homes in which their mother was high on a scale measuring how domineering she was. High-achieving boys and low-achieving girls had non-domineering mothers. The explanation given was that girls saw maternal dominance as affection and concern, whereas the boys saw it as an infringement upon their independence. Although suggestive of cultural factors operating in the home, this study uses some of the stereotypic notions about Mexican Americans discussed above. Mexican Americans are portrayed as homogeneous.

Two studies asked what kinds of Mexican Americans manage to complete high school, college, and/or graduate school. Godoy (1970) interviewed 51 Mexican American high school graduates and 51 college graduates, all leaders in education in California. In comparing the college graduates with the high school graduates, he found that college graduates came from homes where only Spanish was spoken, where the schooling of the parents was less than in homes of high school graduates, and where both parents worked. However, it was found that Mexican Americans in college had fathers with higher occupational status than did Mexican Americans who didn't go to college, had fewer siblings, and were more likely from non-Catholic families. Both groups saw their mother as the most influential person in their lives.

Godoy's finding that occupational status was not commensurate with level of schooling for the Mexican American was corroborated by Blair (1971), who studied rates of return to education for the Mexican American in Santa Clara County, California. Blair found that returns to education for the Mexican American (finishing high school vs. not finishing high school, finishing college vs. not finishing college) were considerably lower than those for Anglos. Blair concluded that there appeared to be a better pay off to the Mexican American in the job market if he dropped out of school before graduating from high school or college.

Long and Padilla (1970) administered a 101-item questionnaire to 50 "successful" Spanish-American graduate students (receiving Ph.D., Ed.D., or M.A. degrees). They found that Spanish American students completing a graduate program came from homes in which both Spanish and English were used, whereas unsuccessful students typically came from homes in which English only was spoken. The authors point out that most previous research had looked only at elementary or secondary school, not at the graduate level. The authors feel that the unsuccessful student is caught between two cultures. It is suggested that his lack of knowledge of Spanish is actually a rejection of Spanish.

4.2.4.2 *Educational and Occupational Aspirations and Expectations*

With respect to aspirations and expectations, there is a prevailing stereotypic notion that Mexican American parents have low aspirations and expectations for their children in the educational system—that in fact, education is a low-priority item in the Mexican American home. Research has shown that this view is held not only by Anglos but by Mexican Americans as well (Anderson and Safar, 1971). Murillo (1971) suggests why some Mexican American parents might relegate the Anglo middle-class school to low priority status. Murillo explains the phenomenon in terms of a value clash. Murillo asserts that in teaching more democratic ideals, the school is a direct threat to the authoritarian structure in the Mexican American home. He feels that the values exposed at school confuse the child and threaten the parents. As he puts it, "Contrary to what many Anglos believe, education is highly valued among Chicanos. Yet the education that the child receives in the Anglo school tends to break down the family unity which is the basis for security in the Mexican American culture" (Murillo, 1971, p. 105).[3] Ramírez, Taylor, and Peterson (1971) point out that when Mexican American parents demonstrate an interest in their child's schooling, the child becomes motivated to achieve. Thus, when they show an interest in the schools, the parents are saying, "I accept the values espoused at school." As Ramirez et al. put it, "(The children) seem to view parental approval of education as permission to accept Anglo values" (Ramírez et al., 1971, p. 227).

Taylor (1970a) found that Mexican American parents do, in fact, value education (using the Minnesota Survey of Opinions—Educational Scale, Spanish translation), contrary to a prevailing stereotype. In comparing the orientations of lower-class Mexican American parents (0-6 years of education) with those of lower-class Anglo parents (10-12 years of education), both groups aspired to two years of college for their children.

The Godoy (1970) study found that parents of college graduates were more concerned that their children obtain an education than were parents of high school graduates. This may suggest that how far the Mexican American student goes in school is related to his parents' emphasis on education.

Coleman (1966), Juárez (1968), Wright (1969), Grebler, Moore, Guzman et al. (1970), Patella and Kuvlesky (1970), and Anderson and Johnson (1971) all studied Mexican American student aspirations and expectations. Coleman found that Mexican Americans had the same occupational aspirations as Anglos, but that fewer planned to attend college. Juárez, in a study of Mexican American and Anglo high school sophomores in Texas, found that both groups had high educational aspirations. The finding that similar aspirations were present across cultures countered the stereotypic notion that Mexican Americans have a low

---

[3]With respect to the Redwood City community, one Mexican American father (with little formal educational background) remarked that he wanted to send his older children to secondary school in Mexico because they would receive a stricter education and subsequently learn more. Two other fathers lamented that the schools were not strict enough, in comparison with those in Mexico.

status orientation. Grebler, Moore, Guzman, *et al.* reported on a study of 3,000 sixth, ninth, and twelfth grade pupils in Los Angeles, which found that Mexican Americans aspired to formal education, but in smaller numbers than did Anglos. Also, Mexican Americans tended to aim at trade schools and junior colleges, whereas Anglos planned on four-year colleges. Also, the expectation that they would continue their education beyond high school was twice as great among Anglos as among Chicanos.

Wright (1969) reports the research findings for occupation aspirations and orientations of low-income Mexican American high school sophomores in four Texas counties. He found that Chicanos aspired to high level jobs, mostly in the low-professional category, but expected to achieve less. At the median level of aspirations, males preferred skilled jobs, females preferred clerical and sales jobs. This report questions the long-standing notion of "class-bound expectations." Most Mexican Americans interviewed desired to be upward mobile. In a different approach to the issue of upward mobility, Patella and Kuvlesky (1970) hypothesized an inverse relationship between desire for upward mobility and identity with the Mexican American subculture. "Identification with the Mexican American subculture" was operationalized as language used in conversations and in the media. Using 600 Mexican American high school sophomores from South Texas, the authors found that their hypothesis was not supported. In other words, those students who desired to be upward mobile were not necessarily those who rejected using Spanish. This finding runs counter to those of other studies which relate upward mobility to language use (see Peñalosa & McDonagh, 1966; Peñalosa, 1966; Mahoney, 1967).

Finally, Anderson and Johnson (1971) found that Mexican Americans, grades 7-12, who were born in the United States had higher educational aspirations (more of a desire to finish high school) than did those born in Mexico. But the authors also found that Mexican American students had less confidence in their ability to fulfill the expectations of parents and of the school than did Anglo students, despite the high educational expectations of children and parents.

4.2.5 *Problems in Educating Mexican Americans in the Schools and Suggestions for Reform*

Indictments of existing educational practices with respect to Mexican American students have become the order of the day and not just from angry Chicano leaders. The National Education Association of the United States issued a now well-known report called *The Invisible Minority* (NEA, 1966). The report called attention to the unsatisfactory results of ignoring Chicano cultural and linguistic traits in the schools and of forcing Mexican-American children to accept Anglo norms. The NEA report spoke of the educational and psychological damage that is done by insisting that the Mexican American's culture heritage is inferior, and by not taking this background into account in teaching methods. A series of other reports and articles followed suit, indicting the present system (see, for instance, California Department of Education, 1968; California State Advisory Committee to the U.S. Commission on Civil Rights, 1968; Bernal, 1969; Hernández, 1970; Ortego, 1970).

Either accompanying criticisms of the present system or in separate publications, there have appeared lists of suggestions for making the existing system more responsive to the needs of the Mexican American student. Bauer (1967) provides a list of needs including the hiring of both Spanish-speaking teachers and of more male teachers in primary grades, teaching Mexican culture and Spanish language in school, instruction via Spanish for non-English speakers, teaching English as a second language, integration of Mexican American and Anglo children in the classroom, and special training for teachers, to name a few. Rodríguez (1969) adds to Bauer's list the specific maintenance of bilingual education programs, special tests for measuring the intelligence and achievement of Mexican Americans, encouraging Mexican American students to go on for higher education, and improving adult education for Mexican Americans. Baty (1972) demonstrated that 10-week workshops can train Anglo teachers to be more optimistic in their expectations about Mexican American students, and more tolerant as well.

Some publications aimed at better educating Mexican American children have stressed recruitment and training of teachers, particularly of bilingual/bicultural ones (see, for example, Wonder, 1965; Past, 1966; Manuel, 1968; Carter, 1969; Saunders, 1969). Others have stressed materials and methods for teaching the Mexican American child (California Department of Education Mexican-American Research Project, 1967; Rivera, 1970). Still others have focused more directly on the bilingual education programs (Zintz, 1969; Andersson and Boyer, 1970; Ulibarrí, 1970; Saville and Troike, 1970; John and Horner, 1971).

Within the last seven years, many of the suggestions noted above have been implemented in schools of the Southwest, largely through the assistance of Federal funds. The Elementary and Secondary Education Act (ESEA) of 1965 has been one prime source of funds, both for compensatory education, English-as-a second-language education, and bilingual education. However, the problems are far from eradicated. In some cases, racism still exists in the schools, teachers still condemn the speaking of Spanish in the classrooms, and Anglo values are still being taught ethnocentrically.

4.3 Summary of Points and Relevance to the Redwood City Study

4.3.1 Recently Mexican Americans have criticized stereotypic treatment of them by predominantly Anglo social scientists in the literature. They assert that Mexican Americans are a heterogeneous group, defying simplistic description.

4.3.2   Research into stereotypes indicates that Anglos and Mexican Americans hold stereotypes of each other, but that more are held by Anglos with respect to Mexican Americans than vice versa.

4.3.3   It is erroneous to equate value orientation with economic status. Class position is just one factor contributing to a Mexican American's value system.

4.3.4   Any realistic attempt to describe the Mexican American must take into account the mixing of races, ethnic groups, and generations within the Mexican American people. Also, such description must consider the extent of various influences bearing on these people, such as the traditional Mexican culture, majority American culture, class position, minority status, and historical, regional, and other variants.

4.3.5   There is an educational gap between the Mexican American and other students in Southwestern schools. Chicano high school drop outs are disproportionately high, as are the numbers of Chicanos relegated to classes for the educable mentally retarded.

4.3.6   The Mexican American's language problem in the schools is also the teacher's problem. The teacher should provide the student with means for learning through the language or languages the student possesses. Sometimes this means teaching through Spanish, sometimes through English (but with emphasis on standard English as a second language or second dialect), and sometimes through both.

4.3.7   In the classroom, there is not always harmony between Anglo and Chicano students. Anglos may not associate with Chicanos and Chicanos may respond in kind. As Chicanos move up through the system, they experience greater failure. The ethnicity of the teacher may not be as important as his ability to speak Spanish and his concern for the Mexican American student.

4.3.8   Low achievement of Mexican American students is attributed to the kinds of schools, the out-of-school environment, level of assimilation, low socioeconomic level, low self-confidence, poor educational progress in school, low education of father, and lack of parental emphasis on education. In some studies, speaking Spanish is seen as a detriment to achievement and mobility. In other cases, speaking both Spanish and English is seen as more of an impetus to success in higher education than just speaking English. Studies of educational aspirations and expectations show that Mexican American students have high aspirations and expectations, and that their parents have high educational hopes for them. However, Chicano students are not as confident as Anglo students that they will fulfill their parents' expectations.

4.3.9   The schools of the Southwest have been indicted for ignoring the linguistic and cultural traits of Chicanos in the curriculum. A series of publications suggesting changes have appeared, and certain changes have already been implemented. However, many changes still need to be made.

As an Anglo undertaking such research, this writer was always conscious of the danger of stereotyping. An attempt was made to let the Mexican American students and parents define their own social and cultural values, without imposing values upon them. In an attempt to keep Anglo biases out of the data collection, a team of Mexican American college students collected all the data for the study, both in school and at the homes of the students.

The Redwood City Bilingual Education Project was aimed at producing a school program sensitive to the needs of the Mexican American students. This Project worked to develop a strong, positive self-concept among the Chicano students. The teachers hired for the Project were generally sympathetic to the special linguistic and cultural needs of the Mexican American children involved. The Project was also designed to foster mutual respect between Mexican American and Anglo students. Parents from both ethnic groups was encouraged to participate in Project activities, both during school and after school hours. A major goal of the Project was that the Chicano student experience success in his studies, not only at school entry but on a continual basis throughout his studies, culminating in the successful completion of his education.

The following chapter will describe the setting for the study, the Redwood City community, and provide the particulars of the research design, including information about the research questions, the sample, the treatments, the instruments, and the data analysis.

5. RESEARCH DESIGN AND PROCEDURES

This chapter begins with a description of the Redwood City Mexican American community. An effort is made to view this specific community in relation to the Anglo majority group in the same neighborhood and in relation to other neighborhoods in the city. Following this socio-demographic description, the research design is presented, including the research questions considered in the study, the composition of the sample, brief reference to treatments (elaborated on in Chapter 5), mention of the instruments used to obtain data, and a description of the data analysis procedures.

5.1 *The Setting: The Redwood City Mexican American Neighborhoods in the Study*

Redwood City is located approximately thirty miles south of San Francisco, just southwest of Highway 101 (see map, Figure 1). According to a 1969 Special Population Census (Clayton, 1970), the City's population totaled 53,858. While the Incorporated Area included 20.5 square miles, the Sphere of Influence[1] was 30.5 square miles (not counting the water areas within Redwood City's boundaries). The Special Population Census gathered information on social and economic characteristics of 25,240 of the 25,714 households in Redwood City's Sphere of Influence. Not only were the findings of Redwood City as a whole reported, but also findings were tabulated separately for each of nineteen neightborhoods that comprised Redwood City.

Although only 4% of household heads in Redwood City had Spanish surnames, they tended to be concentrated in several neighborhoods. The two neigh-

---

[1] The Sphere of Influence is comprised of both Incorporated and Unincorporated areas.

FIGURE 1

REDWOOD CITY
(1 inch = ½ mile)

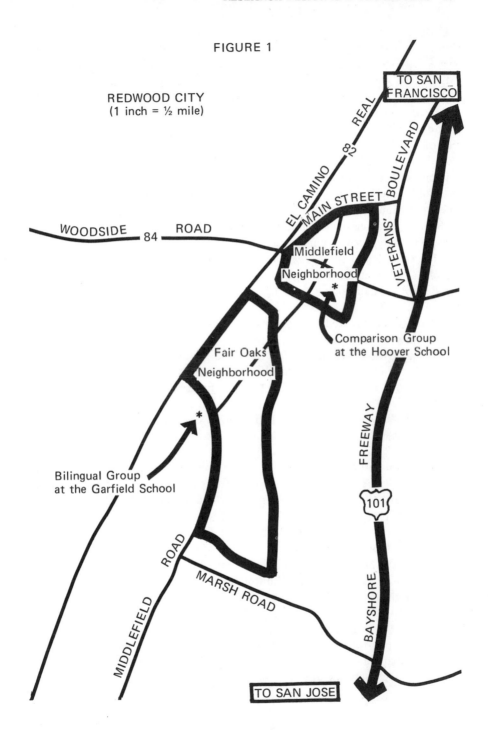

borhoods with the highest number of Spanish-surnamed heads of households were Fair Oaks with 209 (10% of all households in that neighborhood) and Middlefield with 191 (14% of all households in that neighborhood). Between 1964 and 1970, the number of Spanish-surnamed children in the Redwood City schools, grades K through 8, more than doubled: from 532 in 1964 (5.1% of the district total) to 1,308 in 1970 (12.7% of the district total). Most of these Spanish-surnamed children were from the Fair Oaks and Middlefield neighborhoods. In 1970, the Garfield School, in the Fair Oaks neighborhood, had 275 Spanish-surnamed students (33% of the school enrollment) and the Hoover School, in the Middlefield neighborhood, had 190 (49.6% of the school enrollment). Although a Spanish surname does not necessarily indicate that a person is Spanish-speaking or of Mexican origin (Valdez, 1969), these families had, for the most part, recently immigrated from Mexico.

The Garfield School was selected for the Bilingual Project because it had the largest absolute number of Spanish-speaking children. The Comparison group was established at Hoover School, in the adjoining Middlefield neighborhood (see Figure 1).

Throughout this study, frequent mention is made of the "Mexican American community of Redwood City." Actually, this label refers only to Mexican American families that lived in the Fair Oaks and Middlefield neighborhoods and that had children either in the Bilingual Project at the Garfield School or in the Comparison group at the Hoover School. Most of the Spanish-speaking children in grades K-3 at the Garfield School as of the fall of 1971 were in the Bilingual Project. The Comparison group at the Hoover School was comprised of most of the Spanish-speaking students at grades K-2 as of the fall of 1970 (see "Sample," Section 5.2.3, below).

There is no ethnic breakdown of population by neighborhood available for Redwood City before 1969. Even without this information, it would appear that the Fair Oaks and Middlefield communities had absorbed the recent flux of immigration from Mexico in the 1960's. The school data mentioned above tends to support this. Also, the neighborhoods of Fair Oaks and Middlefield had high numbers of short-term residents. According to the 1969 census, 37% of the families in the Middlefield neighborhood and 31% of the families in Fair Oaks had lived in their respective neighborhoods for less than one year.

The original Mexican American population in Redwood City dated back to the early 1930's. Apparently escapees from copper mines in Mexico settled in the area at that time.[2] Mexicans then came during World War II. Many of them found only part-time employment, at the local cannery or elsewhere. Others were fortunate enough to find year-round work at cement factories, asbestos factories, steel factories, and the like.

---

[2] Conversation with Charles J. Bustamante, co-author of Bustamante and Bustamante (1969).

The recent influx of Mexican Americans to Redwood City seems to have started in the mid 1960's. The Fair Oaks and Middlefield neighborhoods were then mostly White with some Black households. As of 1972, the residents were mostly Anglos and Mexican Americans, with their homes interspersed.

The 1969 Special Population Census provided socio-economic data on these neighborhoods, such as the occupation of the principal wage earner, the total family income, and the educational level of the household head. These data are broken down by neighborhood, but unfortunately not by ethnic group. All the same, it is possible to get an idea of how the socioeconomic level of families in the Fair Oaks and Middlefield neighborhoods compared to that of Redwood City as a whole.

With respect to the education level of the household head, both the Fair Oaks and Middlefield neighborhoods had more heads of households with *less* than eighth-grade education than did Redwood City as a whole. They also had at least 10% fewer heads of households with college degrees (see Figure 2). The occupational level of the principal wage earner was also lower than that of Redwood City as a whole, with slightly more people either unemployed or laborers, and 10 to 15% fewer professionals (see Figure 2). Concurrently, the total family income for these two neighborhoods was below that of Redwood City in general. In Middlefield, where there was a 14% concentration of Spanish surnamed, there were also about 12% more families with incomes of under $5,000 than were found in Redwood City as a whole (see Figure 2).

The parents of children in the Bilingual Project and Comparison group were interviewed in their homes in the fall of 1970 and then again in the spring of 1972 (see Section 5.3, Instrumentation). Eighty-one families were interviewed in 1970, and then those 69 families remaining in the area were re-interviewed in 1972. The following information about the Redwood City Mexican American community in the Fair Oaks and Middlefield neighborhoods is based on these interviews.

Comparing data from this study on Mexican American families associated with the Bilingual and Comparison groups to the average of *all* families within the Fair Oaks and Middlefield neighborhoods as described in the 1969 Special Population Census, the following results emerge: Nearly 50% of the Mexican American heads of households were in semi-skilled manual or service occupations (machinists, roofers, gardeners, dishwashers, busboys, etc.), as compared to only 9% in the two neighborhoods taken together (see Figure 2). About 25% of the Mexican Americans were in clerical or skilled manual or service occupations (florists, mechanics, carpenters, cooks, bakers, bartenders, etc.), as compared to 41% of the two neighborhoods taken together (see Figure 2). The remaining 25% were either in unskilled labor or unemployed, a slightly higher percentage than that for the community as a whole (see Figure 2). Only 40 to

FIGURE 2

Fair Oaks and Middlefield Neighborhoods Compared to Redwood City as a Whole

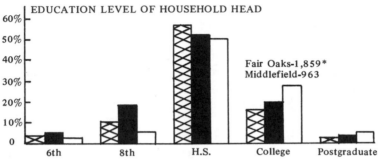

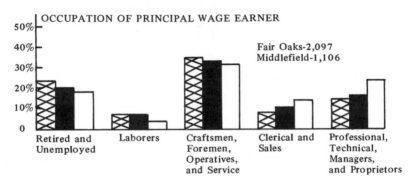

TOTAL NO. OF HOUSEHOLDS
Fair Oaks-2,318
Middlefield-1,405

*Number of Households Responding.

45% of the heads of households had seven or more years of schooling, whereas 80% of all residents in the two neighborhoods together had high school or above. The Mexican American wives had a median three years of schooling. The conclusion that can be drawn from the comparison of the Mexican American families in the study and the neighborhoods in which they live is that while the Middlefield and Fair Oaks neighborhoods were more depressed socioeco-nomically than were other neighborhoods in Redwood City, the Mexican American subgroup was socioeconomically depressed *considerably more* than other groups within their neighborhoods.

Twelve Mexican American heads of households reportedly worked more than 40-hour weeks (up to 60 hours or more) and 40% of the Mexican American wives had jobs. But even long hours and two salaries were usually absorbed quite rapidly since the average household had five children, with some house-holds having as many as nine.

While 93% of the Mexican American families lived in single-family dwellings, the majority of these dwellings were rented (59%). Half of the families re-sponded that they made purchases on credit, particularly from major retail stores. A third of these families said that they obtained loans from banks for their purchases.

At least half of the Mexican American families had immigrated from the State of Michoacan. From two to five families each were from the States of Jalisco and Zacatecas, from Mexico City, and from towns along the United States border. Of those from Mexico, about 65% were from towns, 30% from cities, and only 5% from *ranchos*. Eight sets of parents were born in the United States, mostly in Texas. Two families were from El Salvador and one from Cuba. This finding that only three out of 81 families were non-Mexican Ameri-can Spanish speakers reflects the U.S. Bureau of the Census findings that non-Mexican American Spanish speakers in California numbered only 5% (Public Advocates, Inc. *et al.*, 1971). The families in the study are referred to as "Mex-ican American"[3] because almost all of them were.

The families that immigrated to the United States had lived in this country an average of 11.2 years. They had lived in Redwood City an average of 7.3 years. While in the United States, 34 families had moved three or more times, five families having moved six times. Thus, the Mexican American community was a mobile one, reflecting primarily the difficulty in finding work. Over a third of the families took trips to Mexico every year or two. Another third went to Mexico at least once every three to six years.

In the fall of 1970, 52% of the families said they wanted to stay in the United States permanently, 15% were undecided, and 33% said they wanted

---

[3]See footnote 5, p. 81, for definition of "Mexican American."

to return to Mexico. In the spring of 1972, again 52% said they wanted to stay in the United States, 40% were now undecided, and only 8% said they wanted to return to Mexico to live. However, it was not the same 52% that expressed a desire to stay in the U.S. in 1970 that did so in 1972. Rather, almost half of those expressing a desire to stay in the U.S. in 1970 said two years later that they were undecided or wanted to return to Mexico. And of those who in 1970 said they wished to return to Mexico, most were, at the time of the second interview, either undecided or said that they wanted to stay in the U.S. (see Figure 3). With respect to the twelve families that were no longer in the area for the 1972 interview, school authorities indicated that perhaps half went back to Mexico and half moved elsewhere within the U.S.

The Mexican American families in the study seemed to reflect a group of people that emphasized the nuclear family unit. In only a few cases did family units include persons other than immediate family. Usually, relatives lived elsewhere in the community. When asked what organizations the parents were aware of in Redwood City and nationally, only half of the families said they knew of any—usually Mexican American organizations. However, they were not "joiners." Only six families said that they belonged to one or more of these organizations. Most families (71%) indicated that their family outings were local. They went to parks and beaches in the immediate Bay Area, if they went at all. Often, the heads of households worked on the weekend and didn't have time for excursions. When asked about their visiting patterns in the community, the parents responded that they visited relatives most, Mexican neighbors and non-neighbors somewhat less, and Anglo neighbors and non-neighbors infrequently if at all (see Figure 4).

The fact that these Mexican American parents indicated little interaction with their Anglo neighbors was in large part a reflection of their limited skills in English (and of their Anglo neighbors' lack of Spanish). Only half of the men and 20% of the women said that they could speak English well. Only a third of the men and one-sixth of the women said that their English reading and writing skills were good (see Figure 5). The parents used Spanish almost exclusively at home, and 60% of the husbands were reported to use either Spanish and English or Spanish exclusively with fellow workers at their place of employment. Of those families that went to church (70%), two-thirds said that the priest used only Spanish, 18% said he used both Spanish and English, and only 16% said that he used only English.

5.2 Research Design

5.2.1 Type of Design

This study combines various methodological approaches to research. It is partly a field experiment, in that one group of children received a treatment

FIGURE 3

ULTIMATE DESIRED COUNTRY OF RESIDENCE

MEXICAN AMERICAN PARENT RESPONSES
FROM FALL, 1970, AND SPRING, 1972

N=58

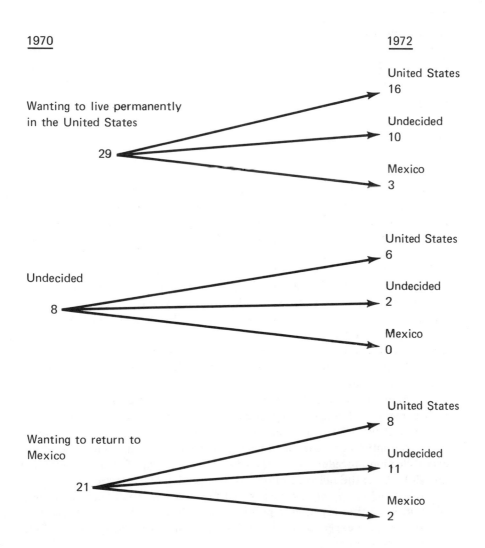

1970

1972

Wanting to live permanently
in the United States

29

United States
16

Undecided
10

Mexico
3

Undecided

8

United States
6

Undecided
2

Mexico
0

Wanting to return to
Mexico

21

United States
8

Undecided
11

Mexico
2

FIGURE 4   MEXICAN AMERICAN VISITING PATTERNS

N=69

Frequency of Visits

	Every Week	Once or Twice a Month	Rarely
Relatives	19*	25	25
Mexican American Neighbors	14	14	41
Mexican American Non-Neighbors	9	12	48
Anglo Neighbors	3	5	61
Anglo Non-Neighbors	3	2	64

*Data in raw scores, based on the 69 households interviewed in the Spring of 1972.

and were compared with another group on a series of tests. It is partly a sociological survey, in that children in the Bilingual and Comparison groups and their families were interviewed. It is also ethnographic research, in that the writer immersed himself in the community and got a feel for the children involved and for their families.

The study is more evaluation than research. Research is concerned with basic theory and perhaps with the design of a program over time with flexible deadlines. Evaluation is concerned with basic theory, but meant to appraise a practical activity by a certain date (Caro, 1971). Wardrop (1971) notes that the role of the evaluator is more difficult than that of the general researcher. Evaluators, in contrast to researchers, work in naturalistic settings and as a result, the traditional research model may be both inadequate and inappropriate for the evaluator.

The evaluation of the Redwood City Bilingual Education Project follows a quasi-experimental design. Campbell and Stanley describe this kind of experiment as follows: "There are many natural social settings in which the research person can introduce something like experimental design into his scheduling of data collection procedures (e.g., the *when* and *to whom* of measurement), even though he lacks the full control over the scheduling of experimental stimuli (the *when* and *to whom* of exposure and the ability to randomize exposures) which makes a true experiment possible. Collectively, such situations can be regarded as quasi-experimental designs" (Campbell and Stanley, 1963, p. 34).

FIGURE 5

REPORTED SPANISH AND ENGLISH PROFICIENCY OF MEXICAN AMERICAN PARENTS

(data in percentages)

SPANISH

	Listening		Speaking		Reading		Writing	
	Father	*Mother*	*Father*	*Mother*	*Father*	*Mother*	*Father*	*Mother*
good	100	100	100	99	90	89	85	85
little	—	—	—	1	6	6	10	10
none	—	—	—	—	4	5	5	5

ENGLISH

	Listening		Speaking		Reading		Writing	
	Father	*Mother*	*Father*	*Mother*	*Father*	*Mother*	*Father*	*Mother*
good	59	30	51	22	38	17	36	14
little	29	34	30	32	29	25	22	16
none	12	36	19	46	33	58	42	70

N=81 (No. of Families in the Fall of 1970).

The specific design is called "the nonequivalent control group design" (Campbell and Stanley, 1963). Experimental and control groups are not randomly selected and possibly not equivalent. Both the experimental and control groups are given a pretest and posttest. As Campbell and Stanley put it, ". . . the groups constitute naturally assembled collectives such as classrooms, as similar as availability permits but yet not so similar that one can dispense with the pretest. The assignment of X (treatments) to one group or the other is assumed to be random and under the experimentor's control" (Campbell and Stanley, 1963, p. 47).

Roberts (1969) points out that the purely experimental designs further scientific understanding of a particular phenomenon, but are so well controlled that they often are not useful in policy determination as are less rigorous studies. Caro (1971) remarks that adequate control is difficult to achieve in an action setting because administrators are reluctant to withhold services from children who may benefit from them. In the Redwood City case, the opposition of school personnel was encountered when it was suggested that Mexican American students be assigned randomly to the Bilingual and Comparison groups.

The overall study conducted by the Evaluator in Redwood City involved two basic types of evaluation: (1) formative evaluation and (2) summative evaluation (see Scriven, 1967). Formative evaluation involves data gathering to help improve the program under development. Such evaluation is intended to provide feedback to teachers at regular intervals, thus allowing for midcourse corrections if certain students aren't progressing adequately under the given instructional approach. Summative evaluation is concerned with producing terminal overall judgments about program worth. Such evaluation deals with the generalized, long-range effects of the project. It usually takes the form of standardized tests or project-made tests of general skills (those not taught only to students in the project), given on a pretest-posttest basis at the start and finish of each school year.

Formative evaluation over the first three years of the Redwood City Project involved specification by teachers of behavioral objectives (and task areas within each objective) that students were expected to meet. Tests were developed by the Project staff to measure progress in meeting language arts, social studies, and science objectives. Commercial unit tests accompanying the State-adopted series were used to assess progress in math. Teachers also filled out an "Individual Student Progress Sheet" on an interim basis. The teachers described what materials each student was using for language arts and for math, what pages he was on in the various materials, and what ability group he was in on the basis of his performance. The teachers also predicted where each student would end up in each type of material by the end of the year, thus making it possible to compare teacher expectations with actual pupil attainment at the end of the year. The specification of a page number for each child in the various materials was considered a reasonable measure of progress, because the materials were either programmed, or similarly sequential, with new material building in sequence incrementally upon previously learned material.

Results of formative evaluation were submitted bi-annually to the Project Office at the Bilingual Education Branch Office in Washington, D.C., and will not be reported here.[4] Tucker and d'Anglejan (1971) emphasize the limited utility of what they call "self-centered" project goals, such as meeting specific teaching objectives, as valid criteria for evaluating the success or failure of a program (e.g., 75% of the children can answer 90% of the questions in certain sections of a book). These authors insist that "more formal evaluation procedures using a control group" are necessary. The approach taken by the Redwod City staff was to combine both types of evaluation into the same study, but only the summative evaluation is reported in this write-up—specifically, the comparison of the group schooled bilingually with a group schooled conventionally.

5.2.2 Research Questions

The following are a series of questions that this research sought to provide answers for:

a. Are Mexican American children who are taught the academic curriculum in Spanish and English for several years as proficient in English language skills as Mexican American children taught only in English?

b. Are Mexican American children who are taught in Spanish and English more proficient in Spanish language skills than comparable children taught only in English?

c. Does a bilingual program promote greater use of Spanish among its Mexican American participants than is found among comparable non-project participants?

d. How well do Mexican American children following a bilingual program perform in relation to a comparison group on tests of a non-language subject matter such as mathematics?

e. What effect does a bilingual program such as this have on the measured academic aptitude of the Mexican American children involved?

---

[4]Copies of these reports are available from the Project Director, Redwood City Bilingual Education Project, 815 Allerton Street, Redwood City, California 94062.

f. How do Mexican American children in a bilingual/bicultural program for several years value the Mexican and Anglo cultures as compared to children who do not receive such a program?

g. What effect does bilingual schooling have upon children's school attendance and attitudes toward school?

h. Are the language attitudes of Mexican American parents with children in a bilingual program for several years affected by their children's participation in the program?

The first two questions above are concerned with whether the teaching of Spanish language skills to Mexican American children is at the expense of English language proficiency, and whether bilingual schooling has any effect upon the maintenance of Spanish language skills. A two-year study cannot begin to assess major changes, but can hopefully give indications of trends in one direction or another.

Another measure of Spanish language maintenance is that of Spanish language use. For this reason, language use is included as a research focus. If the bilingual program is encouraging Spanish language use in an innovative way, then it might be expected that children in the bilingual program will be seen to use as much Spanish after several years in the program as they did at the outset. On the other hand, comparable children in the comparison group may be expected to be using less Spanish after a comparable period of time.

Questions (d) and (e) are concerned with the effect of bilingual schooling on academic aptitude and on math ability. Critics of bilingual education have asserted that instruction through two languages may have a detrimental effect on subject-matter performance and on cognitive development.

Questions (f) and (g) concern themselves with children's attitudes. Since two major problems in the schooling of the Mexican American child are his low self-concept and his high propensity to drop out of school, this study is assessing the attitudes of Mexican American children schooled bilingually and biculturally toward Mexican culture and Anglo culture. Thus, that part of self-concept which relates to cultural identity is being assessed. At the same time, the children's attitudes toward school and toward learning are being measured. Furthermore, the attendance patterns of children in the Bilingual and Comparison groups are being compared to see if a bilingual/bicultural program promotes better school attendance.

Although it may be difficult to detect changes in parental language attitudes as a result of the bilingual schooling of their children, such an attempt will be made. It is thought that the parents' association with the bilingual program through teacher conferences, bilingual program meetings, assemblies, field trips, and other contacts, as well as interchanges with children who are in the project, may result in some interesting posttest results on parents' attitudes.

5.2.3 *Sample*

The sample for this study as of the Spring of 1972 consisted of 90 Mexican American children grades 1-3 and their 70 sets of parents. Forty-five Mexican American and 23 Anglo children received bilingual schooling at the Garfield School in Redwood City, California, while 45 Mexican American children received conventional English-only schooling at a nearby school, the Hoover Elementary School.[5] The 70 sets of parents of the Mexican American children in the Bilingual and Comparison groups were also part of the sample. There weren't as many sets of parents as there were children, because several children came from the same homes. A group of 23 Anglos also received bilingual schooling in the program, but the research findings for this group are not included in this write-up.[6]

The Redwood City Project began in September of 1969 under ESEA Title VII funding with one pilot first-grade group of 20 Mexican Americans and 10 Anglos. In the 1970-71 year, a Follow Up I group of first graders and a Follow Up II kindergarten were added. The decision to begin with first grade rather than with kindergarten was based on the concentrations of Spanish speakers at the various grade levels at the Garfield School. The Spanish-speaking population at the school increased dramatically by grade level with first grade and kindergarten showing the largest concentration. Given this consideration, the Project began with first grade to ensure that many of the neediest first graders got bilingual instruction. One tactical disadvantage of starting the program with first graders, however, was that these students had not benefited from bilingual kindergarten and thus had had reading and math readiness only in English. If Spanish speakers are to be taught how to read in their native *and* dominant language first, then Spanish reading readiness activities should precede English reading readiness. The Project staff had decided that project participants *should* start reading in their native, dominant language first, in keeping with research findings around the world (see the references under 2.2, "Bilingual Education: The Foreign Experience").

The longitudinal study conducted between the fall of 1970 and the spring of 1972, involved the Pilot, Follow Up I, and Follow Up II groups and their re-

---

[5] "Mexican American" refers to Americans of Mexican descent, whether born in the United States or in Mexico. In this sample, they are all native speakers of Spanish. "Anglo" refers primarily to language dominance—i.e., English speaking, rather than to people of Anglo-Saxon origin. Thus, in contrasting Mexican Americans with Anglos, Anglos include Blacks and Asians. In fact, one of the Anglos in the program was Black.

[6] The performance of the Anglos in the Redwood City Bilingual Project was included in interim and end-of-year reports, available from the Project Director, Redwood City School District, 815 Allerton Street, Redwood City, California 94063.

spective comparison groups of Mexican Americans (see Figure 6). The rationale for using two follow up groups for the longitudinal study was as follows: Since bilingual education was new to the Garfield School during the 1969-70 year, special attention was naturally focused on the pupils and on the teachers. This extra attention could have affected the performance of the Pilot group. Some of this novelty had most likely worn off by the 1970-71 year, when a new kindergarten and first grade were added. Thus, it was felt that the assessment of the Follow Up pupils' performance would be under more natural conditions than the initial assessment of the Pilot group had been. The reasoning follows that of Tucker, Otanes, and Sibayan (1970). For much of the analysis, therefore, the Pilot group is looked at separately, as are the Follow Up I and Follow Up II groups, to determine the effects of each "special" treatment.

FIGURE 6

BILINGUALLY-SCHOOLED GROUPS
INCLUDED IN THE STUDY

Group	Years of Bilingual Schooling	Level at Which Began
Pilot	3	First Grade
Follow Up I	2	First Grade
Follow Up II	2	Kindergarten

The Redwood City Bilingual Education Project was selected for the study because the writer was the Internal Evaluator for the Project and had been since October of 1969, the Project's first year. He was a salaried employee of the Redwood City School District. As pointed out repeatedly (see for instance, Caro, 1971), an inside evaluator may tend to be subjective about the project. However, an inside person also has a more detailed knowledge of the project. The evaluator's contacts with the school personnel and Project staff had been very extensive during the year prior to the study. His job responsibilities included not only procuring and constructing tests and interview schedules, training testers, and other evaluative functions, but also attendance at weekly staff meetings; classroom instruction in music, social studies, and physical education; and community liaison work. He visited the homes of all the 30 families participating in the project during the first year. He also served as interpreter at several parent-staff Bilingual Project meetings, particularly during the 1971-72 school year.

Although there were 20 Chicanos at each grade level in the Bilingual Project, there were fewer students included in the longitudinal study. Some of the original students moved away. As of fall 1970, there were 53 Mexican American children in the Bilingual group and 52 in the Comparison group, and 81 sets of parents (see Figure 7). A decision was made to look at children in terms of the group they started with as of the fall of 1970—Pilot, Follow Up I, Follow Up II—or their respective Comparison groups. The Comparison groups were drawn from the Hoover School, a neighboring school ten blocks away from the Garfield School. As mentioned under "Type of Design" (5.2.1, above), the Garfield School Administrative personnel did not agree to have matched pairs of Chicanos randomly placed in the Bilingual Project and in a comparison group. Therefore, it was necessary to go to another school for purposes of comparison.

FIGURE 7

	Bilingual		Comparison	
	Students	Parents	Students	Parents
Number in Fall, 1970	53	40	52	41
Number in Spring, 1972	45	36	45	34

Ideally, the Comparison group should have been composed only of students who were in normal progress through the grades, but since retention in grade had been a common phenomenon for the Mexican American child in the Redwood City schools,[7] it was hard to find a comparison group of children who had *not* been retained in grade or who were not bound to be retained during the study. The Mexican American population in the School District even though concentrated in three schools only, ranged from 35% to 50% of any one classroom. Thus, it was impossible to simply omit those retained in grade and still have enough for a local comparison group. The alternative was to go to another community for the comparison group, but then a number of demographic and environmental variables may have been different.

Seven children in the Bilingual group were retained, but five of these were retained in kindergarten before the Project started. One was retained in kindergarten and one in first grade after the Project began. In the Comparison group, 18 of the 45 students had been retained—four at the end of kindergarten, nine at the end of first grade, five at the end of second grade, and one at the end

---

[7] Apparently the practice as of spring 1972, was not to retain students in grade, at least at the Garfield and Hoover Schools.

of both kindergarten and first grade. Six out of 16 students were retained at the Pilot level, 10 out of 15 at the Follow Up I level, and two out of 14 at the Follow Up II level.

The use of groups—Pilot, Follow Up I, and Follow Up II—rather than grades, is meant to emphasize the number of years of schooling the children had, rather than emphasizing the grade they were in. Grade level is of limited significance when there are retainees. It is well known that many schools have gone to non-graded classes to get away from the stigma attached to being at one level of primary school as opposed to another. An essentially non-graded approach is being used here to look at children in bilingual and conventional schooling programs.

Even with the high retention rate among Comparison students, the average age (computed by year and tenth of year) for the Mexican American Bilingual and Comparison groups showed very little difference across groups (see Figure 8). The age data are based on the children's ages as of October of 1970. The Bilingual Pilot and Follow Up groups were slightly older than their Comparison groups. The Follow Up I Comparison group was slightly older than the Bilingual group. Group differences are consistently the result of one student being more than a half year older than the rest.

FIGURE 8

MEAN AGE (IN YEARS AND TENTHS OF YEARS)*

	BILINGUAL PROGRAM	COMPARISON
	Mexican Americans	*Mexican Americans*
Pilot	8.1	7.9
Follow Up I	6.9	7.2
Follow Up II	5.8	5.7

*As of October, 1970

Figure 9 provides a chart of the students in the Bilingual Project and in the Comparison by group, by ethnicity, and by sex. By chance, twice as many Mexican American males as females were selected for the Bilingual Project. The criteria for selection of both Bilingual and Comparison group Mexican Americans was that the children be Spanish-dominant, and that Spanish be the primary language in the home. School records indicated the primary language spoken in the home. As to the child's language dominance, teachers' ratings were used. Kindergarten teachers' ratings and administrative concurrence were used for selection of the Pilot group for the fall of 1969. A further measure was used for selection of the Follow Up I group. They were given the Dailey Language

FIGURE 9

**THE SEX OF STUDENTS IN THE BILINGUAL AND
COMPARISON GROUPS BY LEVEL**

| Level | BILINGUAL PROGRAM | | | | | | COMPARISON | | |
| | Mexican American | | | Anglo | | | Mexican American | | |
	Male	*Female*	*Total*	*Male*	*Female*	*Total*	*Male*	*Female*	*Total*
Pilot	10	5	15	3	5	8	9	5	14
Follow Up I	10	6	16	5	1	6	8	7	15
Follow Up II	9	5	14	4	5	9	9	7	16
TOTAL	29	16	45	12	11	23	26	19	45

Facility Test (see "Instrumentation" section, 5.3, above). Children with lower English oral proficiency and higher Spanish proficiency were given preference in the program. Then those with balanced scores in both languages were selected, and so forth.

The Mexican American students generally came from families that had recently immigrated from Mexico. Very few children had parents who were born in the United States. Of the children themselves, approximately one-third were born in Mexico, generally the older students. Figure 10 provides data on the birthplace of parents of children in the Bilingual and Comparison groups, and on the birthplace of the children themselves by group level.

For the Pilot Anglos, kindergarten teachers offered the names of their most advanced Anglos in terms of reading readiness. Ten of these children were selected for the Pilot first grade. The rationale was that extra skill in reading would ensure a reasonably homogeneous reading group, simplifying scheduling and reducing the teacher's work load. This simplification was designed to counterbalance the highly differentiated English reading program necessary for the Mexican American students, given their varying command of English. This policy only applied to the Pilot group. The Follow Up I and Follow Up II Anglos represented a cross-section of reading readiness groups so as to offer bilingual schooling to pupils with a wide ability range. Anglo and Mexican American parents had reacted negatively to placing only the most advanced Anglos in the Bilingual Project in the first year. It should also be noted that Anglo children were students with English as their mother tongue. Several of them had a cultural background which differed from that of the rest. One "Anglo" was a Black, and two had Mexican American fathers and Anglo mothers. Neither of these latter two children had any Spanish language ability when they entered the Project.

Other priority considerations for selection of both Mexican American and Anglo students for the Bilingual Project were: (1) that they come from families with high residential stability, (2) that parents give their permission, and (3) that preference be given to children who already had brothers or sisters in the program (so that children could practice language with one another at home—particularly in the case of Anglos learning Spanish, and also to avoid jealousies resulting from one sibling being in the program and not the other).

Chicano parents were generally interested in enrolling their children in the Bilingual Project. Only two sets of parents out of 31 did not want their children in the Project for the 1969-70 school year. Twenty children from the 29 interested families were selected on the basis of the greatest lack of English skills. Since all of the Mexican American children were from relatively low income homes, poverty level was not a criterion for selection. In the case of

FIGURE 10

BIRTHPLACE OF PARENTS OF BILINGUAL AND COMPARISON
GROUP MEXICAN AMERICAN CHILDREN

N = 55 (Total Respondents)

	Bilingual Group Parents		Comparison Parents	
	No.	%	No.	%
Both Parents Born in the U.S.	3	8	5	14
One Parent Born in the U.S.	4	11	3	9
Both Parents Born in Mexico	29	81	26	77

BIRTHPLACE OF BILINGUAL AND COMPARISON GROUP MEXICAN AMERICAN
CHILDREN BY GROUP LEVEL

	BILINGUAL						COMPARISON					
	Pilot		Follow Up I		Follow Up II		Pilot		Follow Up I		Follow Up II	
	No.	%	No.	%	No.	%	No.	%	No.	%	No.	%
Born in the U.S.	6	40	12	75	12	86	7	50	6	40	13	81
Born in Mexico	9	60	4	25	2	14	7	50	9	60	6	19

Anglos, most came from relatively middle-class homes. One-third of the class were Anglos so as to ensure integration in the classroom, with resulting cross-cultural sharing and two-way language modeling.

Every time that a student left the Bilingual Project, another one was brought in to replace him. Thus, the classes always maintained the twenty-Mexican-American-and-ten-Anglo ratio. However, since extensive pretest data were collected on the original students, it was impossible to add new students to the longitudinal study. The Bilingual Project served as an absorption center, of sorts, for newly arrived Mexican immigrant children (perhaps a key function that any bilingual program should perform). Each year the Bilingual Project accepted new non-English-speaking students at all grade levels in which the program was functioning (K-3 as of 1971-72). These students were able to receive all of their instruction in Spanish. Each year a new kindergarten was added as the existing grades advanced. It proved difficult to admit Anglos in the Project at the second- and third-grade levels because of their lack of Spanish language background. However, attempts were made to place Anglo students at these more advanced levels and the students themselves decided whether they wished to remain. Whereas the Mexican American child learned some English out of class, reinforcing his school learning, the Anglo child did not appear to learn very much Spanish out of class.

At the Comparison school, Mexican American children were spread over at least three classrooms at each grade level. This meant that those selected for comparison purposes had to be gathered into one classroom for group tests. During the second year of the study (1971-72), nine of the comparison students were studying in other schools in the Redwood City School District because their families had moved. Their progress was still measured because of the small size of the Comparison group. Needless to say, both the spread over different classrooms within the same school and the following of students to other schools created administrative difficulties and increased evaluation time and costs.

5.2.4 Treatments: The Schooling Program for the Bilingual and Comparison Groups

The treatment for the Mexican American groups involved in bilingual schooling (Mexican American Pilot, Follow Up I, and Follow Up II) varied from year to year and from group to group. It would be misleading to suggest that somehow all the youngsters received the same bilingual training—as if the Project provided a neat package of bilingual instruction. Actually, from the very start of the ESEA Title VII Programs, it was understood that the first three-to-five years would be spent *developing* the program. The federal funds were viewed as "seed money" to help in developing programs that would then be expanded by the local school district, ideally with the help of state and local funds. Thus, whereas bilingual programs in the 1960's before the Bilingual Education Act had often been massive, serving from 700 to 900 students, Title VII programs were generally smaller. The cutback in scope was not meant as a deliberate effort to reduce services to the needy, but merely in the interest of perfecting the bilingual programs—improving teaching methods, teacher training, curriculum materials, and so forth.

Because the Redwood City Bilingual Project was developmental, it is necessary to describe the treatment that each group received so that the research results can be interpreted with that in mind. This description is provided in the following chapter.

5.3 Instrument and Instrument Administration

The instruments in this study measure language proficiency, language use, math achievement, academic aptitude, language attitudes, socioeconomic level, educational environment in the home, and a series of demographic factors.

Ever since Chomsky distinguished between *competence* and *performance* in language ability, i.e., knowledge of a language vs. what one does with what he knows (Chomsky, 1965), tests that purport to assess language competence have been subject to controversy. Sociolinguists warn that what is measured with a given language test is simply performance, not competence. Furthermore, it has been pointed out that only one kind of language performance is probably being tapped at that—namely, the register of language that a child reserves for a classroom or when being interviewed by an authority figure (Ervin-Tripp, 1971). The instruments in this study that measure student language probably are measuring just the language of the classroom or the language reserved for an authority figure. However, since children are forced to spend much of their day in a classroom, their proficiency in the language of the classroom is of great concern. This study employs a wide number of measures, asking the students to perform a variety of different tasks. The use of such a wide array of instruments to measure language skills and language use patterns is intended to help tap the students' language competence better than a single language measure would.

The instruments of the study go beyond strictly language measures. They also include tests of math and academic aptitude, a survey of home factors, and a series of measures on language attitudes.

Because recent literature has singled out the effects that a tester's or interviewer's ethnic background may have on the results of testing and interviewing (Mycue, 1968; Cohen, E. 1970; Wolfram, 1971; Savage and Bowers, 1972), all interviewing and all testing—except for group testing at the Bilingual Project—was carried out by a team of Mexican Americans who were undergraduates at Stanford University. These students were for the most part scholarship students from low-income homes who spoke Spanish natively. Their own backgrounds were in many cases similar to those of the students that they were working with in the study. During the first year of the study, there were fifteen workers. The following year, the same team (minus five) was also responsible for the posttesting. Three new Mexican American testers were hired the second year, but they administered a new instrument, the Language Use Observation Instrument, and acted as assistants in group testing. There were an equal number of males and females on the research staff. The testers and interviewers were given training sessions at Stanford.

While part of the rationale for using Mexican American testers and interviewers exclusively was to guard against possible reactions to Anglo testers, another concern was to help train Mexican American students in psychometric procedures and to give them direct contact with the local schools and with the local community. The students were paid at a higher rate than the Stanford University hourly wage for student work.

Group tests were administered at the Bilingual Project by the teachers themselves. At the Comparison school, group tests were administered in rooms set aside for the testing—usually the classroom of a teacher on a field trip for the day. The staff workers collected the appropriate group of students from their various classrooms, and brought them to this special classroom for the testing session.

Between December 1970 and January 1971, most of the families of students in the Bilingual and Comparison groups were interviewed in their homes by Mexican American college students. Several families that could not be contacted at that time (because they had moved or worked late hours) were reached in February or March. The interviews were conducted in Spanish and lasted generally about an hour. Extensive language census data on the entire family were collected, as well as socioeconomic, educational environment, and demographic information.

In May and June of 1972, those families that had not moved away from Redwood City (70 out of 81) were once again interviewed in their homes, in some cases by the same people who had interviewed them seventeen months earlier.

The posttest interviews were conducted only by interviewers who had taken part in the 1971 interviews. In the spring of 1972, the interviews lasted about 30 minutes.

In homes with phones, families were called to arrange a convenient time for a visit. For the most part, the mother answered the questionnaire, largely because she was more likely to be home for the interviewer. A study by Godoy (1970) reported that Mexican American high school and college graduates felt their mothers influenced them more than did their fathers. Perhaps this finding provides justification for having the mother speak for both parents.

Because of the large number of instruments used in the study, the description of the instruments, details on their administration, results and discussion are presented in a series of five chapters. Chapter 7 deals with Spanish and English Language Proficiency, Chapter 8 deals with Deviations from "School" English and Spanish Grammar,[8] Chapter 9 deals with Language Use, Chapter 10 deals with Mathematics and Academic Aptitude, and Chapter 11 deals with Attitudes toward Language and Culture, and toward School. Supplementary information on each of the instruments used in the study is found in Appendix 1. This information includes specifics on scoring, copies of or sample items from the non-commercial instruments, discussion on how the instruments relate to the research literature (where relevant), and reliability and validity data where available.

5.4 Data Analysis

Data analysis primarily consisted of comparing the Bilingual and the Comparison students and their parents on a series of measures. The statistical techniques used to run these comparisons were one-way analysis of variance (ANOVA) and analysis of covariance (ANCOVA). Analysis of variance is a statistical technique designed to test the null hypothesis that the means of several groups (in this case, two) are the same. Analysis of covariance is an analysis of variance technique for situations in which information on a covariate—in this case a pretest measure—which is strongly predictive of the dependent variable is available. Thus, ANCOVA is used to test the null hypothesis that the means of two groups are the same based on the y scores after "adjustment" using the x scores (Elashoff and Snow, 1970). The covariance procedure reduces possible bias on posttest comparisons resulting from differences in the covariate or pretest scores.

In comparing the students on a measure that was administered only once, analysis of variance was generally computed, using the BMD X64 program (Dixon, 1970) for the most part, but also using the ANOVA statistic available in the SPSS Breakdown program (Nie, Hull, et al., 1972). Both the BMD and SPSS programs allow for unequal group sizes, which was the case at all group levels in this study.

If there was a pretest score or some comparable before-measure, then a Regression Analysis program (SCRDT, 1, n.d.) was run, which computed scatterplots showing posttest plotted against pretest for both Bilingual and Comparison groups at each of the three group levels. The program also provided regression lines for each group and an F test for parallelism. Since an important assumption of analysis of covariance is that the slope of the regression line is the same

---

[8]This mini-study was based on data collected by means of the Storytelling Task discussed in Chapter 7.

for each group (see Elashoff, 1969; Elashoff and Snow, 1970), ANCOVA was run only if the regression lines for the two groups were not significantly different. The BMD X64 program was also used for covariate analysis. If the regression lines for the two groups were significantly different, then ANOVA alone was run.

As it turned out, in only five cases were the regression lines for Bilingual and Comparison groups significantly nonparallel. All instances occurred at the Follow Up II Level, in the analysis of subscales of the Storytelling Task. These significant interactions are discussed in the "Results" section for Chapter 7, Spanish and English Language Proficiency.

As mentioned above, one assumption of analysis of covariance is that the relationship between pre- and posttest scores is similar for both groups—hence, the importance of an F test for parallelism of slopes for the two groups. Another assumption is that the within-group correlation between pre- and posttest scores is high. "High" means .30 or better (see Elashoff and Snow, 1970). The data for this study showed that the within-group correlations were .30 or better 55% of the time (see Appendix 3 for Table of Correlations). In cases where the pre-posttest correlations did not reach .30, the reliability of the measures is called into question, i.e., was an accurate measure of the student's ability obtained? The fact that at times the pre-posttest correlations were higher for either Bilingual or Comparison than for the other group at all three group levels suggests possible problems of validity. In other words, certain instruments or subtests may not have been measuring what they were supposed to be measuring. The possibility of threats to validity is increased when the same or similar measures are used over time because of the problems of selection-maturation interaction and regression effects (see Campbell and Stanley, 1963).

The decision to use ANCOVA was predicated on a desire to take into account initial differences on the various measures and to adjust posttest data accordingly. It was also decided to look at each group level separately—Pilot, Follow Up I, and Follow Up II—rather than to combine all group levels in one analysis. Covariate analysis using all three levels was considered unwise because of the dissimilarity in pre-posttest relationships across group levels and because the three Bilingual groups received different treatments. Although the ANCOVA technique is robust enough to analyze data obtained from non-randomized groups, as in this study, the results must be interpreted with caution because of the uncertainty that the ANCOVA technique removed all the bias.

Contingency-table analysis was used in several instances where the data for two variables being compared fell into several discrete categories. The gamma statistic was used to determine the significance of the crosstabulations. Gamma is a measure of concordance between two variables (see Rosenthal, 1966; Anderson & Zelditch, 1968). Gamma considers whether the two variables are ordered in the same way, whatever that way may be. Thus, two variables need not have a linear relationship to produce a significant gamma. The relationship could, for example, be "L" shaped. Gamma has a special feature that the chi square statistic does not have. That is, gamma provides a measure of significance even if one or more cells in the contingency table has a zero entry.

The crosstabulations were computed using the SPSS Fastabs program (Nie, Hull, *et al.*, 1972). The significance of gamma was computed by means of a Gamma Confidence Interval program, developed by Eleanor Chiang of the Methodology Unit at the Center for Research and Development in Teaching, Stanford University.

Most of the data analysis results appear at the end of the "Results" sections in Chapters 7 and 9-11. However, the mean squares for the significant ANOVA and ANCOVA tests appear in Appendix 4.

As was pointed out above, the Bilingual students at different group levels (Pilot, Follow Up I, Follow Up II) received somewhat different treatments. For this reason, the data were analyzed separately for each group level. This was meant to distinguish children who received one type of exposure to bilingual schooling—both in terms of length of time, starting point, and methods—from students who received another.[9] Such a distinction is meant to make the results more easily interpretable.

5.5 *Summary*

5.5.1 The site for this study of bilingual schooling was Redwood City, California, thirty miles south of San Francisco. The children in the Bilingual and Comparison groups came from families living in two neighborhoods, Fair Oaks and Middlefield, as they were called in a Special Population Census which identified 19 neighborhoods in Redwood City. These two neighborhoods had the highest concentrations of Spanish-surnamed heads of households in Redwood City. School enrollment figures showed that the Mexican American student population had more than doubled since 1964. These neighborhoods were substantially lower in occupational level, educational attainment, and income than Redwood City as a whole. The Mexican Americans, as a subgroup, were considerably lower socioeconomically than were other groups in their neighborhoods. The Anglo families in the community whose children participated in the Bilingual Project were living at a higher socioeconomic level than were the Mexican Americans.

---

[9] No formal analysis was run to compare the achievement of Comparison students retained in grade at each group level with students who were not retained. One problem with such analysis was the unequal number of retainees within each group (6 out of 16 at the Pilot level, 10 out of 15 at the Follow Up I level, and 2 out of 14 at the Follow Up II level). Informal analysis yielded no clear achievement patterns for retainees compared to non-retainees.

5.5.2 The Mexican American population in the Redwood City represented a recent immigrant group (average 11.2 years in the U.S.), exhibited a preference for the nuclear family over the extended family, limited its network of social interactions to visists with relative and to other Mexican Americans, and for the most part, had only imperfect command of English language skills.

5.5.3 Although the overall evaluation design for the Bilingual Project included both formative and summative evaluation, only the summative evaluation was treated in this report. This study examined a series of research issues related to bilingual education, such as the effects of bilingual schooling upon Mexican American students' native and second language learning, upon their language use patterns, upon their performance in a non-language subject matter such as math, upon their academic aptitude, upon their attitudes toward the Mexican and Anglo cultures, and upon their attitudes toward school. The study also looked at the effect of having children in a bilingual program on the language attitudes of the parents. The parents were also asked to report selected socioeconomic, educational, and demographic information on the family.

5.5.4 The sample for the study consisted of 90 Mexican American children and the 70 sets of parents of these children. 45 Mexican Americans, as well as 25 Anglos not in the study, received bilingual schooling at the Garfield School in Redwood City, and 45 Mexican American children received conventional English-only schooling at a nearby school. The students were designated by groups —Pilot, Follow Up I, and Follow Up II—in order to emphasize the number of years of schooling they received while in the Bilingual or Comparison group, rather than the grade they started or ended in. Especially at the Comparison school, many of the Mexican American students were retained in grade.

5.5.5 The Pilot group at the Bilingual Project received three years of bilingual schooling, while the Follow Up I and Follow Up II groups each received two years. Both the Pilot and the Follow Up I groups began their bilingual schooling at the first-grade level, thus missing out on bilingual reading and math readiness at the kindergarten level. The Follow Up II group, on the other hand, started bilingual schooling in kindergarten. All three groups received instruction in math, science, and social studies, both through their vernacular and through their second language. The techniques of bilingual instruction varied from grade level to grade level and from year to year.

5.5.6 The instruments in the study included both measures of performance, such as tests of listening, speaking, reading and writing skills in Spanish and English, and a language use observation instrument, as well as self-report of language use and report by others, parental report of family language proficiency and language use patterns, and measures of language attitudes. Students were also given tests of math and of academic aptitude, and a cultural attitude inventory. Parents were asked to report selected socioeconomic, educational, and demographic information on the family through two questionnaires.

5.5.7   The instruments were administered for the most part on a pre- and posttest basis over a two-year period. The pretesting took place in the fall and winter of 1970 and the posttesting was conducted in the spring of 1972. The bulk of the testing and interviewing was conducted by a team of Mexican American college students.

5.5.8   Data analysis consisted of contrasting the Bilingual and the Comparison students and their respective parent groups on a series of measures. The statistical techniques used to run these comparisons were one-way analysis of variance and analysis of covariance. Covariate analysis was used in order to reduce possible bias in posttest comparisons resulting from differences in pretest scores.

The next chapter provides a detailed description of the school program or "treatment" in the Bilingual education program and at the Comparison school over the period of the study. With respect to the Bilingual education program, reference is made to the staffing, the children, the facilities, the models of bilingual schooling, the scheduling, the instructional materials, and in-service teacher training. Other topics covered include the grouping of students for content subjects, the role of the teacher aides, and the language used by the teaching staff. Mention is also made of the program at the Comparison school.

6. THE SCHOOL PROGRAM

This discussion is meant to illustrate the diversity of bilingual education treatments, to show that bilingual education isn't one thing, but rather a number of possible combinations of treatments. The discussion will follow each of the three groups—the Pilot, the Follow Up I, and the Follow Up II—through their distinct exposures to bilingual schooling. It is hoped that the reader will come away with a feel for what a bilingual program might actually entail in terms of personnel, students, facilities, models of bilingual schooling, scheduling, instructional materials, and in-service teacher training. An attempt will also be made to describe the "treatment" that the Comparison children were getting through their conventional classrooms. Observers were sent into all of the classrooms and made some brief appraisals of how teachers grouped children and of the curriculum materials that they used.

6.1 *Bilingual Project*

6.1.1 *1969-1970 School Year*

6.1.1.1 *The Non-Instructional Staff: Year #1*

During the first year of the Bilingual Project, the non-instructional staff included a Director, a bilingual Coordinator-Master Teacher, a bilingual Evaluator, and a Curriculum Writer. The Director of the Project was in charge of all the District's federal projects, and his involvement in the Project was limited mostly to drawing up a project proposal and getting it funded. The Coordinator was also a Master Teacher who team-taught in the Project. This limited his ability to perform the duties that a full-time coordinator would have performed. The Evaluator and Curriculum Writer, both doctoral students at Stanford University, were hired on a 10% of full-time basis. They replaced a woman who had been Curriculum Writer-Evaluator for August and September of that first year. She had been responsible for the initial evaluation design and baseline testing for the year. Because the Coordinator was also teaching, and the other non-instructional staff were on part-time, the Project was without a full-time manager the first year.

6.1.1.2 *The Instructional Staff: Year #1*

The instructional staff for the first year included two teachers, one a master teacher, and two teacher aides. The master teacher was a male in his mid-forties from Southern Texas, whose mother had been Mexican. He held a Ph.D. in Education and had had extensive experience teaching Spanish (primarily as a second language) in the elementary schools. The other teacher was a Mexican American female from San Francisco, in her early thirties, who had taught for two years before teaching in the Bilingual Project. The master teacher was responsible for the instruction in Spanish, and had a Costa Rican aide for part of the year. The other teacher took charge of instruction in English and had a Mexican American aide. This aide split her time between the two classrooms in the latter part of the year after the Costa Rican aide left. Both aides were women from the local community and were in their thirties. The Mexican American aide had a high school background. The Costa Rican aide had been an elementary school teacher in Costa Rica. Several of the reasons that she left the Project were that she tended to assume the role of teacher, against the wishes of the master teacher in the classroom, and that she expected payment commensurate with her past training and experience rather than what was offered the teacher aide (see Figure 1 for Staffing Chart).

Because it was the first year of the Project, numerous adults and students visited the Project (perhaps too many), and several stayed on to tutor on occasion. The Evaluator taught soccer, ran a mock "TV news program," and taught bilingual songs every Tuesday and Thursday afternoon.

6.1.1.3 *The Children: Year #1*

The initial Pilot group consisted of 20 Mexican American and 10 Anglo first graders. As mentioned in the discussion of the "sample" (5.2.3), the Mexican Americans were either Spanish-dominant or roughly balanced in Spanish and English language skills. The Anglos were non-Spanish speakers. The decision to begin with first grade rather than with kindergarten was based on the concentrations of Spanish speakers at the various grade levels at the Garfield School. The Spanish-speaking population at the school increased dramatically by grade level with first grade and kindergarten showing the largest concentrations (see Figure

FIGURE 1

STAFFING CHART
REDWOOD CITY BILINGUAL EDUCATION PROJECT

1969-1970, Grade 1

Non-Instructional Staff

Director (minimal time)
Coordinator (part time)
Evaluator (part-time)
Curriculum Writer (part-time)

Instructional Staff

Master Teacher (also Coordinator)
Bilingual Teacher
2 Bilingual Teacher Aides

1970-1971, Grades K-2

Non-Instructional Staff

Director (minimal time)
Coordinator (full-time)
Evaluator (part-time)
Bilingual Specialist (part-time)

Instructional Staff

3 Bilingual Teachers
Bilingual Specialist (also on
    Non-Instructional Staff)
3 Bilingual Teacher Aides

1971-1972, Grades K-3

Non-Instructional Staff

Director (minimal time)
Coordinator (full-time)
Evaluator (part-time)
Curriculum Writer (full-time)

Instructional Staff

4 Bilingual Teachers
4 Bilingual Teacher Aides

---

2). Given this consideration, the Project began with first grade to ensure that many of the neediest first graders got bilingual instruction. The neediest kindergarteners were to enter the bilingual program in first grade the following year.

6.1.1.4 *Facilities: Year #1*

Because of limited space in the Garfield School proper, the school rented five classrooms from an adjoining church. Two of these classrooms were used for the Bilingual Project. One was set up as a Mexican culture and Spanish language room, and the other was designed as the English language room. The Mexican culture room had realia from Mexico, as well as from other Latin American countries and from Spain. The rooms were smaller than ordinary school classrooms, thus limiting freedom of movement. There was also a substantial parking lot separating the main school buildings from the church classrooms, thus isolating the Bilingual Project from the rest of the school both physically and

FIGURE 2

BREAKDOWN OF ENROLLMENT FIGURES OF CHILDREN FROM SPANISH-SPEAKING FAMILIES AT GARFIELD, 1969-70

	K	1st	2nd	3rd	4th	5th	6th
No. of Classrooms	6	3	4	4	4	4	4
No. of Spanish-speaking students	38	31	23	26	12	18	17

socially. This separation did not help foster relations between the Bilingual Project and the rest of the school, although other Garfield teachers were invited to visit the Bilingual Project with their classes and some did.

6.1.1.5 Model(s) of Bilingual Schooling in Use: Year #1

The original model adopted for use was that of partial bilingualism (see Fishman and Lovas, 1970). All students, Mexican Americans and Anglos, were expected to acquire fluency and literacy in both languages, but with literacy in the mother tongue restricted to certain subject matter—namely social studies, music, art, and physical education. In actual practice, those Mexican Americans who were Spanish-dominant and unable to follow math and science classes in English (8 out of 20) attended classes in Spanish in the Mexican room, while the others were taught these subjects in English in the other room. This arrangement was consistent with the partial bilingualism model, which opted for English instruction in certain subjects, namely math and science, at the earliest possible time. One problem with the arrangement was that some students preferred to have the instruction in English *not* because they were equally comfortable in English and in Spanish, but because, when given a choice, they perceived it as more prestigious to be in the English language room. One advantage of this arrangement was that Mexican Americans and Anglos were only segregated into separate groups for language instruction.

Language arts was team-taught. The teacher in the Mexican room taught Spanish language arts, and the teacher in the English language room taught English language arts. Since Chicanos had already had English reading readiness in kindergarten but no Spanish reading readiness, it was difficult if not impossible to start them reading in Spanish before reading in English. In actuality, they started reading in both languages at about the same time. This approach seemed to confuse only several of the slower students. The Anglo students were not taught to read in Spanish in that first year of Spanish language arts. It could be argued that many first-grade Chicanos were better able to learn how to read in both languages than were the Anglos because these Chicanos had a grasp of oral English by the time they began reading. The Anglos, on the other hand, could not be said to have had a grasp of oral Spanish at the beginning of first grade.

6.1.1.6 *Scheduling: Year #1*

The classroom schedule underwent several revisions during the first year. The first schedule called for numerous short time segments, ranging from 15 to 25 minutes. The two teachers found that it was difficult to conduct classes for such short periods. Also, much time was spent just switching classes. See Figure 3 for a sample day in the 1969-1970 schedule as it was ultimately set up.

One special event was not indicated in the schedule. A TV news show was initiated and directed by the Evaluator, as part of social studies. Three students were filmed each Tuesday and Thursday morning in a short show-and-tell program, complete with commercials, using closed circuit television equipment available at the Project. The show was viewed by the entire class in the afternoon during social studies.

6.1.1.7 *Instructional Materials: Year #1*

As was true for the other 22 Spanish-English Title VII Bilingual Education Programs in California for 1969-1970, finding instructional materials for teaching Spanish and for teaching the content subjects in Spanish was a real problem. Readers from the González-Pita Company, such as *Pépin en Primer Grado,* were used for teaching·Spanish reading to Spanish speakers. The *¿Cómo Se Dice?* series, published by Ginn and Company, was used to teach oral Spanish to English speakers. The teacher aide in the Mexican room translated some science lessons from the State Series, *Concepts in Science,* into Spanish, but this activity proved to be too time-consuming. Translations of math concepts in the State Series, *Modern School Math,* were made spontaneously, and occasionally with difficulty.

The curriculum for teaching English to Spanish speakers included the *Shuck Loves Chirley* manual by Olguín for pronunciation activities and the *Miami Linguistic Series* for a linguistically-controlled, phonics approach to reading. English for English speakers relied for its curriculum upon the Ginn, Harper-Row, and Bank Street Series provided by the State. These series combine the phonics and the look-say approaches to reading. The English language teacher also supplemented the readers with the language experience approach to reading, having students tell stories and then read their own stories.

The science curriculum was reinforced by means of the "Classroom Laboratory" kit that Harcourt, Brace, Jovanovich put out to accompany the *Concepts in Science* series. The kit provides enough materials so that all the children in the classroom can become involved in a particular experiment.

FIGURE 3

SAMPLE DAY IN THE 1969-1970 SCHEDULE FOR THE REDWOOD CITY BILINGUAL EDUCATION PROJECT

TIME	SPANISH ROOM	ENGLISH ROOM
9:00- 9:10	—	Opening
9:10- 9:40	Spanish for Spanish speakers	English for English speakers
9:40-10:10	Science for Spanish dominant	Science for English speakers and balanced bilinguals
10:10-10:35	Math for Spanish dominant	Math for English speakers and balanced bilinguals
10:35-10:55	Recess	Recess
10:55-11:30	Spanish for English speakers	English for Spanish speakers
11:30-12:00	English for Spanish speakers: "Sesame Street" ETV	English for English speakers
12:00-12:50	Lunch	Lunch
12:50- 1:15	Social Studies for all in Spanish and English	—
1:15- 1:40	—	P.E., Art, or Library (depending on the day)
1:40- 1:50	Recess	Recess
1:50- 2:05	—	Music
2:05- 2:10	—	Evaluation and Dismissal

From its start, the Bilingual Project placed heavy emphasis on the importance of the Mexican heritage of the Mexican American children. Books, filmstrips, films, and records were used whenever possible to teach bicultural social studies. Sometimes, Mexican American parents from the community came to school and talked about aspects of Mexican history and culture. Mexican holidays were celebrated both in the classrooms and in general assemblies. Frequently, students from the Bilingual Project presented songs, dances, and plays to the rest of the school children as part of the holiday celebrations conducted during assemblies. Pictures and stories about some of these presentations appeared in the local papers.

Appendix 2 provides a list of materials used with grades K-3 from 1969 through 1972. The materials listed are not all the materials used in the various bilingual classrooms, but many of the key ones are included.

6.1.1.8 In-Service Teacher Training: Year #1

During this first year, there were no formal training sessions, although there were weekly staff meetings at which teachers discussed problems and needs. The English language teacher attended an extension course in the use of the *Shuck Loves Chirley* pronunciation manual, and the Spanish-language teacher attended various workshops on Mexican American-Anglo relations. The video taping equipment was used to film classroom activities several times a week, and it was suggested that the teachers study these tapes in order to better assess their classroom performance and their students' responses. However, the teachers rarely made use of the tapes for this purpose. Such tapes were primarily used to show segments of classroom activity to parents during the Spring Open House.

6.1.2 The 1970-1971 School Year (The First Year of the Two-Year Study)

6.1.2.1 The Non-Instructional Staff: Year #2

In the second year of the Project, the Director remained the same, as did the Evaluator. A new full-time Coordinator was hired, a Mexican American in his forties from New Mexico, who had had teaching and administrative experience. In place of a curriculum writer, a full-time "Bilingual Specialist" was hired, a woman with a Mexican background (her mother was Mexican), who had had experience as a language specialist. Her duties included home visits with parents, classroom instruction, and curriculum development. Her classroom duties and home visits, however, took up all of her time.

6.1.2.2 The Instructional Staff: Year #2

The instructional staff included (1) the Bilingual Specialist mentioned above, (2) the bilingual woman teacher who had taught the previous year, (3) a male

Anglo instructor in his early thirties, who had learned Spanish while growing up in San Diego and who was in his first year of teaching, and (4) an Anglo female instructor in her thirties, who had lived in various Latin American countries for a number of years. This last teacher had had previous teaching experience abroad and at a preschool in Redwood City. The one remaining Mexican American teacher aide from the previous year was rehired, and two new Mexican American female aides were added to the instructional staff to work in kindergarten and first grade respectively. Thus, there were four bilingual teachers and three bilingual teacher aides. The Coordinator taught Spanish language arts to five Spanish-speaking second graders daily. From time to time, volunteer mothers and students provided tutorial help to students. (See Figure 1 for Staffing Chart.)

6.1.2.3 *The Children: Year #2*

In the second year, the Pilot group moved on to second grade and a Follow Up I group of first graders and a Follow Up II group of kindergarteners were added. There was some discussion as to whether the Bilingual Education Branch of the U.S. Office of Education would allow the Project to expand downward to include kindergarten. The regulations had specified that only upward, vertical expansion would be permitted. The two-pronged expanision not only called for another teacher, but also for more curriculum materials. The Project Office in Washington consented, however, and so a kindergarten was added. Thus, twenty Mexican Americans and ten Anglos in the Follow Up II group were provided an opportunity to receive reading and math readiness in both Spanish and English in kindergarten. The new first grade of twenty Mexican Americans and ten Anglos in the Follow Up I group, on the other hand, had not had bilingual reading and math readiness before commencing bilingual schooling.

6.1.2.4 *Facilities: Year #2*

The church classrooms were still used during the second year for grades 1-3, although space in the main school had been asked for and tentatively granted. A switch would have meant displacing some teachers from their long-established classrooms. A third room was added to the Spanish language and Mexican culture room and the English language room. The kindergarten was given a room in the main school, which brought the Bilingual kindergarten closer to the rest of the school, but isolated this group from the other groups in the Bilingual Project.

6.1.2.5 *Model(s) of Bilingual Schooling in Use: Year #2*

The model followed during the second year was the same partial bilingualism model of the first year. Spanish-dominant first graders received math in Spanish while the balanced bilinguals received math primarily in English along with the Anglos. Second graders all received math essentially in English, as part of the phasing out of the use of Spanish in this subject. The second-grade teacher aide continued to use Spanish more than the teacher did, particularly with complicated explanations of concepts.

Second-grade science was also taught in English, while at the first-grade level it was still taught bilingually. Social studies and music were taught to second graders bilingually, in keeping with the model of maintaining bilingual instruction throughout the elementary grades in one or more subjects.

In the second year, it was possible to start a kindergarten group with reading readiness in both English and Spanish. However, this background preparation was lacking the new group of first graders that year, the Follow Up I group. As with the Pilot group, the Chicano Follow Up I first graders essentially were taught how to read Spanish and English at the same time. The Anglo first graders only learned oral Spanish. The Anglo Pilot second graders started learning how to read in Spanish.

6.1.2.6 *Scheduling: Year #2*

The scheduling for the 1970-1971 year illustrates how three teachers team-taught grades 1 and 2, just as two teachers had team-taught grade 1 the previous year (see Figure 4). The third teacher visited the homes of Project parents during the first hour of each morning, but otherwise provided instruction in a third classroom. The Garfield School initiated early and late shifts of readers in the fall of 1970, as reflected by the schedule. All Spanish-speaking first and second graders came in the early shift, and all English-speaking first and second graders came in the late shift. Kindergarten classes were held only in the morning. Periods were set aside for language arts, work time, math, and music (see Figure 5).

The English language teacher also taught math to second graders. The Spanish language teacher taught math to first graders, and the Bilingual Specialist taught social studies, science, and art to all first and second graders.

For Mexican American and Anglo first and second graders, half the instruction was conducted in Spanish and half in English. At the kindergarten level, more time was spent teaching the children through their own vernacular.

6.1.2.7 *Instructional Materials: Year #2*

The 1970-1971 year saw the introduction of a kindergarten. Appendix 2 provides a list of the materials used. Spanish pre-reading for Spanish speakers was taught using Houghton-Mifflin's *Preparándose Para Leer* and the Laidlaw pre-primers. Spanish for English speakers was taught through the Michigan Oral Language Series *Spanish Guide for Kindergarten.* Laguna Beach materials like *Los*

Tres Osos were used to teach Spanish to both groups. English for Spanish speakers was taught through *Introducing English* and through *Shuck Loves Chirley*. English reading for English speakers was taught through the Behavioral Research Laboratory's *Sullivan Pre-Readers*. Kindergarteners were taught science skills through the Harcourt, Brace, Jovanovich "Classroom Laboratory," accompanying the *Concepts in Science* series.

While first-grade curriculum remained much the same as it had been in the previous year, a new curriculum had to be developed for second grade. In some cases, more advanced volumes in the same series could be used. In other cases, different series had to be purchased, especially for teaching Spanish reading to Spanish speakers (see Appendix 2). The major innovations were in social studies. Commercial series on Mexican Americans, such as "La Raza" by the Southwest Council of La Raza, and Project-developed slide-cassette packages on famous Mexican Americans like César Chávez were used.

6.1.2.8 *In-service Teacher Training: Year #2*

In-service teacher training included a movie on bilingual education, a lecture on stereotypes and caricatures, and training in writing objectives and in individualizing instruction. There were also informal discussions on the direction of the programs, the major emphasis of the curriculum, the objectives of the program, and the management of the program.

6.1.3 *The 1971-1972 School Year*

6.1.3.1 *The Non-Instructional Staff: Year #3*

In the fall of 1971, the Redwood City School District assigned a new Director of Federal Projects. This man then became Director of the Bilingual Education Project. Perhaps as a function of taking over a project already in its third year, the Director had very little contact with the Project. A new principal was assigned to the Garfield School and he took special interest in the Bilingual Education Project. The previous principal had viewed the Project as a separate entity, divorced from the regular school, and had consequently had very little to do with it. The Coordinator and Evaluator remained the same. The Bilingual Specialist from the previous year became full-time Curriculum Writer. The Bilingual Specialist's shift in position was meant to free her from instructional duties so that she could devote time to curriculum development. As it turned out, she taught language arts to Spanish-speaking and English-speaking kindergarteners one hour each morning, limiting her time somewhat, and then she was frequently asked to assume the role of bilingual secretary for the school, putting further constraints on her time.

FIGURE 4

SAMPLE DAY IN THE 1970-1971 SCHEDULE FOR THE
REDWOOD CITY BILINGUAL EDUCATION PROJECT—GRADES 1 AND 2

TIME	SPANISH ROOM	ENGLISH ROOM	BILINGUAL SPECIALIST ROOM
8:30- 9:30	Spanish for Spanish-speaking second graders*	English for Spanish-speaking first graders**	Bilingual Specialist doing home visits
9:30- 9:35	Restroom Break	Restroom Break	"
9:35- 9:45	Homeroom	Homeroom	"
9:45-10:15	Math for all first graders	Math for Anglo and balanced bilingual second graders	Math for Spanish-dominant second graders
10:15-10:30	Recess	Recess	Recess
10:30-11:35	Spanish for Spanish-speaking first graders	English for English-speaking first graders	Social Studies/Science/Art for all second graders
11:35-11:40	Preparation for Lunch	Preparation for Lunch	----
11:40-12:20	Lunch	Lunch	----
12:20- 1:00	Spanish for English-speaking second graders	English for Spanish-speaking second graders	Social Studies/Science/Art for all first graders
1:00- 1:30	P.E. (one day of library)	P.E. (one day of library)	----
1:30- 1:45	Preparation and Dismissal of Spanish speakers in early shift	Preparation and Dismissal of Spanish speakers in early shift	Home Visits
1:45- 2:45	Spanish for English-speaking first graders	English for English-speaking second graders	"

*One group of five were taught by the Coordinator in the office. **During the last three months of the school year, the Bilingual Specialist team taught English to Spanish-speaking first graders along with English teacher.

FIGURE 5

SAMPLE DAY IN THE 1970-1971 SCHEDULE FOR THE REDWOOD CITY BILINGUAL EDUCATION PROGRAM KINDERGARTEN

TIME	KINDERGARTEN
8:30-9:00	2 Groups of English for Spanish speakers 2 Groups of Spanish for English speakers
9:00-9:30	2 Groups of Spanish pre-reading for Spanish speakers 2 Groups of English pre-reading for English speakers
9:30-11:00	Work time: art, games, movies, block play, snack, stories, listening to music, play house, etc.
11:00-11:15	2 Groups of Math (taught bilingually)
11:15-11:30	Music: singing, records, rhythm band, etc.

6.1.3.2 *The Instructional Staff: Year #3*

The kindergarten, first, and second grade teachers for the 1971-1972 year were the same as for the previous year. The teacher aides for the first and second grades were also the same. A new aide for kindergarten had to be selected. For the first half year she was a Bolivian woman who had been a certificated teacher in her country, and for the second half year a Mexican American woman with only five years of formal schooling. The new third grade teacher was a Mexican American male in his fifties from New Mexico. He had had over 15 years of teaching experience at the upper elementary level. A Salvadorian woman in her thirties was hired as his teacher aide. (See Figure 1 for Staffing Chart.)

The Coordinator taught math to one group of first graders every morning, and on Tuesdays the Evaluator taught music to kindergarten, first, and third graders, and soccer to third graders. The Curriculum Writer taught English language arts to kindergarteners each morning for the entire year and Spanish to Spanish-speaking third graders every afternoon for part of the year.

Over the three years of hiring teachers for the Project, only one had been a classroom teacher for the Redwood City Schools previous to her assignment as a teacher in the Bilingual Project. All the other teachers were brought in from outside the district. Although this is to be expected when hiring for such a specialized program, the policy meant that some teachers were forced out of their posts and sent elsewhere, since school enrollments were not going up (if anything, they were going down).

6.1.3.3   *The Children: Year #3*

During the third year of the Project, the Pilot group moved onto third grade, the Follow Up I group to second grade, and the Follow Up II group to first grade. Another kindergarten group was added to the Project, but was not included in the two-year longitudinal study since the study had already be in progress for one year.

6.1.3.4   *Facilities: Year #3*

During the third year, the Bilingual Project finally obtained classroom space in the main school compound. Actually, the Garfield School stopped renting the church classrooms altogether. The Bilingual grades 1-3 were assigned three regular-sized classrooms in the front of the school. The kindergarten classroom remained where it had been, now several classrooms away. The 1-3 grade teachers were overwhelmed by all the space they had to work with. For instance, it was now possible to split the class up into small groups sufficiently far enough apart so that they didn't disturb each other. However, there was no longer an "extra" classroom. During the first year grade 1 had two rooms, during the second year grades 1 and 2 had three rooms, but in the third year grades 1-3 still had three rooms. This meant that teachers for the first time had to operate within self-contained classrooms, although team teaching still went on (see "Scheduling: Year #3," below). The Bilingual staff was given office space on the second floor of the main building over the school office.

6.1.3.5   *Model(s) of Bilingual Schooling in Use: Year #3*

The third year of the Project saw the introduction of a full bilingualism model to replace that of partial bilingualism. As Fishman and Lovas (1970) define it, in a full bilingualism program "students are to develop all skills in both languages in all domains. Typically, both languages are used as media of instruction for all subjects (except in teaching the languages themselves)" (p. 219). What this meant for the Redwood City case was that now math, social studies, science, and all other subjects except language were to be taught in Spanish and English to all Project students grades 1-3. According to Fishman and Lovas, one of the fears of full bilingualism programs is that they often lead to "significant social separation for their maintenance." This was not the case in Redwood City because the classrooms were integrated with twenty Mexican Americans and ten Anglos, and the ability groups were integrated for most subjects. At the third-grade level, Chicano and Anglo students even began to be placed in the same skill groups for English language arts.

The practical scheme for implementing a full bilingualism model involved the use of alternate days bilingual education. The alternate days approach to bilingual schooling calls for the teaching of the subject matter, say, math, in Spanish on Monday, in English on Tuesday, in Spanish on Wednesday and so forth, thus alternating days that instruction is in the student's vernacular (see Tucker, Otanes, and Sibayan, 1970). This alternate days model is not like the morning-afternoon approach where the same content is repeated in the other language. With alternate days bilingual education, each lesson introduced new content. A further innovation introduced along with alternate days bilingual education was the Preview-Review technique (see Krear, 1971a). The lesson was previewed in one language, presented in the other, and then reviewed in the first. This way, although the lesson was presented in only one language on a given day, no student lost out in concept acquisition as a result of limited second-language skills.

The teachers in grades 1-3 chose the alternate days approach over simultaneous translation and other methods. They felt that simultaneous translation meant that they were constantly switching gears linguistically, which interfered with the instructional process. For instance, teachers would sometimes say things that were idiomatically incorrect in their native language because they were translating directly from their second language. Yet the lack of adequate materials in Spanish meant that teachers were often without the terminology in Spanish for teaching math, science, and social studies lessons, particularly at the third-grade level where concepts were already somewhat sophisticated (see 6.1.3.7, "Instructional Materials: Year #3).

The parents of children in the Project were consulted before going to alternate days bilingual education. The Project staff feared that particularly the Anglo parents might object to such an approach because it would put their children at a linguistic disadvantage during lessons conducted in Spanish. The Mexican American students were more balanced in Spanish and English than were the Anglos. The sampling of Anglo parents who were consulted, however, felt that the new approach would help their children learn even more Spanish, so they were in favor of it. Such a model may not have been feasible during the first year or so of the Project because at that time some parents weren't convinced that bilingual schooling would be an asset rather than a detriment. By the third year, the parents were generally quite positive about such schooling.

At the same time that the alternate days approach was being tried out, teachers were also individualizing their instruction according to guidelines specified in teacher training workshops (see 6.1.3.8, "In-service Teacher Training: Year #3"). In all subjects, children were grouped by ability, with frequent integration of Anglo and Chicano children within the same groups, particularly at the third-grade level. Especially in math, it was difficult to speak of *a* lesson to preview and review on a given day because each ability group was working on different concepts. Also, at the first-grade level the Coordinator, teacher aide, and teacher all worked with different groups and had their own patterns for use of Spanish and English. Thus, only in the larger-group activities, as found in social studies and science lessons, was the alternate days approach readily visible to an outside observer (of which there were many). Third-grade math began to be taught increasingly in English only, except to the several students who were recent immigrants from Mexico. Thus, the model in use fluctuated between full and partial bilingualism, depending on the grade level. Also, for some lessons teachers reported that they used simultaneous translation, rather than the alternate days approach, such as when they wanted to teach the same content in both languages. Thus, the model also fluctuated between one of alternate days and simultaneous translation.

Part of the purpose of alternate days bilingual education was to expose the Anglos to more Spanish language and encourage them to use it as a vehicle for learning subject matter. When simultaneous translation was used, the Anglo children didn't have to pay close attention to the content as it was presented in Spanish, because they knew the same content would be repeated immediately in English.

Generally, the alternate days approach to bilingual education worked most smoothly for the Follow Up II group at the first-grade level, since those students had received bilingual schooling during kindergarten the previous year. The Pilot and Follow Up I groups had had all their reading and math readiness in English, and not in Spanish. It appears that the kindergarten year is a very important one for language adjustment, particularly in the case of Anglos being exposed to Spanish for the first time.

6.1.3.6 Scheduling: Year #3

During the 1971-1972 year, team teaching of language continued. In the second-grade room, the Spanish language teacher from the previous year still continued to teach Spanish language arts to Spanish speakers, but only to the first graders. He also taught Spanish language arts to first-through-third-grade Anglos (see Figure 6). Second- and third-grade Anglos were taught Spanish language arts during the same period, putting the second graders at a disadvantage in terms of background and slowing down the third graders in terms of their possible progress. The reasons for this merger were (1) where there were constraints on time, the Mexican American students—the target group for the study and the larger group numerically—were afforded more teacher time, and (2) such a set up would hopefully encourage the older students to "tutor" the younger ones. The third-grade Anglos were also expected to pass along their commitment to Spanish to the second graders. Second- and third-grade Spanish speakers were taught Spanish by the third-grade teacher.

The English language teacher from the previous year taught English language arts to first-, second-, and the late shift of third-grade Spanish speakers. She also taught English language arts to English-speaking first and second graders. The kindergarten teacher taught English language arts to Spanish-speaking second graders and to third graders in the late shift.

Unlike in previous years, however, each teacher taught the content subjects —math, social studies, and science—to his own grade level in his own classroom. As can be seen from the schedule (Figure 6), roughly half the instruction in grades 1-3 was conducted in Spanish and half in English for both Mexican American and Anglo students.

6.1.3.7 *Instructional Materials: Year #3*

The third year marked a major supplement to materials for teaching English language arts. McGraw-Hill *Sullivan Readers* were purchased for use with grades 1-3. This is a programmed reading series using phonically-regular words in beginning reading. This approach to reading, sometimes referred to as the "linguistic approach," only introduces words in which there is a one-to-one correspondence between phonemes (sounds) and graphemes (the letters representing the sounds in the orthography). The series begins with a limited number of basic consonants like *b, t, r, c,* and *p,* and the short vowels *a, e, i, o,* and *u.* Students fill in blanks and proceed at their own rate. The correct answers are found in the margin and the student is to use these answers as feedback to determine whether he has done the reading-writing exercises correctly.

The other major acquisitions were for third-grade instruction. More advanced Laidlaw readers were purchased for use in third-grade Spanish language arts for Spanish speakers. More advanced readers from the González-Pita Company were also purchased. English for all third graders involved the use of the State readers as well as the Sullivan readers (see Appendix #2). For math and science, the State series were used. As had been true for first- and second-grade instruction, there were no Spanish versions of the State series or companion volumes in Spanish. This lack tended to discourage the teachers from using Spanish. Even though two of the teachers were Mexican Americans, they had received their education and professional training in English and had had all their experience teaching in English. Thus, without the aid of appropriate materials in Spanish, they were at a disadvantage when it came to teaching the content subjects in Spanish. Gaarder (1971) found this weakness to be common in Title VII programs across the nation.

As if in recognition of the special knowledge and expertise of the bilingually schooled students in Mexican culture, the Bilingual Project took full charge of the *Cinco de Mayo* (5th of May) assembly at the Garfield School, commemorating the Mexican victory against the French in Puebla in 1862. The students in grades 1-3 in the Bilingual Project presented Mexican songs and dances. This was the first time that the Project had had complete responsibility for an assembly.

FIGURE 6

SAMPLE DAY IN THE 1971-1972 SCHEDULE FOR THE REDWOOD CITY BILINGUAL EDUCATION PROJECT GRADES 1, 2, AND 3

TIME	1ST GRADE ROOM	2ND GRADE ROOM	3RD GRADE ROOM
8:30- 9:30	English for Spanish-speaking second graders in the early shift/English for English-speaking second graders	Spanish for Spanish-speaking first graders	English for Spanish-speaking third graders in early shift/English for English-speaking third graders
9:30- 9:40	Recess	Recess	Recess
9:40-10:40	2 groups of Math for first graders/1 group of English language arts for Spanish-speaking and English-speaking first graders	Social Studies/Science for second graders	Social Studies/Science for third graders (until 10:25) Math for third graders
10:40-10:50	Recess	Recess	Recess
10:50-11:20	2 groups of English language arts for Spanish- and English-speaking first graders/1 group of Math for first graders/1 group of Oral English for Spanish-speaking first graders	Math for second graders	Math for third graders
11:20-11:45	(Continuation of above until 11:30) Music for first graders	P.E.	P.E.

FIGURE 6 (cont.)

TIME	1ST GRADE ROOM	2ND GRADE ROOM	3RD GRADE ROOM
11:45-12:30	Lunch	Lunch	Lunch
12:30- 1:30	Social Studies/Science (until 1:00) P.E.	Spanish for English-speaking second and third graders	Spanish for Spanish-speaking second and third graders in early shift/English for Spanish-speaking second and third graders in late shift*
1:30- 1:40	Recess	Recess	Recess
1:40- 2:40	English for Spanish-speaking third graders in late shift (until 2:15) Math for Anglo first graders/ English for English-speaking first graders	Spanish for English-speaking first graders	Spanish for Spanish-speaking second graders in late shift (until 2:05) Spanish for Spanish-speaking third graders in late shift

*Taught by kindergarten teacher in kindergarten classroom.

6.1.3.8 *In-service Teacher Training: Year #3*

In the third year, teacher in-service training was the most systematic and had the most far-reaching effects upon the staff of all the in-service training. One phase of the training involved viewing of a film series by the Mexican American Education Research Project of the California State Department of Education, called "Unconscious Culture Clashes," narrated by Leonard Olguín. The series was originally screened on educational TV. The sequences discussed acculturation, customs, the difference between words like "education" in English and *educación* in Spanish, and nonverbal cues.

The second phase of training was a series of eight workshops on group participation skills, including topics such as setting up small groups in the classroom and leadership training (teaching students how to lead small groups), developing good discussion skills in children, planning for activities, and organization of group sessions. The workshops were conducted by the Regional Project Office from San Bernardino, California. Largely as a result of these workshops, the teachers in the Bilingual Project adopted more progressive and innovative educational techniques in the classroom. Although many similar techniques had been used in the classroom prior to the workshops, the workshops provided systematic guidelines for training students in small group participation. The workshops also helped eliminate most vestiges of the lock-step teacher-talk-student-listen approach to schooling. An emphasis was placed on reaching the needs of the individual through small groups.

6.1.4. *Grouping of Students for the Content Subjects*

As part of the study of children's language use, three of the Mexican American research assistants did three sets of observations of eight randomly-selected Chicano pupils in each group—Pilot, Follow Up I, and Follow Up II (see "Instruments and Procedures," Chapter 9). The investigators observed these children on three separate days in February of 1972. While the investigators were observing student language use (the results of which are found in Chapter 9), they were also noting how the pupils were grouped each time that they were observed. Observers indicated whether the student was in a whole-class grouping, a small group, or working individually.

Figure 7 indicates the grouping pattern for each level. It can be seen that at the Pilot level, the students were in whole-class, small-group, and individual activities about the same amount of time for math, and were in whole-class activities more often for social studes and science. At the Follow Up I and Follow Up II levels, the students were observed to be exclusively in small groups for math. For social studies and science, the Follow Up I students were observed in whole-group activity most of the time, while the Follow Up II students were either in whole-group or small-group activity.

FIGURE 7

**CLASSROOM GROUPINGS FOR BILINGUAL
PROJECT BY LEVELS – YEAR #3**

Level	Subject	Grouping Pattern	Raw Frequency	Percent
Pilot	MATH	Whole Class	13	34%
		Small Group	11	29%
		Individual	14	37%
	SOCIAL STUDIES/ SCIENCE	Whole Class	21	49%
		Small Group	10	23%
		Individual	12	28%
Follow Up I	MATH	Whole Class	–	–
		Small Group	24	100%
		Individual	–	–
	SOCIAL STUDIES/ SCIENCE	Whole Class	22	92%
		Small Group	2	8%
		Individual	–	–
Follow Up II	MATH	Whole Class	–	–
		Small Group	24	100%
		Individual	–	–
	SOCIAL STUDIES/ SCIENCE	Whole Class	13	52%
		Small Group	10	44%
		Individual	1	4%

6.1.5 *The Ethnic Backgrounds of the Teachers in the Project over the Three Years*

Having Anglo as well as Mexican American teachers in the Project was seen as a benefit rather than a detriment because Chicano students must function biculturally as well as bilingually. Thus, it was considered important to have teachers representing both the majority and the minority cultures. Relations among teachers in the Project were generally warm and friendly. It has been pointed out repeatedly in the recent literature on bilingual education that the bilingual project teacher is generally sympathetic to the linguistic and cultural needs of the non-English-speaking student. There is an element of natural selection involved with the recruitment of teachers for such projects, particularly with respect to the recruitment of Anglos.

6.6.6 *The Role of the Teacher Aide*

The Bilingual Teacher Aide in the Redwood City Project assumed a variety of duties, depending on the relative training, experience, and talents of the aide. Some aides had far more training than others. Two had been teachers in Latin America. Others had had several years of college. Others had had little formal schooling.

The aide's duties depended largely on the teacher's attitudes about the proper role for the aide. One teacher afforded the aide extensive freedom in the classroom. The aide was given total responsibility for instructing her assigned small groups of children in the content subjects. Other teachers afforded their aides some freedom in instruction, but kept them under close supervision. Other teachers refrained from having their aides do any teaching, or restricted them to certain subjects. Aides also performed certain clerical activities, such as preparing classroom instructional materials, correcting work assignments, and scoring tests.

6.1.7 *The Language Used by the Instructional Staff in the Bilingual Program Over the Three Years*

Of the Mexican Americans on the instructional staff, one teacher and one aide had learned their Spanish in San Francisco. Another teacher had learned Spanish in New Mexico. One aide had learned Spanish in Texas, and another had learned Spanish in Mexico. A teacher whose mother was Mexican had learned Spanish in Texas. Three aides had learned their Spanish in each of three Latin American countries, Costa Rica, El Salvador, and Bolivia, respectively. Of the Anglos on the instructional staff, one had learned Spanish in San Diego and the other had learned it while living in Ecuador and Colombia for several years. The Coordinator was a Mexican American from New

Mexico. The Curriculum Writer had a Mexican mother, and had grown up in Argentina. The Evaluator had learned Spanish during Peace Corps training in Puerto Rico and had been in the Peace Corps in Bolivia for two years.

Although they were from disparate Spanish language backgrounds, the staff members agreed to emphasize the variety of Spanish spoken for the most part by the children's parents. Since most of the families with children in the Redwood City primary schools had come from Mexico within the previous ten years, the Spanish spoken in the home was a direct reflection of usage in the Mexican states around Mexico City, where they came from—notably the states of Jalisco, Michoacan and Zacatecas. Henríquez Ureña (1935) referred to this Spanish as central standard (Mexican Spanish). Since the children spoke both standard and nonstandard varieties of Spanish in the classroom, the teachers tried to distinguish between standard and nonstandard forms and suggest when each form was appropriate for use. Since the Spanish readers used in the Project had vocabulary from standard Puerto Rican Spanish, it was also necessary to point out how these forms differed from Mexican Spanish.

Frequently, Mexican American students were used as resource people in questions about Spanish vocabulary. Since the Mexican American and Anglo teachers had spent the major part of their lives in the United States, they were not altogether familiar with the current Mexican lexicon and expressions. After class, students also helped make language-master cards for vocabulary practice. These cards consisted of a picture of an object with a tape on the back. When the card was passed through a special machine, the word for that object would be heard from the tape.

All the teachers spoke a variety of standard English, usually Southwest standard. In general, they used a formal register of English in the classroom. The teacher aides varied in their English proficiency. The aides from Mexico and Bolivia spoke limited English. The aides from Costa Rica and El Salvador spoke heavily-accented English, but with moderate fluency. The Mexican American aide from San Francisco spoke standard English and the Mexican aide from Texas spoke several varieties of English in the classroom, including standard English, a variety of Chicano English (with interference from Spanish in pronunciation and intonation), and Tex-Mex (a mixture of Spanish and English—usually marked by switching in mid-sentence from one language to the other).

As mentioned above, three research assistants did three sets of observations of eight randomly-selected Chicano pupils in each group—Pilot, Follow Up I, and Follow Up II (see "Instruments and Procedures", Chapter 9). While the investigators were observing student language use, they were also indicating what language the instructor—teacher, aide, or other—addressed them in, if the students were addressed by an adult during the one-minute observations.

Figure 8 shows the raw frequencies and percentages of time that Spanish and

English were observed being used in math and in social studies or science, by group level. First, adults were observed to talk to students most in the Follow Up I class and least in the Pilot Class. The frequencies of language use show that adults were observed to use more Spanish than English with the Follow Up I group and more English than Spanish with the other two groups. The adults working with the Pilot group were observed to use the least amount of Spanish altogether—none in social studies and science, and only 31% of the time in math.

The observers commented that in social studies at the Follow Up II level, the teacher often said a sentence in Spanish and then repeated it in English. At the Pilot level, the teacher would start a phrase in Spanish and finish it off in English. Also, on a Spanish language day for a content subject, the Pilot teacher would still use mostly English, at least during the times that the investigator was in the class.

6.2   Comparison School

6.2.1   The Non-Instructional Staff

In the first year of the study (1970-1971), the principal at the Hoover Elementary School, the Comparison school, was an Anglo woman. She was very sympathetic with the aims of the research and was most cooperative. The second year of the study, the principal was a male Guatemalan American. He was less sympathetic with the idea of having his school used for comparative purposes, but he was equally cooperative in providing rooms for testing and interviewing. The change-over in principals may have marked a change in linguistic and cultural atmosphere at the school. During 1970-1971, there were no Spanish-speaking personnel on the administrative staff of the school, whereas in 1971-1972 the principal was able to converse with the Spanish-speaking pupils and with their parents in Spanish. Also, the presence of a principal of Latin American background brought greater prestige to the heritage of the Mexican American students at the school.

6.2.2   The Instructional Staff

The teachers involved with the Comparison group were kindergarten-through-second-grade teachers in 1970-1971, and kindergarten-through-third-grade teachers in 1971-1972. There were two Anglo female kindergarten teachers for the Follow Up II Comparison the first year, and one of them taught a retainee the second year. In the first year, there were three Anglo female first-grade teachers involved, and in the second year one of these left and was replaced by a new Anglo female. Two Anglo females taught the second graders the first year and continued to teach second grade the following year. Two third-grade Anglo teachers, a male and a female, taught the Pilot Comparison students during the

FIGURE 8

ADULT LANGUAGE USE IN BILINGUAL
PROJECT BY LEVELS – YEAR #3

Level	Subject	Language	Raw Frequency	Percent
Pilot	MATH	Spanish	4	31%
		English	9	69%
	SOCIAL STUDIES/ SCIENCE	Spanish	–	–
		English	11	100%
Follow Up I	MATH	Spanish	12	50%
		English	12	50%
	SOCIAL STUDIES/ SCIENCE	Spanish	15	62%
		English	9	38%
Follow Up II	MATH	Spanish	4	25%
		English	12	75%
	SOCIAL STUDIES/ SCIENCE	Spanish	7	39%
		English	11	61%

1971-1972 school year. There were a number of teachers involved at the Comparison school because the low percentage of Mexican Americans in each class (35% to 50%) necessitated going to several classrooms to obtain a full comparison group. The percent of Mexican Americans was similar at the Bilingual school, but a 67% Chicano-33% Anglo classroom ratio had been contrived for the purposes of the Project.

The same language use observations conducted at the Bilingual Projects were conducted at the Comparison school. Investigators looked for the extent to which the teachers used Spanish in their classrooms in February of 1972. The male third-grade teacher knew numbers in Spanish and occasionally used them in math games, but that was the extent of his Spanish. One of the first-grade teachers had a Venezuelan mother, but apparently had not learned very much Spanish. She was not observed to use any Spanish in class. Another first-grade teacher was observed at least three times reprimanding children for speaking Spanish in class. She would say, "Now, this isn't Spanish class. You're not supposed to speak Spanish." However, she was also observed to use Spanish once in referring to the numbers *two* and *three* when speaking to a new boy who did not speak English. In such a situation, she would also use one of her bilingual students as an interpreter—in that instance, letting both boys speak Spanish in class.

None of the classes were observed to have teacher aides, although one third-grade class received occasional help during reading classes from three sixth-grade girls. The school had an English-as-a-second-language (ESL) teacher during the 1971-1972 school year, and an ESEA Title I instructor both years of the study. The ESL teacher worked specifically with those children whose English language proficiency was slight. The Title I instructor and his two teacher aides worked with students who already had a working knowledge of English but who were behind in their studies. Many of these were the Spanish speakers. With the absence of an ESL teacher during the 1970-1971 year, the Title I instructors also taught beginning English. Title I was part of the same federal program that funded the Title VII Bilingual Education Program. Title I had four components: special help in language and the content subjects, counseling, in-service teacher training, and parent involvement. The program was particularly intended for schools with a high proportion of students from low-income homes.

Figure 9 shows the number of Comparison students by group level who were either receiving special help from the ESL teacher or from the Title I instructor. In one or two cases, Comparison children were tutored individually by Stanford University students. Children receiving individual tutoring were also included in the totals in Figure 9. It is important to point out the extra adult assistance that the Comparison students received. Otherwise the reader might think that outcomes attributed to bilingual schooling were more a function of the number of adults attending to the children than the result of the bilingual treatment.

6.2.3 The Children

During the 1969-1970 school year a Pilot Comparison group of 17 Mexican Americans and 10 Anglos was established. Five of the Anglos moved away that year and subsequently the decision was made to eliminate the Anglo Comparison group. Of the 17 in the Mexican American group, four moved away, seven were retained in first grade, and six were promoted to second grade. Those thirteen remaining at the school were included among the Comparison students selected in the fall of 1970, but they were grouped according to where they were at the start of the 1970-1971 year, not according to where they were at the start of the 1969 year (see "Sample." 5.2.3).

6.2.4 Instructional Materials

Teachers in the Comparison classes relied mostly on the State-adopted series for reading and for math. The teachers used the Harper-Row and Ginn readers, which combine the phonic and look-say approaches to reading and generally fall into the category of what are called basal readers. The teachers also used the State-adopted *Modern School Mathematics* series (for complete listings on the State adoptions, see Appendix 2). One third-grade teacher used the Greater Cleveland Math Program in his math classes.

FIGURE 9

COMPARISON STUDENTS RECEIVING SPECIAL
ASSISTANCE THROUGH ESL, TITLE I, OR TUTORING
BY GROUP LEVEL, 1970-1972

	Pilot Comparison	Follow Up I Comparison	Follow Up II Comparison	All Group Levels Combined
ESL*	1	–	7	8
Title I	7	4	–	11
Tutoring	–	1	1	2
Total Receiving Assistance	8	5	8	21
Total in Group	14	15	16	45

*English as a Second Language

6.2.5 *Grouping of Students*

While observing student language use in the classroom, the research assistants also obtained data on the grouping patterns of the Comparison teachers. Figure 10 shows the frequency of whole-class, small-group, and individual groupings for math and for social studes/science at the Pilot, Follow Up I and Follow Up II levels. The frequency of grouping at a particular level is averaged over several classrooms since Comparison students were located in different rooms. Generally, teachers were observed to use whole-class instruction both for math and for social studies/science. The one exception was in the case of Follow Up I Comparison students. The two second-grade teachers were observed to have students work individually on math. The two whole-class and one small-group observation (see Figure 10) were recorded while observing a student who, although assigned to the Follow Up I group, had been retained in first grade.

The data on the Comparison classrooms indicate differences in the grouping of students for the content subjects between the Bilingual and the Comparison groups (compare Figure 7 with Figure 10). The Bilingual teachers were observed to introduce more small groupings and individual activities into their classrooms than were found in the Comparison classrooms. As mentioned under "In-service Teacher Training: Year #3" (6.1.3.8, above), a conscious effort was made at the Bilingual Project to get away from what was considered the more traditional teaching pattern—namely, whole-class instruction.

6.3 *SUMMARY*

6.3.1 As illustrated throughout the chapter, the treatment for the Bilingual group varied not only from year to year but also from group level to group level. Such variation is not surprising when it is remembered that from the very start of the ESEA Title VII Programs, it was understood that the first three-to-five years would be spent developing the program. The federal funds were viewed as "seed money" to help in developing programs that would then be expanded by the local school district.

6.3.2 The Bilingual Project's personnel, students, facilities, scheduling, and in-structional materials changed as the program expanded vertically. In-service teacher training took on new directions, particularly in the third year of the program. The model for bilingual schooling shifted notably from one of partial bilingualism to one of full bilingualism, a clear indication of the developmental nature of the program.

6.3.3 The ethnic and linguistic backgrounds of the Bilingual Project's teachers and aides were markedly diverse, providing the students with exposure to a number of different varieties of Spanish and English.

FIGURE 10

**CLASSROOM GROUPINGS FOR COMPARISON
STUDENTS BY LEVELS – YEAR #3**

Level	Subject	Grouping Pattern	Raw Frequency	Percent
Pilot	MATH	Whole Class	17	66%
		Small Group	5	19%
		Individual	4	15%
	SOCIAL STUDIES/ SCIENCE	Whole Class	2	8%
		Small Group	1	4%
		Individual	21	88%
Follow Up I	MATH	Whole Class	2	8%
		Small Group	1	4%
		Individual	21	88%
	SOCIAL STUDIES/ SCIENCE	Whole Class	18	75%
		Small Group	–	–
		Individual	6	25%
Follow Up II	MATH	Whole Class	20	83%
		Small Group	4	17%
		Individual	–	–
	SOCIAL STUDIES/ SCIENCE	Whole Class	19	79%
		Small Group	5	21%
		Individual	–	–

6.3.4 The Comparison group received conventional English-only instruction. However, almost half of these students also received special attention through ESL or Title I classes, or through individual tutorials. It was observed that the Bilingual students were instructed less as an entire class, and more extensively in small groups or individually, then were the Comparison students.

Now that the Bilingual and Comparison students' school program has been discussed, the reader will be better able to understand the outcomes of the research as reported in Chapters 7 through 11. The next chapter deals with the assessment of Spanish and English language proficiency, and includes measurement of the students' listening, speaking, reading, and writing skills in both languages.

7. SPANISH AND ENGLISH LANGUAGE PROFICIENCY

Are Mexican American children who are taught the academic curriculum in Spanish and English for several years as proficient in English language skills as Mexican American children taught only in English? Are they more proficient in Spanish language skills? These were two of the research questions posed in Chapter 5. This chapter provides answers to these questions, based on the results of research in Redwood City.

A key concern in evaluating the progress of students in a bilingual project, compared with those in conventional schooling, is to assess language proficiency in the students' two languages, both prior to the treatment and after a period of time. In Chapter 1, a three-dimensional model for assessing proficiency in a language variety was presented. The model identified five different elements in each of the four language skills—speaking and writing (the productive skills) and listening and reading (the receptive skills). Four of the elements, namely semantics, syntax, morphemes, and lexicon apply to all four language skills. The fifth element of concern was "phonemes" in the case of listening and speaking and "graphemes" for reading and writing. Language proficiency instruments selected for use with the Redwood City study were meant to assess language ability for all 40 cubes of the model (see Figure 1, Chapter 1). Although the instruments actually used did not achieve so thorough a measurement of proficiency, an attempt was made to obtain as comprehensive an estimate as possible of language proficiency before and after bilingual schooling. All four language skills were tapped, but all of the above-mentioned elements were not covered for each skill.

7.1   *Instruments and Procedures*

7.1.1   *Student's Spanish Language Proficiency*

7.1.1.1   *Listening Skill in Spanish*

With the permission of the Guidance Testing Associates, various items from the *Comprensión Oral, Serie Interamericano* test and the *Prueba de Lectura, Serie Interamericano (Niveles 1-3)* were combined into a single test of Spanish oral comprehension. The Experimental Test of Spanish Oral Comprehension consisted of 45 items which the examiner presented orally and which the students responded to by putting an "X" on or below the picture that was suggested by the oral statement. For example, the examiner said, "¿Cuál gatito está siguiendo a su mamá? Crucen el gatito que está siguiendo a su mamá." ("Which kitten is following its mother? Put an X on the cat that is following its mother.") Then there were four pictures: one of a cat sitting with two kittens near her, one of a kitten following a cat, one of a cat playing with a ball, and one of a boy holding a cat (see Appendix 1.1, for a sample item).

The last three sets of items in the test (10 items in all) were based on each of three stories. The child heard the story twice and then responded to a series of comprehension questions.

7.1.1.2   *Speaking Skill in Spanish*

Two performance measures were used to assess speaking ability—one a test of vocabulary production and the other a test of storytelling ability. Word Naming by Domain, the test of vocabulary production, was based on an instrument developed by Fishman, Cooper, Ma *et al.* (1971), and measured a student's ability to name objects commonly found in settings associated with the domains of home, education, religion, and neighborhood. The settings were the kitchen, the school, the street, and the church. The child was given 45 seconds to name as many Spanish words as he could for objects found in each setting. A sample request was as follows: "¿Cuántas cosas puedes nombrar que se halla en la cocina, como cuchara, sal, arroz?" ("How many things can you name that are found in the kitchen, like spoon, salt, rice?") (see Appendix 1.2).

The Storytelling Task was based on the John T. Dailey Language Facility Test (Dailey, 1968), but the method of presentation and the scoring were altered (see Appendix 1.3). The Dailey Test elicits a series of oral stories based on three pictures—a snapshot, a painting, and a drawing. The snapshot was of an Anglo woman (probably a teacher) outside a white house with Chicano, Black, and Anglo children clustered around her. The painting was "The Holy Family of the Little Bird" by Murillo, and shows a bearded man holding a little child, while a woman and a dog look on. The sketch was of a boy pointing at a cat in a tree.

After the child heard the examiner tell a story based on a sample picture, the child was asked to tell stories in Spanish about the three pictures. The three stories were taped and then rated as a single unit by linguistically trained judges, using a 5-point rating scale adapted from Lambert, Tucker, d'Anglejan, and Segalowitz (1970). The categories included general fluency, grammar, pronunciation, intonation, language alternation, and descriptive ability. The last two categories were added by this researcher, the first to assess the effect of Spanish and English being in contact in the community, and the second to get at cognitive development through storytelling.

The Storytelling Task was administered a second time to a random subsample in posttesting, using three photo cards from *Words and Action* (Shaftel and Shaftel, 1967). The three photos used represented the domains of home, neighborhood, and education, with kitchen, street, and classroom respectively as settings. For this measure, range of vocabulary for each photo was calculated, to obtain a rating of speaking proficiency by domain (see Appendix 1.3 for the details).

7.1.1.3 *Reading Skill in Spanish*

Prueba de Lectura, Serie Interamericana, developed by the Guidance Testing Associates (1967a), includes tests at five levels of difficulty, covering grades 1 through 12. The Level 1 and Level 2 tests were used in this study. The Level 1 test consists of subtests of vocabulary and comprehension. In each exercise, the child chooses a picture which is suggested by a word, a phrase, a sentence, or a paragraph. The Level 2 test has subtests of level of comprehension, speed of comprehension and vocabulary (see Appendix 1.4).

7.1.1.4 *Writing Skill in Spanish*

The Spanish Writing Sample asked students to write a story in Spanish as suggested by a sequence of twelve pictures. The picture sequence technique was based on the work of Petersen, Chuck, and Coladarci (1969). The compositions were scored along seven dimensions, according to a rating scheme adapted from Lewis and Lewis (1965). The scales included: verbal output, range of vocabulary, diversity of vocabulary, accuracy of spelling, grammatical correctness, quality of sentence structure, and effectiveness of expression (see Appendix 1.5).

7.1.1.5 *Parent Rating of Students' Listening, Speaking, Reading, and Writing Skill in Spanish*

As part of a Home Interview Questionnaire, parents were asked to assess the Spanish language skills of their children who were in the Bilingual or Comparison groups. These questions were taken from a language census developed by Fishman, Cooper, Ma *et al.* (1971). The parents were asked whether the child could understand a conversation in Spanish, participate in one, read a newspaper in Spanish, and write a letter in Spanish. Response choices were "yes," "a little," and "no." These four items were combined as an index of student Spanish language proficiency.

As part of the after-measure, parents were also asked whether they had noted a change in the student's ability to speak Spanish with them over the two years of the study. The parents indicated whether their child's Spanish had improved, had stayed the same, or whether he was losing his ability to speak Spanish (see Appendix 1.10).

7.1.2 *Students' English Language Proficiency*

7.1.2.1 *Listening Skill in English*

Listening skill in English was assessed using the Experimental Test of English Oral Comprehension, a parallel test to the Test of Spanish Oral Comprehension (see 7.1.1.1, above). The items were all taken from the Inter-American Oral Comprehension Test and Reading Tests. The examiner presented 45 items orally, and the student had to put an "X" on the one of four pictures which he felt was referred to by the stimulus item. The last three sets of items were based on each of three stories. The child heard the story twice and then had to respond to a series of comprehension questions.

The Experimental Oral Comprehension Test was administered on a pilot basis to a group of non-project Mexican Americans informally, just to make sure that the items and the art work (which was done by a Mexican American college student) were unambiguous. The Pilot Mexican Americans did not receive the posttest, because they had achieved high scores when tested in March of 1971.

The Oral Comprehension Tests were given on a group basis in English first and then in Spanish two to three weeks later. There was only one form of the test (see Figure 1 for Instrument Administration Schedule). Whereas it would have been desirable to divide the class in half and give half the Spanish version first and the other half the English version first, this was not possible because of constraints on space for testing at the Comparison school and because of financial considerations. The English version was used first in order to let the practice effect of having taken the test once work to the benefit of the Spanish version. Whereas many students, particularly the youngest, were Spanish dominant, English was the language expected at school and the idea of Spanish-language tests took a little getting used to, particularly at the Comparison school.

7.1.2.2 *Speaking Skill in English*

The same Word Naming by Domain measure of vocabulary production and the Storytelling Task that were used to measure Spanish speaking skills were also

FIGURE 1

SCHEDULE FOR ADMINISTRATION OF LANGUAGE PROFICIENCY INSTRUMENTS

	Group Levels	Month/Year	Test Form	Group Levels	Month/Year	Test Form
Spanish Language Skills: Experimental Spanish Oral Comprehension	(P) (FUI)	3/71		(FUI) (FUII)	5/72	
Spanish Word Naming by Doman	All Group Levels	10/70-11/70		All Group Levels	4/72	
Spanish Storytelling Task	All Group Levels	9/70-10/70		All Group Levels	4/72-5/72	
Prueba de Lectura, Serie Interamericana	(P) – (1)	5/71	L-1-CES	All	5/72	L-2-CES (P) L-1-CES (FUI) (FUII)
Spanish Writing Sample				(P)	5/72	
English Language Skills: Experimental English Oral Comprehension	(P) (FUI)	2/71		(FUI) (FUII)	5/72	
English Word Naming by Domain	All Group Levels	10/70-11/70		All Group Levels	4/72	
English Storytelling Task	All Group Levels	9/70-10/70		All Group Levels	4/72-5/72	

(continued on following page)

FIGURE 1 (cont.)

	Group Levels	Month/Year	Test Form	Group Levels	Month/Year	Test Form
Murphy-Durrell Reading Readiness Analysis	(FUI) (FUII)	10/70 10/71				
Inter-American Reading Test	(P) (FUI)	5/71	R-1-DE	All	5/72	R-1-DE (FUI) (FUII) R-2-DE (P)
Cooperative Primary Reading Test	(P) (FUI)	5/71	23A 12A	(P, FUI) (FUII)	5/72	23A 12A
English Writing Sample				(P)	5/72	
Student Spanish and English Language Proficiency—Parent Report	Parents All Group Levels	12/70-1/71 (Several families 2/71-3/71)		Parents All Group Levels	5/72-6/72	

GROUPS: Mexican American Bilingual (1)
          Mexican American Comparison (2)

GROUP LEVELS: Pilot (P)
                Follow Up I (FUI)
                Follow Up II (FUII)

used to assess English speaking skill. The students were asked to name, in English, objects commonly found in settings associated with the domains of home, education, religion, and neighborhood. The settings were the kitchen, the school, the street, and the church. The child was given 45 seconds to name as many English words as he could for objects located in each setting. A sample request was as follows: "How many things can you name that are found in the kitchen like spoon, salt, rice?"

The Word Naming by Domain instrument was administered on an individual basis. In pretesting, it was given in the same sitting with the Pupil's Language Use Inventory, and in the posttesting, the Storytelling Task using the Dailey pictures was administered along with the other two instruments. The order of the language that words were named in and the order of the domain for vocabulary were randomized.

In the Storytelling Task, the students were asked to tell stories in English about three pictures—a snapshot, a painting, and a sketch (Dailey, 1968). The stories were taped and then rated by a linguistically-trained judge on a five-point scale for fluency, grammar, pronunciation, language alternation, and descriptive ability. In posttesting, a subsample of students were asked to tell stories about three photo cards from *Words and Action* (Shaftel and Shaftel, 1967). These stories were rated as above, with the addition of a category for range of vocabulary by domain (see 7.1.1.2, above).

The Storytelling Task was piloted in the spring of 1970, when it was used for the purpose of recruiting Mexican American and Anglo students into the Bilingual first grade for the following year (what became the Follow Up I group). In pretesting, the Storytelling Task was administered in a separate sitting, using the Dailey pictures. As mentioned above, this task was combined with other tasks in posttesting (Word Naming by Domain and Pupil's Language Use Inventory), so that children were not removed from the classroom for individual testing more than once. The child was administered the version of the instrument which used the Dailey pictures at school and by two different testers, one giving the test in English and one giving it in Spanish, using the same set of pictures and presenting them in the same order: snapshot, painting, and sketch. Whether the child received the task in Spanish or in English first was randomly determined.

In the posttesting with the *Words and Action* photo cards, using a random subsample of children (roughly five from the Bilingual and five from the Comparison groups at each level), the tester went into the home. This time the *same* tester gave the instrument in both languages, randomizing the first language used in storytelling and the order that the three photo cards—a school scene, a street scene, and a home scene—were presented. *Two* testers were used in pretesting because it was thought that children with limited English might be reluctant to tell stories in English if they knew the tester spoke Spanish. By the time of the posttesting, all students had some English speaking ability and were less likely to refuse to speak English.

7.1.2.3 *Reading Skill in English*

The Murphy-Durrell Reading Readiness Analysis (Murphy and Durrell, 1965) is a readiness test for pre-readers and for children in the early stages of reading. It has subtests on phonemes, letter names, and learning rate. The Phonemes test provides an inventory of the child's ability in identifying sounds in spoken words. There are 24 items, in each of which pupils are to mark two pictures which represent words which start or end with a sound dictated by the teacher. The Letter Names test includes 52 items which measure the ability to identify capital and lower-case letters named by the teacher. The Learning Rate test measures the number of words a child can recognize one hour after a formal instructional presentation. This test contains 18 items.

The Murphy-Durrell Reading Readiness Analysis was uniformly administered to all Follow Up I and II Bilingual and Comparison students. The Pilot Bilingual and Comparison groups had taken different reading readiness tests at their school in 1969 (the Harper-Row and the Ginn, respectively), and the results of the two tests were not comparable.

The Inter-American Tests of Reading, Levels 1 and 2 of the English version, were also administered to Project participants and to the Comparison students. The Level 1 test consists of subtests of vocabulary and comprehension. The Level 2 test has subtests of level of comprehension, speed of comprehension, and vocabulary. In both tests, the child chooses a picture which is suggested by a work, a phrase, a sentence, or a paragraph. The items in the test include both phonically regular and irregular words. The English Tests of Reading parallel the Spanish Tests mentioned above, but at any given administration of both tests, alternate forms were given so that the students did not receive the same items to read in both languages (see Figure 1).

The *Prueba de Lectura, Serie Interamericana,* was given as a pretest only to the Pilot Mexican American and Anglos at the Bilingual Project. In posttesting, this test of Spanish reading was given to all Project participants and Comparison students. In pretesting, the test was not given to the Comparison group because it was thought that they would be at a disadvantage, having not been instructed in Spanish reading. However, it was ultimately decided not to underestimate this ability both because some of these students had been taught to read in Spanish by their parents, and because the close fit between the sounds of Spanish and the orthography heightened the possibility of transfer of reading skills from English to Spanish. Different forms of the English and Spanish versions of the Inter-American Reading Tests were administered on a pre- and posttest basis, and as Figure 1 indicates, the Pilot group was administered the Level 1 test in pretesting (R-1-DE), even though Guidance Testing Associates recommend that the Level 2 test be given to beginning second graders. The procedure followed in this study was in recognition of the fact that Mexican American students in the Bilingual Project were learning how to read in Spanish first, and so would be expected to lag somewhat in their English reading. The Mexican American Comparison students were also given the Level 1 form.

The Cooperative Primary Tests of Reading, developed by the Educational Testing Service (1967), were mandated by the State of California to be given to all students in grades 1-3. Pupils read various materials—words, sentences, stories, and poems—and answer questions about them. The majority of the responses are words or sentences rather than pictures. The test incorporates several unconventional features: no formal time limits, three-choice items rather than four or five, and interspersing of difficult and easy items throughout the test.

The Cooperative Primary Test of Reading was administered to first through third graders. Results were converted into grade equivalent scores (1.2, 2.6, 3.4, etc.) so that scores of students at different *grade* levels (i.e., second vs. third), but at the same *group level* (i.e., Pilot), could be compared.

7.1.2.4 *Writing Skill in English*

Like the Spanish Writing Sample, the English Writing Sample asked students to write a story suggested by a sequence of twelve pictures. The compositions were scored along seven dimensions: verbal output, range of vocabulary, diversity of vocabulary, accuracy of spelling, grammatical correctness, quality of sentence structure, and effectiveness of expression.

The Spanish and English Writing Samples were administered only once, in May of 1972, first in English and then in Spanish two weeks later. This instrument was just administered to the Pilot group, because it was felt that younger children would not have had the training necessary for writing a composition.

7.1.2.5 *Parent Rating of Students' Listening, Speaking, Reading, and Writing Skills in English*

As part of a Home Interview Questionnaire, parents were asked to assess the English language skills of their children who were in the Bilingual or Comparison groups. The parents were asked whether their child could understand a conversation in English, participate in one, read a newspaper in English, and write a letter in English. Response choices were "yes," "a little," and "no." These four items were combined as an index of student English language proficiency.

7.2 Results

7.2.1 English Language Proficiency

In English language skills, the Pilot Comparison group did better in spelling on the Writing Sample (F=11.77, df=1/17, p<.01) than did the Bilingual group.[1] This could be attributed to the fact that the Comparison students spent more time studying English spelling, whereas the Bilingual group divided time between Spanish and English (see No. 7, Table 1, p. 138).

The Follow Up I Comparison group performed better than the Bilingual group in Word Naming by Domain for "kitchen" (F=7.47, df=1/28, p<.05) and for total word naming (F=4.60, df=1/28, p<.05), and in English reading, as measured by the Cooperative Primary Tests (F=10.56, df=1/28, p<.01) (see Nos. 4 and 5, Table 2, p. 142). The Follow Up I group was rated better in English intonation on Storytelling by Domain than the Comparison group (F=4.88, df=1/28, p.<.05) (see No. 2, Table 2, p. 140). Although the Follow Up I Comparison group was clearly better in several English skills—such as naming vocabulary for different domains and in one test of reading, it is important to point out that the Bilingual students were acquiring good intonation patterns in English, a benefit to them in communication. Furthermore, the Bilingual group performed as well as the Comparison group on all other measures of English language proficiency (see Table 2). Thus, the Follow Up I group appeared to be holding its own in the development of English skills.

At the Follow Up II level, the Comparison group was rated higher in descriptive ability on the English Storytelling Task (F=4.51, df=1/27, p<.05) (see Table 3, p. 145). Along with communication ability, pronunciation, and intonation, descriptive ability was one of the subscales on which the pre-post-test regression lines for the Bilingual and the Comparison groups were significantly nonparallel. Because of the significant F, ANOVA rather than ANCOVA was run (see "Analysis of Data," 5.4). The interaction of slopes for the Bilingual and Comparison groups on descriptive ability in English resulted from the fact that the Comparison group made greater gains in terms of the judge's ratings on a five point scale than did the Bilingual students. The more rapid progress of Comparison students in describing the actions in pictures in English was attributed to their treatment: undivided attention paid to English.

---

[1] See Appendix 4 for complete Analysis of Variance and Covariance data.

TABLE 1

MEXICAN AMERICAN STUDENTS' ENGLISH LANGUAGE PROFICIENCY–PILOT LEVEL

Skill Area	Group	N	Pretest Mean	Posttest Mean	Posttest Mean Adjusted For Pretest	F
1. *Oral Comprehension*	P	15	36.27			0.01
	C	14	36.14			
2. *Storytelling:*						
Communicative Ability	P	15	2.92	4.00	4.10	2.55
	C	14	3.46	3.64	3.53	
Grammar	P	15	3.23	3.53	3.55	0.13
	C	14	3.54	3.43	3.41	
Pronunciation	P	15	3.08	3.40	3.46	1.93
	C	14	3.46	3.93	3.86	
Intonation	P	15	3.31	3.73	3.73	0.15
	C	14	3.15	3.86	3.86	
Language Alternation	P	15	4.92	4.87	4.86	2.17
	C	14	5.00	5.00	5.00	
Total	P	15	17.46	19.53	19.75	0.01
	C	14	18.61	19.86	19.63	
Descriptive Ability	P	15	3.23	4.07	4.09	0.73
	C	14	3.39	3.86	3.83	

(continued on following pages)

TABLE 1 (cont.)

Skill Area	Group	N	Pretest Mean	Posttest Mean	Posttest Mean Adjusted For Pretest	F
3. *Storytelling by Domain:*						
Communicative Ability	P	4		3.50		0.69
	C	6		4.00		
Grammar	P	4		3.50		0.12
	C	6		3.67		
Pronunciation	P	4		3.75		0.02
	C	6		3.67		
Intonation	P	4		3.75		0.28
	C	6		3.50		
Language Alternation	P	4		5.00		0.64
	C	6		4.83		
Total	P	4		19.50		0.01
	C	6		19.67		
Descriptive Ability	P	4		3.50		0.96
	C	6		4.00		
Vocabulary Diversity:						
Kitchen	P	4		25.50		0.30
	C	6		21.67		
Street	P	4		25.75		0.01
	C	6		24.83		

TABLE 1 (cont.)

Skill Area	Group	N	Pretest Mean	Posttest Mean	Posttest Mean Adjusted For Pretest	F
Vocabulary Diversity (cont.)						
School	P	4		15.75		2.71
	C	6		22.83		
4. Word Naming by Domain:						
Kitchen	P	15	7.87	10.27	10.44	0.15
	C	14	8.54	10.00	9.89	
Street	P	15	7.53	9.13	9.24	0.01
	C	14	8.39	9.14	9.03	
Church	P	15	6.27	7.80	7.72	0.10
	C	14	5.61	7.29	7.37	
School	P	15	8.67	10.27	10.44	0.34
	C	14	9.77	11.57	11.39	
Total	P	15	30.33	36.80	37.24	0.00
	C	14	32.31	38.00	37.53	
5. CPT Reading Test	P	15	2.07	2.78	2.79	0.43
	C	14	2.12	2.99	2.97	
6. I-A Reading Test:						
Vocabulary	P	15	28.77	25.53	26.75	0.47
	C	14	32.29	29.43	28.13	

(continued on following pages)

TABLE 1 (cont.)

Skill Area	Group	N	Pretest Mean	Posttest Mean	Posttest Mean Adjusted For Pretest	F
6. I-A Reading Test: (cont.)						
Comprehension	P	15	53.31	30.87	31.86	0.20
	C	14	28.43	34.86	33.79	
Total	P	15	53.31	56.40	58.95	0.24
	C	14	60.71	64.29	61.55	
7. *Writing Sample:*						
Verbal Output	P	13		78.38		0.88
	C	6		99.93		
Vocabulary Range	P	13		39.23		0.08
	C	6		37.29		
Vocabulary Diversity	P	13		0.53		0.91
	C	6		0.49		
Spelling	P	13		0.27		11.77**
	C	6		0.12		
Grammar	P	13		0.08		3.70
	C	6		0.05		
Sentence Quality	P	13		2.38		1.66
	C	6		2.93		

**p<.01

TABLE 1 (cont.)

Skill Area	Group	N	Pretest Mean	Posttest Mean	Posttest Mean Adjusted For Pretest	F
7. Writing Sample: (cont.) Expression	P	13		2.46		
	C	6		2.86		0.91
8. *Student Language Proficiency:* Listening, speaking, reading, writing, combined—parent report. (8-point scale with 8 as maximum.)	P	15	5.67	6.67	6.75	
	C	14	6.36	7.50	7.41	2.33

P = Pilot Group
C = Comparison Group

TABLE 2
MEXICAN AMERICAN STUDENTS' ENGLISH LANGUAGE PROFICIENCY—
FOLLOW UP I LEVEL

Skill Area	Group	N	Pretest Mean	Posttest Mean	Posttest Mean Adjusted For Pretest	F
1. *Oral Comprehension*	FUI	16	32.79	38.81	39.13	0.04
	C	15	35.50	39.20	38.86	
2. *Storytelling:*						
Communicative Ability	FUI	16	2.53	3.25	3.24	1.05
	C	15	2.53	3.87	2.88	
Grammar	FUI	16	2.93	3.37	3.36	0.06
	C	15	2.73	3.27	3.28	
Pronunciation	FUI	16	2.67	3.25	3.33	0.71
	C	15	3.07	3.13	3.05	
Intonation	FUI	16	2.80	3.56	3.63	4.88*
	C	15	3.20	3.07	2.99	
Language Alternation	FUI	16	4.75	5.00	4.89	1.29
	C	15	4.87	4.87	4.98	
Total	FUI	16	15.87	18.31	18.36	1.43
	C	15	16.40	17.33	17.28	
Descriptive Ability	FUI	16	2.87	3.56	3.56	1.83
	C	15	2.87	3.13	3.13	

*$p < .05$

TABLE 2 (cont.)

Skill Area	Group	N	Pretest Mean	Posttest Mean	Posttest Mean Adjusted For Pretest	F
3. *Storytelling by Domain:*						
Communicative Ability	FUI	3		3.33		0.07
	C	6		3.17		
Grammar	FUI	3		3.00		1.17
	C	6		3.33		
Pronunciation	FUI	3		3.00		0.29
	C	6		3.33		
Intonation	FUI	3		3.00		0.29
	C	6		3.33		
Language Alternation	FUI	3		5.00		0.00
	C	6		5.00		
Total	FUI	3		17.67		0.07
	C	6		18.17		
Descriptive Ability	FUI	3		3.33		0.09
	C	6		3.50		
Vocabulary Diversity:						
Kitchen	FUI	3		14.67		1.33
	C	6		19.17		
Street	FUI	3		17.33		0.60
	C	6		21.00		

(continued on following pages)

TABLE 2 (cont.)

Skill Area	Group	N	Pretest Mean	Posttest Mean	Posttest Mean Adjusted For Pretest	F
Vocabulary Diversity (cont.):						
School	FUI	3		17.33		0.05
	C	6		15.83		
4. *Word Naming by Domain:*						
Kitchen	FUI	16	7.69	7.50	7.56	7.47*
	C	15	7.92	10.93	10.87	
Street	FUI	16	7.87	7.06	7.02	4.08
	C	15	7.17	9.33	9.38	
Church	FUI	16	6.06	6.87	6.82	1.00
	C	15	5.58	7.93	7.99	
School	FUI	16	7.94	9.31	9.31	2.17
	C	15	8.08	11.46	11.46	
Total	FUI	16	29.56	30.75	30.68	4.60*
	C	15	28.75	39.67	39.74	
5. *CPT Reading Test*	FUI	16	1.46	1.99	2.01	10.56**
	C	15	1.96	2.47	2.45	
6. *I-A Reading Test:*						
Vocabulary	FUI	16	+84.40	31.63	32.27	0.09
	C	15	98.92	33.60	32.91	

*p<.05   **p<.01

TABLE 2 (cont.)

Skill Area	Group	N	Pretest Mean	Posttest Mean	Posttest Mean Adjusted For Pretest	F
I-A Reading Test: (cont.)						
Comprehension	FUI	16	+84.40	27.94	30.06	0.52
	C	15	98.92	30.20	27.93	
Total	FUI	16	+84.40	59.56	62.33	0.11
	C	15	98.92	63.80	60.84	
7. *Student Language Proficiency:*						
Listening, speaking, reading, writing, combined—parent report. (8-point scale with 8 as maximum.)	FUI	16	5.94	6.50	6.51	0.38
	C	15	5.47	6.87	6.86	

FUI = Follow Up I
C = Comparison

+Murphy-Durrel Reading
Readiness Analysis,
Total Score.

TABLE 3

MEXICAN AMERICAN STUDENTS' ENGLISH LANGUAGE PROFICIENCY
FOLLOW UP II LEVEL

Skill Area	Group	N	Pretest Mean	Posttest Mean	Posttest Mean Adjusted For Pretest	F
1. *Oral Comprehension*	FUII	14	23.45	36.07	36.52*	6.59*
	C	16	27.91	33.31	32.92	
2. *Storytelling:*						
Communicative Ability	FUII	14	1.08	2.29		3.44
	C	16	1.46	2.94		
Grammar	FUII	14	2.08	2.86	2.89	0.02
	C	16	3.00	2.87	2.84	
Pronunciation	FUII	14	2.17	2.86		1.49
	C	16	2.23	3.31		
Intonation	FUII	14	1.11	3.07		1.31
	C	16	2.31	3.37		
Language Alternation	FUII	14	3.08	4.71	4.73	0.67
	C	16	4.39	4.87	4.86	
Total	FUII	14	10.58	15.79	15.99	1.48
	C	16	13.54	17.37	17.20	
Descriptive Ability	FUII	14	1.33	2.79		4.51*
	C	16	1.61	3.37		

*p<.05

TABLE 3 (cont.)

Skill Group	Group	N	Pretest Mean	Posttest Mean	Posttest Mean Adjusted For Pretest	F
3. *Storytelling by Domain:*						
Communicative Ability	FUII	4		2.00		9.53*
	C	5		3.40		
Grammar	FUII	4		3.00		0.78
	C	5		3.40		
Pronunciation	FUII	4		2.50		7.00*
	C	5		4.00		
Intonation	FUII	4		2.75		1.10
	C	5		3.40		
Language Alternation	FUII	4		4.75		1.30
	C	5		5.00		
Total	FUII	4		15.00		7.46*
	C	5		19.20		
Descriptive Ability	FUII	4		2.25		5.21*
	C	5		3.40		
Vocabulary Diversity:						
Kitchen	FUII	4		10.50		1.52
	C	5		16.20		
Street	FUII	4		13.75		1.67
	C	5		22.20		

*p<.05

(continued on following pages)

TABLE 3 (cont.)

Skill Area	Group	N	Pretest Mean	Posttest Mean	Posttest Mean Adjusted For Pretest	F
School	FUII	4		9.50		5.36*
	C	5		16.60		
4. Word Naming by Domain:						
Kitchen	FUII	14	3.33	5.64	5.68	3.11
	C	16	4.80	7.63	7.59	
Street	FUII	14	3.67	6.36	6.47	1.93
	C	16	4.90	8.44	8.34	
Church	FUII	14	3.60	4.57	4.45	5.65*
	C	16	3.60	7.69	7.80	
School	FUII	14	5.33	6.64	6.39	4.95*
	C	16	5.44	9.31	9.54	
Total	FUII	14	15.33	23.21	23.04	7.67**
	C	16	18.00	33.69	33.84	
5. CPT Reading Test	FUII	14		1.52		2.55
	C	16		1.86		
6. I-A Reading Test:						
Vocabulary	FUII	14	+49.00	12.50	12.65	1.57
	C	16	51.30	14.69	14.55	

*p<.05
**p<.01

TABLE 3 (cont.)

Skill Area	Group	N	Pretest Mean	Posttest Mean	Posttest Mean Adjusted For Pretest	F
Comprehension	FUII	14	+49.00	9.79	9.83	0.07
	C	16	51.30	10.19	10.15	
Total	FUII	14	+49.00	22.29	22.49	1.09
	C	16	51.30	24.87	24.70	
7. *Student Language Proficiency:*						
Listening, speaking, reading, writing combined—parent report. (8-point scale with 8 as max.)	FUII	14	2.86	5.00	5.28	0.12
	C	16	4.00	5.81	5.57	

+Murphy-Durrell Reading
Readiness Analysis,
Total Score.

FUII = Follow Up II Group
C   = Comparison Group

TABLE 4
MEXICAN AMERICAN STUDENTS' SPANISH LANGUAGE PROFICIENCY
PILOT LEVEL

Skill Area	Group	N	Pretest Mean	Posttest Mean	Posttest Mean Adjusted For Pretest	F
1. *Oral Comprehension*	P	15	36.27			0.00
	C	14	36.21			
2. *Storytelling:*						
Communicative Ability	P	15	2.92	2.93	2.89	0.00
	C	14	2.41	2.86	2.90	
Grammar	P	15	3.00	3.47	3.47	0.34
	C	14	3.00	3.29	3.29	
Pronunciation	P	15	3.77	4.07	4.16	0.69
	C	14	4.33	4.00	3.89	
Intonation	P	15	4.46	4.33	4.36	0.01
	C	14	4.42	4.36	4.33	
Language Alternation	P	15	4.61	4.73	4.73	0.01
	C	14	4.75	4.71	4.71	
Total	P	15	18.77	19.60	19.63	1.05
	C	14	19.17	17.86	17.82	
Descriptive Ability	P	15	3.15	3.47	3.45	1.52
	C	14	3.00	3.00	3.02	

TABLE 4 (cont.)

Skill Area	Group	N	Pretest Mean	Posttest Mean	Posttest Mean Adjusted For Pretest	F
3. *Storytelling by Domain:*						
Communicative Ability	P	4		3.25		0.06
	C	6		3.33		
Grammar	P	4		3.25		0.28
	C	6		3.50		
Pronunciation	P	4		4.25		3.14
	C	6		3.67		
Intonation	P	4		4.25		0.08
	C	6		4.17		
Language Alternation	P	4		5.00		1.60
	C	6		4.67		
Total	P	4		20.00		0.34
	C	6		19.33		
Descriptive Ability	P	4		3.00		0.19
	C	6		3.17		
Vocabulary Diversity:						
Kitchen	P	4		16.00		0.07
	C	6		16.83		
Street	P	4		17.00		0.95
	C	6		22.17		

(continued on following pages)

TABLE 4 (cont.)

Skill Area	Group	N	Pretest Mean	Posttest Mean	Posttest Mean Adjusted For Pretest	F
Vocabulary Diversity (cont.)						
School	P	4		12.75		3.31
	C	6		20.00		
4. *Word Naming by Domain:*						
Kitchen	P	15	7.47	10.60	10.76	0.03
	C	14	9.42	10.64	10.47	
Street	P	15	7.40	7.40	7.33	0.68
	C	14	7.25	8.43	8.50	
Church	P	15	6.93	7.00	7.01	0.22
	C	14	7.00	7.64	7.63	
School	P	15	8.27	8.53	8.53	0.01
	C	14	8.42	8.64	8.64	
Total	P	15	30.13	34.27	34.57	0.00
	C	14	32.08	34.79	34.46	
5. *Prueba de Lectura (Reading):*						
Vocabulary	P	15		21.67		1.80
	C	14		17.64		
Comprehension	P	15		30.93		5.56*
	C	14		22.43		

*p<.05

TABLE 4 (cont.)

Skill Area	Group	N	Pretest Mean	Posttest Mean	Posttest Mean Adjusted For Pretest	F
Prueba de Lectura (Reading): (cont.)						
Total	P	15		52.33		4.26*
	C	14		40.07		
6. *Writing Sample:*						
Verbal Output	P	13		77.54		3.47
	C	6		37.33		
Vocabulary Range	P	13		36.46		3.06
	C	6		21.17		
Vocabulary Diversity	P	13		0.51		8.37**
	C	6		0.68		
Spelling	P	13		0.23		4.70*
	C	6		0.38		
Grammar	P	13		0.09		0.12
	C	6		0.11		
Sentence Quality	P	13		3.23		1.58
	C	6		2.33		
Expression	P	13		3.08		3.89
	C	6		1.83		

*p<.05   **p<.01

(continued on following page)

TABLE 4 (cont.)

Skill Area	Group	N	Pretest Mean	Posttest Mean	Posttest Mean Adjusted For Pretest	F
7. *Student Language Proficiency Proficiency:*						
Listening, speaking, reading, writing combined—parent report. (8-point scale, with 8 as max.)	P	15	5.00	5.60	5.40	0.71
	C	14	4.36	4.71	4.92	

P = Pilot Group
C = Comparison Group

TABLE 5

MEXICAN AMERICAN STUDENTS' SPANISH LANGUAGE PROFICIENCY

FOLLOW UP II LEVEL

Skill Area	Group	N	Pretest Mean	Posttest Mean	Posttest Mean Adjusted For Pretest	F
1. *Oral Comprehension*	FUI	16	31.43	37.37	38.27	0.21
	C	15	35.82	38.80	37.84	
2. *Storytelling:*						
Communicative Ability	FUI	16	2.63	3.00	2.95	0.17
	C	15	2.27	2.73	2.70	
Grammar	FUI	16	3.00	3.19	3.20	2.57
	C	15	3.18	3.73	3.71	
Pronunciation	FUI	16	3.31	4.06	4.08	0.45
	C	15	4.09	4.33	4.31	
Intonation	FUI	16	4.13	4.50	4.49	0.07
	C	15	4.45	4.53	4.55	
Language Alternation	FUI	16	4.37	4.44	4.49	2.94
	C	15	4.55	4.93	4.88	
Total	FUI	16	17.44	19.13	19.20	1.09
	C	15	18.55	20.27	20.19	
Descriptive Ability	FUI	16	3.06	3.63	3.61	4.98*
	C	15	2.91	3.07	3.09	

*$p < .05$

(continued on following pages)

TABLE 5 (cont.)

Skill Area	Group	N	Pretest Mean	Posttest Mean	Posttest Mean Adjusted For Pretest	F
3. *Storytelling by Domain:*						
Communicative Ability	FUI	3		3.00		1.87
	C	6		2.33		
Grammar	FUI	3		4.00		9.00*
	C	6		2.50		
Pronunciation	FUI	3		4.00		3.43
	C	6		3.17		
Intonation	FUI	3		4.33		4.49
	C	6		3.50		
Language Alternation	FUI	3		4.67		0.26
	C	6		4.83		
Total	FUI	3		20.00		5.04
	C	6		16.33		
Descriptive Ability	FUI	3		3.00		0.00
	C	6		3.00		
Vocabulary Diversity:						
Kitchen	FUI	3		15.33		0.48
	C	6		13.17		
Street	FUI	3		18.00		0.01
	C	6		17.67		

*$p < .05$

TABLE 5 (cont.)

Skill Area	Group	N	Pretest Mean	Posttest Mean	Posttest Mean Adjusted For Pretest	F
Vocabulary Diversity (cont.)						
School	FUI	3		16.67		3.27
	C	6		11.50		
4. Word Naming by Domain:						
Kitchen	FUI	16	7.69	7.87	7.89	2.88
	C	15	7.83	9.73	9.72	
Street	FUI	16	6.63	7.06	7.17	1.45
	C	15	7.25	8.53	8.42	
Church	FUI	16	6.13	6.06	6.10	3.72
	C	15	6.58	8.20	8.16	
School	FUI	16	6.19	7.37	7.42	2.62
	C	15	8.00	9.53	9.50	
Total	FUI	16	26.63	28.37	28.68	3.67
	C	15	29.57	36.00	35.68	
5. Prueba de Lectura (Reading):						
Vocabulary	FUI	16		25.56		0.65
	C	15		28.20		
Comprehension	FUI	16		21.81		0.03
	C	15		22.40		

(continued on following page)

TABLE 5 (cont.)

Skill Area	Group	N	Pretest Mean	Posttest Mean	Posttest Mean Adjusted For Pretest	F
Prueba de Lectura (Reading): (cont.)						
Total	FUI	16		47.37		0.24
	C	15		50.60		
6. *Student Language Proficiency:*						
Listening, speaking, reading, writing combined—parent report.(8-point scale, with 8 as max.)	FUI	16	4.38	5.94	6.08	4.04
	C	15	5.13	5.13	4.98	

FUI = Follow Up I Group
C = Comparison Group

TABLE 6
MEXICAN AMERICAN STUDENT'S SPANISH LANGUAGE PROFICIENCY
FOLLOW UP II LEVEL

Skill Area	Group	N	Pretest Mean	Posttest Mean	Posttest Mean Adjusted For Pretest	F
1. *Oral Comprehension*	FUII	14	27.18	34.07	33.97	1.97
	C	16	28.83	35.56	35.65	
2. *Storytelling:*						
Communicative Ability	FUII	14	2.10	2.50	2.49	0.15
	C	16	2.08	2.63	2.63	
Grammar	FUII	14	2.60	3.71	3.71	2.63
	C	16	2.50	3.13	3.13	
Pronunciation	FUII	14	3.30	4.14	4.12	0.46
	C	16	3.42	4.37	4.39	
Intonation	FUII	14	3.50	4.21	4.24	0.36
	C	16	3.92	4.50	4.48	
Language Alternation	FUII	14	4.50	4.64		0.89
	C	16	3.92	4.25		
Total	FUII	14	16.20	19.21	19.21	0.59
	C	16	15.83	19.94	19.94	
Descriptive Ability	FUII	14	2.27	3.00	3.02	0.79
	C	16	2.58	3.31	3.29	

(continued on following pages)

TABLE 6 (cont.)

Skill Area	Group	N	Pretest Mean	Posttest Mean	Posttest Mean Adjusted For Pretest	F
3. Storytelling by Domain:						
Communicative Ability	FUII	4		1.75		2.03
	C	5		2.20		
Grammar	FUII	4		2.00		2.07
	C	5		2.80		
Pronunciation	FUII	4		2.50		3.03
	C	5		3.60		
Intonation	FUII	4		3.00		2.07
	C	5		3.80		
Language Alternation	FUII	4		4.75		1.30
	C	5		4.00		
Total	FUII	4		14.00		1.33
	C	5		16.40		
Descriptive Ability	FUII	4		2.75		1.30
	C	5		3.00		
Vocabulary Diversity:						
Kitchen	FUII	4		6.25		3.13
	C	5		12.80		
Street	FUII	4		7.50		3.06
	C	5		16.00		

TABLE 6 (cont.)

Skill Area	Group	N	Pretest Mean	Posttest Mean	Posttest Mean Adjusted For Pretest	F
Vocabulary Diversity (cont.)						
School	FUII	4		7.75		1.47
	C	5		10.20		
4. *Word Naming by Domain:*						
Kitchen	FUII	14	5.70	7.57	7.58	0.27
	C	16	5.29	8.37	8.36	
Street	FUII	14	5.90	5.50	5.54	3.19
	C	16	4.85	7.44	7.40	
Church	FUII	14	5.40	6.29	6.27	2.01
	C	16	4.71	7.94	7.95	
School	FUII	14	6.80	6.86	6.77	1.93
	C	16	6.07	7.94	8.01	
Total	FUII	14	23.80	26.21	26.09	1.53
	C	16	20.93	30.81	30.92	
5. *Prueba de Lectura (Reading):*						
Vocabulary	FUII	14		13.79		1.29
	C	16		16.06		
Comprehension	FUII	14		13.21		0.24
	C	16		12.50		

(continued on following page)

TABLE 6 (cont.)

Skill Area	Group	N	Pretest Mean	Posttest Mean	Posttest Mean Adjusted For Pretest	F
Prueba de Lectura (Reading): (cont.)						
Total	FUII	14		27.00		0.44
	C	16		28.56		
6. *Student Language Proficiency:*						
Listening, speaking, reading, writing combined—parent report. (8-point scale, with 8 as max.)	FUII	14	3.64	4.43	4.49	0.03
	C	16	4.94	4.44	4.39	

FUII = Follow Up II Group
C   = Comparison Group

TABLE 7

RATING OF STUDENTS' ABILITY TO SPEAK
SPANISH TO PARENTS OVER LAST TWO YEARS
PARENT RATING

	Pilot Level		Follow Up I Level		Follow Up II Level	
	B	C	B	C	B	C
His/Her Spanish has improved	9	5	11	6	9	5
No change	6	5	4	8	5	7
Losing his/her Spanish	0	4	1	1	0	4
TOTAL	15	14	16	15	14	16
G	Gamma = .55*		Gamma = .46**		Gamma = .65**	

B = Bilingual   *$p < .05$
C = Comparison   **$p < .01$

With respect to communicative ability, the Bilingual·students made greater gains than did the Comparison group, and so, an interaction resulted. However, the Bilingual group started out substantially below the Comparison group, so that their gains only brought them even with the Comparison students. On the subscales of pronunciation and intonation, the Bilingual group had several students rated lower on the posttest than on the pretest. Assuming that the judge's ratings were accurate, these several students may have been experiencing a slight dip in phonological aspects of their English speaking ability. No such behavior was observed among Comparison children, but then their entire instruction was in English.

Using a random subsample, the Comparison group was rated higher in communicative ability ($F=9.53$, df=1/7, $p < .05$), pronunciation ($F=7.00$, df=1/7, $p < .05$), total for linguistic aspects ($F=7.46$, df=1/7, $p < .05$), and descriptive ability ($F=5.21$, df=1/7, $p < .05$) on Storytelling by Domain. They had greater vocabulary range in storytelling in the school domain ($F=5.36$, df=1/7, $p < .05$). The Comparison students were also better in word naming for the domains of church ($F=5.65$, df=1/27, $p < .05$) and school ($F=4.95$, df=1/27, $p < .05$), and for total word naming ($F=7.67$, df=1/27, $p < .01$). However, the Bilingual group outscored the Comparison group on Oral Comprehension ($F=6.59$, df=1/27, $p < .05$) (see Nos. 1-4, Table 3, pp. 144-146). Again, the Comparison group appears stronger in English vocabulary. The Bilingual group, although weaker in English vocabulary, comes out strong in English comprehension, indicating that the pupils were gaining skill in the crucial area of understanding spoken English.

Over all group levels, it might be surmised that the Comparison students had a slight edge in English skills. Chapter 8 provides an in-depth analysis of differences between the two groups with respect to grammar in their spoken English.

7.2.2 Spanish Language Proficiency

Across all measures of Spanish language proficiency, there were relatively few significant differences between the Bilingual and Comparison students. The Pilot group outperformed the Comparison students in Spanish reading comprehension ($F=5.56$, $df=1/27$, $p<.05$) and in total reading ($F=4.26$, $df=1/27$, $p<.05$) on the *Prueba de Lectura,* and in spelling, on the Spanish Writing Sample ($F=4.70$, $df=1/27$, $p<.05$). The Comparison group had greater vocabulary diversity on the Spanish Writing Sample ($F=8.37$, $df=1/27$, $p<.01$), however (see Nos. 5 and 6, Table 4, pp. 150-151). The performance of the Bilingual group in Spanish reading and spelling reflects their special training in these areas, and is an indication of their acquisition of literacy skills in Spanish. As for the Comparison group's advantage in diversity of vocabulary on the Writing Sample, it must be pointed out that only six of the fourteen students in the Comparison group wrote compositions in Spanish. The remaining students said that they were unable to do so. Thus, the six who did write compositions were a select group.

The entire Follow Up I group outperformed the Comparison group in one aspect of Storytelling in Spanish, namely descriptive ability ($F=4.98$, $df=1/28$, $p<.05$), and a random subsample was rated higher in grammar than the Comparison group in Storytelling by Domain ($F=9.00$, $df=1/7$, $p<.05$) (see Nos. 2 and 3, Table 5, pp. 153-154). Both results indicate stronger speaking skills in Spanish on the part of the students schooled bilingually for several years, even after adjusting for initial differences.

There were no significant differences between groups at the Follow Up II level (see Table 6, pp. 157-160). The pre-post regression lines for the Bilingual and the Comparison groups were significantly nonparallel for the language alternation subscale of the Storytelling Task. Several Bilingual students used some English mixed in with Spanish in the posttest. No such behavior was observed for Comparison students. This finding is rather unexpected, since the Bilingual students were being taught Spanish formally in class, while the Comparison students were not.[2]

---

[2] For more on this phenomenon of mixing, see Chapter 8. It may be that simultaneous use of Spanish and English in the classroom, as was often practiced in the Bilingual Program, encourages mixing.

When asked whether they had noted a change in their child's ability to speak Spanish with them over the two years of the study, the Bilingual parents at all three levels—Pilot, Follow Up I, and Follow Up II—responded differently from the Comparison parents. Significantly more Bilingual than Comparison parents felt either that the student's Spanish speaking ability had improved or that it had stayed the same (Pilot, gamma=.55, p<.05; Follow Up I, gamma=.46, p< .01; Follow Up II, gamma=.65, p<.01). Nine Comparison parents felt that their child had lost ground in Spanish, while only one Bilingual parent felt that way (see Table 7). These results appear to give some indication of the overall effect of Spanish language instruction on Spanish speaking ability. Children in the Bilingual Project were reportedly holding on to their Spanish speaking skills, while similar Mexican American children in an English-only program were losing their Spanish speaking ability.

Thus, the students in the Bilingual Project appeared to be excelling in several Spanish skill areas—perhaps not as greatly as might have been expected. Since they were receiving formal training in Spanish and using Spanish as the medium of instruction in the classroom, one might have expected to see greater differences between the two groups in reading skills and in measured speaking skill. Still, parent reports of the effects of bilingual vs. English-only schooling on Spanish skills came out strongly in favor of the Bilingual groups.

7.3 Summary of Findings and Discussion

Mexican American children who were taught the academic curriculum in Spanish and English for several years appeared to be *as proficient in most English language skills* as comparable Mexican American children taught only in English.[3] At the Pilot level, where students had been in the Bilingual Project the longest (three years), there was no difference in English oral comprehension, speaking, or reading skill, and only one difference in writing—namely in English spelling. At the Follow Up I level, there was no difference in oral comprehension, and only slight differences in speaking. The Bilingual group was rated as having better intonation patterns in Storytelling, and the Comparison group was seen to produce more words in English for the domain of kitchen and across all domains together in the Word Naming by Domain task. In English reading, there was no difference on one test and a significant difference in favor of the Comparison group on another. At the Follow Up II level, the Bilingual group was better in English oral comprehension, poorer in English speaking skills, and the same in English reading. As far as English speaking skills in Storytelling, the Bilingual group did not equal the Comparison group

---

[3] See Chapter 8 for a discussion of similarities and differences between the two groups with respect to grammatical structures used in spoken English.

in descriptive ability. In Storytelling by Domain, a subsample of the Bilingual group was rated lower in a series of categories—communication ability, grammar, pronunciation, total linguistic aspects, descriptive ability, and vocabulary diversity for the school domain. The Bilingual group was also less proficient in English word naming for the domains of church and school and for total word naming.

The rather extensive advantage of the Comparison group in English speaking skills at the Follow Up II level (mostly first graders by spring, 1972) could be explained by the greater need to speak English at the Comparison school. Particularly at the kindergarten and first-grade levels at the Bilingual Project, most classes were conducted predominantly in Spanish for the Spanish speakers. More English was introduced in the more advanced grades. Also, although Spanish was spoken extensively in the homes of both the Bilingual and the Comparison students, language use results indicate that more English was being used in the homes of the Comparison students, particularly by siblings, in the spring of 1972 (see Chapter 9, "Language Use").

The breakdown of speaking proficiency by domain also provides insights into language patterns. The Follow Up I Comparison group was stronger than the Bilingual group in words for the kitchen, suggesting that they used more English at home when eating, playing around the kitchen, and so forth. The Follow Up II Comparison group produced more different words than the Bilingual group in Storytelling by Domain for the domain of school and more total words for school in Word Naming by Domain, a reflection of their greater use of English at school. This same group also produced more words for the domain of church in English, suggesting that more of these children went to a church where services were conducted in English.

The relatively strong showing of the Bilingual group in English skills is consistent with results from bilingual projects for Spanish-speaking groups elsewhere in the United States.[4] A variety of projects report that Spanish-speaking students are able to develop Spanish literacy skills without losing ground in their development of literacy skills in English. Results from Dade County, Florida (Inclán, 1971), from the Independent School District in San Antonio, Texas (Taylor, 1969), from the Harlandale Independent School District in San Antonio, Texas

---

[4]In this discussion section and in the discussion sections for subsequent chapters, references to findings from other studies on bilingual schooling will be limited to those for other bilingual programs in the United States initiated for Spanish-speaking children from predominantly lower-income families. Research results from other countries, although of theoretical interest, are so dependent upon the sociolinguistic variables operating in their respective communities as to render them all but meaningless for the purposes of comparison with the Redwood City results (see Le Page, 1964; Fishman, Ferguson, & Das Gupta, 1968, on language patterns and language attitudes in countries abroad).

(Pryor, 1967), from Del Rio, Texas (John and Horner, 1971), and from Sacramento, California (Hartwig, 1971) provide evidence that English skills do not suffer because of instruction in and through Spanish.

Just as Cuban students in grades 3-8 in Florida were as good in English reading, using the Inter-American Tests of Reading, as Cuban control students (Inclán, 1971), so Mexican Americans in Redwood City were as good in English reading as Comparison students, using the same tests. However, using another test, the Cooperative Primary Test, the Bilingual Follow Up I group did not perform as well as did the Comparison students. The result might have been due to the emphasis put on Spanish language arts in the Bilingual Project at the Follow Up I level, assuming the results were not just an artifact of the test. If the results were due to an emphasis on Spanish at the Bilingual Project, it would be expected that the difference between the Bilingual and the Comparison groups would be erased over time—i.e., once the Bilingual group had firmly established reading skills in both languages.

The strong showing that the Follow Up I group made in English intonation in Storytelling is consistent with the results of Taylor (1969). She found that fifth-grade Mexican Americans receiving instruction in Spanish scored higher in English oral production (pronunciation, intonation, and fluency together), although the comparison group scored higher in English pronunciation alone. Taylor explained the higher performance in English oral production in that hearing their own language in class reinforced the phonemic and syntactic contrasts between English and Spanish, thus making it easier for these Spanish speakers to learn English. Perhaps as Taylor suggests, the student places extra emphasis on listening and on pronouncing English in a classroom where he is faced with the task of understanding and using both languages.

The Redwood City Bilingual group also came out better than the Comparison group in English oral comprehension at the Follow Up II (first-grade) level, matching the findings of Goodman and Stern (1971) for bilingually-schooled Mexican American first graders. Such a finding would again be consistent with the notion that having to listen to messages in two languages in the classroom may enhance the comprehension of both languages.

Mexican American children who were taught the academic curriculum in Spanish and English for several years were also *slightly more proficient in Spanish language skills* than were Comparison children taught only in English. There were no significant differences in oral comprehension or in word naming. In speaking, the Bilingual Follow Up I group showed greater descriptive ability for Storytelling in Spanish and greater command of Spanish grammar in Storytelling by Domain. In reading, only the Pilot group excelled over the Comparison group, both in reading comprehension and in total reading. The Pilot Comparison group also had better spelling and greater vocabulary diversity in the Spanish Writing Sample. However, since only six out of fourteen Comparison students were able to write a composition in Spanish, the Comparison group's results reflected the efforts of a select few.

It might have been expected that the Bilingual students would outperform the Comparison group in Spanish reading at *all* levels. Perhaps differences at the lower levels will show up in subsequent years. Goodman and Stern (1971) found Mexican American first- and second-grade Bilingual groups in Compton, California, outperformed comparison groups in Spanish reading on the same test as that used in Redwood City. Further comparative results on Spanish language perforance are hard to find, since most bilingual projects are reluctant to test their comparison groups (if they have any) on Spanish language skills. One explanation for a good showing by a comparison group in Spanish reading would be the ease of transfer from reading in English to reading in Spanish. Since the fit between Spanish sounds and the symbols used in print is so close, a student who has good skill in English reading should be able to make the transfer to reading in Spanish with little difficulty. This fact may help explain why Cuban junior high students in the control group performed better in Spanish reading than did the Bilingual group, even though the Bilingual group alone had been trained to read in Spanish and, in fact, read materials for all subjects in Spanish (Inclán, 1971).

Parents of students at all three Bilingual group levels rated their children higher than did Comparison parents in Spanish speaking ability over the two years of the study. Such findings lend considerable weight to the test findings enumerated above, since parents would be in a position to assess the Spanish-speaking skills of their children on a daily basis. The Bilingual parents observed that their children had either improved in their Spanish speaking ability or that they had at least not lost ground. Significantly more Comparison parents, however, reported that their children were either not progressing in their ability to speak Spanish or were actually losing ground in this skill.

The following chapter goes beyond the statistical analysis of speaking skills provided in this chapter, and offers a detailed linguistic analysis of deviant forms appearing in the oral language of the children in the study.

8. DEVIATIONS FROM "SCHOOL" ENGLISH AND SPANISH GRAMMAR

Although efforts have recently been made to describe the syntax of Chicano English and Spanish (Lance, 1969; González, 1968, 1970, Trager-Johnson and Abraham, 1972), not many efforts have been made to look at the grammatical structures of Chicanos in a bilingual program. The literature on testing shows that little had been done to measure oral language proficiency among bilingual primary school children over the past several decades (see the discussion under "Storytelling Task," Appendix 1.3). Evaluation reports from bilingual projects tend to limit their report of oral language proficiency to scales of grammatical proficiency, pronunciation, intonation, and so forth. The mean scale scores of students schooled bilingually are compared to those of students schooled conventionally. This type of analysis formed part of the data report contained above in Chapter 7.

However, it is important not to stop at a statistical report of scale means. There should also be a description of what, for instance, constituted the grammatical deviations that were tallied and that determined the scale scores for grammatical proficiency. The statistical information is helpful to educators involved in bilingual programs and to administrators who have to make decisions about financing such programs. The description of the actual deviant forms, however, is of more direct benefit to those involved in teaching these bilingual children. Such insights can aid the classroom teacher in selecting teaching strategies (see George, 1972; Burt and Kiparsky, 1972, for instance, on teaching strategies derived from error analysis). The following, then, is an analysis of deviant forms, which may stimulate other evaluators of bilingual programs to do similar analyses.

As discussed in Chapter 7, Bilingual and Comparison students were administered the Storytelling Task in the fall of 1970, and then again in the spring of 1972. They were asked to tell stories about three pictures in both Spanish and English. The pictures were taken from the Dailey Language Facility Test (Dailey, 1968). One was a snapshot of an Anglo woman (probably a teacher) outside a white house with Chicano, Black, and Anglo children clustered around her. The second was a painting, "The Holy Family of the Little Bird" by Murillo, with a bearded man holding a little child, while a woman and a dog looked on. The third was a sketch of a boy pointing at a cat in a tree.

The children's stories were taped and transcribed. The stories were analyzed with respect to deviations from "school" English and "school" Spanish. The intent was to determine the extent to which the students' language differed from the language which their teachers would use. Analysis was conducted with an eye to the relative influence of three sources of deviation from school language:

a. child language
b. nonstandard dialect
c. language interference.

In a language contact situation like that of Redwood City, where two languages were used alternately by the same persons (Weinreich, 1953), the sources of the students' deviations were somewhat complex. Weinreich (1953) and others have called attention to *interference* phenomena: deviations from the norms of either language which occur in the speech of bilinguals as a result of their familiarity with more than one language. In Figure 1, these phenomena are labeled "external interference" (areas B and G in Figure 1). The interference is two-way, each language being capable of interfering with the other. This is particularly likely in the speech of young bilingual children who have not fully learned either of their two languages.

Figure 1 shows separate areas of external interference for children and for adults. This is perhaps not altogether accurate, since some deviant forms in the native and second language of both children and adults are based on the same kinds of interference. However, perhaps too much emphasis has been placed on adult interference problems in interpreting children's difficulties (see Cohen, 1970).

The second broad area of language interference is being referred to as "internal interference," deviations from the norm of either language which are a product of developmental problems in language learning or of nonstandard dialect. Developmental problems include over-generalization, ignorance of rule restrictions, and incomplete application of rules (see Richards, 1971). Figure 1 illustrates how some internal interference problems are shared by adults and children (areas D and E), while some are specific to children (areas A and C)

FIGURE 1

Theoretical Framework for
Child and Adult Language Deviations in a
Language Contact Situation

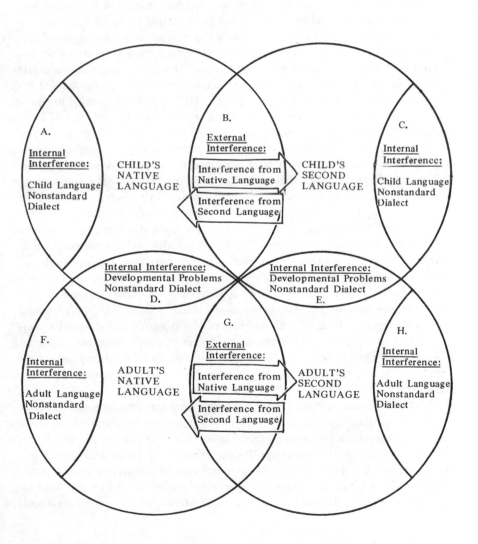

or to adults (areas F and H). When developmental problems pertain to children, who are still in the process of mastering the basic structures of their language, these problems are referred to as "child language." When such problems pertain to children and to adults, they are simply called "developmental." When they pertain exclusively to adults, they are termed for purposes of balance and comparison "adult language." Except for areas of overlap relating to internal interference (Figure 1, areas D and E), adult language patterns are outside the scope of this study, and for the purpose of this study, "child language" refers to the language that children use through third grade.

Interference from a student's native language has perhaps been granted too much importance in explaining difficulties in mastering a second language (see Richards, 1971; Hatch, 1972), particularly the difficulties of young children. Certain problems clearly stem from such interference, especially at the phonological level, but many deviations from the adult norm "derive from the strategies employed by the learner in language acquisition, and from the mutual interference of items within the target language" (Richards, 1971, p. 22). In the language of young native speakers, these errors are seen as a natural part of language development; so presumably are they for young second-language learners. Research on the English language acquisition of native English speakers indicates that Anglos do not have full mastery over English by the early primary grades (Hatch, 1970) even though there has been a popular misconception that by the age of five the native has "mastered" his language. Thus, there is no reason to expect the non-native speaker of English to have any greater mastery.

Although child language "errors" account for many deviations from standard that may appear in children's speech, children are also prey to inherently confusing aspects or peculiarities of the language that may even confuse adults as well, for example, certain irregular verb tenses or the appropriate use of *was* vs. *were*. When such forms occur in adult speech, they are either considered slips of the tongue or dialect forms. There is, of course, a major difference between the child-language errors of a native speaker of a language and those of a non-native speaker. The non-native may make certain "infant" errors, or errors that very young children make, *later* than the native would make them, depending partly on his age and partly on the age at which he started learning the second language.

Dialect forms account for certain deviations from standard language. Children may learn nonstandard dialect forms from many sources, but frequently from age mates or from adults who have perfect mastery of one or another nonstandard dialect of a language. The extensive literature that has appeared with respect to Black English, for instance, suggests the importance of recognizing nonstandard dialects of English as viable, logical, respectable linguistic systems rather than as aberrations to be eradicated (see Labov, 1969). More recently, similar arguments are being made for recognition (and the preservation) of dialect forms of Spanish (see García, 1971; Bowen, 1972). When speaking about the "standard" or "school" language, there is a tacit assumption that there is such a thing. As George (1972) points out, "Both pupils and teachers tend to identify 'errors' by reference to the model, but to assess performance by reference to the local variety." George feels that there is a growing tolerance for local varieties of English. He feels that evaluating errors with respect to standard English would be arbitrary and of little value. In keeping with George's admonitions, this study attempts to use as its models for standard English and Spanish not only those forms incorporated in the "models" for school language, but also forms appearing in locally-acceptable varieties. Clearly, there is always a fine line between nonstandard dialect and the standard.

The categorizing of children's deviations from standard language as child language, interference, or dialect is not intended merely as an academic exercise. The purpose of such a description is to illuminate the forces influencing a child's acquisition of language. As suggested above, such insights can help the classroom teacher in the selection of appropriate teaching strategies. First of all, the teacher can gain a better feel for the source of a child's confusion or difficulty. Although it is not always possible to distinguish a child-language error from interference or dialect, where such distinctions can be made with a certain degree of confidence, then teaching strategies suited to the type of problem can be utilized. For example, if a problem is one of dialect, then the teacher can discuss the appropriateness of the form for the given situation or level of formality. If a deviant form stems from language interference, the teacher can place extra emphasis on the difference between the target and native language with respect to the particular grammatical form. If the error is a result of child-language development, the teacher will know how to provide the appropriate adult model but not to assume that the child is going to automatically produce sentences similar to that model right away. The child may comprehend such forms but not produce them at that stage in his language development.

Although the 360 sets of Spanish and English stories from the Redwood City study provided a considerable corpus of data, it was not always possible to determine whether certain speech segments reflected trends in Chicano child language or whether they were mere flukes or belonged just to one child's idiolect. In some cases, the research literature contains examples of similar speech behavior among other children suggesting that such phenomena are part of a larger trend. In other cases, there is no evidence of similar occurrences elsewhere.

The deviant forms that the children used are coded so that the reader knows whether Bilingual (B) or Comparison (C) children or both produced these forms. A minus sign (-) after the letter code B or C indicates that the item is taken from the stories told in *pretesting* in the fall of 1970. A plus sign (+) after the letter indicates that the item is from the *posttesting* in the spring of 1972. The number and letter preceding the plus or minus sign indicates the number of children who used that form and the group they were in (B or C). For example, (3B-) means that *three* children in the *Bilingual* group during *pretesting* used that particular form. (7C+) means that *seven* children from the *Comparison* group used the form in *posttesting*. At the time of pretesting, the children were in grades K through 2. At the time of posttesting they were in grades 1 through 3. If there are only a few examples of a certain deviant form, then usually all of the examples will be presented. If there are a series of similar forms, then the format will look something like the following:

(6B-)
(7C-)   I don't know *no* stories.
(3C+)   I don't know *no* more.

This means that the kind of double negative indicated by the two examples above was found *at least once* in the speech of six Bilingual students in pretesting, seven Comparison students in pretesting, and three Comparison students in posttesting.

The report of the error analysis will cover seven areas of difficulty: noun phrase constituents, verb phrase and its constituents, conjunctions, negation, interrogation, language alternation, and lexical problems. Table 1 provides a chart of all observed categories of deviation. The source or sources of deviation as suggested throughout the article (child language, interference, nonstandard dialect) are listed along with each category entry, and are entered under the language heading to which they pertain (English or Spanish). In some cases, children had similar errors in both languages. In other cases, the error pertained just to one language, either because no such area of difficulty exists in the other language or because the sampling of language was not extensive enough to include an example of a similar deviant form in that language.

8.1 *Noun Phrase Constituents*

8.1.1 *Noun Phrase*

8.1.1.1 *Regular and Irregular Singular, Plural*

A few students double marked the irregular plural in English:

(1B+)   Once upon a time there was some *peoples* that had a dog and a child.

(1C-)   That's the mother and they are some little *childrens* playing with her.

(1C+)   The boy is on his *feets*.

Students also erroneously used the irregular plural when they should have used the singular:

TABLE 1

CATEGORIES AND SOURCES OF GRAMMATICAL DEVIATION

Key:

CL = Child Language
IE = Interference from English
IS = Interference from Spanish
NSD = Nonstandard Dialect

Error or Deviation Categories	*English – Source of Difficulty*	*Spanish – Source of Difficulty*
1. *Noun Phrase Constituents*		
Noun Phrase		
Regular and Irregular, Singular, Plural	CL	CL, NSD
Mass. vs. Count Nouns	CL	——
Pronoun		
Omission or Double Marking	CL, IS, NSD	CL
Case Confusion	CL, IS, NSD	——
Wrong Gender	CL, IS	——
Wrong Number	CL	——
Relative Deletion	CL	——
Something/Somebody	CL	——
Wrong Reflexive	CL, IS	——
Possessive/Article Confusion	IS	CL

(continued on following pages)

TABLE 1 (cont.)

Error or Deviation Categories	English – Source of Difficulty	Spanish – Source of Difficulty
Determiners		
Article		
Wrong Gender	——	CL, IE, NSD
Wrong Number	CL, IS	CL, IE
Definite/Indefinite Confusion	CL, IS	——
Omission	CL, IS	CL
Demonstrative		
Wrong Gender	——	CL
Wrong Number	CL, IS	CL
Subject or Object Pronoun for Demonstrative	NSD	——
Noun Inversion or Deletion	IS	——
Adjective		
Wrong Number	——	IE
Inverted Order	IS	——
Some/Much-Many	CL	——
Numerals		
Agreement with Noun	CL, NSD	——
2. *Verb Phrase and its Constituents*		
Verb		
Lack of Subject-Verb Agreement	CL, NSD	CL, IE
Omission of the Copula	CL, NSD	CL
Incomplete or Incorrect Present		
Participle in Progressive	CL	CL

TABLE 1 (cont.)

Error or Deviation Categories	English – Source of Difficulty	Spanish – Source of Difficulty
Incorrect Past and Past Participle	CL, NSD	CL, IE, NSD
Problems of Tense	CL, IS	CL
Infinitive with and without "to"	CL, IS	——
Difficulty with Two-Word Verbs	IS	IE
Difficulty with the Reflexive Particle	——	CL, IE
Adverb		
Incomplete Adverbial Phrase or Omission	IS	——
Position	CL, IS	——
Incorrect Adverbial Expression	——	CL
Preposition		
Wrong Preposition	CL, IS	CL
Omission of Preposition	IS	CL, IE, NSD
3. *Conjunction*		
Wrong Form	CL, NSD	NSD
Omission	CL	——
4. *Negation*		
Double or Incomplete Marking of Negation	CL, IS, NSD	IE
5. *Interrogative and Indirect Questions*		
Incorrect or Incomplete Interrogative Form	IS	——
Incorrect Order for Indirect Question	IS	——
6. *Lexical Problems and "Pocho"*	CL, IS	CL, NSD
7. *Language Alternation*	IS, NSD	IE, NSD

(1B-)   The *women* is doing something.

or used the plural -*s* marker with a singular noun:

(2B-)   There's some houses and a *mountains.*
         There's a *trees.*

(3B+)   There's a *mountains.*
         The man's got the baby in his *laps.*

(1C-)   He's down on the *floors.*

One student not only added the plural marker to a singular noun, but to a noun that does not change in the plural:

(1B+)   A man, and a boy, and a *sheeps.*

The above problems are common in child language, although native speakers of English would probably not make such errors by the time they started school (see Menyuk, 1969).

In Spanish, one student double marked the plural:

(1C-)   La bebita andaba con los *pieses* así.

Students also changed the ending of singular nouns, in one case by analogy with other feminine nouns:

(1C+)   Hay *nieva.* (instead of *nieve)*

in other cases to eliminate the word-final consonant:

(1B-)
(1C-)   Aquí está un árbole.

(1C-)   Casitas y un tree – un *arbolo.*

Most of the above errors are common child language forms. The use of *árbole,* however, is dialect. Particularly in New Mexican Spanish, it is common to add an *e* to a word ending in a consonant (Bowen, 1952).

8.1.1.2 *Mass vs. Count Nouns*

Stockwell, Bowen, and Martin (1967) devote a large section in their book to nouns that normally appear as count nouns and as mass nouns in English and in Spanish, and to differences in usage across languages. The data in the Redwood City study revealed few problems with such nouns, and then only with English nouns.

The following utterances were the only ones which clearly showed lack of understanding of how to use mass nouns in English:

(1C-)   I see *a clothes*.

(1C+)   He gave her *a popcorn* and the little baby ate some.

(2B-)   There's *a dirt*.
They're *fruits* in the basket.

In the above cases, the noun was treated as a count noun. These errors are attributed to child language. Native English speakers have difficulties with mass nouns through the second grade (Hatch, 1970; also see Menyuk, 1969).

8.1.1.3 *Pronoun*

8.1.1.3.1 *Omission or Double Marking*

In both English and Spanish, the personal pronoun was omitted when it was object of the verb or of a preposition:

This boy is turning _____ around.
(2C-)   Me and my sister are thinking but we haven't given _____ name yet.

The cat doesn't want us to get _____ down.
(3C+)   That man is putting _____ down.
A basket with clothes on _____ .

(1B+)   And the teacher is holding _____ like that.

In the above examples, "him," "her," or "it" was implied by the context. In "a basket with clothes on," the omission of "it" could have been by analogy to the expression "A man with clothes on," although the appropriate preposition should have been "in," since the clothes were *in* the basket in the picture.

In two cases, the subject pronoun was omitted:

(1B+)   _____ think the baby's eating an apply.

(1C-)   Then _____ puts this in the pants.

Both of these omissions probably reflect interference from Spanish. In Spanish, the subject pronoun is redundant, particularly in first person, since the inflection of the verb indicates person. The first examples could also be a result of analogy, to sentences in English where it is permissible to delete "I," as in "Think it's time to go." Trager-Johnson and Abraham (1972) found that in a translation task from Spanish into English, Chicanos omitted the subject pronoun in English when the Spanish stimulus sentence had subject pronoun deleted. In "spontaneous response," they found such omissions negligible.

There were several instances of double marking the subject by including the subject pronoun after a noun:

(3C-)
(2C+) The boy *he* had a book in his hand.

This usage is a feature of nonstandard speech, particularly that of Blacks (see Baratz, 1969). Lastra (1975) also observed this double marking in the English speech of primary-school Mexican Americans in Los Angeles.

In Spanish, only one example of personal pronoun omission was found:

(1B-) Está un niño detrás de la maestra con un libro y uno más grande está deteniendo _____

The assumption in calling this deviation "personal pronoun omission" is that the student would have used a pronoun (e.g. *deteniéndola* or *deteniendo a ella*) rather than repeating the noun (*a la maestra*). Perhaps the pronominal form develops late enough so that the child would not be expected to know it here. The omissions in the English examples may reflect interference from Spanish in that there might be confusion about where and when to use the personal pronoun. Whereas in English "The man is putting him down" is fine but not "The man is putting down him," in Spanish both "El hombre le está bajando" and "El hombre está bajándole" are acceptable.

8.1.1.3.2 *Case Confusion*

Case confusion only appeared as a problem with storytelling in English. In a few cases the object pronoun was substituted for the subject pronoun:

(3B-)
Him almost break that tree.
Her is telling him to go.
Her got girl right here.

(2C-)
Him one book.
Me and my sister are thinking.

The use of accusative case pronouns in subject position, as shown above, can be considered both a characteristic of child language (through second grade) (see Hatch, 1970), as well as dialect (see Bartley and Politzer, 1972).

Several children substituted both the subject and accusative case pronouns for the genitive form:

(1B-) *He* father said to him to play with the dog . . . *he* cat go outside.

(1B+) He's holding *he* mother.

(1C+) This *he* sister.

(1B-) He's telling *him* friend to come.

(1B+)   Those boys in line waiting for *she* goes open the door.

According to Menyuk (1969), the above forms like "he cat" and "him friend" are child language (nursery school through grade 1). The explanation she gives is that of phonological similarity. In the case of these data, there is a likelihood that *he* was being confused with *his* through phonological similarity if the child perceived the vowel in both words to be the same, i.e. the *i* of *his* to be the same as the *e* of *he*.

One obvious case of Spanish interference was in the following:

(1C-)   Are these the children *from her,* too?

English would require "her children," while "*los niños de ella*" ("the children of her") is acceptable in Spanish.

8.1.1.3.3   *Wrong Gender*

The wrong gender was used in English both in the subject case:

(1B+)   *He's* something like foster mother.

(2C-)
(1C+)   The mother *he's* eating the apple.

(1C-)   The father *it's* taking care of the baby.

and in the genitive case, with the pronoun erroneously feminine:

(2B-)
(1B+)
(3C-)   The boy's happy with *her* mother.
(3C+)

and erroneously maculine:

(1B+)   There was a lady carrying *his* baby.

(1C+)   He's holding his hands at *his* shoulders. (referring to a woman's shoulders)

These gender problems are in part a reflection of child language. Native English-speaking children have trouble keeping their antecedents straight. However, certain characteristics of Spanish suggest that interference may also play a role. Since the subject pronoun is often omitted in Spanish, its obligatory use in English may cause confusion. In the genitive case, "his" and "her" are both expressed as *su*, which would help explain confusion over gender. While there were only two cases of "his" being used for "her," there were nine instances of "her" replacing "his." Since "her" is the marked category, one might have expected more frequent use of "his" for "her," which was not the case.

8.1.1.3.4 *Wrong Number*

In three instances, the plural pronoun replaced the singular, twice in accusative case:

> There's a big tree with leaves on *them*.
>
> (2B+)   The little girl jumped off a tree and she got hurt; all of them are looking at *them*.

and once in the genitive case:

> (1B+)   And this foster mother taking her like in *their* own babies.

In one instance, the singular replaced the plural in the genitive case:

> (1C+)   They already got *his* book for go to school.

This number confusion is probably a reflection of child language. Particularly in longer sentences, children have trouble choosing the correct pronominal form to match the antecedent.

8.1.1.3.5 *Relative Deletion*

There was a tendency on the part of a small group of children to delete the relative pronoun "who" or "that" after a "there's" construction:

> (1B-)
> (1B+)   There's another one _____ is holding her mother.
> (1C-)   There's a boy's holding that lady.
> (3C+)   There's a little boy _____ has a book.

This deletion of the relative pronoun is not typical of child language, nor is it nonstandard dialect. Such deletion is not practiced in Spanish, so it's not a case of interference. The explanation for such forms is not clear. Perhaps such usage reflects an incomplete mastery of the deletion patterns permitted in English.

8.1.1.3.6 *Something/Somebody*

One student used "something" instead of "somebody":

> (1B+)   And *something* like the grandmother and there's *something* like the Jesus likes the baby.

It is possible that this was a fluke, but it may reflect a lack of awareness of the distinction between the indefinite pronoun for people and the one for things. This is probably a child language phenomenon.

8.1.1.3.7 *Wrong Reflexive*

When using the third person plural reflexive pronoun, one student substituted the genitive "their" for the accusative "them" and singularized the reflexive suffix:

(1B+)   Those boys are ready to go to school by *theirself.*

In Spanish, the reflexive particle *se* merely signals that it is reflexive, but provides no further information. The literature on dialect forms for "themselves" verifies "they own selves" (New York Board of Education, 1968) and "theirselves" (Lin, 1965), but not "theirself." However, "hisself" is dialect, so perhaps "theirself" was concocted partly by analogy and partly by number confusion—"self" for "selves."

8.1.1.3.8 *Possessive/Article Confusion*

In Spanish, the article rather than the possessive pronoun is used to modify parts of the body. For example, "Juan lava *las* manos" ("John washes the hands") is used instead of "Juan lava *sus* manos." This difference between Spanish and English seems to have caused difficulties for several students. One student said the following:

(1B+)   *The* hands are back on that girl.

In reference to personal clothing, another student said:

(1C-)   Then puts this in *the* pants.

The possessive "his" was expected from context since the pants were on the boy's person. Another student similarly used an article for a possessive in Spanish:

(1B+)   Los niños se están yendo a la escuela con *los* libros.

Perhaps in Spanish it is acceptable to say *los libros* instead of *sus libros,* but the possessive form would be more frequently used.

Two students used the possessive pronoun with parts of the body in Spanish where the article would be expected, probably showing interference from English:

(1B+)   Esto perro está poniendo *su* mano.
(1C+)   El tiene *su* mano arriba.

8.1.2 *Determiners*

8.1.2.1 *Article*

8.1.2.1.1 *Wrong Gender*

The Spanish article is inflected for gender. Many children inflected both definite and indefinite articles incorrectly:

(1B-)   *el* mano, *la* papá

(1B-)   *el* mano

(4B+)
la perro
el misa
un señora, *un* niña, *la* gato, *la* niño
los clases

(2C+)
un muchachita, *la* muchachito
la hombre

With feminine nouns like *mano* and *clase,* the use of the masculine article would be a likely mistake because of the irregularity of the noun, but with *misa* and *muchachita* the reasons for switching the gender of the article are not so clear. Perhaps they reflect child-language errors. By the same token, the use of *la* with *papá* and even with *hombre* (by analogy with *clase* and other feminine nouns ending in *e*) is likely, but not *la* with *perro, gato, niño,* or *muchachito.* It may be that English with no gender distinctions causes some young bilinguals to be less discriminating about gender in Spanish. Or perhaps these children have an incomplete mastery of Spanish.

There was one occurrence of reduction of *el* to *l* before a word beginning with a vowel:

(1C-)   La casas y un burro y *l'agua.*

This is common in certain dialects of Spanish, particularly of that spoken in New Mexico (see Bowen, 1952).

8.1.2.1.2 *Wrong Number*

Some students also ran into problems with article-noun number agreement. In Spanish, the following were found:

(1B-)   *el* manos

(2C-)
la casas
un chiquíos

(1C+)   *un* papeles

The use of the singular for the plural definite article may be interference from English where the definite *the* isn't inflected for number. The use of the wrong indefinite article may be child language. In English, one child said:

(1B-)   *A* trees.

The picture showed many trees, so it is likely that he wanted to specify more than one tree and used the indefinite article by mistake.

The problem of number exhibited itself in other ways. One child frequently used "one" for "a":

(1B-)   The father and the mother have *one* baby and one dog . . . The boy see *one* book.

Jespersen (1966) points out that "a" is historically a weakened form of "one." Perhaps this child is reintroducing the use of "one" as a stressed form. Of course, it is more likely interference from Spanish, since the article *un* also serves as the number one. One student even used *uno* in its unshortened form:

(1B-)   Allí estaba *uno* muchacho.

8.1.2.1.3 *Definite/Indefinite Confusion*

There appeared a little confusion over whether to use the definite or the indefinite article in English, or whether to use any article at all. For instance, the indefinite article was used for the definite:

(1B+)   The cat is looking on *a* ground.

In apparent confusion over the form "another," one student said:

(1B+)   *The nother* boy picking up books.

Both of the above appear to be examples of child language. Finally, in:

(1B+)   There's something like *the* Jesus likes the baby.

the student was experiencing interference from Spanish, since Spanish does permit the use of the definite article with first names. Phillips (1967) points out that many of the Mexican-American informants in his study of Los Angeles Spanish did not use the definite article with first names, but that such usage may be found. Phillips reported that such usage was much more common if the name was given in English (e.g. "ahorita va a llegar *el* Rick".)

8.1.2.1.4 *Omission*

In English, both the definite and indefinite article where omitted either before the noun subject or before the noun in the accusative case:

(5B-)
(4B+)
(4C-)   And _____ little boy is touching her mother.
(2C+)

(2B-)
(8C-)　　And that one has _____ book to read.

In four of the fifteen omissions of the article before the subject (before "father," "baby," "cat," "dog"), it could be argued that the child was not just referring to a father or a cat, but actually calling the person or animal "father" or "cat" (e.g. "Baby puts his hand up.") However, other data suggest that such omission cannot be explained as a "naming" procedure. For example, one child said, "Father of the baby is playing," in which "father" is not a name but rather a term defining the kinship relation between the two people.

This omission of the article is a child-language phenomenon for the most part. In one case such behavior could be attributed to interference from Spanish:

(1C-)　　_____ other one is lying in the tree.

In Spanish, the indefinite article is not used with *otro, otra* (Whitmore, 1955; Stockwell, Bowen, Martin, 1967). Therefore, if the child were thinking in Spanish, "Otro se está echado en el árbol," he could very well translate this thought into English as, "Other one is lying in the tree."

In Spanish, there were fewer instances of article omission than in English. All of them are listed below:

(1B-)　　Este es _____ gato.

(1B+)　　La señora tiene _____ niña en brazos y _____ niño estaba colgando de la señora.

(2C+)　　Está apuntando a _____ gato que está arriba en una rama del palo.
La mamá está comiendo _____ dulce.

As with the examples from English, the above article omissions are a product of child language. It is possible, however, that both references to *gato* were treating the word as the cat's personal name, and therefore do not reflect omissions at all.

8.1.2.2 *Demonstrative*

8.1.2.2.1 *Wrong Gender*

As with the article, the demonstrative is inflected for gender in Spanish, and therefore is a potential source of difficulty. In fact, two examples of gender difficulty appeared in the data:

(1B+)　　El gato está yendo para *otro* parte.

(1C-)　　Aquí está *este* señorita.

The first error is more readily understandable as child language in that *parte* looks like a masculine noun and thus takes the masculine form of the demonstrative *otro*. The use of *este* with *señorita* is also a child language error in agreement, but it might indicate incomplete learning of Spanish because such agreement is automatic for almost all the other Spanish speakers in the study.

There was one case in Spanish of an analogical reformation of the masculine singular demonstrative:

(1B+)   *Esto* perro está poniendo su mano.

The child's error is logical since the masculine singular should end in *o* (*esto*) and not *e* (*este*). Slobin (1971) points out that this kind of regularization process is a common feature of child language.

8.1.2.2.2 *Wrong Number*

In Spanish, lack of number agreement between the demonstrative and the noun it modified was noted only once:

(1C+)   Veo *este* casitas y árboles.

In English, such problems were more frequent:

(2B-)   *That* children go to school.
       That little pants too big for him.

(1B+)   *This* five kids were in the yard.

(2C-)   And *that's* shoes.
       That was his shoes.

(1C+)   There once was *this* poor people. (referring to one family)

The use of "this" with "poor people" is very likely interference from Spanish, since in Spanish the form would be *esta gente*. The other English examples and the one Spanish example are child language forms, since the demonstrative is not necessarily inflected for number in the early stages of language learning (see Menyuk, 1969).

8.1.2.2.3 *Subject or Object Pronoun for Demonstrative*

There was also one instance of nonstandard dialect in the substitution of the accusative case pronoun for the demonstrative:

(1B-)   The lady's carrying *them* guys.

Lastra (1975) observed the same phenomenon in her data, although she termed it the repetition of the indirect complement.

8.1.2.2.4 *Noun Inversion or Deletion*

There was one example of noun-demonstrative inversion in English:

> (1C-)   School *this*.

The student probably wanted to say, "This is a school." If so, the inverted form may be a result of interference from Spanish, since Spanish would allow the demonstrative to follow the noun it modifies in certain limited contexts (e.g. *el hombre este*).

Another student deleted the noun after the demonstrative, through interference from Spanish:

> (1C-)   And this _____ looking at a story.

Such a deletion is perfectly acceptable in Spanish since *este* implies both "this" and "this one":

> Este (está) leyendo un cuento.

8.1.2.3 *Adjective*

8.1.2.3.1 *Wrong Number*

Whereas in English the adjective is not inflected for number, it is in Spanish. One student neglected to inflect an adjective for plural:

> (1C+)   A ellos también les pasó algo porque ellos le estaban diciendo *mal* cosas al gato.

This therefore could be a result of interference from English.

8.1.2.3.2 *Inverted Order*

In Spanish, descriptive adjectives can precede or follow the noun, often with little change of meaning (Stockwell, Bowen, and Martin, 1967). Such is not the case in English in that the descriptive objective is expected to precede the noun. Thus, we might expect this to be an area of difficulty for Spanish speakers learning English. However, the Chicano children in the Redwood City study avoided such a problem almost entirely. Only two instances were recorded:

> (2C+)   There's two white boys and a man *white* and two boys *black* and one girl *black*.
> There's a mother *white* and there's a girl *negro*.

In the first example, the child had the order correct at first ("two white boys") and then inverted it for the rest of the sentence. Bartley and Politzer (1972) suggest that only Spanish speakers with little control of English will use modifying adjectives *after* the noun.

8.1.2.3.3 *Some/Much-Many*

The unspecified quantity "some" was used *both* with singular as well as with plural count nouns:

(3B+)
> And there *was some house* and some trees.
> *Here's some house,* here's some more.
> The mother sewing to make him some neat shoes and *some* sweater and a cap.

(2C-)
> I see *some* dress.
> There's some pants and *some* shirt.

These errors might be interpreted as child language, but the New York Board of Education (1968) points out that such forms are also nonstandard dialect. They report as nonstandard dialect both forms with "some" followed by a count noun in the singular, (e.g. "Give us some chain.") as well as "some" followed by an incorrectly pluralized mass noun (e.g. "Give me some cashes.") In the Redwood City data, there were only instances of the first of these two kinds of nonstandard forms. One student said the following:

(1C-)
> She's making clothes for the baby because she doesn't have too *much.*

This "much/many" confusion is a feature of child language (Hatch, 1970), but is also nonstandard dialect.

8.1.2.4 *Numerals*

8.1.2.4.1 *Agreement with Noun*

There were a few examples of singular nouns following numerals:

(1B-)
> And these *two house* is staying right here.

(3C-)
> That's a *two* house
> I have *two cat* in my house.
> I see a tree and *three house* and some leaves.

(1C+)
> There are *three house* and six trees.

Generally, the use of a singular noun with a numeral, such as in "two cat," is both nonstandard dialect (New York Board of Education, 1968) and child language as well. The child may feel that pluralization of the noun is redundant. In some languages, the noun is optionally uninflected or the singular is mandatory after a numeral. However, there is also a phonological explanation in the case of "two house" and "three house." The allomorph /-əz/ of the plural morpheme

-s develops later among children than do the /-s/ and the /-z/ allomorphs (Berko, 1958). This explanation may be true for the three children from the comparison group who did not pluralize "house." The one student from the Bilingual group, however, used "dishes" correctly elsewhere in his story, suggesting that his failure to pluralize "house" was not due to incomplete acquisition of the forms of the plural morpheme.

8.2 Verb Phrase and its Constituents

8.2.1 Verb

8.2.1.1 Lack of Subject-Verb Agreement

Perhaps the most noticeable deviation from standard English occurred with the *there* transformation, i.e. sentences derived from the simple declarative pattern and beginning with the expletive "there" (e.g. "Some students are in the room." "There are some students in the room.") Bartley and Politzer (1972) point out that in Mexican-American nonstandard speech, *there* may be used in the singular instead of the plural ("There is some students in the room") or *there* may not be used at all ("Is some students in the room.") The Redwood City data showed only one possible deletion of *there:*

(1B-)   In back of the tree *is* some houses and some trees.

but some definite patterning of the *there* + *is* + plural noun. There were 40 occurrences of *there's* + plural noun, twelve of them involving *there's* + *some* + plural noun. There were two cases of *here's* + plural noun, and then single cases of *there's* + *lots of* or *a whole bunch of* or *a couple of* + plural noun. After checking with several linguists,[1] I decided to consider the above-mentioned forms as not constituting deviation—a good example of departure from some model of standard in favor of the local varieties, a practice that George (1972) recommends. There was one group of utterances that were considered marginally deviant, namely *there's* + numeral + plural noun:

(2B-)   *There's* three boys and one girl.

(4B+)   *There's* four boys and two girls.

There were also two instances of the uncontracted "there is" form:

---

[1] Personal communication with Charles Fillmore, Evelyn Hatch, and J. Donald Bowen.

(2B+)   *There is* four kids and a mother.
        There is four mountains.

Only Bilingual group students used *there's* + numeral + singular noun. A review of the Comparison group's stories to see if the correct plural verb was used indicated that they didn't specify the number of items in a series as did students in the Bilingual group. They simply used an indefinite determiner like "some." There were other instances of lack of agreement between subject and verb, such as:

(2C+)   There *are* a little girl.
        Then the boy *weren't*.

where perhaps the students had been heavily drilled on the use of "there are" and "they weren't," and simply applied them incorrectly. There was another case of assumed hypercorrection:

(1C-)   The cat *are* going to stay up.

There was also confusion over the distinction between *have/has* and *doesn't/don't*:

(1B-)
(4B+)   And the mother *have* a apple.
(1C-)   He *have* a cat.

(1C+)   This one belongs to you but these three *doesn't* belong.

The use of *have* and *doesn't* are nonstandard dialect (Lin, 1965), but also reflect common child language errors.

Another lack of subject-verb agreement in English involved the nonstandard pattern of dropping the *-s* in the third person singular:

(8B-)   He *see* a cat.

(9B+)   The grandma *sit* down.

(6C-)   The little boy sees a cat and *point* to him.

(7C+)   The cat *go* up the tree.

and adding it where it is not used:

(4B-)
(3B+)   He *gots* an old hat on.
(5C-)   The cat is up the tree and *gots* some little flowers.
(4C+)

(1C-)   I *likes* to go.

The New York Board of Education (1972) points out that pupils may use *-s* in almost any position in the present because they are conscious that *-s* is used in school language but aren't quite sure of the limitations governing its use. Whereas such errors are developmental, particularly a form such as "gots" has become so widely used that it is also nonstandard dialect. Smith (1969) also reports its use among Mexican American children. "Gots" is a regularization through analogy of present third-person "got," which is a common dialect form in present tense to indicate possession:

(1B-)   He *got* girl right here.

(1B+)   He *got* something.

(1C-)   He *got* some pants.

It appears that "gots" and "got" are used in free variation in the speech of some children:

(1C-)   He *gots* a book . . . and he *got* the hat.

The tendency to regularize, as noted in "gots" above, continues well into elementary school and has been noted in a number of languages (Slobin, 1971).

In Spanish, lack of subject-verb agreement involved both person and number errors. There were several errors in person:

(1C-)   El *pongo* los pies arriba y luego se sube.

(1C+)   El no más dijo que no *puedo* hablar y el gato dijo que sí, puede.

(1B+)   El papá dice que no *tienes* miedo. (The context called for *tenga.*)

The three items above could be classed as child-language errors. González (1970) found lack of consistent subject-verb agreement in his subjects up to age 5.

Except for one instance, the agreement errors in number involved confusion about how to say "there's" or "there are" in Spanish. The one exception was:

(1C-)   Las flores *va* a salir.

This error is most likely a child language error. As for the other errors, the students used *está, estaba, es* or *tiene* + plural noun in the same way that they used *there's* + plural noun in English, indicating interference from English. The correct Spanish form "there's" and "there are" is *hay.* The forms that appeared included:

(3B-)   Aquí *está* atrás casas y árboles.

(4B+)   Allí *está* un perro, un bebé, un señor, y una señora.

(3C-)
Allí *estaba* uno muchacho.
Una vez *estaba* una niña y su hermano con su mamá.
Está dos casas y una mesa y seis palos.

(1B-)   Acá *es* una pelota.

(1B+)   Está arriba donde *es* un tree.

(1B-)   *Tiene* árbol aquí y casas y montañas.

The fifth example above "Está dos casas . . .", parallels the agreement problem in English of "there's three boys . . ." and is supported by the Spanish form *hay*.

Many students pluralized the verb form of *estar* to agree with the plural nouns, indicating their awareness of subject-verb agreement rules but still showing interference from English in the use of *están* for *hay:*

(3B-)
(3B+)   Aquí *están* unos trapos.
(4C-)
(2C+)   Allí *están* unas casas y montañas.

8.2.1.2 *Omission of the Copula (English—be: Spanish—ser, estar)*

Both the singular and plural forms of the English copula were omitted:

(4B-)
That _____ what he said.
There _____ houses and trees.
And he _____ happy that the cat likes him.
And they _____ too old.

(3B+)
Who's house _____ this?
And he _____ on a hill.
He _____ afraid to go down.

(4C-)
This _____ a school.
Here _____ the book.
Jesus _____ little child.
This _____ God.

(1C+)   These boys _____ in line.

Nonstandard English is often characterized by the omission of *is* and *are* (New York Board of Education, 1968). Thus, the above deviations are probably attributable to nonstandard dialect. Such forms also reflect child language (Menyuk, 1969).[2]

---

[2] An analysis of deviations in the English speech of 15 *Anglo* kindergarteners in Redwood City in a similar storytelling task showed copula omission to be the highest frequency deviation (e.g. "she getting her shoes on, she in her bed, there a hole").

One Mexican American student omitted the verb "to have" in an utterance:

(1C-)   Him _____ one book.

In Spanish, only one omission of the verb *to be* was noted:

(1B+)   Este _____ el misa.

This omission could be considered child language, although González (1970) reports that only two out of the twenty-seven Mexican American children he studied omitted *ser* by the time they were three and a half years old. Interestingly, the children in the González study who omitted the copula were considered linguistically underdeveloped. Clearly, the Redwood City subjects did not omit the copula in Spanish as often as in English. One possible explanation for this is that when the subject pronoun is deleted, which happens frequently, *ser* and *estar* are essential to the meaning of the sentence:

> Es una escuela.
> Está en la colina.

There was one instance of inappropriate insertion of *es:*

(1B+)   El niño se ve como *es* pobre.

This appears to be a result of interference from English because the English equivalent would be, "The boy looks like he *is* poor."

In the case of the copula followed by the present or past possessive, the Spanish data also showed only very limited omission of *estar:*

(2B+)   Niño estaba colgando de la señora y otra niña _____ viendo lo que estaba haciendo.
La mamá está abrazando una niña y una muchacha _____ abrazando la mamá.

(1C-)   Un niño _____ viendo un gato en el árbole.

The first two examples above could be considered applications of anaphorical reference. All three examples reflect child-language behavior.

In English, on the other hand, there were many omissions of the copula with both the present and past progressive, and with "gonna," an informal or dialectal variant of "going to" (see Fasold and Wolfram, 1970):

(10B-)   She _____ carrying her.
(13B+)   And the grandma _____ washing the dishes.
(11C-)   The children _____ coming in the house.
(9C+)

(2B-) His mother _____ gonna go in store and then they

(1B+) _____ gonna come back to the school.

(3C-) When you _____ gonna be big, you _____ gonna go
with school.

There were 43 occurrences of copula omission with the progressive, spread equally across the speech samples of the Bilingual and Comparison students. The high frequency suggests that such forms are a part of the nonstandard English that the children speak. Bartley and Politzer (1972) identify this form as typical from "some" Mexican American speakers. They also point out that this formation of the progressive also occurs in Black English, but with a slightly different meaning. Trager-Johnson and Abraham (1972) found that Mexican American first-grade and junior high students omitted *is* and *are* with the progressive.

8.2.1.3 *Incomplete or Incorrect Present Participle in Progressive*

There were seven instances of *-ing* omission in the progressive particle and one example of the addition of *-ing* where it was not called for:

(2B-)

(3B+) They're *play.*

(1C-) Man's *talk* to the little boy.

(1C+) She's *sit* down.

(1C-) They're all dressed up, maybe to *going* to school.

Trager-Johnson and Abraham (1972) also found the omission of *-ing*, as in "The lions are look happy." The source for this deviation seems to be child language, rather than nonstandard dialect or interference. (Burt and Kiparsky, 1972, also found such forms in the "adult language" of non-native speakers.) The likelihood of interference here is slight since the progressive in Spanish and English operate similarly. There were several cases of wrong or incomplete formation of the progressive in Spanish, also:

(1B-) El niño está *levante* el mano.

(1B+) La niña está *pone* la mano allí a la gato.

The second example, especially, resembles the incomplete progressive forms produced in English.

8.2.1.4 *Incorrect Past and Past Participle*

In English, both the omission of the past marker *-ed* and its inappropriate use with irregular verbs were noted:

(2B-)   The little boy saw him and *point* at him.

(3B+)
        She already *dress* her up.
(1C-)

(1C+)   A boy sees a cat on a tree, and the cat *climb* up the tree.

(1C-)   He was sleeping and he *awaked* and then he *ranned* up there.

(1B+)
        Then he woke up and he *seen* the little kitten up the tree.
(1C+)

The *-ed* omission in the first example above (i.e. *point* instead of *pointed*) is a common child language error, since *-ed* pronounced /-əd/ develops later in a child's repertoire than do the /-t/ and /-d/ (see Berko, 1958). All the same, as the second and third examples indicate, several children omitted the *-ed* /-t/ after *dress* and the *-ed* /-d/ after *climb*. Such simplification of consonant clusters is characteristic of both child language and of nonstandard dialect.

Double marking of irregular past forms appears in the speech of native English speakers through the primary grades (Hatch, 1970). It is noteworthy that only one instance of that behavior was observed in the Redwood City data (in the fourth example above: *ranned, awaked*). Perhaps such double marking calls for a high degree of "nativeness" in a child's control of English, which some of the children did not yet possess.

The use of the past participle "seen" for the simple past "saw," as illustrated by the last example above, is a well-known feature of nonstandard English (see, for instance, Allen, 1969).

Irregular past forms were replaced by the present in the following cases:

(2B-)   Then he *fall* down—down there in the grass.

(1B+)   There was a teacher; she *hold* a little girl.

(1C-)   A cat *get* up in the tree.

Apparently, native English speaking children learn the irregular past forms first. Then, when they have learned the regular past rule, they regularize the previously learned irregular verb. Subsequently, they begin producing the forms in variation (e.g. he ran/ranned/runned) (see Hatch, 1970). Thus, the above verbal behavior of the native Spanish-speaking Mexican American children is a departure from that of native English speakers in that no past form is used at all. Perhaps, the children were not sure of the correct past forms and so either omitted them or thought of them as regular and thus taking the *-ed*, but simply did not pronounce the *-ed* (e.g. student thought *falled*, but said *fall*).

In Spanish, only one student regularized an irregular past form:

(1C-)   Le bebita andaba con los pieses así y el boy—el muchacho se
ponió aquí.

Another student regularized an irregular present form:

(1C-)   Pero no *sabo.*

The use of *sabo* for *sé* for the first person singular by analogy with the other
present tense forms is common among Mexican American children. It could almost be considered nonstandard dialect among young children and yet only one
occurrence of it was noted here. A student regularized an irregular past participle:

(1C+)   Luego se quedó con una mano *ponida* en el suelo.

This was the only noted occurrence of an irregular past participle being regularized. However, students had other problems with the past participle. Two students had gender problems:

(1B-)   Allí está el perrito con la mano *parado.*

(1C+)   Otro está con su mamá *abrazado.*

In the first instance, the student used the -*o* ending in agreement with the -*o* of
mano, even though the feminine article *la* was correctly supplied. The second
case more clearly indicates an agreement problem.

With the possible exception of *sabo* (if, in fact, nonstandard), all the above-
mentioned deviations in Spanish past and past participle forms could be attributed to child language. González (1970) found the regularization of irregular
verb forms to be the most common type of child-language deviation among his
Mexican American subjects. The Redwood City data did, however, include one
relatively frequent deviant form that was a product of English interference:

(2B-)
(2B+)   El señor está *sentando.*
(3C-)   Acá está *sentando* en el suelo.
(3C+)   Un perro y un baby y un señor *se están sentando.*

It appears that the students were thinking "the man (dog, women, etc.) is (are)
sitting down" and translated literally from English. The correct Spanish form for
"he is sitting down" (meaning "he is seated") is *él está sentado.* To express the
idea in Spanish that someone is in the act of sitting himself down, the reflexive
se is necessary. The fact that this reflexive particle was omitted for the most part
is evidence that the child wanted to say that the person or animal was already
seated. In the two cases where the reflexive particle was used, as in the third
sentence above ("Un perro y un baby y un señor se están sentando"), the con-

text indicates that "seated" rather than "sitting themselves down" was intended. There was also one past form that was a dialectal variant:

(1B-)   ¿Dónde te *cortates?*

The use of *cortates* for *cortaste* in the second person is common in New Mexican Spanish (see Bowen, 1952).

8.2.1.5 *Problems of Tense*

A certain amount of tense switching is common among native speakers, even among adults. But when switching occurred in the same sentence, it was recorded as a deviant form.

In English one group of utterances involving tense switching included the following:

(2B-)   The lady's sitting down eating a apple and the clothes *were* on the floor.
And so the cat didn't come up 'cause *he's* scared.

(1B+)   The little boy went to school and he *plays.*

These forms all appear to reflect child language. Such abrupt tense switches would probably not appear in the speech of older students. Another group of utterances involved the use of the *can* modal in the past instead of the present tense:

(3B+)   The man is holding the baby so he *could* see the little sheep.
He's lifting up her hand so the dog *could* get her.

(2C+)   He's telling him to get down so he *could* play with him.
There's a little boy—only his hand *could* see.

One plausible explanation for the use of *could* instead of *can* in all but the last example above is interference from Spanish. The Spanish expression *para que* ("so that") is often followed by the subjunctive. Thus, the expressions above could all be literal translations from Spanish. The last example above, however, doesn't involve a conjunction, and might reflect uncertainty about when to use the modal *could*. Contributing to the child's confusion would be the knowledge that *could* is used in the present tense in utterances like, "Could you help me?" Thus, the erroneous use of *could* for *can* is also a child-language error, resulting from troubles with semantic properties of English modals.

In Spanish, there was one example of a tense switch similar to those in the first group of English utterances with tense switches mentioned above:

(1C-)   El niño se vió un gato que *corre* y se *sube* a un palo.

The utterance appears typical of child language. The three other utterances involving tense switching all occurred in indirect discourse:

(1B-)   Pero mi mommy le voy a decir que me llevaba a esta escuela.

(1B+)   El papá dice que no *tienes* miedo.

(1C+)   El no más dijo que no *puedo* hablar y el dijo que "sí" *puede.*

In the first case, the child used the imperfect indicative *llevaba* instead of the present subjunctive *lleve*. In the remaining two examples, tense as well as number were confused. In the second example, the third person present subjunctive *tenga* was called for by context, instead of the second person indicative *tienes*. In the third example, the third person preterite form *pudo* was required in both cases. The child used the first person present *puedo* and then the third person present *puede*. All these deviations can be seen as tense problems in child language. Lance (1969) found young Chicano bilinguals he studied had similar problems. The use of *puedo* for *pudo* can also be looked at as an error in the handling of radical shifts, in this case the shift in the stem from *ue* to *u* in the preterite.

8.2.1.6 *Infinitive with and without "to"*

In English, when an infinitive is the object of a verb, it sometimes is preceded by the preposition "to" (e.g. "He asked him *to* do it," "He wanted him *to* do it") and sometimes it isn't (e.g. "He made him do it," "He watched him do it.") Predictably, this variation causes problems for non-native speakers of English (Richards, 1970). Such a problem, therefore, is not the result of interference from another language, but simply the result of a confusing aspect of English, and probably found in the language of native English-speaking children at some early stage of development. The Redwood City data included examples of both kinds of errors—eliminating *to* when necessary:

(1B-)   That boy want _____ go home.

(1C+)   They went _____ play outside.

and inserting *to* when not called for:

(1B+)   The kid is make him *to* jump.

Only the first example above could rightfully be explained as interference[3] since the Spanish *quiere irse,* "he wants to go," does not use the preposition *a*. However, in the second and third examples Spanish operates as does English— *fueron a jugar,* "they went to play," and *le hace saltar,* "he makes him jump."

---

[3] See Stockwell, Bowen, and Martin (1967), p. 208.

8.2.1.7 *Difficulty with Two-Word Verbs*

The idea that is described in a two-word verb in English, such as "lift up" or "climb down," is generally expressed by a single-word verb in Spanish, such as *alzar* or *bajar*. Thus, there is a source of interference in English, and Mexican-American children had two kinds of problems related to this. Some omitted the second part of the verb:

(1B-) There's that thing you put the stuff _____ .

(1B+) They don't got a table to eat _____ either.

(1C-) He wants to get the cat down but it won't climb _____ .

(1C+) Then the other boy came _____ behind her.

And two students made a two-word verb out of a single-word verb:

(1C-) He was trying to catch his cat *back*.

(1C+) The lady is carrying *up* the little girl.

Perhaps as a result of the frequency of two-word verbs in English, there were two instances of inappropriate "two-word verb formations" in Spanish:

(2B+) Está una señora viendo *de* lo que está haciendo el niño.
La mamá andaba haciendo *de* comer.

8.2.1.8 *Difficulty with the Reflexive Particle*

The reflexive particle *se* in Spanish, inflected neither for number nor gender, is used quite widely in Spanish, considerably more than a reflexive pronoun is used in English. For instance, in order to express the concept that someone is hanging from someone or something, the Spanish would be *se está colgando de,* but in English "he is hanging himself from" means that someone is committing suicide.

In the Redwood City data, there were cases of omission of the *se* particle, probably through interference from English:

(2B-) El niño está *sentando.*
(3B+) Acá está *sentando* en el suelo.
(1C-) La señora tiene niña en brazos y niño estaba *colgando* de la
(1C+) señora.

As was pointed out in the above section entitled "Incorrect Past and Past Participle," children substituted the present participle for the past participle most likely through direct translation from English:

He is sitting   El está *sentando*
instead of *El está sentado.*

There was also one case where the *se* particle was used where it was not supposed to be:

(1C-)   El niño *se* vió un gato.

and one instance where *se* was used twice:

(1C+)   La mamá *se* está fijándo*se.*

These last two examples reflect overcompensation, through insertion of an unnecessary *se* in the first case and through double marking the reflexive in the second. These deviations are examples of child language.

8.2.2 *Adverb*

The problems with adverbs and adverbial phrases were not very numerous, probably an indication that these forms are learned early and well, and that they are generally quite simple and regular. There were, however, a few difficulties, as discussed below.

8.2.2.1 *Incomplete Adverbial Phrase or Omission*

One student said the following:

(1B+)   There's some rocks, grass, a tree, and some more houses *back.*

This is probably the result of Spanish interference. In Spanish, *atrás* ("towards the back") would stand alone. English usage calls for a locative phrase like "in back, back there, in the back." Another student omitted the locative altogether:

(1C+)   The cat are going to stay *up.*

This also appears to be a case of interference, since in Spanish the word *arriba* takes the place of an adverbial phrase like "up there" or "up in the tree" in English.

8.2.2.2 *Position*

There were three cases of a misplaced adverb:

(1B-)   What's that *again* called?

(1B+)   They eat *altogether* the dinner.

(1C+)   This boy had *once* a cat.

The last two examples are most likely interference from Spanish, since *juntos* and *una vez* respectively could be placed right after the verb in Spanish. Lastra (1975) attributes the misplaced adverbs she found in the spoken English of Mexican American primary students in Los Angeles to interference from Spanish.

The first example is not a result of interference, but perhaps a child-language confusion over the positioning of "again" in an English sentence.

8.2.2.3 *Incorrect Adverbial Expression*

Several Spanish adverbial phrases were incorrect:

> *en la* afuera
> (3B-)   *al* veces
> *en* lado de

The students appear to have learned incorrectly the expressions *afuera, a veces,* and *al lado de.* These are probably child-language errors.

There was also one case of what seemed to be the omission of an adverb such as *así:*

> (1B+)   Este perro está poniendo su mano _____ .

This was also probably a child-language error. There were three instances of the nonstandard *asina* for *así:*

> (2B-)
> (1B+)   El perrito tiene la mano *asina.*

8.2.3 *Preposition*

8.2.3.1 *Wrong Preposition*

In English, not only did the students frequently use the wrong preposition, but even used as many as five different prepositions instead of the appropriate one:

Appropriate Preposition

> He's pointing *on* the cat on a tree top.
> The boy is pointing the finger *in* the cat.
> He's pointing *from* the cat.   *at*
> He's smiling *to* the cat.
> He put the finger like that *with* the cat.

> Another one is sitting *in* the wall.
> He's holding his hands *at* his shoulders.
> One day that teacher took her *to* a trip.   *on*
> The mother has a girl *up* her.

He's up *to* heaven.	
They want to stand *on* the yard.	*in*
He lives *at* a house.	

	And the boy's like that *after* her.	*behind*
(13B-)	The boy is *at back to* her.	
(23B+)	When you gonna be big, you gonna go	
(16C-)	*with* school.	*to*
(13C+)		
	He's facing *down* the ground.	*toward*
	And that one is holding *to* the mother.	*onto*
	He's fixing something *from* his mother.	*for*
	The mother is sitting *in* the baby.	*with*
	They are playing *on* recess.	*during*
	And this foster mother taking her *like in* their own babies.	*like*
	The cat went *up to* a tree.	*up*
	And so the cat didn't come *up* 'cause he's scared.	*down*
	There's another one *beside of* the wall.	*beside*
	The hands are *back on* that girl.	*on the back of*

Several of the above problems are clear cases of interference from Spanish. Since "in" and "on" are both expressed by *en* in Spanish, it would be expected that "in" and "on" would be exchanged and, in fact, they are (e.g. "*on* the yard" and "*in* the wall"). "To" for "onto" is another result of interference since both these forms are represented by *a* in Spanish (e.g. "agarrando *a* la mamá"). The other errors reflect developmental difficulties with the English prepositional system common to all those who learn English as a second language, both children and adults (see Menyuk, 1969; Richards, 1971). Richards (1970) found foreign adults from many language backgrounds had similar problems with English prepositions. Trager-Johnson and Abraham (1972) also noted the misuse of prepositions by Chicano first graders and junior high students.

At least one of the above examples reflects nonstandard dialect usage, namely "beside of" ("There's another one *beside of* the wall.")

In Spanish, there were many fewer cases of misused prepositions, almost exclusively involving the replacement of *al* (*a* + masculine definite article *el*) by some other form:

	El muchacho está apuntando *con* el gato.	
(3B-)	El perro se quiere subir *con* el señor también.	
(2B+)	El muchacho este está apuntando *con* el palo.	*al*
(1C-)	Allí está un niño apuntando *sobre* el gato.	
	Estaba sentando *de* la tierra.	*en*

It is interesting that three of the prepositions erroneously used for *al* with the meaning "at" (*con, en,* and *sobre*) are equivalent in meaning to the English prepositions used erroneously in English instead of "at," namely, "with," "in," and "on." Thus, whatever semantic confusion was involved in the choice of prepositions in English also applied to Spanish. The Spanish errors, like many of the English ones, are products of child language.

8.2.3.2 *Omission of Preposition*

There were numerous cases of preposition omission in English:

		Appropriate Prepositions
	He's pointing _____ the cat.	
	And the mother is looking _____ the baby.	*at*
(3B-)	He gave it _____ that girl.	*to*
(6B+)	They don't got a table to eat _____ either.	*on*
(5C-)		
(3C+)	That little kid don't have no shoes _____ his own.	*of*
	He's sitting _____ the tree.	*in*
	The girl goes _____ tree house.	*(up) into*

Most of the omissions were of "at" before a person (e.g. "the boy") or an animal (e.g. "the cat"). This omission could very well be a result of interference from Spanish. A feature of the Spanish dialect of many of the students was the omission of the preposition *a* before the direct object, when the object was a person, and in one instance, when it was an animal:

(10B-)	
(17B+)	
(7C-)	La mamá está abrazando _____ la niña.
(8C+)	

(1B-)	El niño estaba riéndose *el* gatito aquí arriba del palo.

It would appear that the students were simply carrying this omission over to English (e.g. "The mother is looking the baby.") In one case, the student introduced a "to" where inappropriate:

(1B+)   The boy is turning around *to* the lady.

The student appears to have translated directly from *dando vuelta a la mujer,* because he wanted to say, "turning the lady around."

Another English prepositional omission that can be traced to Spanish interference is "shoes his own," the fifth of the English examples above. This might be a direct translation from the Spanish *zapatos suyos.* The other omissions of prepositions in English may have been due to an attempt to simplify or some other child-language behavior.

Several students omitted the Spanish preposition *a* with *gustan* constructions of the form:

A María le gusta la niña.

The observed forms were as follows:

(2B+)   _____ la negra le gustaba que la mamá la cargara.
Creo que *el* bebito le gusta al perrito.

(1C+)   Compraron un perrito para el niño y *el* niño así le gustaba mucho.

This might be a result of interference from English, since the form in English would be "the baby liked . . ." and not "to the baby liked."

8.3 *Conjunction*

The students used one conjunction in English almost exclusively, namely "and." The run-on narrative using "and" is a common feature of child language (Hatch, 1970). The cases of this usage were so common in the Redwood City data they weren't even considered deviations. Occasionally children used other conjunctions and several times the choice was inappropriate:

It looks *like if* he's trying to kill the little dog.
(3B+)   He can tell a man *so if* he can use a ladder.
I see a tree *where* the cat is in it.

(2C+)   His father was playing with him *when* the mother was looking.
He had an old shirt *that* the boy didn't have none.

The use of "like if" for "as if" is nonstandard dialect. The "so" in "so if" is simply redundant. The substitution of "when" for "while" is probably an early child-language problem in that the child was probably unsure of the semantic field for the conjunction "when."

There was one instance of omission of a conjunction when it should have been included:

(1B+)   He might go up to somebody _____ tell if he'll help him get a cat down.

There was a slight pause between "somebody" and "tell". A pause instead of a conjunction is a characteristic of child language.[4]

In Spanish as in English, there were also several nonstandard forms used as conjunctions:

(1C-)   Hey, there is a cat *porque como* ellos quieren cazar cats.

(1C+)   La mujer está cosiendo y *como que* está comiendo una apples.

The use of *como* and *como que* may reflect the influence of the English "like" as used in nonstandard dialect.

8.4 *Negation*

8.4.1 *Double or Incomplete Marking of Negation*

The double negative has been documented in the literature as a common feature of nonstandard dialect (see, for instance, Hall and Hall, 1969; Bartley and Politzer, 1972). The Redwood City data showed only a few cases of doubly-marked negatives:

(2B-)   I don't know *no* stories.
I don't know *no* more.

(1C-)   That little kid don't have *no* shoes his own.

(2C+)   But they didn't believe that the cat could talk *neither.*
He had an old shirt that the boy didn't have *none.*

Lastra (1973) found examples such as those above in the speech of Mexican American children from Los Angeles, but she gives no indication of their frequency. There was also one substitution of "no" for "not," similar to the pattern that González (1968) found:

(1B-)   Then the boy gonna come back and he *no* gonna see the cat.

This usage reflects direct interference from Spanish, in which the *no* particle indicates negation. However, as Menyuk (1969) reports, two-year-old native speakers use the *no* particle (e.g. "No write this name").

---

[4]Personal communication with Evelyn Hatch.

In Spanish the only observed problem with the negative was one omission of the *no* particle:

(1C-)   El niño se cayó; después _____ está nadie que le ayude.

The omission of the negative particle may be interference from English where the use of *no,* "not," and *nadie,* "nobody," together would constitute a double negative.

8.5   Interrogation and Indirect Questions

8.5.1   Incorrect or Incomplete Interrogative Form

The Storytelling Task did not purposely elicit questions from students, and thus few were used. In several cases where students did ask questions, the following errors resulted:

(2B+)   *How* do you call this in Spanish?
        How _____ you call these?

The substitution of "how" for "what" as the interrogative pronoun is a clear case of language interference. In Spanish, the expression, "What do you call this?" would be " ¿Cómo se llama esto?" using the pronominal form *como,* literally meaning "how."

The elimination of the auxiliary "do" in the second example above is also interference because no separate tense carrier is required in the Spanish equivalent.[5]

8.5.2   Incorrect Order for Indirect Question

In Spanish the elements of the indirect question are ordered in the same way as are those in the direct question:

¿Quién era ese hombre?
Yo quisiera saber quién era ese hombre.

In English, however, the subject-verb order is reversed in the indirect question:

Who *was* that man.
I want to know who that man *was.*

Several students preserved the order used in Spanish while speaking English, suggesting interference from Spanish:

---

[5] Burt and Kiparsky (1972) refer to the underuse of "do" in questions as a mistake common to students of various language backgrounds, but for the above data, interference from Spanish appears to be the most plausible cause of deviation.

(1B-)   I don't know *what's her name.*

(1C+)   She says that a little boy pushed her down and then after that told the teacher *who was the boy.*

8.6 *Lexical Problems and "Pocho"*

A major lexical problem that the students had both in English and in Spanish was that of choosing the appropriate verb. In English, the following forms were used:

		Contextually-Appropriate Verb:
(2B+)	The lady *told* the little girl, "You wanna hear a story?"	*asked*
(2B-)	The boy *see* one book.	*looked at*
(2B-)	The boy is *seeing* the cat.	*looking at*
(1C+)	The other boy came behind her and started *hearing* the story, too.	*listening to*
(2B-)	And these two house *is staying* right here.	*are located*
	He *put* the finger like that with the cat.	*pointed*
(2B+)	The girl's *putting* the lady.	*holding*
	The boys are gonna go to the library to *change* some books.	*exchange*
(1C-)	A cat climbed up the tree and he doesn't want him to *get on* it.	*be on*
(1C+)	The mother *keep* the girl.	*carries*

The first four examples (*tell – ask, see – look at,* and *hear – listen*) indicate confusions common in child language. The use of "change" for "exchange" appears to be the result of interference from Spanish. *Cambiar* means both "to change" and "to exchange." For the other examples, there may be some semantic confusion based on incomplete knowledge of the semantic fields for certain English verbs—the same kind of problems that young native speakers of the language encounter.

In Spanish, the following verbs were used inappropriately:

		Contextually-Appropriate Verb:
(1B+) (1C-)	El niño se está *recargando* en la señora.	*cargando*

(1B-)	Un chavalito está *deteniendo* un libro.	*llevando* *(agarrando)*
(2B+)	El hermano de ella está *viendo* a ver que dice.	*viniendo*
	La maestra está *teniendo* la niña.	*agarrando*
(3C-)	Un niño *viendo* un gato en el árbole y *poniendo* el dedo al gato riéndose.	*apuntando*
(1C-)	Este está *cargado* de la casa.	*el encargado*
(1C+)	El muchachito este está *aguantando* la mujer.	*agarrando*

The substitution of *viendo* for *viniendo* may simply mark a phonological simplification through syllable deletion, rather than a semantic shift from "coming" to "seeing." The same confusion between "putting" and "pointing" seen above in the English examples also appeared in the *poniendo* – *apuntando* confusion. Also, several children expressed the concept of "holding" (*agarrando*) by the verb *tener, detener,* and *aguantar* respectively. This indicates a lack of certainty of the semantic fields for certain verbs in *Spanish,* as well as in English.

In both English and Spanish, children personified domestic animals and referred to their appendages as they did to those of people:

| (1B-) (5B+) (1C-) | The dog is putting his *hand* like this. |
| (1C+) | Dog is lifting up an *arm.* |

| (1B-) | El perrito tiene la *mano* asina. |

One expression in English showed incomplete learning:

| (1C+) | He's pointing on the cat on a *top tree.* |

The child wanted to say "treetop." Another student employed a redundancy common in child language:

| (1B-) | This one going to kindergarten *school.* |

In Spanish, one student called a church a "mass":

| (1B+) | Este el *misa.* |

This usage is understandable in that in Spanish people say that they are going "to mass," rather than "to church" (e.g. *Vamos a la misa.*)

Some of the Spanish verb forms used by the Mexican American students reflected the influence of English. Several have been brought into the Spanish of the Southwest by bilingual Chicanos, and particularly into dialects of Spanish referred to as *pocho* (see Hernández, Cohen, Beltramo, 1975). Examples of these include the following:

(2B+)   El papá está deteniendo el niño y el perro está *guachando* el niño.

(1B-)   La mamá está tachando la niña.

(1C+)   Luego este es un niño de la clase y éste como si lo *pucharon.*

Guachando, "watching," *tachando,* "touching," and *pucharon,* "pushed," all reflect loans in nonstandard dialect. Two other verbs, *holdando,* "holding," and *pointando,* "pointing," were taken from English, but to my knowledge have not been noted elsewhere:

(1B+)
(1C+)   El muchacho grande está *holdando* la muchachita.

(1B+)   El niño está *pointando* al gato.

One student also made a Spanish noun from "branch," *brancho,* which does not appear to be a *pocho* form:

(1B+)   El niño mira en el *brancho* y quiere coger el gato.

8.7 Language Alternation

This discussion of the Spanish and English syntax of Mexican American primary school children would not be complete without mention of language alternation, the use of words and phrases taken directly from one language while speaking another. This phenomenon has also been referred to as "code switching," "speech mixture," and "language mixing" (see Hernández, Cohen, and Beltramo, 1975).

Two patterns were evident in the Redwood City data. First, there was far more introduction of English words and phrases into Spanish storytelling than of Spanish into English storytelling. Second, language alternation primarily consisted of using nouns from one language while speaking the other language, rather than of switching of phrases back and forth between the two languages.

The following were the only cases of use of Spanish nouns while speaking English:

(1B+)   The road for the *casa.*

(2C-)   This *mesa, palo,* and this baby and this *mamá,* and this doggie and this *padre.*
This *palo* and this *flor.*
Little cat and a little *muchachita.*

(1C+)   Right there's the little *palos.*

Particularly in the second example, the student was just beginning to learn English and may not have known the English names for the nouns referred to in Spanish. Lance (1969) and Gumperz and Hernández (1970) both suggest that language switching is not primarily due to lack of knowledge of words in one of the languages. Rather, they feel that certain kinds of lexical items are more susceptible to switching than others, and that subtle social and psychological factors operate in code switching. Whereas these observations are probably accurate for relatively balanced bilinguals, children who are incipient bilinguals (just starting to learn the second language) may switch to their native language out of necessity—the lack of knowledge of the appropriate words in the second language, as illustrated in the examples above.

There was also one example of insertion of both a noun and its article:

(1B-)   He run in *la escuela*.

Another alternation from English involved use of the Spanish possessive pronoun:

(1B+)   And the boy is putting *su* book down.

The remaining examples involved the use of either partial or total Spanish phrases in English:

(1B+)   The teacher is holding like that *que van a entrar a la escuela* . . .
Down there *hay casitas* and the cat is in the tree.

(1C-)   It's about God and God has their little baby down in the floor *donde está el* sheep.

Most of the language alternation while speaking Spanish involved nouns exclusively. The determiners accompanying these nouns were *all* in Spanish, although they did not necessarily agree with the noun in number, nor with its Spanish equivalent in gender (i.e. "*la* house," because "house" in Spanish is feminine, *la casa*). Several switches may actually reflect loans for lack of a Spanish equivalent:

(1B+)
(1C+)   Tienen una *babysitter* para que los cuide.

(1C-)   Hay un *hippy* que está jugando con el baby.

The bulk of the switches involved English words with common Spanish equivalents, and frequently the student actually used the Spanish form earlier or later in the same storytelling session, indicating that he knew the noun in Spanish. Among the English words brought into Spanish were the following:

(1B-)
(1B+) El gato en el *tree.*
(3C-)

(3B-)
(1B+) El papá está sentendo allí agarrando el *baby.*
(1C+)

(1B-) Allí hay muchos *hills,* montañas, árgoles.
(1B+) Veo este casitas y árboles, una *hill,* y este gatito está sentando.

(1B-) El niño, mi *mother,* un libro, una casa, una cama.
(1B-) Pero mi *mommy* le voy a decir que me llevaba a esta escuela.

(1C+) Allí están . . . las *houses.*
(1B-) Están en un *house.*
(1B-) La mata tiene *flowers.*
(1B+) Un *kid,* el mexicanito, acá está agarrando un libro.
(1C-) Aquí está . . . un *pool,* la *leaves,* y el *grass* aquí.
(1C-) Este *boy* quiere llorar.
(1C-) La bebita andaba con los pieses así y el *boy* y el muchacho se ponió así.
(1C-) Aquí están unas hojas . . . y una *church,* una iglesia, un árbol, y aquí está unos *mountains.*
(1C-) El gato lo anda viendo en el *ground.*
(1C-) Su mamá está con un *apple.*

Switches involving other word classes were few. They included the definite article:

(1C-) El niño se está mirando el perro y *the* perro tiene bebitos.

the conjunction, the preposition, and the subject pronoun:

(1B-) Una niña con una señora *and* un niño *with* niñas . . . *she* tiene una sala.

verbs:

(1C+) La mamá está *holding* la muchachita y otros *holding* la mamá . . . Un chavalo está *pointing* a un gato arriba de un tree.

adverbial phrases:

(1C+) La casa acá está *right there.* El muchacho está viendo el gato y él *on top of that arb.*[6]

---

[6] An attempt to shorten *árbol* to make it English, instead of "tree."

and more complete phrases:

(1C-) El niño está apuntando. *Hey, there is a cat* porque como ellos quieren cazar cats.

(1C+) La mamá es *taking care of the children.*
La mamá *is near the* casa.

Since the Mexican-American students in this study were clearly in a language contact situation in which English was the dominant language, it may be expected that most switching would involve bringing words and phrases from the dominant language into the second language. But one finding in the Redwood City data is that language alternation was not very prevalent.

After two years of observation, the number of switches to English while speaking Spanish decreased by half in similar amounts of corpus:

*Cases of Language Alternation
as Presented Above*

	Total Pre	*Total Post*
Bilingual	10	5
Comparison	12	6

The data show no difference between the Bilingual and the Comparison groups in the rate of decrease in switching into English while speaking Spanish. Both groups curtailed such switching by half between pre- and posttestings. The effect that formal training in Spanish had upon switching among the Bilingual group students is a matter for speculation since the Comparison group, without this formal training, also decreased in the extent of their switching by a comparable proportion.

8.8 *Contrasting the Bilingual and Comparison Groups with Respect to Total Deviations*

The reason for coding the deviant responses according to group (Bilingual or Comparison), testing period (pre- and posttest), and number of children involved was to be able to provide summary statements comparing bilingually- and traditionally-schooled children on Spanish and English syntax. Table 2 presents the raw tally of observed deviations from "school" Spanish and from "school" English, and total deviations for all categories. Increase or decrease in deviations from pretest to posttest is indicated next to the raw totals. The totals are based on data from the 45 Bilingual and 45 Comparison students.

To avoid double counting, if a child made the same kind of error more than once, the deviant form was only recorded once. Thus, the totals do not reflect the total number of errors, but rather the total number of students who made a particular kind of error (e.g. in the verb or with prepositions) at least once.

This comparative analysis pointed up several major differences in the performance of the Bilingual and Comparison students, particularly with respect to English. The Comparison group decreased substantially its error with English determiners from pre- to posttest (23 to 6), while the Bilingual group showed no change (11 both times) (see Table 2). In the use of the English verb, the Comparison group showed a decrease in the number of deviations from pretesting to posttesting (42 to 32), whereas deviations among Bilingual students increased (43 to 54). Finally, a similar pattern occurred with prepositions. Fewer Comparison students showed deviations in posttesting than in pretesting (21 to 16), whereas there was an increase in Bilingual students' use of deviant forms (16 to 30). In the case of determiners, the Comparison group had more students using deviant forms in pretesting than did the Bilingual group, but initial deviations were similar for the two groups with respect to verbs and prepositions. With respect to the total number of students using deviant forms over time, the Bilingual group went from 95 to 112 and the Comparison group from 134 to 82.

The findings suggest that the English of the students in the Bilingual Project was not approximating "school" or standard English as closely as that of the Comparison students. In fact, the data suggest that the Bilingual students' English may have been diverging from standard English over time. Other findings for the Redwood City Study (see Chapter 7) show that the Comparison group measured stronger in certain English language skills at certain grade levels than the Bilingual group. For instance, their speaking vocabulary and several other speaking skills were more extensive and their English reading skills were more developed. Such findings were thought to be reasonable, since the Comparison group were immersed in English schooling exclusively. It was thought, however, that their advantage over the Bilingual group would disappear in time. The same may be said about grammatical performance. As the Bilingual group students improve their English generally, their English grammar will improve.

In Spanish, the summary tally also favors the Comparison group with respect to verbs and prepositions (see Table 2). In this case, differences in change scores between the two groups are not nearly as large as for English. All the same, more Bilingual than Comparison students tended to deviate from "school" Spanish in use of verbs and particularly in the use of prepositions (14 to 21, pre to post, for the Bilingual group vs. 8 to 9, for the Comparison group).

These findings suggest several things. The teachers in the Bilingual Project may have been *using* a so-called "school" Spanish but not *teaching* it. Instead, perhaps little attempt was made to correct deviant forms—i.e. to teach the appropriate forms for different situations, eradicating errors based on interference from Eng-

TABLE 2
TABLE OF DEVIATIONS FROM "SCHOOL" SPANISH AND "SCHOOL" ENGLISH*

Categories	Bilingual									Comparison								
	Spanish			English			Combined			Spanish			English			Combined		
	Pre	Post	Diff.	Pre	Post	Diff.	Pre	Post	Diff.	Pre	Post	Diff.	Pre	Post	Diff.	Pre	Post	Diff.
1. *Noun Phrase Constituents*																		
Noun Phrase	2	2	0	13	19	+6	15	21	+6	3	2	-1	20	17	3	23	19	-4
Determiners	7	7	0	11	11	0	18	18	0	4	7	+3	23	6	-17	27	13	-14
2. *Verb Phrase & its Constituents*																		
Verb	16	21	+5	43	54	+11	59	75	+16	14	11	-3	42	32	-10	56	43	-13
Adverb	5	2	-3	1	2	+1	6	4	-2	0	0	0	0	2	+2	0	2	+2
Preposition	14	21	+7	16	30	+14	30	51	+21	8	9	+1	21	16	-5	29	25	-4
3. *Conjunction*	0	0	0	0	4	+4	0	4	+4	1	1	0	0	1	+1	1	2	+1
4. *Negation*	0	0	0	3	0	-3	3	0	-3	1	0	-1	1	2	+1	2	2	0
5. *Interrogative & Indirect Question*	0	0	0	1	2	+1	1	2	+1	0	0	0	0	1	+1	0	1	+1
6. *Lexical Problems & "Pocho"*	3	9	+6	6	9	+3	9	18	+9	5	3	-2	2	4	+2	7	7	0
7. *Language Alternation*	10	5	-5	1	3	+2	11	8	-3	12	6	-6	3	1	-2	15	7	-8
TOTALS	57	67	+10	95	134	+39	152	201	+49	48	39	-9	112	82	-30	160	121	-39

*Data are expressed as the number of students making at least one mistake within the given category.

lish, etc. In an attempt to encourage free bilingual expression, the teachers may have been less likely to correct and to drill on the correct forms. How the Comparison group came out slightly stronger in Spanish is hard to explain. Perhaps there was some transfer from what they learned of "school" English to their use of Spanish, though normal maturation is a more credible explanation. It didn't appear that the Spanish spoken by the parents of the two groups was markedly different, so this shouldn't have been a factor. Research has found there is positive transfer of language skills from one language to another such that the group schooled only in language Y but speaking X at home can also be stronger in language X after a certain number of years than a group schooled in both X and Y (see Revil *et. al.*, 1968, on research findings in the Philippines, 2.2.2).

8.9 *Relative Frequency of Different Kinds of Deviations*

It is difficult to make summary statements about the *source* of the observed deviations because there were often categories for which more than one source was reported (see Table 1 above).

As stated at the outset of this error analysis, deviations from school Spanish or school English may reflect child language, nonstandard dialect, or language interference. Table 1 (see above) listed the 41 categories of deviations, 20 of which were found exclusively in English, 5 exclusively in Spanish, and 16 in both English and Spanish. Altogether, there were 37 categories of deviation in English and 21 categories in Spanish.

Out of the 37 English categories, child language was an explanation for deviation in 27 of the categories, interference from Spanish in 23 of the categories, and nonstandard dialect in 10 of the categories (see Table 3).

For the Spanish categories, child language was an explanation for deviation in 18 of the 21 categories, interference from English in 10 of the 21 categories, and nonstandard dialect in 7 of the categories (see Table 3). The conclusion that might be drawn from these tallies is that child language errors were the predominant source of deviation in both English and Spanish, and particularly in Spanish, for Mexican American K-3 bilinguals in Redwood City. Interference from Spanish was a likely source of deviation in speaking English more frequently than was interference from English a problem in speaking Spanish. This was to be expected since Spanish was the first language of the students in the study and was generally the dominant language for most of them. Nonstandard dialect was the least prevalent source of deviation both in English and in Spanish, but still characterized the children's speech, certainly more than Trager-Johnson and Abraham (1972) found was true for Mexican Americans in San José. They found only a few cases of nonstandard dialect in the deviant forms of the first graders and junior high students they studied.

TABLE 3

RELATIVE FREQUENCY OF SOURCES OF DEVIATION IN SPANISH AND ENGLISH

Grammatical Categories
Where Deviations Found

Source of Deviation	English—from Total of 37 Categories		Spanish—from Total of 21 Categories	
	No.	%*	No.	%
Child Language	27	73**	18	86
Interference	23	62	10	48
Nonstandard Dialect	10	27	7	33

*Percent totals exceed 100% because more than one source of deviation applied to a number of the grammatical categories (see Table 1).

**73% = 27/37.

Of course, there is the problem of what to call child language as opposed to nonstandard dialect. Some forms are clearly both. There is also a grey area between child language and interference. A form may not seem native-like and yet cannot be traced to some pattern in the other language which is causing interference. In this study, it was assumed that such a form might be used by a native speaker of the language at some early stage in his language development. Another approach is to say that these errors are developmental but characteristic of *non*-native learners of the language, the approach taken by Trager-Johnson and Abraham (1972). However, this approach ignores the language acquisition patterns of the native learner and assumes, and perhaps accentuates, a difference between the problems of first- and second-language acquisition for young children. The Redwood City findings suggest that for young children, first- and second-language acquisition problems may be quite similar.

A further analysis of the data was conducted to determine differences in sources of deviation between the Bilingual and the Comparison groups over time. Table 4 presents the raw frequencies and percentages in pre- and posttesting for the occurrence of child language, interference, or nonstandard dialect as the suggested source of deviation for Bilingual and Comparison groups separately. Looking at English deviations, where the Bilingual group had a substantial increase in students' use of deviant forms from pre- to posttesting (95 to 134) and the Comparison group had a substantial decrease (112 to 82), several trends emerged. It can be seen that the bulk of the increase in Bilingual-group deviations were attributed to child language and interference from Spanish. The decrease in Comparison group deviations was a result of fewer deviant forms attributed to child language and to nonstandard dialect. The share of deviations attributed to interference from Spanish increased from pretesting to posttesting for both the Bilingual and Comparison groups (whereas the actual frequency remained about the same)—Bilingual: 28% of total posttest deviations vs. 20% of total pretest deviations; Comparison: 32% of posttest deviations vs. 25% of pretest deviations (see Table 4). This finding suggests that the source of deviation in English *least* susceptible to correction through instruction and maturation is that of interference from Spanish, both for bilingually- and traditionally-schooled students.

A different pattern emerges from the data on Spanish deviations. Whereas the Bilingual group maintained from pre- to posttesting roughly the same proportion of deviant forms attributable to interference from English (44% to 45%), the Comparison group had *fewer* deviant forms proportionately that were attributed to interference from English (50% to 41%; see Table 4). Such a finding suggests that whereas bilingual instruction doesn't appear to affect interference from Spanish in speaking English, it may encourage interference from English in speaking Spanish. According to recent research, the alternate use of two languages in the same classroom (even the teacher's alternate use of two languages in the same sentence) need not cause the students to mix the two languages (see Mackey, 1971). Since most of the switching into English was for one or another noun, perhaps the effect of bilingual instruction is to stimulate greater continued use of English nouns in speaking Spanish, either out of confusion as to the language that the word belongs to or out of lack of knowledge of the word in Spanish. The Comparison students, learning and using their Spanish in domains largely non-overlapping with those in which English was used, may be expected to experience less interference from English in their Spanish over time than the Bilingual students who are constantly in a two-language environment at school.

Further error analyses or studies of deviation should be conducted on data from bilingual children in other areas and situations to better understand what their language is like and to explain sources of confusion. As stated at the outset, a knowledge of the source of the confusion should help the classroom teacher know what teaching technique to employ to handle the various kinds of language problems arising in classrooms characteristic of language contact situations.

8.10   *Summary*

8.10.1   This chapter provided a description of grammatical deviations in the spoken Spanish and English of Mexican American primary school students. Using "school" language as the basis for 'etermining deviation, such deviations were categorized as being products of language interference, child language, or non-

TABLE 4
BILINGUAL AND COMPARISON GROUP DEVIATIONS BY SOURCE

BILINGUAL GROUP

Source of Deviation	Spanish				English				Combined			
	Pre		Post		Pre		Post		Pre		Post	
	No.	%a	No.	%b	No.	%c	No.	%d	No.	%e	No.	%f
Child Language	13	23	20	30	68	72	87	65	81	53	107	53
Interference	25	44	30	45	19	20	37	28	44	29	67	33
Nonstandard Dialect	14	25	21	31	42	44	46	34	56	37	67	33

COMPARISON GROUP

Source of Deviation	Spanish				English				Combined			
	Pre		Post		Pre		Post		Pre		Post	
	No.	%g	No.	%h	No.	%i	No.	%j	No.	%k	No.	%l
Child Language	17	35	14	36	68	61	50	61	85	53	64	52
Interference	24	50	16	41	28	25	26	32	52	32	42	34
Nonstandard Dialect	13	27	13	33	45	40	30	37	58	36	43	35

Note: Total percentage for each of the 12 subdivisions does not add to 100% because more than one source of deviation sometimes applied to the same deviation.

a. % of 57 Bil. Sp. Pretest Deviations.
b. % of 67 Bil. Sp. Posttest Deviations.
c. % of 95 Bil. Eng. Pretest Deviations
d. % of 134 Bil. Eng. Posttest Deviations.
e. % of 152 Bil. Pretest Deviations.
f. % of 201 Bil. Posttest Deviations.
g. % of 48 Comp. Sp. Pretest Deviations.
h. % of 39 Comp. Sp. Posttest Deviations.
i. % of 112 Comp. Eng. Pretest Deviations.
j. % of 82 Comp. Eng. Posttest Deviations.
k. % of 160 Comp. Pretest Deviations.
l. % of 122 Comp. Posttest Deviations.

standard dialect. The deviation analysis was based on Spanish and English speech samples elicited from the Bilingual and Comparison students on a pretest-posttest basis, with a two-year interval in between. The Storytelling Task was used to elicit the speech samples.

8.10.2 Deviations were grouped under the following general categories: noun phrase constituents, verb phrase and its constituents, conjunctions, negative, interrogative and indirect questions, lexical problems and "Pocho," and language alternation. Each deviation was coded to indicate how many children from which group (Bilingual or Comparison) produced the form, and whether it was produced in pre- or posttesting.

8.10.3 The chapter concluded with a series of summary statements, including rough statistical counts. Total deviations made by the Bilingual group were contrasted with those for the Comparison group. The findings showed that the English of the students in the Bilingual Project was not approximating "school" or standard English as closely as that of the Comparison students over time. Furthermore, more Bilingual than Comparison students tended to deviate from "school" Spanish, but not nearly as much as in the case of English. The chapter also included a discussion of the relative frequency of different kinds of deviations, both with the two groups combined and contrasted. Child language accounted for most deviations in English, but interference from Spanish came in a close second, with nonstandard dialect substantially behind. Child language also accounted for most deviations in Spanish, with interference from English and nonstandard dialect both accounting for considerably fewer deviations.

8.10.4 Looking at the Bilingual group in contrast to the Comparison group, the Bilingual group's increase in deviations from school English over time was attributed to child language and interference from Spanish. The decrease in Comparison-group deviations was attributed to a decrease in child language and nonstandard dialect forms. Actually, both Bilingual and Comparison groups showed an increase in deviant forms attributable to interference from Spanish, suggesting that the source of deviation in English *least* susceptible to correction through instruction and maturation is that of interference from Spanish, both for bilingually- and traditionally-schooled students.

8.10.5 With respect to Spanish, the Bilingual group maintained over time roughly the same proportion of deviant forms attributable to interference from English, while the Comparison group had fewer forms attributable to such interference. Thus, whereas bilingual instruction doesn't appear to have affected interference from Spanish in speaking English, it may have encouraged interference from English in speaking Spanish.

While this chapter has dealt with the language forms that the children used, the following chapter will address itself to the issue of which language they chose to use, as assessed through direct observation of the students, interviews with them, and interviews with their parents.

9. LANGUAGE USE

Does a bilingual program promote greater use of Spanish among its Mexican American participants than is found among comparable non-project participants? This question was posed in Chapter 5, and this chapter provides an answer, based on the results of research in Redwood City. Language use is seen as a measure of language maintenance. This study attempts to measure the effects of bilingual schooling on the language use of Mexican American children. If bilingual schooling has an interventionist effect, then perhaps the children in the program might be seen to use Spanish as much several years after being in the program as they did at the outset. On the other hand, children in a comparison group may be expected to be using Spanish less after a comparable period of time.

In this chapter, the instruments used to measure language use are described, and means of administration are discussed. Then the results are presented, followed by an interpretation of the findings.

9.1 Instruments and Procedures

9.1.1 Students' Spanish Language Use

9.1.1.1 The Language Use Observation Instrument

The Language Use Observation Instrument was based on studies by Cooper and Carpenter (1975), Ramírez (1971), and Fillmore (1971). Its intent was to measure the language use of both Mexican American and Anglo children in four different contexts at school: two within the classroom setting (math and social studies/science), and two outside of the classroom setting (lunch and playground). The two classroom settings were intended as more formal, and lunch and playground were intended as more informal. The observers watched children for one minute (after the children started talking) in each of the four settings on three different days. The observer noted the language that the child used—Spanish or

English; to whom the child addressed his remarks—to a Mexican American or Anglo teacher or teacher aide (combined into one category, "adult," for the purposes of analysis), or to a Mexican American or Anglo student; the grouping arrangement the child was in—whole class, small group, or individual; and the language that the adult was using at the time (if an adult was present).

9.1.1.2 *Pupil's Language Use Inventory*

Based on an instrument developed by Fishman, Cooper, Ma *et al.* (1971), the Pupil's Language Use Inventory asked for the student's self-report of his language use by domain. The child was asked the language he used and the language used by others to address him when he was with various members of his family at home, with classmates at school, with peers in the neighborhood, and at church with his companions. Response choices included "Spanish," "English," and "both." All the items relating to the student's own language use were combined as an index of *student* language use—*student* report (items 1b, 2b, 4b, 5b-8, in the Pupil's Language Use Inventory, Appendix 1.7). Items relating to the language use of other family members were combined as an index of *family* language use—*student* report (items 1a, 2a, 3, 4a, 5a).

9.1.1.3 *Parent Rating of Students' Language Use*

As part of a Home Interview Questionnaire, parents were asked about the student's language use patterns by domain (based on Fishman, Cooper, and Ma *et al.*, 1971). The parents were asked what language the student used at home to speak with adults, to speak with children, to read books or magazines, and to write letters, and what language he used to talk with peers in the neighborhood. These items were combined as an index of *student* language use—*parent* report (see Home Interview Questionnaire, 1970 & 1972, Appendix 1.10).

9.1.2 *Students' English Language Use*

9.1.2.1 *The Language Use Observation Instrument*

This was the same instrument mentioned above under Spanish Language Use. The instrument was used to measure the English and Spanish language use of Mexican American and Anglo students in four contexts at school—math class, social studies or science class, lunch, and playground.

The Ramírez (1971) study served as the pilot study for the Language Use Observation Instrument. Ramírez' results helped determine the modifications that were necessary (see Appendix 1.6). A random subsample of eight Mexican American children from the Pilot, Follow Up I, and Follow Up II levels respectively were selected for observation, and were observed in February and March of 1972. One Mexican American observer was assigned to each subgroup of Mexican Americans.

9.1.2.2 *Pupil's Language Use Inventory*

This is the same instrument mentioned above under Spanish Language Use. This interview sheet was used to obtain a student's self-report of the language he used and the language used by others to address him when he was with family at home, with classmates at school, with peers in the neighborhood, and with companions at church. Items relating to the student's own language use were combined as an index of *student* language use—*student* report. Items relating to the language use of other family members were combined as an index of *family* language use—*student* report.

The Pupil's Language Use Inventory was administered individually to all Mexican Americans in the Bilingual and Comparison groups along with other individual measures. Students were interviewed by Mexican American college students, using the Spanish form of the questionnaire (see Appendix 1.7). The interviews were conducted in small office rooms at both schools. The questionnaire was administered in October and November of 1970 and then again in April of 1972.

9.1.2.3 *Parent Rating of Students' Language Use*

This is the same instrument mentioned above under Spanish Language Use. Parents were asked what language the student used at home with adults and with children, for reading and writing, and the language he used with peers in the neighborhood. These items were combined as an index of *student* language use—*parent* report. Interviews with parents were conducted twice, in order to obtain a before measure (winter, 1970-1971) and an after measure (spring, 1972) (see Figure 1).

9.2 *Results*

At the Pilot level, the Bilingual students reported that other family members (parents, older and young brothers and sisters) used significantly more Spanish with them than Comparison students reported their families doing (F=4.88, df=1/26, p<.05), after adjusting for initial differences.[1] Both student groups reported more Spanish than English being used by other family members, but the Bilingual students reported more use of Spanish altogether. This could be a reflection of the students' training in Spanish at school. This training may stimulate the student to speak more Spanish at home, and consequently he is responded to in Spanish more frequently. Parents' report indicated that the Bilingual students *were* using more Spanish at home than the Comparison students, after adjusting for initial differences (F=4.60, df=1/26, p<.05). The Bilingual students were reported using more Spanish than English, but the Comparison group was said to use more English than Spanish. However, the Language Use Observation Instrument showed the Bilingual group used *more English* with other Mexi-

[1] See Appendix 4 for complete Analysis of Variance and Covariance data.

can American students out of class (on the playground and at lunch) than did the Comparison students (F=20.08, df=1/12, p<.01) (see Table 1, pp. 224-225). Perhaps this phenomenon was a reflection of the in-class language pattern. At the Bilingual school, Spanish was used extensively in class, so English was preferred out of class "for a change," whereas at the Comparison school, English was more or less mandatory in class, but in the playground and at lunch the child could speak Spanish.

At the Follow Up I level, only one significant difference in language use was observed. The Bilingual group was observed to use more Spanish to adults in the classroom than were the Comparison students (F=5.31, df=1/12, p<.05) (see Table 2, p. 229). This pattern would be expected since students at the Comparison school were not encouraged to speak Spanish to adults. They did, however, speak Spanish to the principal (who was Latin American), and the observers included those interactions on the rating sheet. One phenomenon true only at the Follow Up I level and only for the Bilingual group was that the students reported an *increase* in their use of Spanish from pretest to posttest. On a 14-point scale (with 14 being maximum use of Spanish), the Bilingual students had a mean pretest score of 6.94, and a mean posttest score of 8.37 (see Table 2, p. 228).

At the Follow Up II level, the Bilingual students reported themselves using more Spanish than the Comparison group reported for themselves (F=12.13, df=1/27, p<.01). Furthermore, whereas the Comparison group reported using English more than Spanish, the Bilingual group reported using Spanish more than English. This report was corroborated by the parental report which also indicated that the Bilingual students used Spanish more than did the Comparison students (F=6.27, df=1/27, p<.05), and similarly, the Comparison group was reported to use each language about the same, while the Bilingual group used Spanish more than English. Contrasting the Bilingual and Comparison groups on the Language Use Observation Instrument, the Bilingual group was observed using Spanish more with adults in class (F=7.87, df=1/12, p<.05) and with other Mexican American students out of class (F=20.01, df=1/12, p<.01), while the Comparison group was observed to use English more with other Mexican American students out of class (F=15.48, df=1/12, p<.01) (see Table 3, pp. 230-231). The results of the observation appear quite reasonable: if the Bilingual students used more Spanish out of class with Mexican Americans, they also used less English.

Whereas Tables 1-3 indicate the percent of observations of Mexican American students speaking English to Anglo students in class and out of class, use of *Spanish* to Anglos is not indicated because the incidence was so slight. At the Pilot level, Mexican American students were not observed to use Spanish with Anglo students either in class or out of class. At the other two levels, such use was very limited.

FIGURE 1

SCHEDULE FOR ADMINISTRATION OF LANGUAGE USE INSTRUMENTS

	BEFORE MEASURE		AFTER MEASURE	
	Group Levels	Month/Year	Group Levels	Month/Year
SPANISH AND ENGLISH LANGUAGE USE:				
Language Use Observation Instrument	All Group Levels, Random Subsample	2/72-3/72		
Pupil's Language Use Inventory	All Group Levels	10/70-1/71	All Group Levels	4/72
Parent Report of Student Spanish and English Language Use	Parents All Group Levels	12/70-1/71 (*2/71-3/71)	Parents All Group Levels	5/72-6/72

*Several families

Groups: Mexican American Bilingual
          Mexican American Comparison

Group Levels: Pilot
          Follow Up I
          Follow Up II

TABLE 1

MEXICAN AMERICAN STUDENTS' LANGUAGE USE

PILOT LEVEL

	Group	N	Pretest Mean	Posttest Mean	Posttest Mean Adjusted For Pretest	F
Student Language Use—Student Report (14-Point Scale)	P	15	8.27	7.07	7.08	0.24
	C	14	8.36	6.79	6.77	
Student Language Use—Parent Report (10-Point Scale)	P	15	6.07	5.40	5.28	4.60*
	C	14	4.64	3.21	3.34	
Family Language Use—Student Report (12-Point Scale)	P	15	7.33	6.87	7.03	4.88*
	C	14	7.64	6.14	5.97	

P = Pilot Group

C = Comparison Group

*p<.05

TABLE 1 (cont.)

LANGUAGE USE OBSERVATION INSTRUMENT
(DATA EXPRESSED AS % USE IN CLASS, OUT OF CLASS)

	Group	N	Pretest Mean	Posttest Mean	Posttest Mean Adjusted For Pretest	F
INCLASS Spanish to Mex. Am. Student in Class	P	7		0.08		1.48
	C	7		0.04		
English to Mex. Am. Student in Class	P	7		0.42		0.77
	C	7		0.33		
English to Anglo Student in Class	P	7		0.17		0.15
	C	7		0.15		
Spanish to Adult in Class	P	7		0.06		1.83
	C	7		0.00		
English to Adult in Class	P	7		0.27		3.24
	C	7		0.48		
OUTOFCLASS Spanish to Mex. Am. Student out of Class	P	7		0.16		2.15
	C	7		0.33		
English to Mex. Am. Student out of Class	P	7		0.63		20.08**
	C	7		0.37		
English to Anglo Student out of Class	P	7		0.21		0.86
	C	7		0.30		

**p < .01

The language use results are most promising for the prospects of bilingual education. If a bilingual program is intended to encourage bilingual youngsters to use their language of heritage, then these results show that, in fact, this is going on. Student report, parental report, and direct observation, all provided evidence to that effect.

9.3 *Summary of Findings and Discussion*

The Bilingual Project did promote greater use of Spanish among its Mexican American participants than was found among comparable non-project participants. On the basis of parental report, the Bilingual Pilot group was reported to be using more Spanish than the Comparison group at the end of the study. The Bilingual group was also reportedly using more Spanish than English, while the Comparison group was using more English than Spanish. Students' report of the language that family members used in speaking to them showed that, while both the Bilingual Pilot and Comparison students were addressed predominantly in Spanish, the Bilingual students were still addressed significantly more in Spanish than were the Comparison students. Also the Bilingual Project students were observed using English more often out of class (on the playground and at lunch) when addressing other Mexican American students than were the Comparison students.

The Bilingual Follow Up I students were observed to use Spanish more frequently to adults in class than were the Comparison students.

Students' report of language use showed far more use of Spanish by the Bilingual Follow Up II group than by the Comparison students. The Bilingual group maintained almost the same high level of Spanish use over two years of bilingual schooling, while the Comparison group shifted to about equal use of English and Spanish during two years of English-only schooling. Parental report also showed the Bilingual group to be maintaining the predominant use of Spanish, while the comparison group had shifted to the predominant use of English. The Bilingual students were observed to use Spanish more frequently with adults in class and with other Mexican American students out of class than were Comparison students. The Comparison students used more English in addressing other Mexican American students out of class than did the Bilingual students.

It appears that the Bilingual Project in Redwood City did contribute to the maintenance of the Spanish language by encouraging the use of Spanish among the students involved. The fact that the students were given formal schooling in Spanish and used Spanish as a vehicle for learning the subject matter appeared to have acted as in incentive for them to continue to use Spanish regularly in a variety of social interactions. An irony of bilingual schooling is that program staffs are now encouraging children to behave in a way that had been shunned for fifty years or more in most U.S. schools: to use their native language at school. In a sense, the new pattern is one of reverse socialization. Whereas school children had been subjected to the English-only rule whereby they were punished, even suspended or expelled, for using a language other than English in school (see Espinosa, 1917; Bernal, 1969; Carter, 1970; Ortego, 1970; Cannon, 1971),[2] now they are being encouraged to use that language in school.

One finding, however, runs counter to the other findings. Bilingual Pilot students were observed to use more English with other Mexican American students out of class (on the playground and at lunch) than did the Comparison students. As suggested in the Results section, this finding may simply indicate a desire for a change, since Spanish was spoken so extensively in class. All the same, this group represents the students with the most bilingual schooling, and the results of the language use observation may reflect a trend toward greater use of English. Note that student self-report of language use did not differ significantly between the Bilingual Pilot and Comparison groups. Both groups reported using English and Spanish about the same amount of time. Perhaps a bilingual program has only an interim effect on language use. If so, perhaps the students in the bilingual project eventually succomb to social pressures to use English at the expense of Spanish, particularly within a school population of predominantly monolingual English speakers—as was the case at the Garfield School in Redwood City.

It appears that no other study of a bilingual project in the U.S. has contrasted the language use patterns of students in the project with comparison students. Thus, it is not possible to relate these findings to those of other projects. Hopefully, other such studies will appear in the near future. The language use studies on Spanish speakers that are available pertain to patterns in Texas and New Mexico (see Mahoney, 1967; Thompson, 1971; Timmins, 1971), and generally conclude that Spanish language use is on its way out, except in certain rural areas. However, these results do not pertain to California. Neither do they pertain to students enrolled in bilingual programs nor to the communities in which these students live. It should also be remembered that the Bilingual students were for the most part from families that had immigrated to the United States from Mexico within the previous ten years. Thus, these children were also first- and second-generation Spanish speakers. For this reason, one would expect Spanish to be used considerably, both among the Bilingual and the Comparison children. The significant differences in the language use patterns of these two groups were attributed to the interventionist effects of bilingual program.

This chapter has concerned the sociolinguistic assessment of language use patterns. The next chapter turns to paper-and-pencil tests used to measure the effects of bilingual schooling upon the acquisition of mathematical skills and upon the development of certain intellectual abilities.

---

[2] See also the U.S. Commission on Civil Rights Report III, *The Excluded Student,* 13-20, 1972, for more on "no Spanish" rules.

TABLE 2
MEXICAN AMERICAN STUDENTS' LANGUAGE USE
FOLLOW UP I LEVEL

	Group	N	Pretest Mean	Posttest Mean	Posttest Mean Adjusted For Pretest	F
Student Language Use—Student Report (14-Point Scale)	FUI	16	6.94	8.37	8.61	0.58
	C	15	9.47	8.40	8.14	
Student Language Use—Parent Report (10-Point Scale)	FUI	16	5.50	4.25	4.40	0.10
	C	15	7.67	4.33	4.17	
Family Language Use—Student Report (12-Point Scale)	FUI	16	7.13	6.81	6.89	0.04
	C	15	7.63	7.07	6.99	

FUI = Follow Up I Group
C   = Comparison Group

TABLE 2 (cont.)

LANGUAGE USE OBSERVATION INSTRUMENT
(DATA EXPRESSED AS % USE IN CLASS, OUT OF CLASS)

	Group	N	Pretest Mean	Posttest Mean	Posttest Mean Adjusted For Pretest	F
IN CLASS Spanish to Mex. Am. Student in Class	FUI	7		0.26		0.37
	C	7		0.19		
English to Mex. Am. Student in Class	FUI	7		0.34		0.11
	C	7		0.30		
English to Anglo Student in Class	FUI	7		0.13		0.11
	C	7		0.16		
Spanish to Adult in Class	FUI	7		0.09		5.31*
	C	7		0.00		
English to Adult in Class	FUI	7		0.18		2.41
	C	7		0.35		
OUT OF CLASS Spanish to Mex. Am. Student out of Class	FUI	7		0.37		0.46
	C	7		0.28		
English to Mex. Am. Student out of Class	FUI	7		0.46		0.09
	C	7		0.43		
English to Anglo Student out of Class	FUI	7		0.17		1.07
	C	7		0.29		

FUI = Follow Up I Group
C = Comparison Group
*p<.05

TABLE 3

MEXICAN AMERICAN STUDENTS' LANGUAGE USE

FOLLOW UP II LEVEL

	Group	N	Pretest Mean	Posttest Mean	Posttest Mean Adjusted For Pretest	F
Student Language Use—Student Report (14-Point Scale)	FUII	14	11.00	10.29	10.01	12.13**
	C	16	10.06	7.37	7.62	
Student Language Use—Parent Report (10-Point Scale)	FUII	14	6.07	5.86	5.77	6.27*
	C	16	5.75	3.25	3.32	
Family Language Use—Student Report (12-Point Scale)	FUII	14	8.64	7.86	7.73	2.14
	C	16	6.94	6.63	6.73	

FUII = Follow Up II Group

C   = Comparison Group

*p<.05

**p<.01

TABLE 3 (cont.)

LANGUAGE USE OBSERVATION INSTRUMENT

(DATA EXPRESSED AS % USE IN CLASS, OUT OF CLASS)

	Group	N	Pretest Mean	Posttest Mean	Posttest Mean Adjusted For Pretest	F
Spanish to Mex. Am. Student in Class	FUII	7		0.34		1.11
	C	7		0.25		
English to Mex. Am. Student in Class	FUII	7		0.17		2.67
	C	7		0.30		
English to Anglo Student in Class	FUII	7		0.12		1.63
	C	7		0.06		
Spanish to Adult in Class	FUII	7		0.13		7.87*
	C	7		0.00		
English to Adult in Class	FUII	7		0.24		2.30
	C	7		0.39		
Spanish to Mex. Am. Student out of Class	FUII	7		0.63		20.01**
	C	7		0.13		
English to Mex. Am. Student out of Class	FUII	7		0.22		15.48**
	C	7		0.64		
English to Anglo Student out of Class	FUII	7		0.15		1.52
	C	7		0.23		

FUII = Follow Up II Group

C = = Comparison Group

*$p < .05$

**$p < .01$

10. MATHEMATICS AND ACADEMIC APTITUDE

How well do Mexican American children following a bilingual program perform in relation to a comparison group on tests of a non-language subject matter such as mathematics? What effect does a bilingual program have on the measured academic aptitude of the Mexican American children involved? Critics of bilingual education have asserted that instruction through two languages may have a detrimental effect on subject-matter performance and on cognitive development. Assessment of progress in math and measurement of skill in non-verbal ability tasks were conducted in this study in an attempt to provide answers to the above questions.

In this chapter, the instruments used to measure math skills and academic aptitude are discussed, the results are presented, and the findings interpreted.

10.1 Instruments and Procedures

10.1.1 Mathematics Achievement

The Cooperative Primary Test of Mathematics, developed by the Educational Testing Service (1967), measures knowledge of major mathematical concepts, independent of a particular curriculum program or method. The concepts tested are: number, symbolism, operation, function and relation, approximation and estimation, proof, measurement, and geometry. This test has the same format as the CPT Reading Test, with similar unconventional features, such as the interspersing of easy and difficult items throughout the test. The test has two levels, one for administration at the end of grade 1, and one for administration at the end of grades 2 and 3.

The Cooperative Primary Test of Math was given at the Pilot and Follow Up I levels as a pretest in May of 1971, and at all three group levels as a posttest in May of 1972. The test is in English, but the teachers at the Bilingual Project and the testers at the Comparison school repeated some hard-to-interpret items in Spanish. The Cooperative Primary Math Test was chosen rather than some other math achievement test because it had the same format as the Cooperative Primary Reading Test which the students had taken the previous year.

10.1.2 *Academic Aptitude*

The Nonverbal Subtests of the Inter-American Tests of General Ability were used as a measure of academic aptitude. At Level 1, the nonverbal subtests are Association (16 items) and Classification (16 items). At Level 2, the nonverbal subtests are Classification (24 items) and Analogy (16 items). The directions for the subtests were given in both Spanish and English, and then the students worked on their own. The student had to choose one out of four items as being the correct match for something pictured to the left, or as the one item that did not belong in the series. According to the test manual, Level 1 is meant for first graders and Level 2 is meant for second and third graders.

The Inter-American Nonverbal Ability Subtests had been piloted during the 1969-1970 school year. It was found that administering the entire General Ability Test in Spanish and English was time consuming and that the verbal section overlapped with other verbal measures already in the study. Thus, the Nonverbal Subtests were used exclusively. As can be seen in Figure 1, the different group levels received pretesting in academic aptitude, as measured by the Nonverbal Ability Subtests, at different times and using different forms of the test. An attempt was made to test all students in academic aptitude at the beginning of their first-grade year and at the end of each academic year. However, data on the academic aptitude of Pilot Comparison students for the start of first grade (Fall, 1969) were only available for some of the children. Thus, results from the spring of 1971 testing were used as pretest data for the Pilot group.

The instructions for the Nonverbal Ability Subtests were given in both Spanish and English. See Appendix 1.8 for the details of the tests.

10.2 *Results*

At both the Pilot and Follow Up I levels, there were no significant differences in math performance between the Bilingual and Comparison students. These findings suggest that bilingual schooling does not impair the acquisition of subject-matter content. At the Follow Up II level, the Bilingual group scored better than the Comparison group (F=10.67, df=1/28, p<.01)[1] indicating that bilingual schooling may in fact enhance the acquisition of math skills (see Tables 1-3, pp. 235, 238-239). It should be noted that the Follow Up II group received all

---

[1] See Appendix 4 for complete Analysis of Variance and Covariance data.

FIGURE 1
SCHEDULE FOR ADMINISTRATION OF MATH & ACADEMIC APTITUDE INSTRUMENTS

	Group Levels	Month/Year	Test Form	Group Levels	Month/Year	Test Form
Mathematics Ability						
Cooperative Primary Math Test	P FUI	5/71	23A 12A	ALL	5/71	23B (P) (FUI) 12B (FUII)
Academic Aptitude						
Inter-American Nonverbal Ability Subtests	P FUI FUII	4/71 10/70-11/70 10/71	GA-2-CE HA-1CEs-A GA-1-DE-A		4/72	HG-2-DEs (P) (FUI) GA-1-CE-A (FUII)

Groups: Mexican American Bilingual
Mexican American Comparison

Group Levels: Pilot = P
Follow Up I = FUI
Follow Up II = FUII

TABLE 1

MEXICAN AMERICAN STUDENTS' MATHEMATICS, ACADEMIC APTITUDE

PILOT LEVEL

Skill Area	Group	N	Pretest Mean	Posttest Mean	Posttest Mean Adjusted For Pretest	F
CPT Math Test	P	15	141.21	152.00	153.19	1.31
	C	14	144.61	151.36	150.08	
Nonverbal Ability Subtests	P	15	29.93	29.93	28.04	1.32
	C	14	24.25	28.29	30.30	

P = Pilot Group   C = Comparison Group

of its math training bilingually or in Spanish exclusively, whereas the Pilot and
Follow Up I groups received math readiness in kindergarten exclusively in
English.

As in the case of math performance, there were no significant differences in
nonverbal ability, taken as a measure of academic aptitude, at either the Pilot or
the Follow Up I levels (see Tables 1 and 2, pp. 235, 238). This finding indicates
that bilingual schooling does not hinder the development of nonverbal reasoning
skill. At the Follow Up II level, the Bilingual group excelled in nonverbal ability
($F=7.41$, $df=1/27$, $p<.05$), even after adjusting statistically for initial differences
(see Table 3, p. 239). Thus, the bilingual treatment appears to have enhanced the
nonverbal reasoning powers of the students in the program over time. Such a
finding is most encouraging, given the fears of the critics of bilingual education
that such a program will impair the cognitive functioning of its participants.

10.3 *Summary of Findings and Discussion*

The Mexican American children following the bilingual program performed as
well as, or better than, comparison children on tests in a non-language subject
matter, namely mathematics. At the Pilot and Follow Up I levels, there were no
significant differences. At the Follow Up II level, the Bilingual group came out
ahead. These findings are consistent with findings for Spanish speakers in other
bilingual programs in the United States.

In Sacramento, California, first and third graders schooled bilingually came
out better than control groups (Hartwig, 1971). Cuban students schooled bilingually in Florida came out as well in math as control students (Inclán, 1971).
Treviño (1968) followed one group of Spanish speakers in Texas from grade 1
through grade 3. At the end of first grade, the group schooled bilingually was
better in math fundamentals than a control group. At the end of third grade,
the bilingual group appeared to have become stronger at verbal problems and
to have lost ground comparatively in mechanical problems. However, a new
control group was used for testing at the third-grade level, which may explain
the gain on one subtest and the loss on the other.

The Redwood City Bilingual students demonstrated that they were able to
learn mathematical concepts bilingually—although predominantly in Spanish,
using English-medium textbooks. Furthermore, the test itself was in English,
although complex verbal problems were translated into Spanish. The results
for the Bilingual students are impressive in relation to those of comparable students
in an English-only school. Clearly, it is most important to compare the performance of these bilingually-schooled youngsters to that of the proper reference
group, i.e. other similar Mexican American students. It is useful, however, to
relate the scores of the Bilingual and Comparison students to the national
norms, particularly for the purposes of comparison across group levels. At the

Pilot level, the Bilingual group scored at the 66th percentile nationally and the Comparison group scored at the 61st percentile. The Bilingual Follow Up I group scored at the 22nd percentile and the Comparison group at the 37th percentile; the Bilingual Follow Up II group at the 34th percentile, and the Comparison group at the 20th percentile. If examined across group levels, percentile rankings suggest that Mexican American youngsters improve with respect to the national norms the longer they are in school. Their improved performance is probably due to a number of factors, among which are improved ability in English and greater familiarity with test-taking situations.

The Bilingual Project also had no apparent detrimental effect upon the academic aptitude of the Mexican American children involved. In fact, that program seemed to have enhanced academic aptitude in the case of the youngest group of children involved. At the Pilot and Follow Up I levels, there were no significant differences on the Inter-American Nonverbal Ability Subtests, taken as a measure of academic aptitude. At the Follow Up II level, the Bilingual group outperformed the Comparison group, even after adjusting for initial differences.

What is particularly interesting about the Follow Up II results is that on the *pretest* measure of academic aptitude, the Comparison group outscored the Bilingual group by a mean of three points, while on the *posttest,* the Bilingual group outscored the Comparison group by three points. It appears that the Bilingual group had not only overcome an initial deficit, but had progressed beyond the Comparison group by the end of the two-year study.

Some critics claim that instructing children bilingually from an early age may cause them to suffer intellectual retardation. The results of this study do not lend support to that view. It should be further noted that students from lower socioeconomic backgrounds have been thought to be especially susceptible to this kind of retardation if bilingually schooled. Yet, all of the students in the study were from such backgrounds, and appeared to suffer no such deficiencies.

It is unfortunate that other studies on bilingual programs in the U.S. have not reported academic aptitude or intelligence scores on a pre-posttest basis. For the most part, projects have used nonverbal ability or intelligence data only for the purpose of collecting baseline data, rather than collecting such data at regular intervals. Tucker and d'Anglejan (1971) stress the importance of gathering data longitudinally to determine whether children who are instructed bilingually from an early age suffer intellectual retardation in comparison with their monolingually instructed counterparts. Lambert and Tucker (1972) report no such intellectual deficit among English Canadian students schooled bilingually in French and English in Montreal, Canada.

The next chapter deals with the children's attitudes toward Mexican and Anglo culture and toward school, and with parental attitudes toward the Spanish and English languages.

TABLE 2
MEXICAN AMERICAN STUDENTS' MATHEMATICS, ACADEMIC APTITUDE
FOLLOW UP I LEVEL

Skill Area	Group	N	Pretest Mean	Posttest Mean	Posttest Mean Adjusted For Pretest	F
CPT Math Test	FUI	16	133.87	139.37	140.56	2.95
	C	15	136.69	146.07	144.80	
Nonverbal Ability Subtests	FUI	16	21.00	26.69	26.95	0.03
	C	15	22.29	27.60	27.31	

FUI = Follow Up I Group   C = Comparison Group

TABLE 3

MEXICAN AMERICAN STUDENTS'
MATHEMATICS, ACADEMIC APTITUDE
FOLLOW UP II LEVEL

Skill Area	Group	N	Pretest Mean	Posttest Mean	Posttest Mean Adjusted For Pretest	F
CPT Math Test	FUII	14		135.21		10.67**
	C	16		131.81		
Nonverbal Ability Subtest	FUII	14	16.64	23.64	24.25	7.41*
	C	16	19.61	20.25	19.71	

FUII = Follow Up II Group
C   = Comparison Group

*p<.05
**p<.01

11. ATTITUDES TOWARD LANGUAGE AND CULTURE, AND SCHOOL

How do Mexican American children in a bilingual/bicultural program for several years value the Mexican and the Anglo cultures and the dominant languages of these cultures as compared to children who do not receive such a program? What effect does bilingual schooling have upon children's school attendance and attitudes toward school? Are the language attitudes of Mexican American parents with children in a bilingual program for several years affected by their children's participation in the program? Mexican American children in American schools are characteristically portrayed as placing low or negative value on their Mexican heritage and on the Spanish language. Their school attendance is by and large erratic, and they drop out of school early. This chapter treats the effects of a bilingual program upon these prevalent patterns. This chapter also discusses the effects of the bilingual program upon the language attitudes of the parents of children in the program. The parents are likely to have frequent contact with the program directly, and also, to share some of its effects indirectly through their children.

11.1 *Instruments and Procedures*

11.1.1 *Student Attitudes*

11.1.1.1 *Attitudes Toward The Mexican American and the Anglo Cultures*

The Cross-Cultural Attitude Inventory (Jackson and Klinger, 1971) was designed to measure the degree of positive or negative feelings students have for the Mexican American and the Anglo cultures. The test constructors attempted to choose items that were not associated with economic factors, since the culture of the Mexican American is, according to the authors, "too often associated with a culture of material poverty." Items were selected to represent sports, games, food, clothing, language, facial characteristics and the like. The items chosen had to be graphically representable, recognizable by the students, and symbols of the Mexican American and Anglo cultures respectively. There were eleven items forming an index which represented Anglo culture, eleven items forming an index which represented Mexican culture, and two items, "book" and "school," which were combined as an index of attitude toward school.

The test was primarily designed for three to twelve year olds. The students had to react to a picture of each item as it appeared in their booklet by marking an "X" over the face which reflected their feelings about the item. There were five faces depicted along a continuum, with the first having the most happy face (a big smile) and the last having the saddest face (a big frown) (see Appendix 1.9 for a sample item).

11.1.1.2 Attitudes Toward Spanish

Students' attitudes toward Spanish were assessed directly by an item in the Cross-Cultural Attitude Inventory. The students reacted to the word "sí" (printed with big letters in a booklet) by marking an "X" over the face which reflected their feelings about the item. Also, as part of a Home Interview Questionnaire, parents reported the student's language preference when speaking with adults and when speaking with children. The response categories were "Spanish," "English," and "both." These ratings were meant to help assess the student's feelings about using Spanish, regardless of his actual use patterns.

11.1.1.3 Attitudes Toward English

Student attitudes toward English were assessed directly by an item in the Cross-Cultural Attitude Inventory. The students reacted to the word "yes" (printed with big letters in a booklet) by marking an "X" on the face which reflected their feelings about the item. Also, as mentioned above under Attitudes Toward Spanish, parents reported the student's language preference when speaking with adults and when speaking with children. The response categories were "Spanish," "English," and "both." These ratings were meant to help assess the student's feelings about using English, regardless of his actual use patterns.

11.1.1.4 Attitudes Toward School

A behavioral measure of attitude toward school is attendance. Illness was not counted an an "official absence" on the school rosters for the Redwood City School District. Thus, absences were for other reasons, such as a desire on the part of the child to stay home or go elsewhere. In part, the student's record was also a measure of the parents' attitude toward school, because the parent may have desired to keep the child at home.

There are two items on the Cross-Cultural Attitude Inventory that are intended to measure student attitudes toward school. One is a picture of a book and the other a picture of a school. As mentioned above, the two items were combined in an index to measure attitude toward school.

The Cross-Cultural Attitude Inventory was administered on a group basis only once, in January of 1972. At that time, the test was being piloted throughout the Southwest by the National Consortia for Bilingual Education at Fort Worth, Texas, and the data collected at the Redwood City Project went into this effort.

11.1.2 Attitudes of Parents

The Language Orientation Questionnaire, based on an instrument by Gardner and Lambert (Gardner and Lambert, 1959; Gardner, 1960), was used to obtain parents' reactions to seven reasons for their children to learn Spanish. A sample item was "Your children's learning Spanish will enable them to maintain friendships among Mexican Americans." The parent was asked to rate this statement on a five-point continuum from "very good reason" to "very bad reason" for their child to learn Spanish. Parents were also asked to select from among the seven reasons the two best reasons and the least acceptable reason for their child to learn Spanish.

The same Language Orientation Questionnaire described above was used to obtain parental reactions to seven suggested reasons for their children to learn English. A sample item would be "Your children's learning English will enable them to make friendships among Anglos (gavachos)." The parents were also asked to select the two best reasons and the least acceptable reason for their child to learn English.

The parents of students in the Bilingual and Comparison groups were asked to fill out the Language Orientation Questionnaire at the end of the home interview session, both in the winter of 1971 and in the spring of 1972. The parents tended to answer the Spanish version of the Language Orientation Questionnaire (see Figure 1 for Schedule for Administration of Attitudinal Instruments).

The second time that the parents filled out the questionnaire, they were also asked what they thought the effect would be on their child's ability to use English, if the teachers used Spanish in the classroom. See Appendix 1.11 for a copy of the Language Orientation Questionnaire.

11.2 Results

11.2.1 Attitudes of Students

The findings on the Cross-Cultural Attitude Inventory showed differences in favor of the Bilingual group with respect to attitude toward Mexican culture at

FIGURE 1

SCHEDULE FOR ADMINISTRATION OF ATTITUDINAL INSTRUMENTS

	Group Levels	Month/Year	Group Levels	Month/Year
Attitudes toward Spanish and English, toward Mexican & Anglo Cultures, toward School:				
Cross-Cultural Attitude Inventory	All group levels.	1/72		
Parental Language Attitudes:				
Language Orientation Questionnaire	Parents all group levels.	12/70-1/71. (Several families 2/71-3/71)	Parents, all group levels.	5/72-6/72

Groups: Mexican American Bilingual
Mexican American Comparison

Group Levels: Pilot
Follow Up I
Follow Up II

the Pilot level (F=6.16, df=1/26, p<.05).[1] There were no significant differences at the other two levels although the Bilingual Follow Up II group mean was noticeably higher than that of the Comparison group (F=2.63, df=1/24) (see Tables 1-3, pp. 245-247). These results indicate that the students who had been in the Bilingual Project the longest had a more positive attitude toward Mexican culture than the Comparison students, since the Pilot group had had *three* years as compared with two years for the Follow Up I and II groups. Perhaps it takes more than two years of bicultural education for cultural attitudes to mature.

On the student ratings of Spanish and English (the items "sí" and "yes") from the Cross-Cultural Attitude Inventory, there were no significant differences at any of the group levels. The only difference approaching significance was a slightly higher rating of "sí" by the Bilingual Pilot group than by the Comparison group at that level. Such a trend in the data would be expected since the Pilot group were participants in a program that endorsed the Spanish language and which used Spanish extensively in class.

Parents reported on student language preference, both at the outset of the program and at the end of 1972. The Follow Up I group was reported to prefer Spanish significantly more at the end of 1972, than was the Comparison group (F=6.41, df=1/28, p<.05) (see Table 2, p. 246). In fact, the Bilingual group's language preference switched from Spanish to English, whereas the Comparison students switched from preference of Spanish to preference for English. It is likely that the preference rating for the Bilingual group would also have been "English" if not for the Bilingual Project. Results for the other two levels, although not significant, also showed Bilingual students preferring Spanish more than Comparison students did. At the Follow Up II level, the Bilingual parents noted that their children's preference for Spanish remained constant, whereas the Comparison students reportedly switched to preference for English (see Table 3, p. 247).

One measure of attitude toward school is attendance. At both the Pilot and Follow Up II levels the Bilingual students had significantly fewer absences, both for the 1970-1971 year and for the 1971-1972, than did the Comparison students (Pilot, *1970-71:* F=10.61, df=1/27, p<.01; *1971-72:* F=5.50, df=1/27, p<.05; Follow Up II, *1970-71:* F=4.61, df=1/28, p<.05; *1971-72:* F=6.25, df=1/28, p<.05) (see Table 1, p. 245, and Table 3, p. 247). This is a strong unobtrusive measure of the students' interest in the bilingual program and of their desire to come to school regularly in order to participate.[2]

---

[1] See Appendix 4 for complete Analysis of Variance and Covariance data.

[2] Correlation analysis, using Pearson's Product-Moment Correlation (SPSS Program), did not reveal any substantial (p<.01) or systematic relationship between the number of times a student was absent and his performance on any of the achievement measures.

TABLE 1

STUDENT ATTITUDES TOWARD LANGUAGE, CULTURE, AND SCHOOL

PILOT LEVEL

Variable	Group	N	Pretest Mean	Posttest Mean	Posttest Mean Adjusted For Pretest	F
Attitude toward Mexican Culture	P	15		47.93		6.16*
	C	13		42.54		
Attitude toward Anglo Culture	P	15		46.53		0.71
	C	13		44.77		
Attitude toward School (10-Point Scale)	P	15		9.13		6.79*
	C	13		7.21		
Attendance	P	15	+1.07	++2.40		+10.61**
	C	13	8.64	5.93		++ 5.50*
Sí	P	15		4.00		1.21
	C	13		3.46		
Yes	P	15		4.27		0.21
	C	13		4.46		
Language Preference—Parent Report (4-Point Scale)	P	15	2.20	1.93	1.93	0.86
	C	13	2.00	1.43	1.43	

P = Pilot Group   *p<.05
C = Comparison   **p<.01

+ 1970-71
++ 1971-72

TABLE 2

STUDENT ATTITUDES TOWARD LANGUAGE, CULTURE, AND SCHOOL

FOLLOW UP I LEVEL

Variable	Group	N	Pretest Mean	Posttest Mean	Posttest Mean Adjusted For Pretest	F
Attitude toward	FUI	14		44.86		0.23
Mexican Culture	C	14		46.21		
Attitude toward	FUI	14		47.86		0.31
Anglo Culture	C	14		46.50		
Attitude toward	FUI	14		7.94		0.23
School	C	14		8.47		
Attendance	FUI	16	+2.69	++10.37		+2.99
	C	15	7.80	11.33		++0.11
Sí	FUI	14		3.93		0.09
	C	14		3.79		
Yes	FUI	14		4.21		0.31
	C	14		3.93		
Language Preference—Parent	FUI	16	1.94	2.13	2.23	6.41*
Report (4-Point Scale)	C	15	2.73	1.13	1.03	

FUI = Follow Up I Group   +1970-71   *p<.05
C   = Comparative Group   ++1971-72

TABLE 3
STUDENT ATTITUDES TOWARD LANGUAGE, CULTURE, AND SCHOOL
FOLLOW UP II LEVEL

Variable	Group	N	Pretest Mean	Posttest Mean	Posttest Mean Adjusted For Pretest	F
Attitude toward Mexican Culture	FUII	13		49.08		2.63
	C	13		45.08		
Attitude toward Anglo Culture	FUII	13		48.69		1.53
	C	13		45.92		
Attitude toward School	FUII	13		8.07		0.50
	C	13		7.19		
Attendance	FUII	14	+7.93	++5.69		+4.61*
	C	16	17.00	11.14		++6.25*
Sí	FUII	15		4.23		0.08
	C	13		4.38		
Yes	FUII	13		4.23		0.02
	C	13		4.15		
Language Preference—Parent Report (4-Point Scale)	FUII	14	2.43	2.43	2.41	2.86
	C	16	2.31	1.50	1.52	

FUII = Follow Up II Group
C = Comparison Group

+ 1970-71
++ 1971-72

*p<.05

On the school attitude index in the Cross-Cultural Attitude Inventory, the Bilingual group came out significantly higher on attitude toward school at the Pilot level (F=6.79, df=1/26, p<.05) (see Table 1, p. 245). Once again, the Pilot group had been in the Bilingual Project longer than the groups at the other two levels, and the Pilot Comparison group had been receiving conventional English-only schooling longer than the other two Comparison groups. The school-attitude rating appears, then, to be a clear indication of support for the Bilingual Program.

11.2.2 *Attitudes of Parents*

At the Pilot level, Bilingual parents rated "completing their education" significantly more positively as a reason for their children to learn *Spanish* than did the Comparison group (F=10.41, df=1/26, p<.01). Also, they rated "completing their education" (F=4.58, df=1/26, p<.05) and "conversing with more and varied people" (F=5.39, df=1/26, p<.05) more positively as reasons for their children to learn *English* (see Table 4, pp. 249-250). Both groups rated all reasons highly.

At the Follow Up I level, Bilingual parents rated "preserving their language and culture" (F=8.71, df=1/17, p<.01) and "completing their education" (F=4.69, df=1/17, p<.05) more highly as reasons for their children to learn Spanish than did the Comparison parents, and also rated "making friends" (F=8.73, df=1/17, p<.01) and "necessary for business or educational goals" (F=11.91, df=1/17, p<.01) more positively as reasons for their children to learn English (see Table 5, pp. 252-253). There were no significant differences between Bilingual and Comparison parents at the Follow Up II level (see Table 6, pp. 254-255).

Analysis of variance was run in order to compare the *pretest* ratings of Bilingual and Comparison parents at all three group levels to see if there were significantly different attitudes at the outset. The analysis of covariance technique is intended to adjust for such initial differences, but ANOVA on pretest scores was conducted to provide a further insight into parent language attitudes. The results showed no significant differences between Bilingual and Comparison parents on the ratings of reasons for their children to learn English, and significant differences only at the Follow Up I level on three of the reasons for learning Spanish.

The Bilingual parents rated "maintaining Mexican American friendships" (F=6.00, df=1/18, p<.05), "thinking and acting as Mexican Americans" (F=6.52, df=1/18, p<.05), and "conversing with more people" (F=6.00, df=1/18, p<.05) significantly higher than did the Comparison parents as reasons for their children to learn Spanish. On the posttest, these differences were not significant. In one case, on the "thinking and acting as Mexican Americans" item, the Bilingual parents went from a mean 4.9 to a 3.8 rating, while the Comparison parents

TABLE 4
LANGUAGE ATTITUDES OF MEXICAN AMERICAN PARENTS

PILOT LEVEL

Reasons for child to learn *Spanish:*	Group	N	Pretest Mean	Posttest Mean	Posttest Mean Adjusted For Pretest	F
Preserve native language and culture	P	15	4.47	4.80	4.80	1.24
	C	14	4.50	4.57	4.57	
Useful in getting a job	P	15	4.60	4.80	4.81	3.37
	C	14	4.43	4.36	4.35	
Maintaining Mexican American friendships	P	15	4.67	4.67	4.66	1.11
	C	14	4.50	4.43	4.43	
Thinking and acting as Mexican Americans	P	15	4.33	4.47	4.47	0.03
	C	14	4.29	4.43	4.43	
Completing their education	P	15	3.60	4.67	4.68	10.41**
	C	14	3.86	3.50	3.48	
Conversing with more people	P	15	4.40	4.60	4.60	0.33
	C	14	4.43	4.43	4.43	
Necessary for business and ed. goals	P	15	4.40	4.60	4.59	0.62
	C	14	4.14	4.36	4.37	

**$p < .01$

P = Pilot Group
C = Comparison Group

(continued on following page)

TABLE 4 (cont.)

Reasons for child to learn *English:*	Group	N	Pretest Mean	Posttest Mean	Posttest Mean Adjusted For Pretest	F
For making friends with Anglos	P	15	4.33	4.73	4.73	3.17
	C	14	4.29	4.29	4.29	
Useful in getting a job	P	15	4.73	4.87	4.85	1.50
	C	14	4.57	4.57	4.58	
For respect of Anglo community	P	15	4.60	4.40	4.37	2.36
	C	14	4.36	3.71	3.75	
To think and behave like Anglos	P	15	3.87	4.13	4.11	3.82
	C	14	3.79	3.21	3.24	
To complete their education	P	15	4.27	4.47	4.47	4.58*
	C	14	3.93	3.64	3.64	
Conversing with more people	P	15	4.33	3.80	4.80	5.39*
	C	14	4.36	4.36	4.35	
Necessary for business and ed. goals	P	15	4.60	4.80	4.79	3.03
	C	14	4.50	4.43	4.44	

*p<.05

P = Pilot Group
C = Comparison Group

went from a 3.9 to a 4.6 rating (5 being the highest rating and 1 being the lowest). Although the parent groups reversed their ratings of this item on the posttest, the difference was not significant.

The parental language orientation ratings indicated that parents of children in the Bilingual program endorsed certain integrative and instrumental reasons for learning both Spanish and English more than did Comparison parents. In other words, the Bilingual parents saw Spanish as both a means of preserving language and culture, and also as a means of becoming better educated. They also saw English both as a means of making friends and as a means for becoming better educated and for getting a job.

Parents were also asked to rank-order the two best and one worst reason for their children to learn Spanish and English. Bilingual and Comparison parents across all three levels chose "preserving native language and culture" as one of the two best reasons for their children to learn Spanish (see Table 7, p. 256). The two groups differed on the other best reason. The Bilingual parents saw Spanish as useful in getting a job, whereas the Comparison parents ranked "thinking and acting as a Mexican American" as their chief reason. The striking difference here was that the Bilingual parents expressed a belief that Spanish could be useful in finding a job. Such a feeling was perhaps an outgrowth of their exposure to the bilingual program—of their awareness that there were jobs for Spanish speakers within the California job market and that their children would have better access to these jobs through studying Spanish in school.

A Spearman-Rho rank order correlation was performed on the rankings by the two groups of best and worst reasons for learning Spanish and English. The Bilingual and Comparison parents were found to have significantly different rankings (rho=.50, n.s.) for the seven items on *best* reasons for learning Spanish (see Table 7, p. 256). The statistical test merely reinforced the fact that the two sets of parents were not in agreement on the rankings for these items.

On ratings of the *worst* reasons for learning Spanish, the Bilingual parents' most common choice was "thinking and acting as a Mexican American," and the most common choice for the Comparison parents was "completing their education." Perhaps due to the fact that the Comparison parents had not been exposed to the schooling of their children in Spanish, they were less likely to see its advantages in terms of "completing their education." Even with this disagreement, a rank order correlation showed that Bilingual and Comparison parents did not differ significantly in their rankings of worst reasons for their children to learn Spanish (rho=.78, p<.05) (see Table 7).

With respect to reasons for learning English, both groups of parents ranked "useful in getting a job" and "necessary for business and educational goals"— two instrumental reasons—as the best reasons, and "to think and behave like Anglos" as the worst reason. Rank order correlations for best and worst reasons

TABLE 5

LANGUAGE ATTITUDES OF MEXICAN AMERICAN PARENTS

FOLLOW UP I LEVEL

Reasons for child to learn *Spanish:*	Group	N	Pretest Mean	Posttest Mean	Posttest Mean Adjusted For Pretest	F
Preserve native language and culture	FUI	10	4.90	4.90	4.89	8.71**
	C	10	4.60	4.30	4.30	
Useful in getting a job	FUI	10	4.80	4.70	4.63	0.03
	C	10	4.20	4.60	4.67	
Maintaining Mexican American friendships	FUI	10	5.00	4.80	4.77	0.29
	C	10	4.60	4.60	4.63	
Thinking and acting as Mexican Americans	FUI	10	4.90	3.80	3.64	3.17
	C	10	3.90	4.60	4.76	
Completing their education	FUI	10	4.40	4.60	4.61	4.69*
	C	10	4.00	3.80	3.79	
Conversing with more people	FUI	10	5.00	4.50	4.57	1.12
	C	10	4.60	4.30	4.23	
Necessary for business and ed. goals	FUI	10	4.80	4.60	4.57	0.89
	C	10	4.50	4.30	4.33	

*p<.05
**p<.01

FUI = Follow Up I Group
C   = Comparison Group

TABLE 5 (cont.)

Reasons for child to learn *English:*	Group	N	Pretest Mean	Posttest Mean	Posttest Mean Adjusted For Pretest	F
For making friends with Anglos	FUI	10	4.80	4.90	4.89	8.73**
	C	10	4.60	4.10	4.11	
Useful in getting a job	FUI	10	4.80	4.90	4.89	3.81
	C	10	4.70	4.50	4.50	
For respect of Anglo community	FUI	10	4.50	4.30	4.24	0.04
	C	10	4.20	4.10	4.16	
To think and behave like Anglos	FUI	10	4.60	3.90	3.76	0.48
	C	10	4.00	3.90	4.03	
To complete their education	FUI	10	4.20	4.00	4.01	0.00
	C	10	4.30	4.00	3.99	
Conversing with more people	FUI	10	4.70	4.60	4.60	0.73
	C	10	4.50	4.40	4.40	
Necessary for business and ed. goals	FUI	10	4.70	5.00	4.98	11.91**
	C	10	4.50	4.40	4.41	

FUI = Follow Up I Group   **p<.01
C   = Comparison Group

TABLE 6
LANGUAGE ATTITUDES OF MEXICAN AMERICAN PARENTS
FOLLOW UP II LEVEL

Reasons for child to learn *Spanish:*	Group	N	Pretest Mean	Posttest Mean	Posttest Mean Adjusted For Pretest	F
Preserve native language and culture	FUII	11	4.55	4.55	4.55	1.13
	C	10	4.80	4.80	4.79	
Useful in getting a job	FUII	11	4.36	4.73	4.72	0.27
	C	10	4.50	4.60	4.61	
Maintaining Mexican American friendships	FUII	11	4.45	4.64	4.62	0.61
	C	10	4.70	4.10	4.82	
Thinking and acting as Mexican Americans	FUII	11	4.18	4.55	4.58	2.16
	C	10	4.60	4.10	4.06	
Completing their education	FUII	11	3.90	3.82	3.87	0.27
	C	10	4.40	3.60	3.55	
Conversing with more people	FUII	11	4.45	4.64	4.63	0.01
	C	10	4.70	4.60	4.61	
Necessary for business and ed. goals	FUII	11	4.36	4.55	4.55	0.03
	C	10	4.40	4.50	4.50	

FUII = Follow Up II Group
C   = Comparisong

TABLE 6 (cont.)

Reasons for child to learn *English*:	Group	N	Pretest Mean	Posttest Mean	Posttest Mean Adjusted For Pretest	F
For making friends with Anglos	FUII	11	4.36	4.55	4.53	0.11
	C	10	4.70	4.60	4.61	
Useful in getting a job	FUII	11	4.45	4.73	4.76	0.15
	C	10	4.80	4.70	4.67	
For respect of Anglo Community	FUII	11	4.27	4.55	4.57	0.44
	C	10	4.70	4.40	4.37	
To think and behave like Anglos	FUII	11	3.73	3.91	4.09	0.00
	C	10	4.50	4.30	4.10	
To complete their education	FUII	11	3.90	3.82	3.85	0.08
	C	10	4.40	3.70	3.67	
Conversing with more people	FUII	11	4.36	4.45	4.53	0.05
	C	10	4.70	4.70	4.61	
Necessary for business and ed. goals	FUII	11	4.36	4.91	4.95	0.04
	C	10	4.70	4.90	4.86	

FUII = Follow Up Group II
C   = Comparison Group

TABLE 7

RANK ORDERING OF BEST AND WORST REASONS
FOR LEARNING SPANISH AND ENGLISH

Reasons for child to learn *Spanish:*	Ranks for Best Reason		Ranks for Worst Reason	
	B	C	B	C
Preserve native language and culture	1	1	7	6.5
Useful in getting a job	2	3	5.5	4
Maintaining Mex. Am. friendships	4	4	4	5
Thinking and acting as Mex. Ams.	6.5	2	1	2
Completing their education	5	6.5	3	1
Conversing with more people	6.5	6.5	2	3
Necessary for bus. and ed. goals	3	5	5.5	6.5
Rank order correlations	rho = .50		rho = .78*	

B = Bilingual Parents   C = Comparison Parents   *p<.05

Reasons for child to learn *English:*	Ranks for Best Reason		Ranks for Worst Reason	
	B	C	B	C
For making friends with Anglos	3.5	6.5	3.5	6.5
Useful in getting a job	1	1	6.5	6.5
For respect of Anglo community	3.5	3	3.5	3
To think and behave like Anglos	7	5	1	1
To complete their education	5	4	2	2
Conversing with more people	6	6.5	5	4.5
Necessary for bus. and ed. goals	2	2	6.5	4.5
Rank order correlations	rho = .74*		rho = .76*	

B = Bilingual Parents   C = Comparison Parents   *p<.05

showed that the two groups ranked the seven items similarly (best reason, rho=
.74, p<.05; worst reason, rho=.76, p<.05) (see Table 7).

In general, it would appear that the parents who have had their children in
the Bilingual program were more positive than the Comparison parents about

TABLE 8

PARENT ATTITUDE TOWARD
TEACHER'S USE OF SPANISH IN THE CLASSROOM

PILOT LEVEL

	Bilingual Parents	Comparison Parents
Will increase child's learning of English	7	3
Will not effect child's learning of English	8	7
Will decrease child's learning of English	0	4
TOTAL	15	14

Gamma = .64**

**p<.01

the virtues of Spanish for not only integrative reasons, such as to preserve language and culture, but also for instrumental reasons, such as to become better educated and to get a job. The results suggest the positive effects of the program upon the parents' language attitudes.

Finally, Bilingual parents at the Pilot level differed from Comparison parents in their attitudes towards the effects of using Spanish in the classroom upon English language ability. Significantly more Bilingual parents felt either that the teacher's use of Spanish would increase their child's learning of English or that his English ability would come out of the same (Gamma=.64, p<.01). Four Comparison parents out of fourteen felt that use of Spanish would decrease their child's learning of English, while none of the Bilingual parents shared that view (see Table 8). These Bilingual parents had had their children in the Project the longest (three years), and so had consequently had the most time to see the effects of using Spanish in the classroom upon English language skills. They had obviously not noticed any adverse effects of Bilingual instruction. This finding also speaks well for bilingual schooling.

11.3 *Summary of Findings and Discussion*

After three years in a bilingual/bicultural program, the children in the program viewed the Mexican culture more positively than did comparison students who had not benefited from such a program. Although there were no significant differences at the other two group levels, the Bilingual Pilot group mean was noticeably higher than that of the Comparison group. It may be that children have to spend a minimum of three years in a bicultural program for pronounced cultural attitudes to appear. All three group levels of students in the Bilingual Project rated Anglo culture as positively as did students in the Comparison groups, suggesting that there need not be a loss of esteem for Anglo culture when Mexican culture is an integral part of the curriculum. Rather, the Bilingual Project appears to be instilling a sense of dual culturalism or biculturalism within the participants.

It should be remembered that the children in the study were for the most part first-generation Americans. This fact lends even more significance to differences in attitudes toward Mexican culture. Derbyshire (1969) studied the attitudes and behaviors of East Los Angeles Mexican American teenagers born in Mexico, or whose parents were born in Mexico, with those of second- and third-generation Americans. He found that immigrant teenagers dissociated themselves from "Mexicans," whereas second- and third-generation Mexican American teenagers highly identified themselves as "Mexican." The author speculates that the strong identification with Mexican values is functional to identity maintenance for established Mexican American adolescents, but not necessary for new immigrants. As Derbyshire puts it, ". . . after one or two generations in the United States, it may be adaptively necessary for Mexican American adolescents to overly view themselves as highly Mexican in order to defend against 'the cultural stripping' process of American society" (p. 102). Dworkin (1965, 1971) found that Mexican American adults who were born in Mexico and had lived in the United States for a shorter period of time were less negative toward their Mexican background than were Mexican Americans born in the United States or who were born in Mexico but had lived in the United States for a longer period of time. Clearly, the adolescents of the Derbyshire study are closer in age to the children in the Redwood City study than are the adults in the Dworkin study. If it can be assumed that there is a "cultural stripping" process in effect from the time that the first-generation Mexican American student enters school in Redwood City (and my own observations would support that notion), then the Bilingual Project can truly be accredited with turning the tide against cultural stripping.

There were no differerences between the Bilingual and Comparison students with respect to how they rated English and Spanish, as represented by the items "yes" and "sí" on the Cross-Cultural Attitude Inventory. The parents of the Bilingual Follow Up I students, however, noted an increase in preference for Spanish on the part of their children over the two years of the study, whereas the Comparison parents noted a sizeable decrease. At the Follow Up II level, the Bilingual parents noted that their children's preference for Spanish remained constant, whereas the Comparison students reportedly switched to preference for English.

Bilingual schooling appeared to have a most healthy effect upon school attendance and upon attitudes toward school. The Bilingual students at the Pilot and Follow Up II levels had significantly fewer absences during both school years of the study than did the Comparison students. This finding is particularly relevant, since a number of administrators remark that they could solve the problem of educating the minority students better if they could only get them to attend classes more regularly. It appears that the Bilingual Project provides an incentive for the Mexican American minority student to come to school.

The Bilingual group also came out significantly higher on attitude toward school at the Pilot level, where the students had been in the Project the longest. Of course, it could be argued that since this was the first group, special attention was lavished upon them with a resultant Hawthorne effect. However, this measure was taken after the children had been in the Project for 2½ years, and in the meantime, three other groups had been added. Thus, the feeling of uniqueness should have worn off, and the attitudes toward school most likely reflected actual feelings about attending classes at the Bilingual Project.

The language attitudes of parents of children in the Bilingual Project appear to have been affected by their children's participation in the program. At both the Pilot and Follow Up I levels, the Bilingual parents were more supportive of certain instrumental (economic) and integrative (social) reasons for their children to learn Spanish and reasons for their children to learn English than were Comparison parents, even after adjusting for differences in ratings at the start of the study. Lambert and Gardner (1972) point out that, while their research in Canada has shown that having integrative motives for learning a language as opposed to instrumental ones helps a person learn the language better, in the case of ethnic minorities in North America, the learning process is different. They note that for a student learning Spanish as a foreign language, an integrative motive is more important, whereas for an ethnic minority both high instrumental and integrative orientations toward learning English would be expected. The Redwood City study also indicated that parents had high instrumental and integrative orientations toward learning Spanish.

In rank ordering the two best, and one worst, reasons for their child to learn Spanish and English, Bilingual and Comparison parents agreed on one integrative reason for learning Spanish: to preserve language and culture. Most Bilingual parents also endorsed an instrumental motive, "to get a job," while most Comparison parents endorsed another integrative reason, "thinking and acting as a true Mexican American." This difference is attributed to the influence of the Bilingual Project. The Bilingual parents' belief that Spanish could be useful in finding a job is seen as an outgrowth of their exposure to the Bilingual Project. They had seen role models for their children in the professional educators who used Spanish in their work.

As for the worst reason for their children to learn Spanish, most Bilingual parents chose an integrative item, "thinking and acting as a Mexican American," while most Comparison parents chose the instrumental motive, "completing their education." It is difficult to understand why the Bilingual parents would rate "thinking and acting as a true Mexican American" so low, except perhaps as a reaction to the wording used. In Spanish, the term used was *verdadero chicano*. Many parents voiced an objection to being called *chicanos* and several changed the wording to *mexicano* on the questionnaire. This could explain why they marked the item down. The explanation for the Comparison parents' low rating of learning Spanish to "complete their education" is more evident. They did not feel that their children needed to have Spanish to round out their education—but they had *not* had the benefit of seeing that their children could improve their Spanish language skills without jeopardizing progress in English, in math, and in other areas.

Parents of the Bilingual Project group were significantly more positive about the effects upon their children's English language development of using Spanish as a medium of instruction in the classroom. They felt that the use of Spanish would either increase their children's learning of English or that their English ability would come out the same. Comparison parents tended to feel that use of Spanish in the classroom would either decrease, or have no effect on, their ability in English. Few Comparison parents, however, felt that use of Spanish would enhance the learning of English. This difference in views is striking. It lends further support to the contention that exposure to a bilingual program actually affects the views of the parents.

12. CONCLUSIONS
AND RECOMMENDATIONS

12.1 *Summary Responses to Research Questions*

12.1.1 *Are Mexican American children who are taught the academic curriculum in Spanish and English for several years as proficient in English language skills as comparable Mexican American children taught only in English?* Yes, in most skill areas. The bilingually-schooled children lagged behind in English vocabulary development, however.

12.1.2 *Are the bilingually schooled children more proficient in Spanish language skills than comparable children taught only in English?* Yes, to a limited extent. Differences were few. It may be that such differences will become greater as the children in the Bilingual Project are exposed to more years of Spanish-medium instruction in the classroom.

12.1.3 *Does a bilingual program promote greater use of Spanish among its Mexican American participants than is found among comparable non-project participants?* Yes. Greater Spanish language use by the bilingually-schooled youngsters were verified both by the student's own report, by parental report, and by direct systematic observation.

12.1.4 *How well do Mexican American children, following a bilingual program, perform in relation to a comparison group on tests of a non-language subject matter such as mathematics?* At least as well as the Comparison students, and at one group level, significantly better.

12.1.5 *What effect does a bilingual program such as this have on the measured academic aptitude of the Mexican American children involved?* No adverse effects. To the contrary, the Bilingual students came out better than the Comparison students at one level and the same at the other two levels.

12.1.6 *How do Mexican American children in a bilingual/bicultural program for several years value the Mexican and the Anglo cultures and the dominant languages of these two cultures, as compared to similar children who do not receive such a program?* The Mexican American students who had been in the Bilingual Project the longest (three years) were significantly more positive toward the Mexican culture than were the Mexican American Comparison students. There were no significant differences in the ratings of Anglo culture, suggesting that the bilingually-schooled students did not gain appreciation for Mexican culture at the expense of their esteem for Anglo culture. As for language attitudes, the Bilingual and Comparison students did not differ on their ratings of Spanish and English, but the Bilingual parents noted a sustained preference for Spanish on the part of their children over the two-year study while the Comparison parents reported an increased preference for English on the part of their children.

12.1.7 *What effect does bilingual schooling have upon children's school attendance and upon attitudes toward school?* For the most part, the school attendance of the Mexican American students in the Bilingual Project was much better than that of Mexican Americans students in the Comparison group, indicating a desire on their part to go to school. Furthermore, those students who had been in the Bilingual Project the longest had more positive attitudes toward school than did Comparison students who had been schooled conventionally for the same period of time.

12.1.8 *Are the language attitudes of Mexican American parents with children in a bilingual program for several years affected by their children's participation in the program?* It would appear so. The Bilingual group parents were more positive than the Comparison parents about the virtues of the Spanish language, not only as a means of preserving their heritage, but also for practical reasons such as enhancing their children's education and helping them to get a job.

12.2 *Limitations*

Since this is "yet another" study of a bilingual education program, it faces the criticism that has been leveled at programs in the past: how do you determine what can be attributed to bilingual schooling? When studying students in the natural setting, with no random selection of students for experimental and control groups, it might be suggested that any findings supposedly in favor of bilingual education are merely artifacts of the selection of students. This criticism was in part controlled for by the use of analysis of covariance to statistically equate the Bilingual and Comparison groups on most measures, using the pretest score as the covariate. However, the results in Redwood City are not expected to be directly generalizable to other Mexican American communities anyway. Rather, they should be suggestive of what would happen if similar bilingual education programs were initiated in similar communities.

Secondly, because the program was developmental, it was impossible to evaluate the effects of "the" treatment. Many different approaches were tried. Many incipient bilingual education programs forgo extensive evaluation altogether for this very reason. An extensive evaluation was undertaken anyway to establish a set of methodological procedures for the Redwood City Project evaluation and for use with bilingual programs in general, and to provide Redwood City with initial feedback as to the effectiveness of its various treatments.

Thirdly, there was no attempt to control for teacher differences. Other bilingual studies have admitted the same weakness, but none to my knowledge have systematically considered this variable. In terms of teaching experience, the teachers in the Comparison school had many more years of experience in teaching reading in English than teachers in the Bilingual Project. Yet, teachers at the Bilingual Project might have been more committed to teaching Mexican American children, since they willingly applied for the job.

Fourthly, the sample was not only non-random but also relatively small. These factors would help explain some of the statistical findings, such as certain low correlations between pre- and posttest scores. All statistical results must be interpreted carefully because of the shortcomings of the sample. However, the evaluator was limited to those students in the Bilingual Project, and to the students of similar background at a neighboring school.

Finally, the study did not cover a large enough span of years to warrant any truly summary statements about the effects of bilingual education in Redwood City. The conclusions are based on a two-year study, at the end of which one group had completed three years of bilingual schooling. The other two groups had completed two years.

12.3 Conclusions

Bilingual education programs in the United States are attempting to eliminate the stigma that has been attached to being bilingual. These programs strive to make each bilingual child *functionally* bilingual—namely, able to understand, speak, read, and write in both his first and second language effectively. The bilingual student should emerge from such a program with the feeling that both of his languages are useful to him. Such programs are attempting to demonstrate that bilingualism need not be a detriment, but rather, an advantage in a world with ever-increasing multilingual demands. The initiation of bilingual programs is also intended to produce individuals who feel proud of their cultural heritage and who enjoy going to school, because from the first day they enter the classroom, they experience success, not failure.

It is still too early to assess the ultimate effects of bilingual schooling in Redwood City. Yet the early indications were that bilingual education in this Mexican American community in California was a viable, significant innovation. Mexican American youngsters were becoming literate in both Spanish and English; they were using their Spanish without shame; their performance in the academic subjects was as good as or better than that of comparison youngsters in an English-only program, and they felt better about being Mexican American and about their school experience. Furthermore, the successful experiences of the children appeared to have a positive spin-off effect upon the parents. These parents gained greater conviction themselves that there was an important place for the knowledge of Spanish in an increasingly miltilingual society.

12.4 *Recommendations*

12.4.1 Answers to the research questions posed in this study should continue to be obtained at regular intervals in Redwood City in order to find out more about the long-range effects of bilingual schooling in this community. It is important to know whether deficits in English language that the Bilingual group may now have are overcome with time. By the same token, Spanish language proficiency should be measured regularly to see if the group instructed through Spanish actually continues to acquire skills in Spanish that are superior to those of children who do not receive such schooling. Language use patterns should also be followed regularly to determine whether the Bilingual Project does play an interventionist role in stimulating the continued use of Spanish. In addition, math and academic aptitude scores should be examined regularly over time. Finally, language attitudes of the students and of their parents, as well as students' attitudes toward culture and toward school, should be assessed at regular intervals to see if longevity in a bilingual program such as this produces increasing differences between project participants and comparison students.

12.4.2 At least two other kinds of analysis should be performed on the Redwood City data. First, Spanish language proficiency and English language proficiency should be compared across skills (reading, writing, listening, and speaking) and across domains (home, neighborhood, church, and school) to see in which skills and in which domains proficiency in one language is better than proficiency in the other. Such analysis should be performed on the Bilingual and Comparison groups both separately and combined as one group. Secondly, language proficiency data should be analyzed by domain and by skill area for each language separately to assess the relative strengths and weaknesses within each language. These analyses were not undertaken in the present study so as not to detract from the major focus, namely a comparison of bilingual and English-only instruction.

12.4.3 Even without the benefit of long-range research results, the results of this study are encouraging enough to recommend that bilingual education programs should be implemented and continued elsewhere. The preliminary results of this study are highly supportive of bilingual/bicultural schooling. Not only does the student gain bilingual language skills and the incentive to use his native language, but he also expresses a greater appreciation of his own culture, more-positive attitudes toward school, and an increased desire to attend classes.

12.4.4 If the effort is expended to initiate a bilingual program, a similar effort should be made to evaluate the effectiveness of the program. Part of this evaluation effort should include summative evaluational techniques such as those described and implemented in this study. Instruments like the Storytelling Task, the Writing Sample, and Word Naming by Domain could easily be modified for use elsewhere. Particularly in the case of storytelling, almost any interesting pictures, slides, or film could be used to stimulate children to speak.

Other projects for Mexican Americans should be encouraged to use the Inter-American Tests of Reading, both in Spanish and in English, so as to allow for meaningful comparison of results from one locale to another. The Inter-American Tests of General Ability should also be used. Unfortunately, an effort by the California State Department to norm the Inter-American Reading and General Ability Tests for California was aborted. More work still has to be done on tests of oral comprehension. As of yet there are few group tests of listening comprehension available for testing children in the early school grades, although the Inter-American Test Series should soon include such tests.

The observation of language use behavior is a promising technique and is recommended for all bilingual projects. It might be even more useful to extend observation into non-school domains, such as into the home, the neighborhood, etc. The Cross-Cultural Attitude Inventory should definitely be used more to establish its validity and also to acquire data for the purposes of comparison across projects. Its principal author, Steve Jackson, has revised the test and is distributing it commercially.[1]

The various report measures—the Pupil's Language Use Inventory, the Home Questionnaire, and the Language Orientation Questionnaire—all have their benefits, particularly when coupled with performance measures. As illustrated by the study, such instruments become increasingly valuable when they are used over time, rather than on a one-time basis.

As suggested at the beginning of this book, bilingual schooling is more than just the learning of two languages. Bilingual schooling implies a whole new con-

---

[1] Learning Concepts, 2501 N. Lamar, Austin, Texas 78705.

cept in innovative education. For too long the Mexican Americans have been second-class students in the public schools. The possibilities for innovative schooling for *la raza* are countless. But first, educators and the public must be favorably disposed. As Rodríguez (1969) so eloquently puts it, "What is not spelled out in any . . . recommendations, however, is the imperative need for drastic additudinal change both within the dominant cultural group and within the Mexican American Community. And this attitudinal change must be the primary concern of the public school. Every person in the school dealing with a student must become culturally cognizant of the significance of recognizing the enriching values of cultural heritage. It must permeate their very being that the person with a bilingual, bicultural asset is 'advantaged' and from that position can be a vital factor in the enrichment of the school, the community, all of society" (p. 36).

Appendix 1. INSTRUMENTATION SUPPLEMENT

1.1 Experimental Tests of Spanish and English Oral Comprehension.
1.2 Word Naming by Domain.
1.3 Storytelling Task.
1.4 Tests of Reading, Inter-American Series.
1.5 Writing Sample.
1.6 Language Use Observation Instrument
1.7 Pupil's Language Use Inventory.
1.8 Nonverbal Subtests of the Tests of General Ability, Inter-American Series.
1.9 Cross-Cultural Attitude Inventory.
1.10 Home Interview Questionnaire.
1.11 Language Orientation Questionnaire.

1.1 *Experimental Tests of Spanish and English Oral Comprehension*

With the permission of the Guidance Testing Associates (Austin, Texas), various items from the Inter-American Test of Oral Comprehension and from the Inter-American Tests of Readings (Levels 1-3) were combined into a single Experimental Test of Oral Comprehension, with parallel versions in Spanish and in English. The Experimental Test consisted of 45 items which the examiner presented orally and which the students responded to by putting an "X" over the one of four pictures that was suggested by the oral statement.

The reason that an experimental test was designed was simply that previous experience in administering the Inter-American Test of Oral Comprehension showed that this test was geared for a pre-school or kindergarten level *only* and could not be used to measure gains in oral comprehension *over time*. Subsequent to development of the Experimental Test, the Guidance Testing Associates came out with their own experimental Level 2 test of oral comprehension. As of 1972, they were still piloting it, and used the Follow Up II first graders of the Bilingual Projects in the piloting.

The last three sets of items (10 altogether) were based on each of three stories. The child heard the story twice and then had to respond to a series of comprehension questions. All the items had to be carefully selected so that the questions had answers that could be depicted.

A reliability check was performed on the English and Spanish versions of the tests after their administration as pretests in the study. The English version of the test had a split-halves reliability correlation coefficient of .88 (N=101), while the Spanish version had a reliability coefficient of .73 (N=96).

Below is a sample item in both Spanish and English, with the corresponding pictures that the child was to choose from:

"Marta tiene su pájaro en una de las jaulas. Si no lo hiciera así, podría irse volando. De hecho, puede irse volando hoy porque el hermanito de Marta ha dejado la puerta abierta. ¿Cuál es el pájaro de Marta?"

"Martha keeps her bird in one of the cages. If she did not, it might fly away. In fact, it could fly away today, for Martha's little brother has left the door open. Which is Martha's bird?"

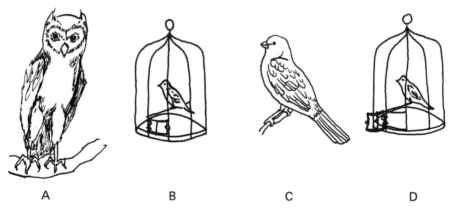

A   B   C   D

1.2 *Word Naming by Domain*

Based on an instrument in Fishman, Cooper, Ma et al. (1971), this measure called for the students to name objects commonly found in settings associated with the domains of home, education, religion, and neighborhood. These domains were selected for the study of a Puerto Rican community in Jersey City after a year of participant observation and focused interviews and discussions with informants (see Greenfield and Fishman, 1971). It was decided to determine whether these same domains distinguished bilingual behaviors among Mexican Americans—another group of Americans with a Latin background.

To the Latin American immigrant in the United States, the home and the church often serve as sources of preservation of Spanish, and the school and the neighborhood streets as sources of English language acquisition. If the children had been of working age, the context of work would have been added.

The settings chosen within the four domains of home, education, religion, and neighborhood were the kitchen, the school, the street, and the church, respectively. The child was given 45 seconds to name as many words as he could for objects found in the specified setting. He was given the task in both Spanish and English.

The scorer recorded a hash mark every time the child said a word. The child's score for each of the four contexts in both languages was the total number of hash marks. If the child repeated a word, he still got credit for two words. The first language the child did the task in and the order in which the contexts were presented was carefully randomized using a table of random numbers.

The instrument has several uses. First, it indicates the relative size of the child's active vocabulary in Spanish and English. By looking at the Spanish and English scores, the examiner can obtain an estimate of the child's so-called bilingual balance—his relative proficiency in Spanish and English. Furthermore, the total output of the child, in just one language or in both, can be compared with that of other children. Finally, the scores by context can indicate which contexts the child has more vocabulary for in Spanish and English. Frequently, a person is labeled a bilingual, but his actual areas of strength in both languages are not spelled out. This task helps determine the relative strengths of the child in active vocabulary output in four representative contexts.

The Word Naming by Domain task sheet appears below:

"Now we're going to play a game. How may things can you name that are found _____ like _____ ?"

in the kitchen	spoon, salt, rice
in the street	car, tree, dog
in church	candle, priest, cross
in school	,table, paper, pencil

"Ahora vamos a jugar en juego. ¿Cuántas cosas puedes nombrar que
se halla_____ como _____ ?"

en la cocina	cuchara, sal, arroz
en la calle	carro, árbol, perro
en la iglesia	bela, padre, cruz
en la escuela	mesa, papel, lápiz

Present the domains and sample words in the order indicated in your roster.
Also, present the exercise in Spanish or English first according to the roster.

There is a 45-second limit for each word naming task. Remember, there are
8 tasks in all. Do 4 in one language and then 4 in the other.

As the child names objects, make a hash mark for each one. You can use
scrap paper for this. After the 45 seconds are up, add up the hash marks. (It
doesn't matter if the child repeats an object twice—just count every word.)

1.3 Storytelling Task

Before describing the Storytelling Task itself, an attempt will be made to
place this test within the context of oral proficiency test development. In the
last several years, particularly because of the advent of bilingual schooling, the
need for tests to determine the relative oral proficiency of children in English
and in their mother tongue has become acute. Mackey (1970) emphasizes the
importance of determining the relative proficiency of a child in his two languages as he starts a bilingual education program and as he progresses in it.

There is little contention with Lado's belief that speaking skills are of prime
importance and need to be measured (Lado, 1961). However, there is considerable debate as to how to measure these skills. Lado (1961) advocates a *discrete-
point* approach to measuring proficiency, in which the test elicits specific items
that can be marked as correct or incorrect. In support of Lado, Mackey (1967)
asserts that a student may avoid sentence structure and vocabulary of which he
is unsure when given a spontaneous language test. However, Spolsky (1969),
Upshur (1969), and Brière (1971) reject discrete-point proficiency tests because
they feel that these tests do not give an overall assessment of proficiency, namely, how well the individual communicates. Perren (1967) points out that testing
for specific language elements requires that the test maker isolate and objectively
score what are considered to be representative, important elements of speech.
Such tests also require the establishment of relative weights for these elements
in a total score. He comments that "at present, there seems to be considerable
justification for deliberately using tests of gross skills of communication rather
than concentrating exclusively on tests of their assumed constituent elements"
(Perren, 1967, p. 28).

The literature on oral proficiency tests show that little has been done to measure the Spanish-English language skills of bilingual primary school children. Most of the instruments have been measures of general communicative ability or fluency, rather than discrete-point tests. Carrow (1957) reports that she had children retell a story that they had just heard, rather than have them make one up, as a measure of fluency. Lambert and Macnamara (1969) used the same technique in Montreal. John, Horner, and Berney (1970) report having developed a similar test.

Stemmler (1976) designed a test of spontaneous language and methods of thinking, called the Language Cognition Test. Spontaneous language is elicited by giving the child objects to describe, such as a cap, a ball, and a pen, and by asking him to tell a story about a picture. Ott (1967) devised the Self Test, which includes prerecorded questions designed to elicit three levels of speech: literal, inferential, and imaginative. Peterson, Chuck, and Coladarci (1969) used cartoon strips to elicit speech from primary students. Taylor (1969) used a tape cassette-film strip device developed by Language Arts, Inc., of Austin, to elicit stories. Children are told to pretend that they are radio announcers and are to describe the filmstrip frames as they see them.

There appear to be only several discrete-point tests for measuring the Spanish and English oral proficiency of bilinguals. Cervenka (1967) developed a battery to test Spanish and English speaking and listening. He used nine subtests measuring phonological, syntactic, and semantic control of both languages. At least one other test of oral Spanish and English has been devised (Moreno, 1972), the Oral Spanish and English Proficiency Placement Test. It is based on the Region One Curriculum Kits (1970), and is intended to be used along with them. The Michigan Oral Language Series (1970) published a discrete-point test of oral English for native Spanish speakers. It seeks information on the following: the uses of *be, do, have;* the past tense and past participle; subject-verb agreement; the double negative; comparisons; possessives; plurals, and pronunciation. At this very moment other tests are being devised, and still other tests exist and are being used, but have not been published or even discussed in the literature.[1]

Many of the above-mentioned instruments would appear to effectively elicit speech samples of at least one kind: classroom speech. It is true, as Labov (1970)

---

[1] The Dissemination Center for Bilingual Bicultural Education, 6504 Tracor Lane, Austin, Texas 78721, and the New York City Consortium on Bilingual Education, Hunter College Division, Box 93, 695 Park Avenue, New York, New York 10021, have collected information on both published and unpublished evaluation instruments used by Title VII Bilingual Education Programs.

One highly promising test designed to measure children's oral proficiency in English and Spanish grammatical structures, called the Bilingual Syntax Measure, should be available by summer of 1975 (Harcourt Brace Jovanovich, Inc.).

points out, that children may be much more fluent when speaking among their peers in a more agreeable place than the classroom. Yet educators have been primarily concerned with children's speech behavior in school, and the above instruments appear to measure this type of speech. That is not to say that educators should not be interested in children's speech behavior outside of class. Indeed, they should be. Perhaps, development of language skills in the classroom should depend more on the language base acquired outside of class, i.e., the nonstandard dialects of both English and Spanish that are spoken out of class.

Just in assessing classroom speech, there is little consensus as to what kind of scoring should be used. Taylor (1969) used a simple word count to determine fluency. Five frames of a filmstrip were shown and thirty seconds were allowed for discussion of each frame. Carrow (1957) analyzed three-minute samples of speech in terms of length and subordination of clauses, number and types of grammatical errors, number of words and number of different words. Stemmler's Language Cognition Test (Stemmler, 1967) and the Michigan Oral Language Productive Test (Michigan Oral Language Series, 1970) include separate tests for measuring cognitive development.

Results from testing with the Cervenka bilingual instrument show that it is difficult to elicit specific item responses from six- and seven-year-old children (e.g., sentence completion, asking of questions, etc.). Furthermore, Cervenka (1967, p. 48) reports that young children lack the necessary language consciousness to judge whether a structure is "correct" or "incorrect"—a task that is called for in one of his subtests on grammar (e.g., "correct" or "incorrect": "They singed very well yesterday." "A fly is more small than a mouse." "A tree is taller than I." "Where live birds?"). However, the children may not be lacking language consciousness, but rather an understanding of how to perform the required task.[2] Other difficulties associated with using such discrete-point tests have been enumerated by Perren (1967).

It would appear that both discrete-point tests and tests of general communicative ability are useful in assessing the bilingual skills of young children. The value of the test of communicative skills is that it provides a measure of fluency in each of two languages, *independent of specific vocabulary, pronunciation, or grammar.* The value of the discrete-point test is its ability to give the teacher an idea of the student's *specific language needs.* The overall-skills test helps determine which language needs more development and in what general areas. The discrete-point test may suggest what items to teach. But the problem is to construct a good discrete-point test. As Harris points out, "The technique of eliciting and rating highly structured speech samples shows much promise, but such testing is still in the experimental stage and requires very great test-writing skill and experience" (Harris, 1969, p. 90).

---

[2] For more on this, see A.V. Cicourel *et. al. Language Use and School Performance.* New York: Academic Press, 1974.

For the Redwood City study, a test of general communicative ability was developed. This test, the Storytelling Task, was adapted from the John T. Dailey Language Facility Test (Dailey, 1968), and used some of the Dailey materials as well as photo cards from *Words and Action: Roleplaying Photo-Problems for Young Children* (Shaftel and Shaftel, 1967).

The Dailey Language Facility Test elicits a series of stories in English and in Spanish, in response to three pictures—a snapshot, a painting, and a drawing. The snapshot is of a school scene (a teacher and students outside), the painting is of a home scene (a father holding a baby, a mother and dog watching), and the drawing is of a neighborhood scene (a boy sitting on the ground pointing at a cat in a tree). Although three domains, home, education, and neighborhood, are represented by these pictures, the pictures also represent three different media—a photo, a painting, and a sketch. Therefore, analysis of language competence by domain on these pictures might simply have been picking up students' reactions to the different media, and so, was not carried out.

A second storytelling task was also administered to a subsample, using three pictures representing the same domains. However, the pictures were photo cards (2' x 1½') from *Words and Action* (Shaftel and Shaftel, 1967). These photos are from a series of problem-solving photographs that are meant to stimulate speculation and verbal response. The photos selected represented the domains of home, education, and neighborhood as did the Dailey pictures. One is of a father walking in the door to see his boy spill a box of cereal on the kitchen floor. A second shows an older and a younger boy both tugging at the same block in a classroom. The third shows a policeman preventing a small child from darting into the street after a rubber ball. For this task, it is possible to obtain a measure of language competence by domain because all stimuli are photos.

The script that the examiner used both with the Dailey pictures and with the *Words and Action* photos was adapted from that used in the Dailey Test. The Dailey script asks the child to tell a story without telling him what a story is. The script for this research provided that the child first saw a snapshot and heard a story about it (actually told by a junior high school student and included in the Dailey manual) (Dailey, 1968, p. 13). Then the child was asked to tell his own story.

The Dailey Test uses a single 0-9 rating scale for each of the three pictures. For this study, the scoring system was based on the measurement of storytelling by Lambert, Tucker, d'Anglejan, and Segalowitz (1970). This system involved the rating, for Spanish and English, of general fluency, grammar, pronunciation, rhythm and intonation, and language alternation, and included a rating for descriptive ability. Each of the six categories of ratings had a 1-to-5 rating continuum. The use of six rating categories was thought to provide a greater possible dispersion of scores than the simple 0-9 Dailey scale and also provided for separate scrutiny of specific areas of language difficulty, such as language alternation.[3] The category of language alternation was included as a measure of language independence. It gives not only an indication of how much a bilingual alternates between his two languages, but of whether words and phrases from one language are more likely to be inserted into speech in the other language rather than vice versa (on language alternation, see Espinosa, 1917; Lance, 1969). For the analysis of the *Words and Action* data, a seventh category, range of vocabulary, was added. The range of vocabulary was simply the total number of different words used in the story. The range of vocabulary was calculated for each of the three stories prompted by the photos.

All the children's stories were taped. Then a Mexican American and an Anglo rater with some training in linguistics transcribed the tapes and rated the Spanish and the English stories respectively. The raters were instructed to interpret grammatical "errors" liberally. Nonstandard forms in common use, like "me either" instead of "me neither," or "gonna" for "going to," were not considered errors in grammer. Substitution of one pronoun for another ("he" for "she") or misuse of verb tenses ("he hitted"), or confusion of use of verb tenses with the negative ("he didn't found") *were* considered errors.

The raters did not actually begin the task of rating until the inter-rater reliability correlation coefficient was greater than .80. After several practice sessions, the mean inter-rater reliability coefficient for six student ratings was .87.

It is possible to criticize this method of elicitation of speech, especially if it takes place entirely within the academic framework, since it may severely limit the speech of youngsters who would otherwise exhibit an extremely wide range of expression (Labov, 1969). For this reason, a subsample of children were retested in their own homes (sometimes in the child's room, sometimes in the livingroom, sometimes outside the house). Testing at home still doesn't eliminate the fact that the child is being asked to produce speech for an adult authority figure. (The tester was a twenty-year-old male Chicano.) However, it can be argued that since the children have to face adult authority figures every day at school, it may be helpful to have a sample of their speech in such a setting.

Copies of the script for the Storytelling Task and the rating sheet used to assess the stories are presented below.

Script for the Storytelling Task

1. What is your name?
    ¿Cómo te llamas?

---

[3] Language alternation refers here to the entire range of language shift, from switching out of one language into another in the middle of a sentence to the mixing of single words from one language into sentences in another.

2. How old are you?
   ¿Cuántos años tienes?

3. Do you like to hear stories?
   ¿Te gustan las historias?

4. Let me tell you a story about this picture (Plate I)[4]:
   Déjame decirte una historia de este retrato:

Once there was a little girl and her shoes were too small. So they had to buy her some new shoes. One of her sisters had just gotten out of bed and her other sister was already dressed. Her mother took her and got her a pair of shoes. They tried the shoes on her. They fit and the little girl was very happy. And the shoes lasted a long, long time.

Una vez había una muchachita y sus zapatos no le quedaban porque estaban muy pequeños. Así es que le tenían que comprar un par de zapatos nuevos. Una de sus hermanas apenas se había levantado de la cama y su otra hermana ya estaba vestida. Su mamá la llevó a comprar un par de zapatos. Le probaron los zapatos. Le quedaron y la muchachita estaba muy feliz. Los zapatos duraron mucho tiempo.

5. Now could you tell me a story about a picture if I show it to you?
   Ahora tú dime una historia de un retrato.

   (If no) See if you can tell me a story about this picture.
            Trata de contarme una historia de este retrato.

   (If yes) Good, tell me a story about this picture.
                    (Use plates IV, V, VI)
             Bueno, cuéntame una historia de este retrato.

6. (If prompting needed) Tell me what you see in the picture.
                          Dime lo que ves en el retrato.

7. What are they doing in the picture?
   ¿Qué están haciendo en el retrato?

8. What else can you tell me about the picture?
   ¿Qué más me puedes contar del retrato?

---

[4]Plate I in the Dailey Language Facility Test.

Rating Sheet for Storytelling Task

Rater's Initials _____   Total Score _____
Student's Number _____   Level _____
Language (put 'X') _____ Spanish _____ English _____

General Ability to Communicate

_____ 5. Wide vocabulary, good control of grammar, no hesitation.
_____ 4.
_____ 3.
_____ 2.
_____ 1. Practically incomprehensible, very limited vocabulary, much prompting needed in a conversation.

Grammar

_____ 5. No noticeable errors in grammar.
_____ 4.
_____ 3.
_____ 2.
_____ 1. Many grammatical errors.

Pronunciation

_____ 5. No trace of an accent.
_____ 4.
_____ 3.
_____ 2.
_____ 1. Almost impossible to understand because of heavy accent.

Intonation

_____ 5. Child has all the appropriate intonation patterns of the language.
_____ 4.
_____ 3.
_____ 2.
_____ 1. Intonation not at all native-like.

Language Alternation

_____ 5. Child does not mix languages at all—either in phrases or with
_____ 4. separate words.
_____ 3.
_____ 2.
_____ 1. Extensive mixing of words and phrases from the two languages.

Descriptive Ability

_____ 5. Generalizing about action or object (e.g., "dogs like to chase balls.")
_____ 4. Setting the action in a chronological order (e.g., "the dog catches the ball.")
_____ 3. Inferring relationships among objects (e.g., "the dog is chasing the ball.")
_____ 2. Describing objects ("red ball").
_____ 1. Naming objects ("ball").

NOTE: Rating #3 for the first five categories means moderate ability in its respective category. #4 means almost, but not quite, native-like. #2 means skills are very limited in that category, but some proficiency is noticeable.

1.4 *Tests of Reading, Inter-American Series*

The Inter-American Tests of Reading include tests at five levels of difficulty, covering grades 1 through 12. The tests are published in English and Spanish parallel editions. English- and Spanish-speaking educators from Puerto Rico, Mexico, and Texas participated in the test construction. The publishers report that "the language of the tests was chosen to avoid local idioms, and instead, to use 'standard' language that could be understood generally" (Guidance Testing Associates, 1967a). They also maintain that an effort was made to find language of similar difficulty for the two editions. A semantic frequency list correlating the six thousand most frequent English and Spanish words (Eaton, 1940) was used as a resource.

The Level 1 test consists of subtests of vocabulary and comprehension. In each exercise of the tests, the child chooses a picture which is suggested by a word, a phrase, a sentence, or a paragraph. The Level 2 test has subtests of level of comprehension, speed of comprehension, and vocabulary. In the first two subtests, the child chooses a picture to which a phrase, sentence, or paragraph refers. In the third test, vocabulary, the child chooses a word suggested by a picture. The Inter-American English Reading Tests are meant to test the reading progress of students who have had a basal approach to reading, as there are phonically irregular words.

The tests were developed in Texas, and although their main use is in testing Mexican American and other Spanish-speaking school children of the Southwest, they have been used in Puerto Rico, on the East Coast of the U.S., and elsewhere. The reliability of the English version of the test, through correlation of CE and DE forms, was .90 for Level 1 and Level 2 when given to second graders, and .83 when Level 2 was given to third graders. The reliability of the

Spanish version was .86 for Level 1, .74 for Level 2 given to second graders and .71 for Level 2 given to third graders (Guidance Testing Associates, 1967b). Thus, it can be seen that the reliability dropped when the Spanish version of the test was given. It appears that the reliability check was run on school children in Puerto Rico.

As a check for concurrent validity (the relationship of test scores to an accepted contemporary criterion of performance), the Level 2 test results for grades 2 and 3 were correlated with performance on the Metropolitan Reading Test and on the Stanford Achievement Primary II, Reading (Word Meaning and Paragraph Meaning) Test. Guidance Testing Associates (1967b) present correlation coefficients by subtests only. The correlation of the subtests of the Inter-American Reading Test, Level 2, with subtests from the Metropolitan Reading Test range from .61 to .87, with a mean of .69. Correlations with the Stanford Reading Test range from .30 to .82, with a mean of .68.

No national norms are provided for these tests. The publishers (Guidance Testing Associates, 1967a) suggest that local norms be established. The State of California began a program to provide norms for the Inter-American Tests, but it was never completed.

1.5 *Writing Sample*

Although this study placed major emphasis on assessing primary-school students' oral comprehension, speaking, and reading skills, it was felt necessary to have some measure of writing skill. Part of the difficulty with such a measure was the age and writing ability of the children. It was decided to assess the writing ability of only the older students, the nine and ten year olds. The means of stimulating the writing sample was through a sequence of twelve pictures that tell a story. The instrument was administered to the Pilot Mexican American and Anglo students and to the Pilot Comparison group. It was realized that the Pilot Comparison group would have difficulty in writing Spanish because they had not been taught Spanish writing skills.

The compositions were scored along seven dimensions, adapted from Lewis and Lewis (1965). They were: verbal output (number of words), range of vocabulary (number of different words), diversity of vocabulary (type-token ratio), accuracy of spelling (ratio of number of errors to total number of words), grammatical correctness (ratio of number of errors to total number of words), quality of sentence structure (5-point scale with "5" being very complete sentences, much variety in sentence structure), and effectiveness of expression (5-point scale, with "5" being very colorful use of words; high unity of composition). Grammatical errors were considered to be only those forms that a native speaker of the language would not use in any register of any dialect. Thus, dialect forms used by native speakers of Spanish and English respectively were counted as correct.

Below is the set of directions for the exercise. The sequence of pictures that were used to elicit the composition is on page 280.

Writing Sample
(English & Spanish)

Give every student a copy of the picture story and a piece of lined writing paper. Make sure that the students are seated so as not to encourage copying from someone else. When all are ready say:

"Now we are going to write a story from these pictures. Look at all the pictures from the top left to the bottom right. Then write down on your paper the story that these pictures tell.

"Ahora vamos a escribir una historia sobre estos retratos. Ve todos los retratos desde él que está arriba y a la izquierda hasta él de abajo a la derecha. Luego, escribe en tu papel la historia que los retratos cuentan."

Do not give help to the student (i.e., vocabulary words, actions, etc). Collect the papers at the end of 45 minutes.

1.6 Language Use Observation Instrument

Fishman (1969) points out that self-report as a means for determining language use is in need of empirical validation. Self-report data, particularly from young children, may suffer from the Hawthorne effect. The children know they are in a program in which a premium is put on Spanish, so they may *say* they speak it more than they actually do. One means of determining language use other than by asking the respondent is that of observing him in language use situations and recording the language he uses. This technique has not been widely employed in sociolinguistic research because of the time and money involved in such efforts. Recently, however, sociolinguists have attempted to measure language use directly. Two language use observation studies were conducted in Ethiopia, one on language use in the market (Cooper and Carpenter, 1975) and one on language use in the court (Cooper and Fasil, 1972). Several pilot language use observation studies were also conducted by Stanford University students. Ramírez (1971) looked at the language use of 12 Chicano males in the Bilingual Follow Up I Group in Redwood City. Fillmore (1971) observed the language use of 30 Anglo students, 10 each from grades 1, 3, and 5 in an elementary school with 80% Mexican American and 20% Anglo students, in Alviso, California.

It is on the basis of results from the Ramírez and Fillmore pilot studies that this current language use observation instrument was drawn up. Mexican American students were randomly selected from the Pilot, Follow Up I, and Follow Up

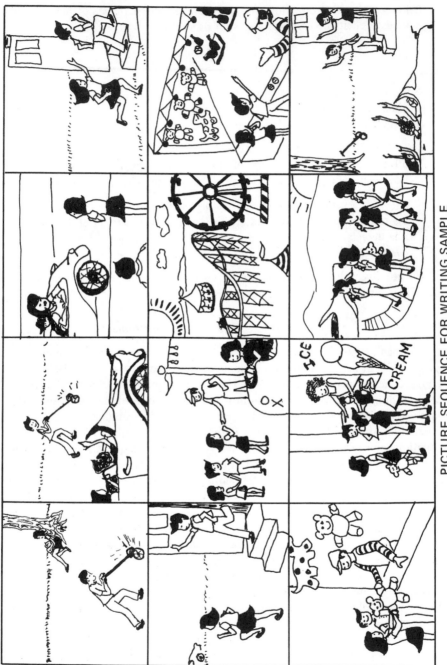

PICTURE SEQUENCE FOR WRITING SAMPLE

STUDENT LANGUAGE USE OBSERVATION INSTRUMENT

Student	Observation Period	MATH	Grouping Pattern	Adult/ Language	SOCIAL SCIENCE	Grouping Pattern	Adult/ Language	PLAY-GROUND	LUNCH
Juan Perez	1st	S→AT, E→MA	SG	AT/S	E→AS, S→MS	W	AT/S	E→AG, S→MS	E→MS, S→AS
	2nd								
	3rd								
	1st								
	2nd								
	3rd								

Sample Entry

ETC.

KEY:

Languages

S = Spanish
E = English

Students

MS = Mex. Am. Stud.
AS = Anglo Stud.

Adults

MT = Mex. Am. Teacher
MA = Mex. Am. Aide
AT = Anglo Teacher
AA = Anglo Aide

Grouping

W = Whole Class
SG = Small Group
I = Individual

II groups at the Bilingual and Comparison schools—four boys and four girls from each group. One Mexican American observer was assigned to observe the eight Mexican American children within each of the six subgroups. Language use was observed in four different contexts: two within a classroom setting (Math and Social Studies/Science), and two outside the classroom setting (Lunch and Playground). Fishman (1966b), in specifying his bilingual dominance configuration, indicated that levels of formality (intimate, casual, formal) may affect the bilingual's choice of language. The two classroom settings were intended to be formal, and lunch and playground were intended to be more informal. Houston (1969) found that Black children used a school register in the classroom and a non-school register outside the classroom. Perhaps there is a close analogy between register switching, as in Houston's study, and language switching, as in the present study.

Furthermore, language switching may be affected by different topics and different interlocutors (see Mackey, 1962). Thus, the observers were further instructed to indicate whether an adult was present when the language use was observed, who this adult was, and what language this adult was speaking. At the Bilingual program, there were Mexican American teachers, Anglo teachers, and Mexican American (and other Latin American) teacher aides. At the Comparison school, there were only Anglo teachers, and no aides.

The observers were to observe each child for one minute (after he started talking) in each of the four settings on three different days. The observer marked down on his observation sheet to whom the child addressed his remarks (Mexican American or Anglo teacher or teacher aide, Mexican American or Anglo student), the classroom grouping—if in class (whole class, small group or individual grouping at the time of observation), the ethnic background of the adult leading the group (if there was one) and the language that the adult was using at the time.

The Ramírez pilot instrument had provisions for indicating the language that the addressee used in responding to the student under observation. But his results showed that it was different to get meaningful data because often no single person was addressing remarks at the student. Rather, students would all offer information to an adult at the same time.

Incidental information picked up by this instrument includes the patterns of communication in the classroom—who speaks to whom. For instance, who do Mexican American children address their remarks to?

A copy of the instrument is on page 281.

1.7 *Pupil's Language Use Inventory*

Based on an instrument in Fishman, Cooper, Ma *et al.* (1971), the Pupil's Language Use Inventory asked the pupil for his own self-report of the languages he used and the languages used by others to address him when he was at home with his parents, his older siblings, and his younger siblings; when he was in the neighborhood with his peers; when he was at school with his friends; and when he was with his companions at church. The domains of family, neighborhood, education, and religion were chosen in replication of a study by Greenfield and Fishman (1971), and based on a year of participant observation and focused interviews and discussions with representative informants of a Puerto Rican barrio in Jersey City. The intent was to see if the domains that differentiated language use patterns for one group of children of Latin American background also applied to another group, from a Mexican American barrio in California.

The child was asked to report on language use when a person, such as a parent or sibling, and a place, such as the home or the neighborhood streets, were supplied. No attempt was made to add another variable, namely the topic that the child would be discussing with this person. Greenfield and Fishman (1971) used the following set up:

Domain	Interlocutor	Place	Topic
Family	Parent	Home	How to be a good son or daughter.
Friendship	Friend	Beach	How to play a game.
Religion	Priest	Church	How to be a good Christian.
Education	Teacher	School	How to solve a math problem.
Employment	Employer	Workplace	How to do your job in the most effective way.

The authors found that *topic* was not as important as *person* and *place* in one experiment, and in another experiment only person was important—neither topic nor place. Oliver (1970) also found that topic was not important in a study of language use in New Mexico. Specifying the right topics is a problem. Ervin-Tripp (1964) found topic important, but only topics that were specific to Japanese culture—festivals, the Japanese New Year Day, cooking and housekeeping, a doll festival, street storytellers. Ervin-Tripp (1967) suggests that the content of the discussion does not necessarily determine the language being used; that friendship patterns often determine the choice of language.

Response categories to questions on the Pupil's Language Use Inventory were "Spanish," "English," or "both." The Spanish version of the questionnaire was used, although an English translation was provided on the form (see below). The questionnaire was written so as to be intelligible to kindergarteners, as well as to students in grades 1-3. The Spanish translation was made by Mexican American college students. The questionnaire included provision for noting who the children associated with at school and at home, and who they went to church with. This information was used to determine the extent to which the Mexican American children interacted with Anglos, and hence, had reason to use English. A similar questionnaire, with more questions about school language use, was used by Timmons (1971).

A copy of the instrument used in the Redwood City study follows:

Pupil's Language Use Inventory

NOTE: Give this questionnaire in whatever language the child seems to be most comfortable. When in doubt, repeat the question in the other language. (2 = Spanish; 1 = Both, 0 = English)

1a. In what language does your mother usually talk to you at home?
¿En qué te habla tu mamá en casa?

1b. What language do you use to talk to her?
¿En qué le respondes?

2a. What language does your father use to talk to you at home?
¿En qué te habla tu papá en casa?

2b. What language do you use to talk to him?
¿En qué le respondes?

3. What language do your parents speak when they talk to each other at home?
¿En qué hablan tu mamá y tu papá cuando platican los dos en casa?

4a. What language do your older brothers and sisters use when they talk to you at home?
¿En qué te hablan tus hermanos mayores en casa?

4b. What language do you use when you talk to them?
¿En qué les hablas a ellos?

5a. What language do your younger brothers and sisters use when they talk to you at home?
¿En qué te hablan tus hermanos menores en casa?

5b. What language do you use to talk to them?
¿En qué les hablas a ellos?

6. Who are the kids you hang out with in school?
¿Quiénes son tus amigos en la escuela?

When you are with _____ in the school playground, what
language do you usually speak?
Cuando andas con _____ ¿en qué hablan ustedes?

7. What kids do you hang out with where you live?
    ¿Quiénes son tus amigos en donde vives?

    When you're with _____ what language do you use?
    Cuando andas con _____ ¿en qué hablan ustedes?

8. Who do you go to church with?
    ¿Con quién vas a la iglesia?

    When you're standing outside the church along with _____ ,
    what language do you speak?
    Antes de entrar a la iglesia con _____ , ¿en qué hablan
    ustedes?

1.8 *Nonverbal Subtests of the Tests of General Ability, Inter-American Series*

The Inter-American Tests of General Ability were developed in Texas by
Guidance Testing Associates (1967a, 1967b), with the major purpose being to
provide bilingual children an opportunity to be tested on their intellectual development both in Spanish and in English.

During the 1969-1970 year, the Level 1 Test of General Ability was administered to the Mexican American Pilot first graders and to the Comparison group
(at that time) in both English and Spanish. It was determined that the verbal
part of the test was too time-consuming and did not provide any new data not
already provided by the Inter-American Tests of Reading, the Word Naming by
Domain instrument, and the Storytelling Task. Therefore, only the Nonverbal
Ability Subtests were administered in the subsequent two years. Another rationale for using only the Nonverbal Ability Subtests was that research had shown
bilinguals to perform better on nonverbal tests than on verbal tests, when compared with monolinguals (see Darcy, 1953, 1963; Jensen, 1961; Diebold, 1968).
Jensen (1961) found that Mexican Americans classified low on I.Q. performed
better on language-independent tests than did low I.Q. Anglo children. Galvan
(1967) also suggests that nonverbal tests are a better indicator of intelligence
than are verbal tests.

At Level 1, the Nonverbal Ability Subtests consist of Association (16 items)
and Classification (16 items). At Level 2, the Nonverbal Ability Subtests involve
Classification (24 items) and Analogy (16 items). In the Redwood City Study,
the instructions for the subtests were given in both Spanish and English. The
students had to choose one out of four items as either being the correct match
for something pictured to the left, or as the one item that did not belong in

the series. The two subtests at each level were timed such that the student was given either five or six minutes to complete each subtest.

According to the author of the tests,[5] the General Ability Tests measure achievement and infer ability on this basis. The Nonverbal Ability Subtests are being used in this study as a measure of academic aptitude, or more specifically as a measure of the child's ability to cope with school-related tasks. The middle-class school system asks students to perform classification, association, and analogy type tasks on a daily basis. The Nonverbal Ability Subtests were administered on a pretest-posttest basis to determine how children in a bilingual project differed in academic aptitude over time from students in a conventional school program.

Mean reliability figures for alternate forms over several administrations of the Nonverbal Ability Subtests (Guidance Testing Associates, 1967b) were as follows. For the Spanish version, correlation of form CEs with DEs produced coefficients of .81 when Level 1 was given to grade 1 (.62 when given to first-grade Mexican Americans from Texas), .64 when Level 2 was given to grade 2, and .55 when Level 2 was given to grade 3. On the English version, the correlation coefficients were .77 when Level 1 was given to grade 1, .66 when Level 2 was given to grade 2, and .62 when Level 2 was given to grade 3.

As measures of concurrent validity, results from the General Ability Tests were correlated with results using well-known intelligence tests. The correlation of the Nonverbal Ability Subtests, Level 1 (English Form CE), with the Goodenough-Harris Draw-A-Man Test was .52, when testing first graders. The correlation of the Nonverbal Ability Subtests, Level 2, with the Otis Quick Scoring Mental Ability Test, Alpha, were .65 (Form CE) and .64 (Form DE) for second graders, and .76 (Form CE) and .69 (Form DE) for third graders. Both reliability and validity data were generally based on student groups with from 50 to 100 students per group (see Guidance Testing Associates, 1967b, for actual tables).

The publishers of the Inter-American General Ability Tests provide no national norms for interpreting the results of testing. Instead, they urge the testers to establish their own local norms and they provide guidelines for how to do this. Between 1970 and 1972, the California State Office of Bilingual Testing and Assessment was engaged in a project to norm the Inter-American Tests for Mexican Americans and Anglos in California. Unfortunately, the project was never completed.

There has been much controversy recently about just what is being measured when Mexican American children are given so-called tests of intelligence. The San Francisco Chronicle of May 25, 1972, pointed out that, while about 15% of the children in California schools were Mexican Americans, they made up 40% of those in classes for the mentally retarded. It is well known that they

---

[5] Personal communication with Dr. Herschel Manuel.

were put there on the basis of results from standardized tests. The Bay Area Bilingual Education League organized a convocation of evaluators and administrators to critique existing intelligence tests. The keynote address by De Avila (1972) pointed out weaknesses in many of the standardized tests on the market. The report issued on the basis of the conference included a professional critique of the Inter-American General Ability Tests (see BABEL, 1972).

1.9 Cross-Cultural Attitude Inventory

The Cross-Cultural Attitude Inventory was developed by Steve Jackson and Ron Klinger (1971), Region XIII Education Service Center, Austin, Texas, with the assistance of Dr. Carl F. Hereford, University of Texas at Austin. The instrument provides information regarding cross-cultural perceptions. The inventory contains 24 items (pictures), eleven "Mexican American" and eleven "Anglo" items. Two items, "school" and "book" are neutral. The items are concerned with games/recreation, clothing, food, language, etc. Responses are made directly on the test booklet corresponding to five positions (ranging from a very happy face to a very sad face). Jackson recently revised the instrument (see p. 265 above), but did not provide reliability or validity data.

Below is a list of the 24 items on the test, in English and in Spanish. The test administrator reads the name of the item in both languages before the students mark their reactions. Following the list of items are two sample items from the test, an Anglo and a Mexican American "little boy."

Items Used in Test

In the order in which they appear in the test, the items are:

In English	In Spanish
Little girl (M.A.)	Muchachita
The English word *yes*	La palabra en inglés *yes*
Chicken soup	Caldo de pollo
Mexican flag	Bandera de México
Little boy (Anglo)	Muchachito
Tortilla	Tortilla
Little boy (M.A.)	Muchachito
Hamburger	Hamburguesa
The Spanish word *sí*	La palabra en español *sí*
Jalapeño pepper	Jalapeño chile
Bullfighter	Torero
Book	Libro
Pin-the-tail-on-the-donkey	Juego de burro
American flag	Bandera de los Estados Unidos
Piñata	Piñata

Cowboy hat	Sombrero de vaquero
Football player	Jugador de fútbol
Little girl (Anglo)	Muchachita
School	Escuela
Taco	Taco
Menudo	Menudo
Mexican hat	Sombrero
Bread	Pan
Pickle	Pepino

1.10 *Home Interview Questionnaire*

A Home Interview Questionnaire was designed for use with parents of children in the Bilingual Project and at the Comparison school. One form of the questionnaire was administered in the fall of 1970 to obtain baseline and pretest data, and then another form of the questionnaire with posttest questions that had been overlooked earlier was administered in the spring of 1972. The Home Interview Questionnaire contained questions on language proficiency and language use, on the socioeconomic level and educational environment of the home, demographic questions, and several miscellaneous questions. Copies of both forms are at the end of this section. (A discussion of the Language Orientation Questionnaire, also part of the home interview, appears in the next section.)

Questions 32-39 of the fall-1970 questionnaire (see below) pertained to the language proficiency of all members of the household. Questions 20-27 of the spring-1972 questionnaire applied only to the language proficiency of children in the Bilingual and Comparison groups. These questions were taken from a language census employed in a study of a Puerto Rican neighborhood in Jersey City (see Fishman, Cooper, Ma *et al.,* 1971).

Questions 40-50 of the fall-1970 questionnaire dealt with the language use of all members of the household. Questions 28-35 of the spring-1972 questionnaire applied only to the language use of children in the Bilingual or Comparison groups.

While language proficiency questions dealt with what a person *could* do with Spanish and English, language use questions referred to what he *typically did.* The type of language use inquiries employed in this study went further than those found in other research projects (see, for instance, Mahoney, 1967; Anderson and Johnson, 1968, 1971; Patella and Kuvlesky, 1970; Peñalosa, 1966; and Nall, 1962).

How to measure the socioeconomic level of a family has always been a matter of controversy in social science research. There have been and still are a variety of scales in use (see Kahl and Davis, 1954; Labov, 1966). In the Red-

SAMPLE ITEMS FROM THE CROSS-CULTURAL ATTITUDE INVENTORY

wood City study, it was decided to use a modified version of the Warner scale (W. L. Warner *et al.,* 1949). This scale provides seven levels of employment, with each level divided into seven categories including professionals, proprietors, business men, clerks, manual workers, protective and service workers and farmers. Some of these categories do not have entries at all levels. For instance, there are no specific jobs named for the protective and service worker categories at the top three levels of the occupational scale. Another category was added, namely "housewife or unemployed." Occupational status and parents' education were combined to produce a more traditional scale of socioeconomic level.

At the same time, a series of educational environment questions were asked. These questions were based on research by Lambert and Macnamara (1969) in turn based on the work of Bloom (1964). In a large-scale survey to assess the relation between the socioeconomic level, aptitude, and achievement, Bloom found that a knowledge of the educational environment in the home was a more powerful predictor of children's achievement in school than was socioeconomic level.

Questions 6 and 7 on the fall-1970 questionnaire and questions 3, 4, 6 and 18 on the spring-1972 form pertained to socioeconomic level. Questions 8, 13a-f, 14-17, 22-26, 30, and 31 on the fall-1970 form applied to the educational environment in the home.

Questions 10-17 in the spring-1972 questionnaire were intended as measures of how the family functioned as a decision-making unit and as a unit which had to process resources. Particularly since most of the Mexican American families in the study had limited resources, the questions sought to find out how different families coped with the situation of having limited resources. The questions were concerned with (1) the extent to which the family was familiar with the local community and with other areas of California, (2) the family's network of friends and associates, and (3) the family's sphere of influence. Lipset and Zetterberg (1956) stress the importance of the power ranking of a person in a community, and not just his socioeconomic status. Particularly in the case of minorities, a person may have a low-prestige occupation by majority-society standards, but command a degree of power and prestige in his local minority community. A recent study of school children in the *barrios* of four Latin American countries suggested that a *barrio* family's ability to manage limited resources and attain local power or respect in the *barrio* had an effect on the school success of children from that family.[6]

Finally, the Home Interview Questionnaire had demographic questions: on the fall-1970 form, 1-5, 8-12, 18-21; and on the spring-1972 form, 1, 2, 5-9. It

---

[6]"The Study of Factors Associated with the School Success of Barrio Children in Latin American Countries (Argentina, Brazil, Paraguay, and Colombia)," ASCOFAME, Bogota, Colombia. Personal Communication from Robert F. Arnove, Assistant Professor, Indiana University.

also had several miscellaneous questions: 27-29 on the fall-1970 form, and 38-41 on the spring-1972 form.

With respect to the reliability of the Home Interview Questionnaire, Fishman (1971a) found that his language census questionnaire had high reliability. Upon requestioning 20% of the households one month later, he found a mean of 91% agreement between responses the first and the second time on demographic variables. There was a median census-recensus item correlation of .81 for the language proficiency and use items.

The Redwood City study relied on three methods of checking the reliability of the Home Interview Questionnaire. First, the writer knew 20 of the original 81 Mexican American families personally, having spent at least an hour in each of their homes the year prior to this two-year study. Thus, he was able to check the data results by Mexican American interviewers against his own observations and knowledge of the families. Second, two pretest interviews were repeated two weeks later and results were checked with earlier results. There was a mean 96% agreement between the responses on the first and second interviews. Third, the Bilingual Specialist in the Bilingual Project administered a Parent Profile questionnaire to all the Mexican American parents in the Project during the 1970-1971 school year, and this questionnaire had seven items that were identical to those asked in the Home Interview Questionnaire. Thus, it was possible to cross-check the Parent-Profile responses against those in the Home Interview Questionnaire. There were very few discrepancies. In cases where discrepancies existed, they were usually attributed to the fact that a different parent answered each of the questionnaires.

With respect to the validity of the language proficiency and language use information, Gumperz and Hernández (1970) have pointed out that language use questions tend to reflect the analyst's—not the native's—theory of speaking. Whereas a person may say he uses Spanish in a given situation, he may actually be switching from one to the other. Fishman and Terry (1971) suggest that whereas retrospective reports of language behavior may not reflect each family member's sociolinguistic performance minute by minute, they do provide a substantially accurate overall perception of the person as a bilingual. In the Redwood City study, an effort was made to obtain convergent measures of language proficiency and use as a check for validity. For instance, both the parents and the students reported on each other's language use, and both groups described the language use of the students' siblings.

Below are the pre- and posttest forms of the Home Interview Questionnaires:

Home Interview Questionnaire: Fall, 1970

A.   *Información de los que viven en la casa (Information on People Living in the Home)*

1.   Nombre
     (Name)

2. Relación al padre
   (Relationship to Family Head)
3. Sexo 1=M 0=F
   (Sex)
4. ¿Cuándo nació?
   (Birthdate)
5. ¿Dónde nació? 1=Mexico 0=USA
   (Birthplace)
6. Empleo
   (Occupation)
7. Educación 0=no formal education; 1=K-3, 2=4-6; 3=7+
   (Education)

B. *Información cerca de los hijos (Information on the Children in the Family)*

8. ¿Ha tenido _____ educación antes de kindergarten?
   0=no 1=sí
   (Has _____ had pre-school?)
9. ¿Dónde está situada la escuela?
   (Where is the school located?)
10. ¿Fue _____ al kindergarten? 0=no 1=sí
    (Has _____ been to kindergarten?)
11. ¿Dónde fue al kindergarten?
    (Where was it located?)
12. ¿Cuántos años asistió _____ al kindergarten?
    (For how many years did _____ go to kindergarten?)
13. Antes que _____ comenzó el kindergarten, ¿podía su niño:
    a. recitar el alfabeto?
    b. reconocer las letras?
    c. leer?
    d. contar?
    e. escribir su nombre?
    f. nombrar los colores?
    3=esp.; 2=esp. e ing.; 1=ing.; 0=ninguno
    (a. recite the alphabet?)
    (b. recognize letters?)
    (c. read?)
    (d. count?)
    (e. print his name?)
    (f. name colors?)
    (3=sp.; 2=sp. & eng.; 1=eng.; 0=none)

14. ¿En qué idioma le (leía) Ud. a _____ ?
3=esp.; 2=esp. e ing.; 1=ing.; 0=ninguno
(In what language do (did) you read to _____?)

15. ¿Con qué frecuencia lee (leía) Ud. a _____ ?
(How often do (did) you usually read to _____?)

16. ¿Con qué frecuencia ayuda (ayudaba) Ud. a _____ con su tarea de escuela?
(How often do (did) you help _____ with his homework?)

17. ¿Conoce Ud. la maestra de _____?
(Have you met _____'s current teacher?)
1=sí 0=no

C. *Información General (General Information)*

18. ¿Cuánto tiempo ha vivido Ud. en Redwood City?
(How long have you lived in Redwood City?)

19. ¿En dónde vivía Ud. antes de venir a Redwood City?
(Where did you live before moving to Redwood City?)

20. ¿Visita Ud. a sus parientes en México? ¿Con qué frecuencia?
(Do you go to Mexico for visits? How often?)

21. Eventualmente, ¿desearía Ud. vivir (residir) en México?
(Would you eventually like to return to Mexico to live?)

22. ¿Tiene diccionarios en la casa? Inglés _____ Español _____
Otro _____
(Do you have dictionaries in your home? English _____
Spanish _____ Others _____)

23. ¿Qué revistas o periódicos tiene en su casa?
(What magazines or newspapers do you have at home?)

24. ¿Tienen los niños materiales educativos como libros, pinturas, papeles, pizarras o tizas en la casa?
(Do the children have educational materials like books, paints, papers, chalk boards or chalk in the home?)

25. Más o menos ¿cuántas horas por día pasan sus niños mirando la televisión? ¿Miran algunos programas en español? ¿Escuchan programas españoles en la radio?
(About how many hours a day do your children watch TV programs? Do they watch any programs in Spanish? Do they listen to Spanish radio programs?)

26. ¿Les preguntan sus niños algunas veces el significado de ciertas palabras? ¿Palabras en español? ¿En inglés? ¿Tratan Uds. de explicarles el significado?
(Do your children ever ask you what certain words mean? Spanish words? English words? Do you try to explain?)

27. ¿En qué región cree Ud. que se habla el español más correcto?
¿Quién habla el español más correcto aquí donde Ud. vive? ¿Trata
Ud. de enseñar a sus niños a hablar de esa manera?
(Where do you think the best Spanish is spoken? Who do you think
speaks the best Spanish around here? Do you ever try to get your
children to speak that way?)

28. ¿En qué región se habla el inglés más correcto? ¿Quién habla
el inglés más correcto aquí donde Ud. vive? ¿Trata Ud. de enseñar
a sus niños a hablar de esa manera?
(Where do you think the best English is spoken? Who do you think
speaks the best English around here? Do you ever try to get your
children to speak that way?)

29. ¿Se ponen tristes sus niños cuando se enferman y no pueden ir a
la escuela? ¿Cuáles se ponen tristes?
(If your children are sick and can't go to school, are any of them
disappointed? Which ones?)

30. Aunque no tiene Ud. cita con la maestra, ¿va Ud. a visitar la
escuela?
(Do you go to school for things other than teachers' conferences?)

31. ¿Cree Ud. que puede tener alguna influencia sobre la educación de
su niño en la escuela?
(Do you feel that you can influence what your child gets out of
school?)

D. *La Habilidad en los Idiomas (Proficiency in Spanish and English)*
2=sí 1=poco 0=no

32. ¿Puede entender _____ una conversación en español?
(Can _____ understand a conversation in Spanish?)

33. ¿Puede participar _____ en una conversación en español?
(Can _____ engage in an ordinary conversation in Spanish?)

34. ¿Puede leer _____ un periódico en español?
(Can _____ read a newspaper in Spanish?)

35. ¿Puede escribir _____ cartas en español?
(Can _____ write letters in Spanish?)

36. ¿Puede entender _____ una conversación en inglés?
(Can _____ understand a conversation in English?)

37. ¿Puede participar _____ en una conversación en inglés?
(Can _____ engage in an ordinary conversation in English?)

38. ¿Puede _____ leer un periódico en inglés?
(Can _____ read a newspaper in English?)

39. ¿Puede _____ escribir cartas en inglés?
(Can _____ write letters in English?)

E.   *Uso de los Idiomas (Spanish and English Language Use)*
     2=esp.; 1=esp. e ing.; 0=ing.

40. ¿Qué idioma usa _____ con más frecuencia en casa para conversar con adultos?
     (What language does _____ use most frequently at home for conversation with adults?)

41. ¿Qué idioma usa _____ con más frecuencia en casa para conversar con niños?
     (What language does _____ use most frequently at home for conversation with children?)

42. ¿Qué idioma usa _____ con más frecuencia para leer libros o periódicos en casa?
     (What language does _____ use most frequently to read books or newspapers at home?)

43. ¿Qué idioma usa _____ generalmente para escribir cartas?
     (What language does _____ commonly use at home for writing letters?)

44. ¿Qué idioma usa _____ generalmente para conversar con sus amigos en el trabajo?
     (What language does _____ use most at work for conversation with fellow workers?)

45. ¿Qué idioma usa generalmente en el trabajo para conversar con el jefe?
     (What language does _____ use most at work for conversation with the boss?)

46. Generalmente, ¿en qué idioma conversa _____ con personas de su edad en esta vecindad (en la calle)?
     (What language does _____ commonly use when talking to people of the same age in the neighborhood (in the street)?)

47. ¿Qué era (es) el idioma de instrucción en la escuela de _____?
     (What was (is) the language of instruction in _____'s school?)

48. ¿En qué idioma prefiere conversar _____ con adultos?
     (What language does _____ like most for conversation with adults?)

49. ¿En qué idioma prefiere conversar _____ con niños?
     (What language does _____ like most for conversation with children?)

50. ¿En qué idioma da la misa el padre (ministro) cuando _____ va a la iglesia?
     (In what language does _____'s priest (minister) give the service when _____ attends services?)

Home Interview Questionnaire: Spring, 1972

RESPONDENT'S NAME _____ CASE I.D. _____

DATE OF INTERVIEW _____

NOTES: Use NR for "no response."
Use NA for "not applicable."

1. ¿Ha tenido usted niños desde el otoño de 1971? _____
    ¿Cuántos? _____
    (Have you had any children since the fall of 1971? _____
    How many?)
2. ¿Ha cambiado de trabajo el encabezado de la casa desde el otoño
    de 1971? _____
    (Has the head of the household changed his job since the fall of
    1971?) _____
3. Hágame el favor de describir el ambiente donde trabaja el
    encabezado de la casa. ¿Qué hace en su trabajo? _____

    _____

    (Please describe the head of the household head's job setting. What
    does he do at work?)
4. ¿Cuántas horas por semana trabaja el encabezado de la casa?
    _____

    (How many hours does the head of the household work per week?)
5. Si es usted originalmente de Mexico, ¿de cuál estado vino? _____
    (If you are originally from Mexico, what state are you from?)
6. ¿Vivía usted en una cuidad _____, un pueblo _____ o un
    rancho _____?
    (Did you live in a city, a town, or a rural area?)
7. ¿Cuántos años ha vivido usted en los Estados Unidos?
    (How many years have you lived in the United States?)
8. ¿Cuántas veces se ha cambiado de casa desde que vino a los
    Estados Unidos? _____
    (How many times have you moved since coming to the United
    States?)
9. Eventualmente, ¿desearía usted vivir en México? _____
    (Eventually, would you like to go to Mexico to live?)
10. ¿Cuáles organizaciones en Redwood City conoce usted?

    _____

    _____

    (What organizations are you aware of in Redwood City?)

11. ¿Pertenece a organizaciones locales o nacionales? ¿A cuáles?

_____

(What organizations do you belong to?)

12. ¿Cuántas veces visita usted las siguientes personas?

	3 veces o más a la semana	1 o 2 veces a la semana	Cada 2 semanas más o menos	Cada mes	Casi nunca
Parientes					
Vecinos mexicanos					
Mexicanos que no son vecinos					
Vecinos americanos					
Americanos que no son vecinos					

(How much of the time do you visit the following people: Relatives, Mexican American Neighbors, Mexican Americans who are not neighbors, Anglo neighbors, Anglos who are not neighbors? 3 or more times per week, 1 to 2 times per week, every 2 weeks or so, monthly, rarely.)

13. ¿Cuáles sitios en Redwood City conocen sus niños? _____

_____

(What places in Redwood City are your children familiar with?)

14. Cuando ustedes van de paseo, generalmente ¿adónde van?

_____

(When you go on an excursion (trip), generally where do you go?)

15. Cuando usted tiene un problema médico o un problema financiero, ¿con quién va? _____

(When you have a medical or financial problem, who do you go to?)

16. ¿Ha comprado algo en crédito? Sí _____ No _____

(Have you bought anything on credit?)

17. ¿Cuáles comerciantes del barrio le dan crédito? _____

_____

(Which businessmen in the community give you credit?)

18. Hágame el favor de describir su casa.

_____ a. es de sólo una familia

_____ b. es de varias familias

_____ c. está comprada

_____ d. está rentada

(Please describe your home: a. single-family, b. several-family, c. bought, d. rented.)

19. ¿Ha tomado usted o su esposo clases en inglés?
    _____ ninguna clase
    _____ 1 mes o menos
    _____ 6 meses
    _____ 1 año o más
    _____ al momento está tomando clases
(Have you or your husband taken any English classes? None, 1 month or less, 6 months, 1 year or more, currently taking.)

LA HABILIDAD EN LOS IDIOMAS 2=sí 1=poco 0=no

Just ask of: _____, _____, _____

20. ¿Puede entender (*student*) una conversación en español?
(Can _____ understand a conversation in Spanish?)
21. ¿Puede participar _____ en una conversación en español?
(Can _____ engage in an ordinary conversation in Spanish?)
22. ¿Puede leer _____ un periódico en español?
(Can _____ read a newspaper in Spanish?)
23. ¿Puede escribir _____ cartas en español?
(Can _____ write letters in Spanish?)
24. ¿Puede entender _____ una conversación en inglés?
(Can _____ understand a conversation in English?)
25. ¿Puede participar _____ en una conversación en inglés?
(Can _____ engage in an ordinary conversation in English?)
26. ¿Puede _____ leer un periódico en inglés?
(Can _____ read a newspaper in English?)
27. ¿Puede _____ escribir cartas en inglés?
(Can _____ write letters in English?)

USO DE LOS IDIOMAS 2=esp. 1=esp. e ing. 0=ing.

28. ¿Qué idioma usa _____ con más frecuencia en casa para conversar con adultos?
(What language does _____ use most frequently at home for conversation with adults?)
29. ¿Qué idioma usa _____ con más frecuencia en casa para conversar con niños?
(What language does _____ use most frequently at home for conversation with children?)
30. ¿Qué idioma usa _____ con más frecuencia para leer libros o periódicos en casa?
(What language does _____ use most frequently to read books or newspapers at home?)

31. ¿Qué idioma usa _____ generalmente para escribir cartas?
(What language does _____ commonly use at home for writing letters?)

32. Generalmente, ¿en qué idioma conversa _____ con personas de su edad en esta vecindad (en la calle)?
(What language does _____ commonly use when talking to people of the same age in the neighborhood (in the street)?)

33. ¿Qué es el idioma de instrucción en la escuela de _____?
(What is the language of instruction in _____'s school?)

34. ¿En qué idioma prefiere conversar _____ con adultos?
(What language does _____ like most for conversation with adults?)

35. ¿En qué idioma prefiere conversar _____ con niños?
(What language does _____ like most for conversation with children?)

36. Si el professor usa español en la clase de sus niños, ¿qué efecto tendrá esto en la habilidad de ellos para usar el inglés?
_____ Le aumentará la habilidad que tiene para aprender el inglés.
_____ Le disminuirá la habilidad que tiene para aprender el inglés.
_____ Su habilidad en el inglés saldrá lo mismo.
(If the teachers use Spanish in your child's classroom at school, what effect will this have on his ability to use English? It will increase his learning of English, it will decrease his learning of English, his English ability will come out the same.)

37. Durante los últimos dos años, ¿tuvo _____ un cambio en su habilidad de hablar con usted en español?
_____ Su español se ha mejorado.
_____ No ha cambiado.
_____ Ha estado perdiendo su habilidad de hablar el español.
(Over the past two years, has there been a change in _____'s ability to speak with you in Spanish? His Spanish has improved, no change, he's losing his ability to speak Spanish.)

38. ¿Se siente a gusto cuando visita la escuela?
(Do you feel comfortable when you visit your children's (child's) school?)

39. ¿Siente usted que los maestros en la escuela entienden los problemas de los mexicanos?
(Do you feel that the teachers at school understand the problems of the Mexican Americans?)

40. ¿Qué le gusta del programa escolar de sus niños? _____

_____

_____

(What do you like about your children's (child's) program at
school?)

41. ¿Qué le disgusta? _____

_____

(What don't you like?)

1.11 *Language Orientation Questionnaire*

The Language Orientation Questionnaire is based on a questionnaire developed
by Gardner and Lambert (Gardner and Lambert, 1959; Gardner, 1960). The instrument asked for parents and siblings of students in the Bilingual and Comparison groups to react to suggested reasons for the students to learn English as a
second language.

Research on language attitudes (Gardner and Lambert, 1959; Gardner, 1960;
Feenstra, 1968; Feenstra and Santos, 1970; Gardner and Santos, 1970; Lambert,
Tucker, d'Anglejan, and Segalowitz, 1970; Gardner and Lambert, 1972) has
identified the existence of two general orientations for learning a language, an
integrative one and an instrumental one. The integrative motive reflects a desire
for more contact with the people who speak the language. The instrumental
motive reflects a desire to obtain a good job or to better oneself educationally.
The items chosen for the questionnaire were assigned, on an *a priori* basis, to
one of these two sets of motives for language learning.

This is perhaps the first time that the language orientation questions were
used with a single group to rate both reasons for learning a second language
and reasons for learning (or preserving) a mother tongue. A rating of orientation toward mother tongue was included because primary-school Mexican Americans may not necessarily retain their mother tongue. In fact, many Chicano
youngsters today cannot speak Spanish. The Redwood City Bilingual Project
was attempting to preserve the Spanish language skills and cultural heritage of
the Chicano student. The use of the Language Orientation Questionnaire in pre-
and posttesting parental language attitudes was considered one means of determining whether having their children in a bilingual project affected the language
attitudes of Mexican Americans in the community.

In pretesting the instrument on parents and in using it for baseline language attitude data on siblings, it was observed that there was not very much dispersion of ratings. Most items were rated as "very good reasons," "good reason," and "neither good nor bad." Thus, in posttesting parental attitudes, parents were also asked to select the two most important reasons and the one least acceptable reason for their children to learn Spanish and English.

On the following pages can be found copies of the Language Orientation Questionnaire in Spanish and English, and a copy of the instructions for rank ordering of items on the posttest.

Language Orientation Questionnaire: Spring-1972 Interview

Administer the Language Orientation Questionnaire only to the adult(s) who answer(s) the Home Interview Questionnaire.

After the respondent has rated the 7 reasons for having his children learn Spanish, ask him to select the *2 best reasons* (las dos razones mejores) and the one (1) least acceptable reason (la razón menos aceptable) for their children to learn Spanish and English. Circle the numbers of the top two reasons and "X" the least acceptable reason. For example:

1.
②
3.
④
5.
X
7.

2 and 4 are rated at the top;
6 is rated lowest.

After the respondent has finished the questionnaire, ask him the following question:

¿Cuánta importancia le da a que sus niños aprendan el español comparada con la importancia que le da a que hablen inglés?

_____ más importante
_____ igual de importante
_____ menos importante

(How important is it for your children to learn Spanish as compared to English? More important, equally important, less important.)

LANGUAGE ORIENTATION QUESTIONNAIRE: SPANISH FORM

A. ¿Es ésta una buena razón para que sus hijos aprenden el español?

	muy buena razón	buena razón	ni buena ni mala razón	mala razón	muy mala razón
1. Les ayudará a preservar su idioma y su cultura.					
2. Les ayudará a encontrar un buen trabajo.					
3. Les ayudará a tener amistades entre todos de su raza.					
4. Les permitirá siendo verdaderos chicanos.					
5. Nadie está completamente educado si no puede hablar el español correctamente.					
6. Les permitirá a conocer y conversar con más y diferentes personas.					
7. Lo necesitan para cumplir sus objectivos educacionales o comerciales.					

8. ¿Qué tan necesario es que sus niños puedan hablar y entender el español?
Muy necesario _____ algo necesario _____ no es necesario _____.

9. ¿Qué tan necesario es que sus niños puedan leer español?
Muy necesario _____ algo necesario _____ no es necesario _____.

10. ¿Qué tan necesario es que sus niños puedan escribir el español?
Muy necesario _____ algo necesario _____ no es necesario _____.

LANGUAGE ORIENTATION QUESTIONNAIRE: SPANISH FORM (cont.)

	muy buena razón	buena razón	ni buena ni mala razón	mala razón	muy mala razón
B. ¿Es ésta una buena razón para que sus hijos aprenden el inglés?					
1. Les ayudará a hacer amigos entre los angloamericanos.					
2. Les ayudará a encontrar un buen trabajo.					
3. Necesitan un buen conocimiento del inglés para tener el respeto de la comunidad angloamericana.					
4. Les ayudará a pensar y actuar como angloamericanos.					
5. Nadie está completamente educado si no puede hablar el inglés correctamente.					
6. Les permitirá a conocer ye conversar con más y diferentes personas.					
7. Lo necesitan para cumplir sus objectivos educacionales o comerciales.					

8. ¿Qué tan necesario es que sus niños puedan hablar y entender el inglés?
Muy necesario _____ algo necesario _____ no es necesario _____ .

9. ¿Qué tan necesario es que sus niños puedan leer el inglés?
Muy necesario _____ algo necesario _____ no es necesario _____ .

10. ¿Qué tan necesario es que sus niños puedan escribir el inglés?
Muy necesario _____ algo necesario _____ no es necesario _____ .

RESPONDENT'S NAME _____ HOUSEHOLD # _____

LANGUAGE ORIENTATION QUESTIONNAIRE: ENGLISH FORM

	very good reason	good reason	neither good nor bad	bad reason	very bad reason
A. Is this a good reason for your children to learn Spanish?					
1. It will help them to preserve their own native language and culture.					
2. It will someday be useful to them in getting a good job.					
3. It will enable them to maintain friendships among Mexican Americans.					
4. It will enable them to continue to think and behave as true Mexican Americans (Chicanos).					
5. No one is really educated unless he is fluent in the Spanish language.					
6. It will allow them to meet and converse with more and varied people.					
7. They need it for some specific educational or business goals.					

8. How important is it for your children to be able to speak and understand Spanish? Very important _____ Somewhat important _____ Not important _____.

9. How important is it for your children to be able to read Spanish? Very important _____ Somewhat important _____ Not important _____.

10. How important is it for your children to be able to read Spanish? Very important _____ Somewhat important _____ Not important _____.

LANGUAGE ORIENTATION QUESTIONNAIRE: ENGLISH FORM (cont.)

	very good reason	good reason	neither good nor reason	bad reason	very bad reason
B. Is this a good reason for your child to learn English?					
1. It enables them to make friendships with Anglos (Gavachos).					
2. It will someday be useful to them in getting a job.					
3. They need a good knowledge of English to be respected in the Anglo community.					
4. It will enable them to think and behave as Anglos do.					
5. No one is really educated unless he is fluent in English.					
6. It will allow them to meet and converse with more and varied people.					
7. They need it for some specific educational or business goals.					

8. How important is it for your children to be able to speak and understand English? Very important _____ Somewhat important _____ Not Important _____ .

9. How important is it for your children to be able to read English?
Very important _____ Somewhat important _____ Not important _____ .

10. How important is it for your children to be able to write English?
Very important _____ Somewhat important _____ Not important _____ .

RESPONDENT'S NAME _____ HOUSEHOLD # _____

Appendix 2. INSTRUCTIONAL MATERIALS, K-3, 1969-1972

The list of materials presented in this section is organized by grade level, starting with third grade, and then, within each grade level, by subject: Spanish for the Spanish speaking, Spanish for the English speaking, English for the Spanish speaking, English for the English speaking, Mathematics, Social Studies, and Science.

Recently, many new bilingual materials have appeared on the market. Two of the best sources of information on such materials are the Materials Acquisition Project, San Diego City Schools, 2950 National Avenue, San Diego, California 92113, and the Bay Area Bilingual Education League (BABEL), 1414 Walnut Street, Berkeley, California 94709. It is fair to say that many of the materials that have been found to be better than the ones used in the Redwood City Project, became available only recently. As the number of programs and intensity of interest in bilingual instruction have increased, more and more commercial publishers have started publishing materials for bilingual education programs.

GRADE 3

Spanish for the Spanish Speaking

Books, workbooks: 1. Laidlaw Readers, Palo Alto, California
   1° grado — *Aprendamos a leer*
   2° grado — *Camino de la escuela, Nuestros amigos*
   3° grado — *Del campo al pueblo, Sorpresas y maravillas, Aventuras maravillosas*
   4° grado — *Nuestro mundo maravilloso, Cuaderno de trabajo*

2. *El mundo de las palabras,* 2° y 3° grado, Ediciones Anaya, Book 2, Madrid, Spain

3. *Aventura del lenguage,* Casado, Lisardo, Jose Mata Honorio Muro Texts for Grades 3 and 4

4. *Mi diccionario ilustrado,* 3° grado, Scott Foresman & Co.

Spanish for the English Speaking

Books, workbooks:

1. *Mi cuaderno de español,* Book 2, M. MacRae, Houghton-Mifflin Co.

2. *Somos Amigos.* Tirsa Saavedra Scott, Ginn & Co.

3. Laidlaw Readers (see above)

Audiovisual:

1. *Cantemos en español,* Book 1, Vol. 1 & 2. B. & M. Krones. Holt, Rinehart & Winston, Inc.

2. *Sing and Speak Spanish,* Album 2. M. MacRae, Houghton-Mifflin Co.

3. *Somos Amigos,* Parts 1 & 2, Tirsa Saavedra Scott, Ginn & Co.

English for the Spanish Speaking

Books, workbooks:

1. *Sullivan Reading Series.* Programmed Reading Books 1-22. McGraw-Hill Book Co.

2. *Michigan Oral Language Series,* Primary Parts 1-4. MLA/ACTFL Edition.

3. My Weekly Reader Education Center, Columbus, Ohio
Reading Success Series, Books 1-6
Table and Graph Skills Series
Imagine and Write, Books 2-5

4. The MacMillan Reading Program, MacMillan & Co.
4th grade — *The Magic Word*
3rd grade — *More Than Words, Better than Gold*
2nd grade — *Enchanted Gates, Shining Bridges*

5. *Basic Goals in Spelling.* California State Series, McGraw-Hill Book Co.

6. *Better Handwriting for You* — 3rd grade. California State Series

7. *Beginning Dictionary.* Thorndike-Barnhart.

Audiovisual: 1. Spanish Vocabulary Cards—Spanish-English Visual
                         Education Association, Inc.

English for the English Speakers

Books, workbooks: 1. *Sullivan Reading Series.* McGraw-Hill Book Co.

                      2. *Ginn Elementary English.* Ginn & Co.

                      3. *Basic Reading Program.* Harper-Row Co.

                      4. *The Bank Street Readers.* MacMillan Co.

                      Note: Also Nos. 3-7 above under "English for the
                         Spanish Speaking."

Mathematics

Books, workbooks: 1. *Modern School Mathematics: Structure and Use.*
                         Houghton-Mifflin Co.

                      2. *Matemática 3 y 4.* McSwain Brown Co.

Social Studies

Books, workbooks: 1. *The Social Sciences: Concepts and Values.*
                         California State Series

Audiovisual: 1. "La Raza" Filmstrip series.

                      2. César Chávez Unit: Slides, cassettes. In Spanish and
                         English. Prepared by project staff.

Science

Books, workbooks: 1. *Concepts in Science.* Harcourt, Brace, Jovanovich,
                         Inc.

GRADE 2

Spanish for the Spanish Speaking

Books, workbooks: 1. Ediciones escolares. Madrid, Spain. Jesus González-
                         Pita. *Victoria, La escuela nueva.*

                      2. Laidlaw Brothers Readers. Palo Alto, Calif.
                         Aprendamos a leer
                         Nuestros amigos
                         Camino de la escuela

	3. Laguna Beach Books. Kenworthy Education Service, Inc.

       Los tres osos
       Los cuatro cantantes de Guadalajara
       Doña Cigarra y Doña Hormiga
       Caperucita roja
       El flautista de Jamelín
       Doña Zorra y Doña Cigueña

Audiovisual:

1. Records accompanying the Laguna Beach books.

2. Songs in Spanish for Children. Columbia #CL1897

Spanish for the English Speaking

Books, workbooks:

1. *Mi cuaderno de español.* M. W. MacRae. Houghton-Mifflin Co.

2. *Somos Amigos,* Tirsa Saavedra Scott. Ginn & Co.

3. *Zoo Risa.* McNally & Loftin

Audiovisual:

1. SVE Education Filmstrips — Elementary Spanish for Young Americans (6 filmstrips, 3 records, guides #A188SR)

2. Somos Amigos, Parts I & II — records.

3. Flashcard kit — Spanish (21 categories) — Wible Language Institute

English for the Spanish Speaking

Books, workbooks:

1. *Sullivan Programmed Readers.* McGraw Hill Book Co.

2. *The Bank Street Readers.* Harper Row Co.

3. *Basic Goals in Spelling.* McGraw Hill Book Co.

4. *Michigan Oral Language Series.* MLA/ACTFL Edition.
Bilingual Conceptual Development Guide
English Guide
Interdisciplinary Oral Language Guide, Primary Parts I-IV.

Audiovisual:

1. Audiovisual English (10 filmstrips, 5 records, teacher's guide). Collier-MacMillan English Program.

2. Language Development Cards and Charts. The Economy Co.

Language Development Cards, Groups A & B
Wall Charts (Number and Color)
Pocket Chart (Calendar, Weather, Special Days)

English for the English Speaking

Books, workbooks:

1. *Sullivan Programmed Reading.* McGraw Hill Book Co.

2. *Ginn Elementary English.* Ginn & Co.

3. *Basic Reading Program*, Grade 2. Harper & Row Co.

4. *The Bank Street Readers*, Grade 2. MacMillan & Co.

5. *Basic Goals in Spelling.* McGraw Hill Book Co.

Audiovisual:

1. GAF Corporation. Library Chest #2163 — 20 Viewmaster Reels.

2. Language Development Kit, Peabody, Level 3. American Guidance Services, Inc.

3. Flashwords. Milton Bradley Co.

Mathematics

Books, workbooks:

1. *Modern School Mathematics: Structure and Use.* Houghton-Mifflin Co.

Audiovisual:

1. Addition and Subtraction Flashcards — #9372. Milton Bradley Co.

2. Counting Devices. Jumbo Counting Frame #771 Palfrey

3. Judy Clock #JU701. Robert Morrison Sales Co.

Social Studies

Audiovisual:

1. "La Raza" Filmstrip Series. Multimedia Productions, Inc., Palo Alto, Calif. Southwest Council of La Raza, Parts 1-4.

2. United States Flashcards #9002. Milton Bradley Co.

3. César Chávez Unit: Slides, cassettes. In Spanish and English. Prepared by project staff.

Science

Books, workbooks:

1. *Concepts in Science — 2.* Harcourt, Brace, Jovanvich, Inc.

Audiovisual:

1. Concepts in Science — Classroom Laboratory 2.

Music

Books, workbooks:	1. Latin American Game Songs #M-4-B. Ruth de Cesare. Mills Music, Inc.
Audiovisual:	1. Latin American Game Songs. Bowmar Records Mills Music, Inc.

GRADE 1

Spanish for the Spanish Speaking

Books, workbooks:
1. *Victoria.* J. Gonzáles-Pita Co.
2. Organización Distribuidora Ibérica. Madrid, Spain.

Audiovisual:
1. Foldaway Play Screen #RH271E. Creative Playthings.

Spanish for the English Speaking

Books, workbooks:
1. *Teaching Spanish in the Grades.* M. MacRae. Houghton-Mifflin Co.
2. *Mi cuaderno de español,* Book 1. M. MacRae. Houghton-Mifflin Co.
3. *¿Cómo se dice?* Tirsa Saavedra Scott. Ginn & Co.

Audiovisual:
1. ¿Cómo se dice? Records. Ginn & Co.
2. Cantemos niños. B & M. Krones. Holt, Rinehart & Winston, Inc.
3. Flashcards: Spanish for Beginners #9007. Milton Bradley Co.
4. Instructional Charts for Caperucita roja, Los tres osos. Laguna Language Series. Kenworthy Education Service, Inc.

English for the Spanish Speaking

Books, workbooks:
1. *Oral English, Learning a Second Language.* The Economy Co.
2. *Shuck Loves Chirley.* Leonard Olguín. Golden West Publishing House, Huntington Beach, Calif.
3. *Miami Linguistic Readers.* D. C. Heath & Co.
4. *Structural Reading Series.* Singer Co., N.Y.
5. *Spanish-English Readingtime.* Kits 1-4 MacMillan Co.

	6. *Sullivan Programmed Reading,* McGraw Hill Book Co.

6. *Sullivan Programmed Reading,* McGraw Hill Book Co.

7. *Better Handwriting for You.* Noble & Noble, Inc.

Audiovisual:

1. Tapes accompanying Spanish-English Readingtime. MacMillan Co.

2. Listen and Do (Records 1-16). Houghton-Mifflin Co.

3. Disneyland Records. Walt Disney Productions

4. Auditory Discrimination Program (12 picture cards, 3 cassettes). Keith Gilmore

5. Filmstrips accompanying Sullivan Programmed Readers. McGraw Hill Book Co.

English for the English Speaking

Books, workbooks:

1. *Sullivan Programmed Readers.* McGraw Hill Book Co.

2. *Ginn Elementary English.* Ginn & Co.

3. *Basic Reading Program.* Harper & Row

4. *The Bank Street Readers.* MacMillan Co.

5. *SRA Reading Laboratory 1a.* Science Research Associates

6. *Language Development Kit,* Peabody, Level 2. American Guidance Service, Inc.

7. *Basic Goals in Spelling.* McGraw Hill Book Co.

8. *Better Handwriting for You,* Noble & Noble, Inc.

Audiovisual:

1. Disneyland Records. Walt Disney Productions.

2. Magnetic Alphabet Board #AA400. Robert Morrison Sales Co.

3. Filmstrips accompanying Sullivan Programmed Reading. McGraw Hill Book Co.

Mathematics

Books, workbooks:

1. *Modern School Mathematics: Structure and Use.* Houghton-Mifflin Co.

Audiovisual:

1. Jumbo Counting Frame #771. Palfrey's

2. Judy Clock #JU701. Robert Morrison Sales Co.

Social Studies

Books, workbooks: 1. *Principles and Practices in the Teaching of the Social Sciences. Concepts and Values, Level 1.* Harcourt, Brace, Jovanovich, Inc.

Science

Books, workbooks: 1. *Concepts in Science-1.* Harcourt, Brace, Jovanovich, Inc.

Audiovisual: 1. Concepts in Science Classroom Laboratory 1. Harcourt, Brace, Jovanovich, Inc.

Music

Books, workbooks: 1. Exploring Music. Holt and Rinehart

KINDERGARTEN

Spanish for the Spanish Speaking

Books, workbooks: 1. *Laidlaw Reading Series.* Laidlaw Bros. Palo Alto, Calif.
En el hogar y en la escuela
Camino de la escuela
Aprendemos a leer

2. *Preparándose para leer.* Houghton Mifflin Co.

3. *Laguna Beach Stories.* Richard McKean Publishers

Spanish for the English Speaking

Books, workbooks: 1. *Michigan Oral Language Series.* Spanish Guide for Kindergarten. MLA/ACTFL Edition.

2. *Laguna Beach Materials.* Richard McKean Publishers

Audiovisual: 1. Beginning Conversational Spanish. Sterling Educational Films

English for the Spanish Speaking

Books, workbooks: 1. *Introducing English.* Houghton Mifflin Co.

2. *Michigan Oral Language Series, English Guide for Kindergarten.* MLA/ACTFL Edition.

3. *Region One Curriculum Kit (Rock)* – Levels I & II. Melton Book Co., Inc., Dallas, Texas

                        4. *Peabody Language Development Kit,* Levels 1 and 2. American Guidance Service, Inc.

                        5. *Shuck Loves Chirley.* Leonard Olguín. Golden West Publishing House, Huntington Beach, Calif.

Audiovisual: 1. Beginning Conversational English. Sterling Educational Films.

English for the English Speaking

Books, workbooks: 1. *Readiness in Language Arts.* Sullivan Associates Behavioral Research Laboratory.

                        2. *Building Pre-Reading Skills, Kit A.* California State Series.

                        3. *Peabody Language Development Kit.* Levels 1 and 2. American Guidance Service, Inc.

Mathematics

Books, workbooks: 1. *Modern School Mathematics: Structure and Use.* Houghton Mifflin Co.

Audiovisual: 1. Try Tasks 1, 2, & 3. Experiences for Young Children. California State Series.

Social Studies

Audiovisual: 1. Viewmaster. 21 picture wheels and cassette tapes on Fantasyland, Marineland, Adventureland, Tomorrow Land, Frontierland and the San Diego Zoo. Bilingual recordings.

Science

Books, workbooks: 1. *Concepts in Science – K.* Harcourt, Brace, Jovanovich, Inc.

Audiovisual: 1. Concepts in Science – Classroom Laboratory K. Harcourt, Brace, Jovanovich, Inc.

Appendix 3.
CORRELATIONS OF TEST SCORES

Pretest with Posttest	P N=15	PC N=14	FUI N=16	FUIC N=15	FUII N=14	FUIIC N=16
Span. Oral Comprehension	––	––	.75**	.55*	.67**	.19
Eng. Oral Comprehension	––	––	-.01	.49	.64*	.47
Span. Storytelling Task						
Communicative Ability	.29	.29	.23	.50*	.17	-.12
Grammar	.30	.12	.38	.00	-.09	-.21
Pronunciation	.32	.54*	.14	-.07	-.20	.16
Intonation	-.06	.26	-.41	.23	-.11	.53
Lang. Alternation	.08	-.26	––	––	-.29	.72
Total	.16	.23	.16	.27	-.16	.34
Descriptive Ability	.23	.49	.41	.00	.26	.27
Eng. Storytelling Task						
Communicative Ability	.69**	.20	.29	.35	.73**	.46
Grammar	-.14	.35	.41	-.25	.02	.16
Pronunciation	.31	.71**	.59*	-.02	-.13	.70**
Intonation	-.17	.25	.35	.34	-.14	.56*
Total	.46	.55*	.52*	-.16	.01	.74**
Descriptive Ability	.50*	.16	.53*	.24	.72**	.15
Span. Word Naming						
Kitchen	.07	.20	.20	.02	-.26	.13
Street	.54*	.37	.62**	.08	-.24	.03
Church	.11	.51	.50*	-.10	-.14	.13
School	.11	-.10	.34	-.21	.32	.56*
Total	.32	.18	.69**	-.09	-.05	.23
Eng. Word Naming						
Kitchen	.55*	.31	.56*	.22	.81**	.33
Street	.56*	-.23	.28	.00	.21	.42
Church	.34	.19	.56*	.41	.89**	.50
School	.40	.17	.25	-.06	.59	.14
Total	.61**	.16	.60**	.08	.70	.58*
Eng. Reading[1]						
Vocabulary	.83**	.73**	.14	.55*	.50	.43
Comprehension	.43	.48	.76**	.58*	.53	.43
Total	.71**	.65**	.66**	.62*	.53	.44

P   = Pilot
PC   = Pilot Comparison
FUI   = Follow Up I Level
FUIC = Follow Up I Comparison
FUII = Follow Up II
FUIIC = Follow Up II Comparison

[1]Murphy-Durrell Reading Readiness
Analysis was Pretest for FUI &
FUII Levels.

* p <.05
** p <.01

	P	PC	FUI	FUIC	FUII	FUIIC
Pretest with Posttest	N=15	N=14	N=16	N=15	N=14	N=16
Cooperative Primary Test of Reading	.57*	.41	.18	.85**	——	——
Cooperative Primary Test of Math	.82**	.39	.38	.68**	——	——
Nonverbal Ability	.57*	.69**	.33	.38	.55*	.60
Stud. Span. Proficiency	.60**	.62**	.36	.46*	.15	.05
Stud. Eng. Proficiency	.38	.58*	-.05	-.08	.54*	.40
Stud. Lang. Use – Stud. Report	.70**	.61**	.54*	.62**	.44	.63**
Stud. Lang. Use – Parent Report	.14	.35	.38	.10	.20	.54*
Family Lang. Use – Student Report	.83**	.53*	.46*	.12	.43	.14
Stud. Lang. Preference	.28	-.07	.45*	.10	.28	.35

Appendix 4.
MEAN SQUARES FOR ANALYSIS OF VARIANCE AND COVARIANCE

VARIABLE	Mean Square/ School Group	MS/ School Group w/ Covariate	*MS/ Error	d.f.	F
Ch. VIII, Table 1					
Span. Reading Comp.	523.77	––	94.23	1/27	5.56
Span. Reading Total	1,088.77	––	255.71	1/27	4.26
Writing Sample –					
Vocab. Diversity	0.12	––	0.01	1/17	8.37
Writing Sample – Spelling	0.09	––	0.02	1/17	4.70
Table 2					
Storytelling Task –					
Descriptive Ability	2.41	2.08	0.42	1/28	4.98
Storytelling by Domain –					
Grammar	4.50	––	0.50	1/7	9.00
Table 5					
Writing Sample – Spelling	0.15	––	0.01	1/17	11.77
Table 6					
Storytelling Task – Intonation	1.90	2.93	0.60	1/28	4.88
Word Naming by Domain –					
Kitchen	91.26	84.27	11.28	1/28	7.47
Total	615.54	634.23	137.91	1/28	4.60
CPT Reading Test	1.78	1.30	0.12	1/28	10.56
Table 7					
Oral Comprehension –	56.83	89.04	13.50	1/27	6.59
Storytelling –					
Descriptive Ability	2.59	––	0.57	1/27	4.51
Storytelling by Domain –					
Communicative Ability	4.35	––	0.46	1/7	9.53
Pronunciation	5.00	––	0.71	1/7	7.00
Total	39.20	––	5.26	1/7	7.46
Descriptive Ability	2.94	––	0.56	1/7	5.21
Vocabulary Diversity – Sch.	112.02	––	20.89	1/7	5.36
Word Naming by Domain –					
Church	72.50	83.43	14.76	1/27	5.65
School	53.21	72.76	14.70	1/27	4.95
Total	819.01	871.24	113.58	1/27	7.67

VARIABLE	Mean Square/ School Group	MS/ School Group w/ Covariate	*MS/ Error	d.f.	F
Ch. X, Table 1					
Student Language Use – Parent Report	34.59	25.87	5.62	1/26	4.60
Family Language Use – Student Report	3.79	7.88	1.61	1/26	4.88
Lang. Use Obser Eng. to Mex. Am. Students out of Class	0.17	––	0.03	1/12	20.08
Table 2					
Lang. Use Observation – Span. to Adult in Class	0.02	––	0.005	1/12	5.31
Table 3					
Stud. Lang. Use – Stud. Report	63.26	41.01	3.38	1/27	12.13
Stud. Lang. Use – Parent Report	50.75	44.63	7.11	1/27	6.27
Lang. Use Observation – Span. to Adult in Class	0.06	––	0.007	1/12	7.87
Span. to M.A. Student out of Class	0.87	––	0.04	1/12	20.01
Eng. to M.A. Student out of Class	0.63	––	0.04	1/12	15.48
Ch. XI, Table 3					
CPT Math Test	86.41	––	8.10	1/28	10.67
Nonverbal Ability	85.95	148.95	20.11	1/27	7.41
Ch. XII, Table 1					
Attitude toward Mexican Culture	202.72	––	32.93	1/26	6.16
Attitude toward School	26.67	––	3.93	1/26	6.79
Attendance (1970-71)	415.65	––	39.19	1/27	10.61
Attendance (1971-72)	90.16	––	16.39	1/27	5.50
Table 2					
Lang. Preference – Parent Report	7.61	10.34	1.61	1/27	6.41
Table 3					
Attendance (1970-71)	614.44	––	133.39	1/28	4.61
Attendance (1971-72)	222.21	––	35.54	1/28	6.25

VARIABLE	Mean Square/ School Group	MS/ School Group w/ Covariate	*MS/ Error	d.f.	F
_____Table 4					
Reas. for Learning Span. –					
Complete Education	9.86	10.36	0.99	1/26	10.41
Reas. for Learning Eng. –					
Complete Education	4.91	5.01	1.09	1/26	4.58
Converse with More People	1.42	1.46	0.27	1/26	5.39
_____Table 5					
Reasons for Learning Span. –					
Preserve Native Language					
and Culture	1.80	1.54	0.18	1/17	8.71
Reasons for Learning Eng. –					
Making Friends with					
Anglos	3.20	2.97	0.34	1/17	8.73
For Bus. & Ed. Goals	1.80	1.57	1.13	1/17	11.91

*If Covariate, MS/Error is from
Computation using MS/School
Group with Covariate.

REFERENCES

Allen, Virginia F.
    1969   "Teaching Standard English as a Second Dialect." *Florida Foreign Language Reporter* 7.1:123-127, 164.

Altus, Grace T.
    1953   "WISC (Wechsler) patterns of a selective sample of bilingual school children." *Journal of Genetic Psychology* 83:241-248.

Anderson, James G. and William M. Johnson
    1968   *Socio-cultural Determinants of Achievement Among Mexican-American Students.* Las Cruces, New Mexico: New Mexico State U. ED 017 394.

Anderson, James G. and Dwight Safar
    1971   "The Influence of Differential Community Perceptions on the Provision of Equal Educational Opportunities." In. N.N. Wagner and M. J. Haug, eds. *Chicanos: Social and Psychological Perspectives.* St. Louis: C.V. Mosby. Pp. 244-252.

Anderson, James G. and William M. Johnson
    1971   "Stability and Change among Three Generations of Mexican-Americans: Factors Affecting Achievement." *American Educational Research Journal* 8.2:285-309.

Anderson, Theodore R. and M. Zelditch, Jr.
    1968   *A Basic Course in Statistics with Sociological Applications.* New York: Holt, Rinehart, & Winston.

Andersson, Theodore
    1965   "A new focus on the bilingual child." *Modern Language Journal* 49:156-160.

Andersson, Theodore
    1968   "Bilingual Elementary Schooling: A Report to Texas Educators." *Florida Foreign Language Reporter* 6.2:3, 4, 6, 25.

Andersson, Theodore
    1969a   "Bilingual schooling: oasis or mirage?" *Hispania* 52:69-74.

Andersson, Theodore
    1969b   *Foreign Languages in the Elementary School: A Struggle Against Medio-
                crity.* Austin, Texas: University of Texas Press.

Andersson, Theodore
    1969c   "What is an Ideal English-Spanish Bilingual Program?" *Florida Foreign Lan-
                guage Reporter* 7.1:40, 168.

Andersson, Theodore and Mildred Boyer
    1970   *Bilingual Schooling in the United States.* 2 Volumes, Washington, D.C.:
              Superintendent of Documents, U.S. Government Printing Office. ED 039
              527.

Andersson, Theodore
    1971   "Bilingual Education: The American Experience." *Modern Language
              Journal* 55.7:427-440.

Arnold, Richard D.
    1968   *San Antonio Language Research Project. 1965-66 (Year 2) Findings.*
              Austin, Texas: R & D Center for Teacher Education, Texas U. Ed. 022 528.

BABEL
    1972   *Bilingual Testing and Assessment: Proceedings of BABEL Workshop and
              Preliminary Findings.* Multilingual Assessment Project, Bay Area Bilingual
              Education League, 1414 Walnut Street, Berkeley, Ca. 94709.

Badillo, Herman
    1972   "A Guest Editorial: The Politics and Realities of Bilingual Education."
              Foreign Language Annals 5.3:297-301.

Baratz, Joan C.
    1969   "Teaching Reading in an Urban Negro School System." In J.C. Baratz and
              R.W. Shuy, eds. *Teaching Black Children to Read.* Washington, D.C.: Center
              for Applied Linguistics. Pp. 92-116.

Barker, George C.
    1947   "Social Functions of Language in a Mexican-American Community." *Acta
              Americana* 5:185-202.

Bartlett, D. W.
    1969   "Preface," In *Description and Measurement of Bilingualism.* L.G. Kelly, ed.
              Toronto, Canada: U. of Toronto Press. Pp. v-vi.

Bartley, Diana E. and Robert L. Politzer
    1972   *Practice-Centered Teacher Training: Standard English as a Second Dialect.*
              Philadelphia: Center for Curriculum Development, Inc.

Baty, Roger M. and Stanford International Development Education Center
    1972   *Re-Educating Teachers for Cultural Awareness: Preparation for Educating
              Mexican-American Children in Northern California.* New York: Praeger.

Bauer, Evelyn
    1967   *The Relationship of Cultural Conflict to the School Adjustment of the
              Mexican-American Child.* USOE-funded ESL Project at UCLA. Sacramento,
              California: California State Department of Education.

Berko, Jean
    1958   "The Child's Learning of English Morphology." *Word* 14:150-177.

Bernal, Joe J.
    1969   "I am Mexican-American." *Florida Foreign Language Reporter* 7.1:32, 154.

Blair, Philip M.
    1971   "Rates of Return to Schooling of Majority and Minority Groups in Santa
              Clara County, California." Unpublished Ph.D. Dissertation, Stanford
              University.

Bloom, Benjamin S.
    1964   *Stability and Change in Human Characteristics*. New York: John Wiley and
              Sons.

Bordie, John G.
    1970   "Language Tests and Linguistically Different Learners: The Sad State of
              the Art." *Elementary English* 47:814-828.

Bowen, J. Donald
    1952   "The Spanish of San Antonito, New Mexico." Unpublished Doctoral Dis-
              sertation, University of New Mexico.

Bowen, J. Donald
    1972   "Local Standards and Spanish in the Southwest." In R.W. Ewton, Jr. and
              J. Ornstein, eds. *Studies in Language and Linguistics 1972-73*. The Univer-
              sity of Texas at El Paso, Texas Western Press, Pp. 153-164.

Brière, Eugène J.
    1971   "Are We Really Measuring Proficiency with Our Foreign Language Tests?"
              Foreign Language Annals 4.4:385-391.

Burma, John
    1954   *Spanish-speaking Groups in the United States*. England: Duke University
              Press.

Burns, Donald H.
    1968   "Bilingual Education in the Andes of Peru." In J.A. Fishman, C.A. Ferguson,
              and J. Das Gupta, eds. *Language Problems of Developing Nations*. New York:
              Wiley and Sons. Pp. 403-413.

Burt, Marina K. and Carol Kiparsky
    1972   *The Gooficon: A Repair Manual for English*. Rowley, Massachusetts: New-
              bury House.

Bustamante, Charles J. and Patricia L. Bustamante
    1969   *The Mexican-American and the United States*. Mountain View, California:
              Patty-Lar Publications Ltd. P.O. Box 4177.

California. Department of Education
    1967   *Prospectus for Equitable Educational Opportunities for Spanish-Speaking
              Children*. Sacramento, California: Mexican-American Research Project. ED
              020 038.

California. Department of Education
    1968   *The Education of the Mexican American*. Summary of the Proceedings of
              the Lake Arrowhead and Anaheim Conferences of August, 1966 and April,
              1967. Sacramento, California.

California State Advisory Committee to the U.S. Commission on Civil Rights
    1968   *Education and the Mexican-American Community in Los Angeles*. Unpub-
              lished.

Campbell, D. T. and J. C. Stanley
    1963   *Experimental and Quasi-Experimental Designs for Research.* Chicago: Rand McNally & Co.

Cannon, Garland
    1971   "Bilingual Problems and Developments in the United States." *Publications of the Modern Language Association,* pp. 452-458.

Carlson, Hilding B. and Norman Henderson
    1950   "The Intelligence of American Children of Mexican Parentage." *Journal of Abnormal and Social Psychology* 45:544-551.

Caro, Francis G.
    1971   "Issues in the Evaluation of Social Programs." *Review of Educational Research* 41.2:87-114.

Carrow, Sister Mary Arthur
    1957   "Linguistic functioning of bilingual and monolingual children." *Journal of Speech and Hearing Disorders* 22:371-380.

Carter, Thomas P.
    1969   *Preparing Teachers for Mexican-American Children.* University Park, New Mexico: New Mexico State University. ED 025 367.

Carter, Thomas P.
    1970   *Mexican Americans in School: A History of Educational Neglect.* New York: College Entrance Examination Board.

Casavantes, Edward J.
    1969   "A New Look at the Attributes of the Mexican American." Southwest Cooperative Educational Laboratory, Albuquerque, N.M. ED 028 010.

Casavantes, Edward J.
    1971   "Pride and Prejudice: A Mexican American Dilemma." In N.N. Wagner and M.J. Haug, eds. *Chicanos: Social and Psychological Perspectives.* St. Louis: C.V. Mosby. Pp. 46-51.

Cervenka, Edward J.
    1967   *Final report on Heat Start evaluation and research: 1966-67, Section VI: The measurement of bilingualism and bicultural socialization of the child in the school setting: the development of instruments.* Austin, Texas: Child Development Evaluation and Research Center, Univ. of Texas. ED 019 122.

Chandler, John T. and John Plakos
    1969   "Spanish-Speaking Pupils Classified as Educable Mentally Retarded." Sacramento, California: Mexican-American Education Research Project, Division of Instruction, California State Department of Education.

Chomsky, Noam
    1965   *Aspects of the Theory of Syntax.* Cambridge: M.I.T. Press.

Christian, Chester, Jr.
    1971   "Differential Response to Language Stimuli Before Age 3: A Case Study." Conference on Child Language, Chicago, November 22-24. Laval, Québec: Les Presses de l'Université. Pp. 1-14.

Clayton, Mary
    1970   *Population—1969, Redwood City, California.* Redwood City, California: Redwood City Planning Department.

Cohen, Albert K. and Harold M. Hodges
    1963   "Characteristics of the Lower Blue Collar Class." *Social Problems.* 10:303-333.

Cohen, Andrew D.
    1970   A Sociolinguistic Approach to Bilingual Education: The Measurement of Language Use and Attitudes toward Language in School and Community, with Special Reference to the Mexican American Community of Redwood City, California. Committee on Linguistics, Stanford, California. ED 043 007.

Cohen, Elizabeth G.
    1970   *A New Approach to Applied Research: Race and Education.* Chicago: Merrill.

Coleman, James S. *et al.*
    1966   *Equality of Educational Opportunity.* U.S. Department of Health, Education, and Welfare, Office of Education. A publication of the National Center for Educational Statistics. Washington, D.C.: U.S. Government Printing Office.

Cooper, Robert L.
    1968   "An elaborated language testing model." *Language Learning* 3:57-72.

Cooper, Robert L.
    1970   "Testing." In R.C. Lugton, ed. *Preparing the EFL Teacher.* #7. Philadelphia, Penn.: The Center for Curriculum Development, Inc.

Cooper, Robert L.
    1971   "Word Naming and Word Association." In J. Fishman, R. Cooper, R. Ma *et al. Bilingualism in the Barrio.* Indiana U. Publications, Lang. Science Mongraphs #7. The Hague, Netherlands: Mouton & Co. Pp. 286-294.

Cooper, Robert L. and Susan Carpenter.
    1972   "Language in the Market." In M.L. Bender, J.D. Bowen, R.L. Cooper, and C.A. Ferguson *et al. Language in Ethiopia.* Nairobi: Oxford U. Press, Ch. 18.

Cooper, Robert L. and Fasil Nahum
    1972   "Language in the Court." In M.L. Bender, J.D. Bowen, R.L. Cooper, C.A. Ferguson *et al. Language in Ethopia.* Nairobi: Oxford U. Press, Ch. 19.

Córdova, Ignacio R.
    1969   *The Relationship of Acculturation, Achievement, and Alienation among Spanish American Sixth Grade Students.* New Mexico State University, Las Cruces, New Mexico. ED 025 369.

Dailey, John T.
    1968   *Language Facility Test, Test Administrator's Manual.* Alexandria, Va.: The Allington Corporation, 801 N. Pitt Street #701.

Darcy, Natalie T.
    1953   "A review of the literature on the effects of bilingualism upon the measurement of intelligence." *Journal of Genetic Psychology* 82:21-57.

Darcy, Natalie T.
    1963   "Bilingualism and Intelligence; review of a decade of research." *Journal of Genetic Psychology* 103:259-282.

Davis, Frederick B.
    1967   *Philippine Language-Teaching Experiments.* Quezon City, Philippines: Alemar-Phoenix.

De Avila, Edward A.
    1972   "Some Cautionary Notes on Attempting to Adapt IQ Tests for Use with
            Minority Children and a Neo-Piagetian Approach to Intellectual Assessment."
            In *Bilingual Testing and Assessment; Proceedings of BABEL Workshop and
            Preliminary Findings.* Multilingual Assessment Project, Bay Area Bilingual
            Education League, 1414 Walnut Street, Berkeley, Ca. 94709. Pp. 65-105.

Del Buono, Xavier
    1972   "A Contrastive Analysis of Funded Projects." Presentation at Annual Cali-
            fornia TESOL Convention, Hilton Hotel, San Francisco, March 17-18, 1972.

Department of Education, Manila
    1953   *The relative effectiveness of the vernacular and of English as media of in-
            struction.* Bulletin nos. 9, 12, 14, 16. Manila: Bureau of Public Schools.

Derbyshire, Robert L.
    1969   "Adaptation of Adolescent Mexican Americans to United States Society."
            American Behavioral Scientist. Pp. 88-103.

Diebold, A. Richard
    1961   "Bilingualism and Biculturalism in a Huave Community." Unpublished Doc-
            toral Dissertation, Department of Anthropology, Yale U.

Diebold, A. Richard
    1968   "The Consequences of Early Bilingualism in Cognitive Development and
            Personality Formation." In E. Norbeck, D. Price-Williams, and W. McCord,
            eds. *The Study of Personality: An Interdisciplinary Approach.* New York:
            Holt, Rinehart, and Winston, Inc. Pp. 218-245.

Dixon, W. J., ed.
    1968   *BMD: Biomedical Computer Programs.* Berkeley & Los Angeles: University
            of California Press.

Dworkin, Anthony G.
    1965   "Stereotypes and Self-Images Held by Native Born and Foreign Born Mexi-
            can-Americans." *Sociology and Social Research* 49:214-224.

Dworkin, Anthony G.
    1971   "National Origin and Ghetto Experience as Variables in Mexican American
            Stereotypes." In N.N. Wagner and M.J. Haug, eds. *Chicanos: Social and
            Psychological Perspectives.* St. Louis: C.V. Mosby. Pp. 80-84.

Eaton, Helen S.
    1940   *Semantic Frequency List for English, French, German, and Spanish.* Chi-
            cago: University of Chicago Press.

Edelman, Martin
    1968   "The Contextualization of Schoolchildren's Bilingualism." In J.A. Fishman,
            R.L. Cooper, and R. Ma *et al. Bilingualism in the Barrio.* Two Volumes,
            Final Report. Yeshiva University. Contract No. OEC-1-7-062817-0297, U.S.
            Department of Health, Education, and Welfare. ED 026 546, 525-537.

Edelman, Martin, R.L. Cooper, and J.A. Fishman
    1971   "Young Puerto Rican Schoolchildren." In J.A. Fishman, R.L. Cooper, R.
            Ma *et al. Bilingualism in the Barrio.* Indiana U. Publications. Lang. Science
            Monographs #7. The Hague, Netherlands: Mouton & Co. Pp. 298-304.

Educational Testing Service
    1967   *Handbook: Cooperative Primary Test.* Princeton, New Jersey.

Elashoff, Janet D.
    1969   "Analysis of Covariance: A Delicate Instrument." *American Educational Research Journal* 6.3:383-401.

Elashoff, Janet D. and Richard E. Snow
    1970   *A Case Study in Statistical Inference: Reconsideration of the Rosenthal-Jacobson Data on Teacher Expectancy.* Technical Report No. 15, Stanford Center for Research and Development in Teaching. Stanford, California: School of Education, Stanford Univ.

Ervin-Tripp, Susan M.
    1964   "An analysis of interaction of language, topic, and listener." *American Anthropologist* 66.2:86-102.

Ervin-Tripp, Susan M.
    1967   "An Issei Learns English." *Journal of Social Issues* 23.2:78-90.

Ervin-Tripp, Susan M.
    1971   "Social Dialects in Developmental Sociolinguistics." In R. Shuy, ed. *Sociolinguistics: A Crossdisciplinary Perspective.* Washington, D.C.: Center for Applied Linguistics. Pp. 35-64.

Espinosa, Aurelio M.
    1911   *The Spanish Language in New Mexico and Southern Colorado.* Historical Society of New Mexico Publication No. 16. Santa Fe, New Mexico: New Mexican Printing Company.

Espinosa, Aurelio M.
    1917   "Speech Mixture in New Mexico: the Influence of the English Language on New Mexican Spanish." In H.M. Stephens and H.E. Bolton, eds. *The Pacific Ocean in History.* New York: MacMillan Co. Pp. 408-428.

Fasold, Ralph W. and Walt Wolfram
    1970   "Some Linguistic Features of Negro Dialect." In R.W. Fasold and R.W. Shuy, eds. *Teaching Standard English in the Inner City.* Washington, D.C.: Center for Applied Linguistics. Pp. 41-86.

Feenstra, Henry J.
    1968   "Aptitude and motivation in second-language acquisition." Unpublished Doctoral Dissertation. The University of Western Ontario, London, Ontario.

Feenstra, Henry J. and Emma H. Santos
    1970   "Aptitude, Attitude and Motivation in Second Language Acquisition: A Look at Two Cultures." Occasional Paper #5, Language Study Center, Philippine Normal College, Manila.

Ferguson, Charles A.
    1959   "Diglossia." *Word* 15:325-340.

Ferguson, Charles A.
    1971   "Problems of Teaching Languages with Diglossia." In A.S. Dil, ed. *Language Structure and Language Use: Essays by Charles A. Ferguson.* Stanford, California: Stanford University Press. Pp. 71-86.

Fillmore, Lily Wong
    1971   "A Study of Incidental Second Language Learning by Anglo Minority Group Children in a Mexican American Community." Unpublished paper, Stanford University.

Fishman, Joshua A.
    1964   "Language Maintenance and Language Shift as a Field of Inquiry." *Linguistics* 9:32-70.

Fishman, Joshua A.
1965   "Who speaks what language to whom and when?" *Linguistique* 2:67-88.

Fishman, Joshua A.
1966a   "The Implications of Bilingualism for Language Teaching and Language Learning." In A. Valdman, ed. *Trends in Language Teaching.* New York: McGraw-Hill. Pp. 121-132.

Fishman, Joshua A.
1966b   *Language loyalty in the United States.* The Hague, Netherlands: Mouton & Co. ED 036 217.

Fishman, Joshua A.
1967   "Bilingualism with and without Diglossia; Diglossia with and without Bilingualism." *Journal of Social Issues* 23.2:29-38.

Fishman, Joshua A.
1969   "Some Things Learned: Some Things Yet to Learn." *Modern Language Journal* 53:255-258.

Fishman, Joshua A.
1971a   "A Sociolinguistic Census of a Bilingual Neighborhood." In J.A. Fishman R.L. Cooper, and R. Ma *et al. Bilingualism in the Barrio.* Indiana U. Publications, Language Science Monograph #7. The Hague, Netherlands: Mouton & Co. Pp. 157-176.

Fishman, Joshua A.
1971b   "Sociolinguistic Perspective on the Study of Bilingualism." In J.A. Fishman, R.L. Cooper, and R. Ma *et al. Bilingualism in the Barrio.* Indiana U. Publications, Lg. Science Monograph #7. The Hague, Netherlands: Mouton & Co. Pp. 557-582.

Fishman, Joshua A.
1971c   *Sociolinguistics: A Brief Introduction.* Rowley, Mass.: Newbury House.

Fishman, Joshua A., Charles A. Ferguson, and Jyotirindra Das Gupta, eds.
1968   *Language Problems of Developing Nations.* New York: John Wiley and Sons, Inc.

Fishman, Joshua A. and John Lovas
1970   "Bilingual Education in Sociolinguistic Perspective." *TESOL Quarterly* 4.3:215-22.

Fishman, Joshua A., Robert L. Cooper, and Roxana Ma *et al.*
1971   *Bilingualism in the Barrio.* Indiana U. Publications, Lang. Science Monograph #7. The Hague, Netherlands: Mouton & Co.

Fishman, Joshua A. and C. Terry
1971   "The Contrastive Validity of Census Data on Bilingualism in a Puerto Rican Neighborhood." In J.A. Fishman, R.L. Cooper, and R. Ma *et al. Bilingualism in the Barrio.* Indiana U. Publications, Language Science Monograph #7. The Hague, Netherlands: Mouton & Co. Pp. 177-195.

Gaarder, A. Bruce *et al.*
1966   *Bilingualism: From the Viewpoint of the Administrator and Counselor.* Report I presented at the Third Annual Conference on Bilingualism, Southwest Council of Foreign Language Teacher, El Paso, Texas.

Gaarder, A. Bruce
1967   "Organization of the Bilingual School." *Journal of Social Issues* 23.2:110-120.

Gaarder, A. Bruce
   1969   "Statement before the Special Subcommittee on Bilingual Education of the Committee on Labor and Public Welfare, U.S. Senate, Thursday, May 18, 1967." *Florida Foreign Language Reporter* 7.1:33-34, 171.

Gaarder, A. Bruce
   1970   "The First Seventy-Six Bilingual Education Projects." In J.E. Alatis, ed. *Monograph Series on Language and Linguistics.* No. 23, 21st Annual Roundtable. Washington, D.C.: Georgetown University Press. Pp. 163-178.

Gaarder, A. Bruce
   1971   "Language Maintenance or Language Shift: The Prospect for Spanish in the United States." Paper presented at the Child Language Conference, Chicago, November 22-24.

Galarza, Ernesto, Herman Gallegos, and Julian Samora
   1969   *Mexican Americans in the Southwest.* Santa Barbara, California: McNally & Loftin, published in cooperation with B'nai B'rith.

Galvan, Robert R.
   1967   "Bilingualism as it relates to intelligence test scores & school achievement among culturally deprived Spanish-American children." Unpublished Doctoral Dissertation, East Texas State University, Commerce, Texas.

García, Ernest
   1971   "Chicano Spanish Dialects and Education." *Aztlan* 2.1:67-77.

Gardner, Robert C. and W.E. Lambert
   1959   "Motivational Variables in Second-Language Acquisition." *Canadian Journal of Psychology* 13:266-272.

Gardner, Robert C.
   1960   "Motivational variables in second-language acquisition." Unpublished Doctoral Dissertation, McGill University, Montreal, Canada.

Gardner, Robert C. and E.M. Santos
   1970   "Motivational Variables in Second-Language Acquisition: A Philippine Investigation." Dept. of Psych. Research Bulletin #149, University of Western Ontario, London, Canada.

Gardner, Robert C. and Wallace E. Lambert
   1972   *Attitudes and Motivation in Second-Language Learning.* Rowley, Massachusetts: Newbury House.

Garretson, O.K.
   1928   "Study of the causes of retardation among Mexican children." *Journal of Educational Psychology* 19:31-40.

George, H.V.
   1972   *Common Errors in Language Learning: Insights from English.* Rowley, Massachusetts: Newbury House.

Gill, L.J. and B. Silka
   1962   "Some Non-Intellectual Correlates of Academic Achievement among Mexican-American Secondary School Students." *Journal of Education Psychology* 53:144-149.

Glazer, Nathan and Daniel P. Moynihan
   1963   *Beyond the Melting Pot.* Cambridge, Mass: M.I.T. Press.

Godoy, Charles E.
1970   *Variables Differentiating Mexican-American College and High School Graduates.* Mexican-American Research Project, California State Department of Education, Sacramento, California.

González, Gustavo
1968   "A Linguistic Profile of the Spanish Speaking First-Grader in Corpus Christi." Unpublished Master's Thesis. University of Texas at Austin.

González, Gustavo
1970   "The Acquisition of Spanish Grammar by Native Spanish Speakers." Unpublished Doctoral Dissertation, University of Texas at Austin.

Goodman, Frank M. and Carolyn Stern
1971   *Bilingual Program Evaluation Report, ESEA Title VII, 1970-71.* Compton City Schools, 604 S. Tamarind St., Compton, California. ED 054 672.

Gordon, Milton M.
1964   *Assimilation in American Life: The Role of Race, Religion, and National Origin.* New York: Oxford U. Press.

Gordon C. Wayne, Audrey J. Schwartz, *et al.*
1968   *Educational Achievement and Aspirations of Mexican-American Youth in a Metropolitan Context.* Occasional Report No. 36. Los Angeles, California: Center for the Study of Evaluation at UCLA.

Grebler, Leo, J.W. Moore, R.C. Guzman *et al.*
1970   *The Mexican-American People: The Nation's Second Largest Minority.* New York: The Free Press, Division of Macmillan Co.

Greenfield, Lawrence and J. A. Fishman
1971   "Situational Measures of Normative Language Views of Person, Place and Topic Among Puerto Rican Bilinguals." In J.A. Fishman, R. L. Cooper, R. Ma *et al. Bilingualism in the Barrio.* Indiana U. Publications, Lg. Science Monograph #7. The Hague, Netherlands: Mouton & Co. Pp. 233-251.

Gudschinsky, Sarah C.
1971   *Literacy in the Mother Tongue and Second Language Learning.* Conference on Child Language, Chicago, Nov. 22-24. Conference Preprints, pp. 341-355. Laval, Québec: Les Presses de l'Université.

Guerra, Manuel H.
1969   *The Retention of Mexican American Students in Higher Education with Special Reference to Bicultural and Bilingual Problems.* Published for the National Training Program for Teachers, Counselors and Administrators Involved in the Recruitment, Retention and Financial Assistance of Mexican Americans in Higher Education. California State College, Long Beach, California 90801.

Guerra, Manuel H. and Y. Arturo Cabrera
1966   *An Evaluation and Critique of the Mexican American Studies Project; A Ford Foundation Grant Extended to the University of California at Los Angeles.* Prepared for the Education Council of the Mexican American Political Association, Los Angeles, California.

Guidance Testing Associates
1967a   *Manual—Tests of General Ability and Tests of Reading Inter-American Series Forms CE, DE, CEs, DEs.* 6516 Shirley Avenue, Austin, Texas 78752.

Guidance Testing Associates
    1967b   *Technical Report. Tests of General Ability and Tests of Reading. Inter-*
               American Series Forms CE, DE, CEs, DEs. 6516 Shirley Avenue, Austin,
               Texas 78752.

Gumperz, John J.
    1964   "Linguistic and Social Interaction in two communities." In J.J. Gumperz
               and D. Hymes, eds. *The Ethnography of Communication.* Washington, D.C.:
               American Anthropological Association. Pp. 137-153.

Gumperz, John J.
    1967   "On the Linguistic Markers of Bilingual Communication." *Journal of Social
               Issues* 23.2:48-57.

Gumperz, John J.
    1969   "How Can We Describe and Measure the Behavior of Bilingual Groups?" In
               L.G. Kelly, ed. *Description and Measurement of Bilingualism.* Toronto, Can-
               ada: U. of Toronto Press. Pp. 242-249.

Gumperz, John J. and Eduardo Hernández
    1970   "Cognitive Aspects of Bilingual Communication." In W.H. Whiteley, ed.
               Language Use and Social Change. London: Oxford University Press, Pp.
               111-125.

Hall, R.M.R. and B. L. Hall
    1969   "The Double Negative: A Non-Problem." *Florida Foreign Language Re-
               porter* 7.2:113-115.

Harris, David P.
    1969   *Testing English as a Second Language.* New York: McGraw-Hill.

Hartwig, Keith E.
    1971   *Early Childhood Bilingual Education, Final Evaluation 1970-1971.* Sacra-
               mento City Unified School District ESEA Title VII Project, P.O. Box 2271,
               Sacramento, California 95810.

Hatch, Evelyn
    1970   "More Problems for the Elementary School ESL Teacher." *Workpapers:
               Teaching English as a Second Language.* University of California at Los
               Angeles. Pp. 87-92.

Hatch, Evelyn
    1972   "Some Studies in Language Learning." *Workpapers: Teaching English as a
               Second Language.* University of California at Los Angeles. Pp. 29-36.

Haugen, Einar I.
    1953   *The Norwegian Language in America: A Study in Bilingual Behavior.* 2 Vol-
               umes. Philadelphia: U. of Penn. Press.

Haugen, Einar I.
    1956   *Bilingualism in the Americas: A Bibliography and Research Guide.* Univer-
               sity of Alabama, The American Dialect Society.

Heller, Celia
    1966   *Mexican-American Youth, Forgotten Youth at the Crossroads.* New York:
               Random House.

Henríquez Ureña, Pedro
    1935   *El español en Méjico, los Estados Unidos y la América Central.* Buenos Aires,
               Argentina: Biblioteca de Dialectología Hispanoamericana, IV. Pp. xvii-xx.

Hernández, Deluvina
    1970   *Mexican American Challenge to a Sacred Cow.* Mexican American Cultural Center, Monograph No. 1. University of California at Los Angeles.

Hernández-Ch., Eduardo, Andrew D. Cohen, and Anthony F. Beltramo, eds.
    1975   *El Lenguaje de los Chicanos: regional and social characteristics of language used by Mexican Americans.* Washington, D.C.: Center for Applied Linguistics.

Hoffman, Moses N.H.
    1934   *The Measurement of Bilingual Background.* New York: Teachers College, Columbia University.

Horn, Thomas D.
    1966a   *A Study of the Effects of Intensive Oral-Aural English Language Instruction, Oral-Aural Spanish Language Instruction, and Non-Oral-Aural Instruction on Reading Readiness in Grade One.* Cooperative Research Project No. 2548. Austin, Texas: The University of Texas. ED 010 048.

Horn, Thomas
    1966b   "Three Methods of Developing Reading Readiness in Spanish-speaking Children in First Grade." *Reading Teacher* 20:38-42.

Houston, Susan
    1969   "A Sociolinguistic Consideration of the Black English of Children in Northern Florida." *Language* 45:599-607.

Hymes, Dell
    1967   "Models of the Interaction of Language and Social Setting." *Journal of Social Issues* 23.2:8-28.

Inclán, Rosa G.
    1971   "An Updated Report on Bilingual Schooling in Dade County, Including Results of a Recent Evaluation." Conference on Child Language. Chicago, Nov. 22-24.

Jackson, Steve, and Ron Klinger
    1971   *Test Manual: Cross-Cultural Attitude Inventory.* Austin, Texas: Dissemination Center for Bilingual Bicultural Education (6504 Tracor Lane, Austin 78721).

Jakobovits, Leon A.
    1970   *Foreign Language Learning.* Rowley, Massachusetts: Newbury House.

Jensen, Arthur R.
    1961   "Learning Abilities in Mexican-American and Anglo-American Children." *California Journal of Educational Research* 12.4:147-159.

Jespersen, Otto
    1966   *Essentials of English Grammar,* University, Alabama: University of Alabama Press.

Jiménez, Randall C.
    1971   "Attributes of the Chicano as Presented in Educational Literature." In *A Preliminary Annotated Bibliography with Selected Articles about the Chicano.* Prepared by Mexican American Graduate Studies Department, San José State College, San José, California. Pp. 14-26.

John, Vera P., Vivian M. Horner, and Tomi D. Berney
    1970   "Story Retelling: A Study of Sequential Speech in Young Children." In H. Levin and J.P. Williams, eds. *Basic Studies in Reading.* New York: Basic Books. Pp. 246-262.

John, Vera P. and Vivian M. Horner
    1971   *Early childhood Bilingual Education*. New York: Modern Language Association Materials Center, 62 Fifth Avenue.

Johnson, G. B.
    1953   "Bilingualism as measured by a reaction-time technique and the relationship between a language and a non-language intelligence quotient." *Journal of Genetic Psychology* 82:3-9.

Jones, W.R.
    1960   "A critical study of bilingualism and nonverbal intelligence." *British Journal of Educational Psychology* 30:71-76.

Jones, R.M.
    1969   "How and When Do Persons Become Bilingual?" In L.G. Kelly, ed. *Description and Measurement of Bilingualism*. Toronto, Canada: University of Toronto Press. Pp. 12-25.

Juárez, Rumaldo Z.
    1968   *Educational Status Orientations of Mexican American and Anglo American Youth in Selected Low-Income Counties of Texas*. Washington, D.C.: U.S. Department of Agriculture.

Kahl, J.A. and Davis J.A.
    1955   "A Comparison of indexes of socio-economic status." *American Sociological Review* 20:317-325.

Kelly, Louis G., ed.
    1969   *Description and Measurement of Bilingualism*. Toronto, Canada: University of Toronto Press.

Keston, M.J. and C.A. Jiménez
    1954   "Study of the Performance on English and Spanish Editions of the Stanford-Binet Intelligence Test by American-Mexican Children." *Journal of Genetic Psychology* 85:263-9.

Kjolseth, Rolf
    1972   "Bilingual Education Programs in the United States: For Assimilation or Pluralism?" In Bernard Spolsky, ed. *The Language Education of Minority Children: Selected Readings*. Rowley, Mass.: Newbury House. Pp. 94-121.

Kloss, Heinz
    1971   "Laws and Legal Documents Relating to Problems of Bilingual Education in the United States." ERIC ED 044 703.

Krear, Serafina E.
    1971a   "Development of Pre-Reading Skills in a Second Language or Dialect." Paper presented at the Conference on Child Language, Chicago, Nov. 22-24. Preprints Pp. 240-263. Laval, Québec: Les Presses de l'Université Laval.

Krear, Serafina E.
    1971b   "The Role of the Mother Tongue at Home and at School in the Development of Bilingualism." In N.N. Wagner and W.J. Haug, eds. *Chicanos: Social and Psychological Perspectives*. St. Louis: C.V. Mosby, Pp. 229-231.

Labov, William A.
    1966   *The Social Stratification of English in New York City*. Washington, D.C.: The Center for Applied Linguistics.

Labov, William
    1969   "The Logic of Non-Standard English." *Florida Foreign Language Reporter* 7.1:60-74, 169.

Labov, William
    1970   "The Educational Campaign Against Negro Children." Paper presented at the TESOL Convention, San Francisco, California, March 18-21.

Lado, Robert
    1961   *Language Testing.* London: Longmans, Green & Co., Ltd.

Lambert, Wallace E. and E. Anisfeld
    1969   "A Note on the Relationship of Bilingualism and Intelligence." *Canadian Journal of Behavioral Science* 1:123-128.

Lambert, W.E. and J. Macnamara
    1969   "Some cognitive consequences of following a first-grade curriculum in a second language." *Journal of Educational Psychology* 60.2:86-89.

Lambert, W.E., G.R. Tucker, A. d'Anglejan and S. Segalowitz
    1970   "Cognitive and Attitudinal Consequences of Following the Curricula of the First Three Grades in a Foreign Language." Mimeo, McGill U.

Lambert, W.E., M. Just, and N. Segalowitz
    1970   "Some Cognitive Consequences of Following the Curricula of the Early School Grades in a Foreign Language." In J.E. Alatis, ed. *Report of the Twenty-First Annual Round Table Meeting on Linguistics and Language Studies.* Washington, D.C.: Georgetown U. Press. Pp. 229-279.

Lambert, W.E. and G.R. Tucker
    1971   "The Home-School Language Switch Program Grades K Through Five." A report presented at the Conference on Child Language, Chicago, Nov. 22-24. Preprints pp. 139-147. Laval, Québec: Les Presses de l'Université Laval.

Lambert, W.E. and G.R. Tucker
    1972   *Bilingual Education of Children: The St. Lambert Experiment.* Rowley, Massachusetts, Newbury House.

Lance, Donald M.
    1969   "Dialectal and Nonstandard Forms in Texas Spanish." In D.M. Lance *et al. A Brief Study of Spanish-English Bilingualism Final Report. Research Project ORR-Liberal Arts-15504.* Texas A&M University, College Station, Texas. ED 032 529. Pp. 45-67

Lance, Donald M. *et al.*
    1969   *A Brief Study of Spanish-English Bilingualism: Final Report, Research Project ORR-Liberal Arts-15504.* Texas A & M University, College Station, Texas. ED 032 529.

Lastra, Yolanda
    1975   "El Habla y la Educación de los Niños de Origen Mexicano en Los Angeles." In E. Hernández-Ch., A.D. Cohen, and A.F. Beltramo, eds. *El Lenguaje de los Chicanos: regional and social characteristics of language used by Mexican Americans.* Arlington, Va.: Center for Applied Linguistics.

Leibowitz, Arnold
    1969   "English Literacy: Legal Sanction for Discrimination." *Notre Dame Lawyer* 45:7-67.

Leibowitz, Arnold H.
    1971   *Educational Policy and Political Acceptance: The Imposition of English as the Language of Instruction in American Schools.* Washington, D.C.: CAL/ERIC. ED 047 321.

Leopold, W.F.
1949   *Speech Development of a Bilingual Child: A Linguist's Record.* 4 Vols.,
Evanston, Ill.: Northwestern U. Press.

Le Page, R.B.
1964   *The National Language Question: Linguistic Problems of Newly Independent
States.* London: Oxford U. Press.

Lewis, Hilda P. and Edward R. Lewis
1965   "Written language performance of sixth-grade children of low SES from bilingual and from monolingual backgrounds." *Journal of Experimental Education*
33.3:237-242.

Lewis, Oscar
1966   "The Culture of Poverty." *Scientific American* 215.4:19-25.

Light, Richard L.
1971   "The Schools and the Minority Child's Language." *Foreign Language Annals*
5.1:90-94. ED 047 320.

Lin, San-Su C.
1965   *Pattern Practice in the Teaching of Standard English to Students with a Non-
Standard Dialect.* New York: Bureau of Publications, Teachers College, Columbia University.

The Linguistic Reporter
1971   "TESOL Conference in New Orleans." Spring, 1971, pp. 10-11.

Linn, George B.
1967   "Linguistic functions of bilingual Mexican-American children." *Journal of
Genetic Psychology* 3.2:183-193.

Lipset, Seymour M. and Hans L. Zetterberg
1956   "A Theory of Social Mobility." In *Transactions of the Third World Congress
of Sociology.* Vol. II, Pp. 155-177.

Long, K.K. and A.M. Padilla
1970   "Evidence for Bilingual Antecedents of Academic Success in a Group of
Spanish-American College Students." Department of Psychology, West
Washington State College. Mimeo.

López, Al
1970   *"North from Mexico* by Carey McWilliams." *Chicanismo,* February 13, 1970,
Stanford University. P. 5.

Lynn, Klonda
1945   "Bilingualism in the Southwest." *Quarterly Journal of Spanish* 31:175-180.

Ma, Roxana and Eleanor Herasimchuk
1971   "The Puerto Rican Speech Community." In J. Fishman, R.L. Cooper, R.
Ma *et al. Bilingualism in the Barrio.* Indiana U. Publications, Lg. Science
Monograph #7. The Hague, Netherlands: Mouton & Co. Pp. 357-364.

Mackey, William F.
1962   "The Description of Bilingualism." *Canadian Journal of Linguistics* 7:51-85.

Mackey, William F.
1967   *Language Teaching Analysis.* Bloomington: Indiana U. Press.

Mackey, William F.
1970   "A Typology of Bilingual Education." *Foreign Language Annals* 3.4:569-608.

Mackey, William F.
   1971   "Free Language Alternation in Early Childhood Education." Conference on
           Child Language, Chicago, Nov. 22-24. Laval, Quebec: Les Presses de l'Uni-
           versité Laval. Preprints Pp. 396-432.

Mackey, William F.
   1972   *Bilingual Education in a Binational School.* Rowley, Massachusetts: Newbury
           House.

Macnamara, John
   1966   *Bilingualism and primary education.* Edinburgh: Edinburgh U. Press.

Macnamara, John
   1967a   "The Bilingual's Linguistic Performance—A Psychological Overview." *Jour-
           nal of Social Issues* 23.2:58-77.

Macnamara, John
   1967b   "The Effects of Instruction in a Weaker Language." *Journal of Social Issues*
           23.2:120-134.

Macnamara, John
   1969   "How can one measure the extent of a person's bilingual proficiency?" In
           L. Kelly, ed. *The Description and Measurement of Bilingualism.* Toronto,
           Canada: U. of Toronto Press. Pp. 80-97.

Macnamara, John and T.P. Kellaghan
   1967   "Reading in a Second Language." In M.D. Jenkinson, ed. *Improving Read-
           ing Throughout the World.* Newark, Delaware: International Reading Asso-
           ciation, Pp. 231-240.

Madsen, William
   1964   *The Mexican-Americans of South Texas.* New York: Holt, Rinehart and
           Winston.

Mahoney, Mary K.
   1967   "Spanish and English Language Usage by Rural and Urban Spanish-American
           Families in Two South Texas Counties." Unpublished M.S. Thesis, Texas A
           & M Univ.

Malherbe, E.G.
   1946   *The Bilingual School.* London: Longmans, Green & Co., Ltd.

Malherbe, E.G.
   1969   "Commentary to R.M. Jones, 'How and When Do Persons Become Bilin-
           gual?' " In L.G. Kelly, ed. *Description and Measurement of Bilingualism.*
           Toronto, Canada: U. of Toronto Press. Pp. 41-51.

Mallory, Gloria E.
   1971   "Sociolinguistic Considerations for Bilingual Education in an Albuquerque
           Community Undergoing Language Shift." Unpublished Doctoral Disserta-
           tion, The University of New Mexico.

Manuel, Herschel T.
   1930   *The education of Mexican and Spanish-speaking children in Texas.* Austin,
           Texas: University of Texas.

Manuel, Herschel T.
   1963   *The preparation and evaluation of interlanguage testing materials.* Report of
           Cooperative Research Project No. 681. Austin, Texas: U. of Texas.

Manuel, Herschel T.
   1965   *Spanish-speaking Children of the Southwest: Their Education and the Public
           Welfare.* Austin: University of Texas.

Manuel, Herschel T.
    1968   "Recruiting and Training Teachers for Spanish-Speaking Children in the
             Southwest." *School and Society* 96:211-214.

Martínez, Oscar
    1970   *"Mexican-Americans of South Texas* by William Madsen." *Chicanismo,*
             February 13, 1970, Stanford University. P. 5.

Mayeske, George W.
    1969   *Educational Achievement Among Mexican-Americans: A Special Report
             from the Educational Opportunities Survey.* Technical Note 22, Department
             of H.E.W., National Center Educational Statistics, Washington, D.C.

McKim, Lester W.
    1970   *FLES: Types of Programs.* No. 16. ERIC Focus Reports on the Teaching of
             Foreign Languages. New York: Mod. Lang. Assoc. Materials Center, 62 Fifth
             Ave.

McWilliams, Carey
    1949   *North from Mexico: The Spanish-Speaking People of the United States.*
             New York: J.P. Lippincett Co.

Menyuk, Paula
    1969   *Sentences Children Use.* Cambridge, Massachusetts: M.I.T. Press.

Michigan Oral Language Series
    1970   *Michigan Oral Language Productive Test: Structured Response.* ACTFL Edi-
             tion, Modern Language Association, 62 Fifth Avenue, N.Y., N.Y. 10011.

Modiano, Nancy
    1966   "Reading Comprehension in the National Language: A Comparative Study
             of Bilingual and All Spanish." Unpublished Dissertation, New York Univer-
             sity, New York.

Modiano, Nancy
    1968   "National or Mother Language in Beginning Reading?" *Research in the Teach-
             ing of English* 2:32-43.

Moore, Joan W.
    1967   "Political and Ethical Problems in a Large-Scale Study of a Minority Popu-
             lation." In G. Sjoberg, ed. *Ethics, Politics and Social Research.* Cambridge,
             Massachusetts: Schenckman Publishing Co. Pp. 225-244.

Moreno, Steve
    1970   "Problems Related to Present Testing Instruments." *El Grito* 3:25-29.

Moreno, Steve
    1972   *Oral Spanish and English Proficiency Placement Test.* Moreno Educational
             Company, 3226 Galloway Drive, San Diego, California 92122.

Murillo, Nathan
    1971   "The Mexican American Family." In N.N. Wagner and M.J. Haug, eds.
             Chicanos: Social and Psychological Perspectives. St. Louis: C.V. Mosby.
             Pp. 97-108.

Murphy, Helen A. and Donald D. Durrell
    1965   *Murphy-Durrell Reading Readiness Analysis: Manual of Directions.* New York:
             Harcourt, Brace & World, Inc.

Mycue, Elena Ines de Los Santos
    1968   "Testing in Spanish and the Subsequent Measurement of English Fluency."
             Unpublished M.A. Thesis. College of Education. Texas Woman's University.
             ED 026 193.

Nall, Frank C., II
1962   "Role Expectations: A Cross-Cultural Study." *Rural Sociology* 27:28-41.

Nava, Julian
1970   *Mexican Americans: A Brief Look at Their History.* Anti-Defamation League of B'nai B'rith, 315 Lexington Avenue, New York, N.Y. 10016.

NEA
1966   *The Invisible Minority: Report of the NEA-Tucson Survey on the Teaching of Spanish to the Spanish-Speaking.* National Education Association of the United States, Department of Rural Education, Washington, D.C.

New York Board of Education
1968   *Nonstandard Dialect.* Champaign, Illinois: National Council of Teachers of English.

Nie, Norman H. and C. Hadlai Hull *et al.*
1972   *Statistical Package for the Social Sciences: Update Manual.* National Opinion Research Center, University of Chicago.

Oliver, Joseph D.
1970   *Social Determinants in Communication Events in a Small Bilingual Community in New Mexico.* Washington, D.C.: Center for Applied Linguistics. ED 044 675.

Orata, P. T.
1953   "The Iloilo experiment in education through the vernacular." In *The Use of Vernacular Languages in Education.* Monographs on Fundamental Education VIII. Paris: UNESCO. Pp. 123-131.

Ornstein, Jacob
1971   *Sociolinguistics and the Study of Spanish and English Language Varieties and Their Use in the U.S. Southwest, With a Proposed Plan of Research.* Available from SWCEL, 117 Richmond Drive, N.W., Albuquerque, New Mexico 87106.

Ortego, Phillip D.
1970   "Montezuma's Children." *The Center Magazine.* Center for the Study of Democratic Institutions, Box 4068, Santa Barbara, California 3.6:23-31.

Ott, Elizabeth H.
1967   "A Study of Levels of Fluency and Proficiency in Oral English of Spanish-Speaking School Beginners." Unpublished Doctoral Dissertation, College of Education, University of Texas at Austin.

Ott, Elizabeth H.
n.d.   *Basic Education for Spanish-Speaking Disadvantaged Pupils.* Austin, Texas: Southwest Educational Development Laboratory. ED 020 497.

Owens, Thomas R.
1972   "Analysis of a Spanish Bilingual Preschool Program." Paper presented at the American Educational Research Association Annual Meeting. Chicago, Illinois, April 4-8.

Palomares, Uvaldo H. and Emery J. Cummins
1968   *Assessment of Rural Mexican-American Pupils Preschool and Grades One Through Twelve.* Wasco, California. Mexican-American Research Project, California State Department of Education.

Parsons, Theodore W., Jr.
1965   "Ethnic Cleavage in a California School." Unpublished Doctoral Dissertation, Stanford University.

Pasamanick, Benjamin
    1951   "The Intelligence of American Children of Mexican Parentage: A Discussion
            of Uncontrolled Variables." *Journal of Abnormal and Social Psychology*
            46:598-602.

Paschal, F.C. and L.R. Sullivan
    1925   "Racial Influences in the Mental and Physical Development of Mexican Chil-
            dren." *Comparative Psychology Monographs* 3.14.

Past, Ray *et al.*
    1966   *Recruitment and Preparation of Bilingual Teachers*. Report III, 3rd Annual
            Conference on Bilingualism, Southwest Council of Foreign Language Teach-
            ers, El Paso, Texas, November, 1966.

Patella, Victoria M. and W.P. Kuvlesky
    1970   "Language Patterns of Mexican Americans: Are the Ambitious Un-Mexican?"
            Paper presented at the Rural Sociological Society meeting. Washington, D.C.
            August 26-30.

Peal, Elizabeth and W.E. Lambert
    1962   "The Relation of Bilingualism to Intelligence." *Psychological Monographs*
            76.27.

Peñalosa, Fernando
    1966   "A Socioeconomic Class Typology of Mexican Americans." *Sociological In-
            quiry* 36:19-30.

Peñalosa, Fernando
    1967   "The Changing Mexican American in Southern California." *Sociology and
            Social Research* 51.4:405-417.

Peñalosa, Fernando
    1970   "Toward an Operational Definition of the Mexican American." *Aztlan*
            1.1-1-12.

Peñalosa, Fernando and E.C. McDonagh
    1966   "Social Mobility in a Mexican-American Community." *Social Forces* 44:
            498-505.

Perren, George
    1967   "Testing Ability in English as a Second Language." *English Language Teach-
            ing* 12.1:22-29.

Petersen, Robert O.H., H.C. Chuck, and A.P. Coladarci *et al.*
    1969   *Teaching Standard English as a Second Dialect to Primary School Children
            in Hilo, Hawaii*. Final Report to the Office of Education, U.S. Department
            of H.E.W. Hawaii District, State of Hawaii. Department of Education, P.O.
            Box 1922, Hilo, Hawaii 96720.

Philippine Normal College
    n.d.   "The Philippine Normal College Bilingual Experiment: Grade One Class of
            1969-70." Philippine Normal College, Manila, The Philippines.

Phillips, Robert N., Jr.
    1967   "Los Angeles Spanish: A Descriptive Analysis." Unpublished Doctoral Dis-
            sertation, University of Wisconsin.

Pryor, Gus C.
    1967   *Evaluation of the Bilingual Project of Harlandale Independent School Dis-
            trict, San Antonio, Texas, in the First Grades of Four Elementary Schools
            During 1966-67 School Year*. San Antonio, Texas, Harlandale Independent
            School District, ED 023 508.

Public Advocates, Inc. & Mexican-American Legal Defense and Educational Fund
  1972   *Official U.S. Census Bureau Preliminary Spanish Language/Spanish Surname Population Statistics: California's and the Southwest's Largest Minority – One in Six a Chicano.* Public Advocates, Inc. 433 Turk Street, San Francisco, California 94102.

Ramírez, Arnulfo G.
  1971   "Language Usage in a Bilingual School Setting." Unpublished manuscript Stanford University, Stanford, Calif.

Ramírez, Manuel, III, C. Taylor, and B. Peterson
  1971   "Mexican-American Cultural Membership and Adjustment to School." In N.N. Wagner and M.J. Haug, eds. *Chicanos: Social and Psychological Perspectives.* St. Louis: C.V. Mosby. Pp. 221-228.

Region One Curriculum Kits
  1970   Levels I and II. Melton Book Company, Inc., 111 Leslie Street, Dallas, Texas.

Revil, Jovencio T., H.P. Hachero, S.G. Alondogan, E.B. Ortega, and D.B. Demaluan
  1968   *A Follow-Up Study of the Rizal Experiment Relative to Achievement in English, Philipino, and Content Subjects at the End of Second Year High School.* Philippine Normal College, Manila, Philippines.

Richards, Jack
  1971   "A Non-Contrastive Approach to Error Analysis." *English Language Teaching* 25.3:204-219.

Riley, John E.
  1968   *The Influence of Bilingualism on Tested Verbal Ability in Spanish.* Unpublished paper, Texas Woman's University. ED 026 935.

Rivera, Feliciano
  1970   *A Mexican American Source Book with Study Guideline.* Educational Consulting Associates, Menlo Park, California.

Rivera, Jaime S.
  1970   Chicanos: Culture, Community, Role–Problems of Evidence, and a Proposition of Norms Toward Establishing Evidence." *Aztlan* 1.1:37-51.

Roberts, Karlene H.
  1969   *Understanding Research: Some Thoughts on Evaluating Completed Educational Projects.* An Occasional Paper from ERIC at Stanford. Stanford, California. Standford, California: Institute for Communication Research.

Rodríquez, Armando
  1969   "The Mexican-American – Disadvantaged? Ya Basta!" *Florida Foreign Language Reporter* 71:35-36, 160.

Romano, Octavio I.
  1968   "The Anthropology and Sociology of the Mexican-Americans: The Distortion of Mexican-American History." *El Grito* 2.1:13-26.

Rosenthal, Irene
  1966   "Distribution of the Sample Version of the Measure of Association, Gamma." *Journal of the American Statistical Association* 61:440-453.

Rowan, B. *et al.*
  1950   "Teaching of Bilingual Children." *Education* 70:423-426.

Rubin, Joan
  1968   *National Bilingualism in Paraguay.* Mouton: The Hague.

Sánchez, George I.
  1932a   "Group Differences and Spanish-speaking Children." *Journal of Applied Psychology* 16:549-58.

Sánchez, George I.
  1932b   "Scores of Spanish-speaking children on repeated tests." *Pedagogical Seminary and Journal of Genetic Psychology* 42:223-231.

Sánchez, George I.
  1934   "Bilingualism and Mental Measures." *Journal of Applied Psychology* 18:765-72.

Saunders, Jack O.
  1969   *The Blueprint Potentials of the Cooperative Teacher Education Preparation Utilizing the Talented Mexican American.* University Park, New Mexico: New Mexico State University. ED 025 372.

Savage, James E., Jr. and N.D. Bowers
  1972   "Testers' Influence on Children's Intellectual Performance." Paper presented at the American Educational Research Association Annual Meeting. Chicago, Illinois.

Saville, Muriel R. and Rudolph C. Troike
  1970   *A Handbook of Bilingual Education.* Washington, D.C.: Center for Applied Linguistics ERIC Clearinghouse. ED 035 877.

Schwartz, Audrey J.
  1969   *Comparative Values and Achievement of Mexican-American and Anglo Pupils.* Center for the Study of Evaluation Report No. 37. Los Angeles California: UCLA Graduate School of Education.

SCRDT 1
  n.d.   Regression Analysis. Stanford Center for Research and Development in Teaching. Stanford, California: School of Education, Stanford, University.

Scriven, Michael
  1967   "The Methodology of Evaluation." In R.W. Tyler, R.M. Gagné, and M. Scriven, eds. *Perspectives of Curriculum Evaluation.* Chicago: Rand-McNally. Pp. 39-83.

Shaftel, Fannie and George Shaftel
  1967   *Words and Action: Role-palying Photo-Problems for Young Children.* New York: Holt, Rinehart and Winston, Inc.

Simmons, Ozzie G.
  1961   "The Mutual Images and Expectations of Anglo-Americans and Mexican-Americans." *Daedalus 90:286-299.*

Slobin, Dan I.
  1971   *Psycholinguistics.* Glenview, Illinois: Scott, Foresman and Co.

Smith, Gail M.
  1969   "Some Comments on the English of Eight Bilinguals." In Donald Lance *et al. A Brief Study of Spanish-English Bilingualism: Final Report.* Texas A&M University. Pp. 16-24. ED 032 529.

Spolsky, Bernard
  1969   "Language Testing—The Problem of Validation." *Florida Foreign Language Reporter* 7.1:100-102, 163-164.

Stemmler, Anne O.
1966 "An Experimental Approach to the Teaching of Oral Language and Reading." In J.A. Emig, J.T. Fleming, H.M. Popp, eds. *Language and Learning.* New York: Harcourt, Brace, & World, Pp. 53-72.

Stemmler, Anne O.
1967 "The LCT, Language Cognition Test Research Edition—A Test for Educationally Disadvantaged School Beginners." *TESOL Quarterly* 1:35-43.

Stockwell, Robert P., J.D. Bowen, and J.W. Martin
1967 *The Grammatical Structures of English and Spanish.* Chicago: The University of Chicago Press.

Swain, Merrill, ed.
1972 *Bilingual Schooling: Some Experiences in Canada and the United States.* Symposium Series #1, The Ontario Institute for Studies in Education, Toronto, Ontario, Canada.

Taylor, Marie E.
1970a *Educational and Cultural Values of Mexican-American Parents: How They Influence the School Achievement of Their Children.* Mexican-American Educational Research Project. Sacramento, California: State Department of Education.

Taylor, Marie E.
1970b *An Overview of Research on Bilingualism.* Mexican-American Education Research Project. Sacramento, California: State Department of Education.

Taylor, Thomasine E.
1969 "A Comparative Study of the Effects of Oral-Aural Language Training on Gains in English Language for Fourth and Fifth Grade Disadvantaged Mexican-American Children." Doctoral Dissertation, University of Texas, Austin.

Thompson, Roger M.
1971 "Language Loyalty in Austin, Texas: A Study of a Bilingual Neighborhood." Unpublished Doctoral Dissertation, The University of Texas at Austin.

Timmins, Kathleen M.
1971 "An Investigation of the Relative Bilingualism of Spanish Surnamed Children in an Elementary School in Albuquerque." Unpublished Doctoral Dissertation, The University of New Mexico.

Tobier, Arthur, ed.
1969 "Bilingualism." *The Center Forum* 4.1. New York: Center for Urban Education.

Trager-Johnson, Edith C. and Frank Abraham[1]
1972 "Basic Chicano English and Spanish Syntax: Some Interactions and Implications." Departments of English and Linguistics, University of California at Santa Barbara and San José State College, San José, California. Mimeo.

Treviño, Bertha G.
1968 "An analysis of the effectiveness of a bilingual program in the teaching of math in the primary grades." Unpublished Doctoral Dissertation, U. of Texas.

Tucker, G.R., F.T. Otanes, and B.P. Sibayan
1970 "An Alternate Days Approach to Bilingual Education." In J.E. Alatis, ed. *Report of the 21st Annual Round Table Meeting on Linguistics and Language Studies.* Washington, D.C.: Georgetown U. Press. Pp. 281-299.

---

[1]Appeared as "Basic English and Spanish Syntax of Spanish-Speaking Americans. Some Interactions and Implications," in R. Nash, ed. *Readings in Spanish-English Contrastive Linguistics.* Hato Rey, Puerto Rico: Inter American University Press, 72-122, 1973.

Tucker, G. Richard, W.E. Lambert, A. d'Angelejan, and F. Silny
    1971   "Cognitive and Attitudinal Consequences of Following the Curriculum of the First Four Grades in a Second Language." Mimeo, McGill University.

Tucker, G. Richard and Alison d'Anglejan
    1971   "Some Thoughts Concerning Bilingual Education Programs." *Modern Language Journal* 55.8:491-493.

Tucker, G.R., W.E. Lambert, and Alison d'Anglejan
    1972   "Are French Immersion Programs Suitable for Working Class Children?" Mimeo, McGill University. (Appeared in *Language Sciences,* 1973, 25:19-26).

Ulibarrí, Horacio
    1968   *Educational Needs of the Mexican-American.* University Park: New Mexico State University. ED 016 538.

Ulibarrí, Horacio
    1970   *Bilingual Education: A Handbook for Educators.* Dallas, Texas: Southern Methodist University Press. ED 038 078.

UNESCO
    1953   *The use of vernacular languages in education. Monographs on fundamental education VIII.* Paris. Pp. 17-44.

Upshur, John A.
    1969   "Productive Communication Testing: Progress Report." Paper presented at the Second International Congress of Applied Linguistics, Cambridge, U.K., Sept. 8-12.

U.S. Commission on Civil Rights
    1968   *The Mexican American.* Prepared by Helen Rowan, Washington, D.C.

U.S. Office of Education
    1971   *Programs Under Bilingual Education Act (Title VII, ESEA). Manual for Project Applicants and Grantees.* Bureau of Elementary and Secondary Education, Health, Education and Welfare. OMB-51-R0838.

Valdez, R. F.
    1969   "The Fallacy of the Spanish Surname Survey." *California Teachers Association Journal* 65.3:29-32.

Valencia, Atilano A.
    1969   "Bilingual/Bicultural Education: A Perspective Model in Multicultural America." Southwestern Cooperative Educational Laboratory, Inc. OE Contract No. OEC-4-062827-3078.

Valentine, Charles A.
    1968   *Culture and Poverty: Critique and Counter Proposals.* Chicago: University of Chicago Press.

Wagner, Nathaniel N. and Marsha J. Haug
    1971a   *Chicanos: Social and Psychological Perspectives.* St. Louis: C.V. Mosby Co.

Wagner, Nathaniel N. and Marsha J. Haug
    1971b   Introduction to "Part 2, Interethnic Perceptions." In *Chicanos: Social and Psychological Perspectives.* St. Louis: C.V. Mosby. Pp. 53-54.

Wardrop, J.L.
    1971   "Determining 'most probable' causes: A call for re-examining evaluation methodology." From symposium entitled, "Critique of the report of the Phi Delta Kappa Study Committee on Evaluation." ED 048 337.

Warner, W. Lloyd and Leo Srole
   1945   *The Social Systems of American Ethnic Groups.* Yankee City Series III,
          New Haven, Yale University Press.

Warner, W.L., M. Meeker, and K. Eells
   1949   *Social Class in American: A Manual for Procedure for the Measurement of
          Social Status.* Chicago: Social Science Research Associates.

Weinreich, Uriel
   1951   "Research Problems in Bilingualism with Special Reference to Switzerland."
          Unpublished Doctoral Dissertation, Department of Linguistics, Columbia
          University.

Weinreich, Uriel
   1953   *Languages in Contact: Findings and Problems.* New York: Linguistic Circle
          of New York. 6th Printing, The Hague, Mouton & Co. 1968.

Whitmore, Katherine R.
   1955   *The New Handbook for Intermediate Spanish.* New York: W.W. Norton &
          Co.

Williams, Jane C.
   1968   *Improving Educational Opportunities for Mexican-American Handicapped
          Children.* Office of Education, U.S. Department of H.E.W., Washington,
          D.C. ED 018 326.

Wolfram, Walt
   1971   "Social Dialects From a Linguistic Perspective." In R. Shuy, ed. *Sociolin-
          guistics: A Cross disciplinary Perspective.* Washington, D.C.: Center for
          Applied Linguistics. Pp. 86-135.

Wonder, John P.
   1965   "The Bilingual Mexican-American as a Potential Teacher of Spanish."
          Hispania 48.1:97-99.

Worrall, Anita D.
   1970   "Bilingualism and Cognitive Development." Unpublished Doctoral Disser-
          tation, Cornell University.

Worrall, Anita D.
   1971   "Bilingualism and Cognitive Development." Mimeo, Cornell U. (Appeared
          in *Child Development* December, 1972.)

Wright, Carrie E. and H.T. Manuel
   1929   "The language difficulty of Mexican children." *Journal of Genetic Psychol-
          ogy* 36:458-466.

Wright, David E., Jr.
   1969   *Occupational Orientations of Mexican-American Youth in Selected Texas
          Counties.* Texas A&M University. ED 023 512.

Zintz, Miles
   1969   "What Teachers Should Know About Bilingual Education." In H. Ulibarrí
          and J.G. Cooper, *Interpretive Study of Bilingual Education.* Albuquerque,
          New Mexico: College of Education, University of New Mexico. ED 028
          427.

INDEX

AUTHOR INDEX

ABRAHAM, F., 167, 177, 193, 201, 214-215
ALLEN, V. F., 194
ALTUS, G. T., 43, 46
ANDERSON, J. G., 61, 63-64, 288
ANDERSON, T. R., 92
ANDERSSON, T., 1, 19-21, 29, 31-32, 35, 36, 65
ARNOLD, R. D., 34, 36
ARNOVE, R. F., 290

BADILLO, H., 31
BARATZ, J. C., 178
BARTLETT, D. W., 7
BARKER, G. C., 2
BARTLEY, D. E., 178, 186, 188, 193, 204
BATY, R. M., 65
BAUER, E., 65
BELTRAMO, A. F., 208
BERKO, J., 188, 194
BERNAL, J. J., 33, 65, 227
BERNEY, T. D., 271
BLAIR, P. M., 62
BLOOM, B. S., 290
BORDIE. J. G., 8, 46
BOWEN, J. D., 171, 176, 182, 184, 186, 188, 196-197
BOWERS, N. D., 47, 89
BOYER, M., 1, 19-21, 29, 31, 65
BRIÈRE, E. J., 270
BURMA, J., 58
BURNS, D. H., 26
BURT, M. K., 167, 193, 205
BUSTAMANTE, C. J., 70
BUSTAMANTE, P. L., 70

CABRERA, Y. A., 52
CAMPBELL, D. T., 76, 78, 92
CANNON, G., 31-33, 227
CARLSON, H. B., 42-43
CARO, F. G., 76, 78, 82
CARPENTER, S., 219, 279
CARROW, M. A., 45, 271-272
CARTER, T. P., 33, 51, 59-60, 64, 227
CASAVANTES, E. J., 54-55
CERVENKA, E. J., 271-272
CHANDLER, J. T., 45-46
CHÁVEZ, C., 105
CHIANG, E., 93
CHOMSKY, N., 89
CHRISTIAN, C. C., 11
CHUCK, H. C., 127, 271
CICOUREL, A. V., 272
CLAYTON, M., 68
COHEN, A. D., 168, 208
COHEN, A. K., 54
COHEN, E. G., 89
COLADARCI, A. P., 127, 271
COLEMAN, J. S., 61, 63
COOPER, R. L., 2, 14-15, 17, 126-127, 219-220, 268, 279, 282, 288
CÓRDOVA, I. R., 61
CUMMINS, E. J., 46

DAILEY, J. T., 126, 131, 168, 273
D'ANGLEJAN, ALISON, 22, 27-28, 32, 79, 127, 237, 273, 300
DARCY, N. T., 41, 285
DAS GUPTA, J., 22, 164
DAVIS, F. B., 22, 25